Romantic Motives

HISTORY OF ANTHROPOLOGY

Romantic Motives

ESSAYS ON
ANTHROPOLOGICAL SENSIBILITY

Edited by

George W. Stocking, Jr.

HISTORY OF ANTHROPOLOGY
Volume 6

THE UNIVERSITY OF WISCONSIN PRESS

The University of Wisconsin Press
114 North Murray Street
Madison, Wisconsin 53715

3 Henrietta Street
London WC2E 8LU, England

Library of Congress Cataloging-in-Publication Data
Romantic motives: essays on anthropological sensibility / edited by
George W. Stocking, Jr.
286 p.   cm. — (History of anthropology ; v. 6)
Includes bibliographies and index.
1. Anthropology—Philosophy. 2. Anthropology—History.
3. Romanticism.
I. Stocking, George W., Jr., 1928–   . II. Series.
GN345.R65   1989
306'.01—dc20   89-40268
ISBN 0-299-12360-X

HISTORY OF ANTHROPOLOGY

EDITOR
George W. Stocking, Jr.
Department of Anthropology, University of Chicago

EDITORIAL BOARD
Talal Asad
Department of Anthropology, New School for Social Research
James A. Boon
Department of Anthropology, Princeton University
James Clifford
Board of Studies in the History of Consciousness,
University of California, Santa Cruz
Donna J. Haraway
Board of Studies in the History of Consciousness,
University of California, Santa Cruz
Curtis M. Hinsley
Department of History, Northern Arizona University
Dell Hymes
Department of Anthropology, University of Virginia
Henrika Kuklick
Department of History and Sociology of Science,
University of Pennsylvania
Bruce G. Trigger
Department of Anthropology, McGill University

INFORMATION FOR CONTRIBUTORS

Normally, every volume of *History of Anthropology* will be organized around a particular theme of historical and contemporary anthropological significance, although each volume may also contain one or more "miscellaneous studies," and there may be occasional volumes devoted entirely to such studies. Since volume themes will be chosen and developed in the light of information available to the Editorial Board regarding research in progress, potential contributors from all areas in the history of anthropology are encouraged to communicate with the editor concerning their ongoing work.

Manuscripts submitted for consideration to HOA should be typed twenty-six lines to a page with 1¼-inch margins, with *all* material double-spaced, and documentation in the anthropological style. For exemplification of stylistic details, consult the published volumes; for guidance on any problematic issues, write to the editor. Unsolicited manuscripts will not be returned unless accompanied by adequate postage. All communications on editorial matters should be sent to the editor:

> George W. Stocking, Jr. (HOA)
> Department of Anthropology
> University of Chicago
> 1126 E. 59th St.
> Chicago, Illinois 60637 U.S.A.

All communications relating to standing orders, orders for specific volumes, missing volumes, changes of address, or any other business matters should be addressed to:

> Marketing Department
> The University of Wisconsin Press
> 114 North Murray Street
> Madison, Wisconsin 53715

Contents

Romantic Motives

ROMANTIC MOTIVES
AND THE HISTORY
OF ANTHROPOLOGY

In its most general historical self-definition, anthropology has characteristically insisted on its status as an "ology"—glossed not simply as discourse, but as discourse which, like other proliferatingly institutionalized "ologies" of the nineteenth and twentieth centuries, claims to be a "science." Although its character varied somewhat in different national anthropological traditions, in general we may say that "anthropology" in the nineteenth century laid claim to being "the science of man." And despite the transformations of the ensuing century and the periodic questionings of many of its practitioners and critics, it has not since abandoned that self-description (which has of course considerably enhanced its claims for support from outside the discipline).

Legitimating origin accounts of the discipline tend to emphasize three cultural moments of especially powerful formative significance: some focus on the decades after 1850 (Penniman 1935; Service 1985); others look a century farther back (Evans-Pritchard 1950; Harris 1968); a few seek ancestral intellectual totems among the ancient Greeks (Kluckhohn 1961). It is immediately striking that each of these three formative moments was also a moment in the history of a general intellectual orientation which may be called developmental, progressive, or (loosely) evolutionary, and which construes the history of humankind as an ever-increasing knowledge of and control over the rest of the natural world through the processes of human reason (Bock 1956). From this perspective, all three moments may be regarded as part of a broader tradition that we associate with the Enlightenment. That, at least, was clearly the view of one of the discipline's major founding figures, E. B. Tylor, who decorated the title page of of *Primitive Culture* (1871) with an epigraph from one of the major works of Enlightenment "conjectural history." Although the early-twentieth-century "revolution in anthropology" (*HOA* 2; Jarvie 1964; Stocking 1989) was in many respects to transform the discipline, its historiography (expressing, no doubt, a very strong inclination within the disciplinary *imago*) still reflects this identification with the Enlightenment tradition—most strikingly, perhaps, in the tendency to regard the early nine-

3

teenth century simply as an anthropological dark age dominated by racialism, and in the virtual neglect, within the Anglophone sphere, of the Germanic roots of cultural anthropology.

There is, however, another side of the modern anthropological tradition which, variously manifest, has strongly influenced both the self- and public representation of the discipline. Perhaps most strikingly expressed in the image of "the anthropologist as hero"—Lévi-Strauss in the Brazilian jungle (Sontag 1966), Malinowski or Mead alone among the natives on a South Sea island—this disciplinary alter ego reflects what has been called the "ethnographicization" that accompanied the revolution in anthropology of the early twentieth century (Stocking 1989). Rather than being, archetypically, an activity of the armchair or the study, anthropology came out of doors into the open air; what was most critical to the definition of the discipline was not so much the comparative perspective that it offered on the varieties of humankind as the detailed descriptive information that it could provide about particular groups outside the Western European tradition. This conception of anthropology might have been expected to produce a disciplinary historiography marked by quite different moments, and rooted less in Western speculations about scientific progress than in Western traditions of exploration and natural history. But, in fact, the history of the discipline as an "ography," or descriptive discourse, if not unwritten, is certainly much more lightly inscribed (cf. HOA 1; Boon 1982; Clifford 1988; Duchet 1971; Geertz 1988).

The grounding of anthropological knowledge in the ethnographic text, and prior to that, in the interactive and reflexive experiential processes by which ethnographic texts are generated, calls our attention to other aspects of the contrapuntal anthropological tradition we are trying here to evoke (Geertz 1973; Clifford & Marcus 1986; Ruby 1982). Thus, on various occasions in the history of anthropology (as indeed in the history of the human sciences generally), it has been argued that there is a radical dichotomy between two forms of knowledge. What for American anthropologists may be regarded as the *locus classicus* of that distinction is a short essay on "The Study of Geography," which Franz Boas published a century ago. Written during the period when he was moving away from that discipline toward the one in which he was to play such an influential intellectual and institutional role (cf. Stocking 1968, 1974), the essay distinguished two modes of scientific inquiry. On the one hand, there was the approach of the physicist, whose fragmenting analytic method resolved phenomena into their elements, in order by comparison to establish or verify general laws. On the other, there was that of the cosmographer (or the historian), who sought an integrative, holistic understanding of each phenomenon, without regard "for the laws which it corroborates or which may be deduced from it" (Boas 1887:642; cf. below, pp. 30–32, 267–68). Granting that the terms of the opposition might be otherwise stated (e.g., as "nomothetic" and "idiographic"), and that some might deny its existence or insist on its ultimate resolvability, it seems clear that some such methodological tension has been a persisting one within the modern anthropological tradition (cf. Stocking 1988).

However, to treat the polarity simply at the level of methodology would be to take a narrower view than Boas' argument implied. For Boas, the opposition between the physical and the historical methods could also be expressed in terms of a more general opposition between objectivity and subjectivity, manifested not only in the method of inquiry, but in the constitution of its object and in the motivation of the inquirer. Whereas physicists investigated phenomena that had "an objective unity" in the external world, cosmographers studied phenomena whose elements "seem to be connected only in the mind of the observer"(Boas 1887:645) – as, one might suggest, the geography of the Black Forest, or the culture of the Eskimo. At a deeper level, however, both forms of inquiry were subjectively grounded. Motivated by the "aesthetic" disposition, physicists sought to "bring the confusion of forms and species into a system." Motivated by the "affective" impulse, or "the personal feeling of man toward the world," cosmographers were devoted to the phenomenon itself, "without regard to its place in a system," and sought "lovingly" to "penetrate into its secrets until every feature is plain and clear" (1887:644-45; cf. Stocking 1974). From this perspective, the polarity of method in anthropology is grounded in another opposition, which has perhaps less to do with intellect *per se* than with emotion and feeling. And although Boas himself may not have intended it, to discuss anthropological method in these terms is clearly to open the door to a wider range of culturally conditioned preconditioning subjectivities. Extending somewhat – but not entirely forsaking – the literary historical meanings of the term, we might say that what is at issue is a matter of "sensibility" (Lerner 1974).

The fact that Boas chose Comte, a son of the French Enlightenment tradition, and Goethe, a father of the German Romantic tradition, to exemplify his two opposing methodological orientations brings us back toward the broader cultural historical context in which such a tension must be viewed. And the terms of Boas' opposition are of course clearly resonant of those which have traditionally been used to characterize "romanticism," whether construed narrowly as literary movement (cf. Weinberg 1974), or more broadly, as one of a small number of frameworks of assumption that have characterized major phases of Western European cultural history (cf. Jones 1973) – and which, as Boas' argument would suggest, remain enduring options of intellectual sensibility within the modern anthropological tradition (cf. Horton 1973; Shweder 1984).

Defining "romanticism" is a problem that has vexed students of literature and of the history of ideas for over half a century (Lovejoy 1924; Lucas 1936;

Bloom 1970). This volume is not intended as a contribution to that literature. Our approach has been to exemplify rather than to define, and in pursuing this approach, we have deliberately chosen a broad construction of what in our preliminary announcements was called, rather loosely, "the romantic motif in anthropology." The essays we have gathered in response to that call deal with a broad range of topics. The first, bringing modern Western anthropology back in touch with its earliest philosophical roots, considers what might be characterized as a fundamental contradiction (to which the Boasian tension is obviously related) between the conditions of possibility of social community and the conditions of possibility of scientific knowledge—an issue whose broader "romantic" resonance is only too obvious. The second, bringing anthropology in touch with contemporary literary criticism, deals with general issues of authorship and authenticity by focussing on one of the earliest of those eighteenth-century fabricators of "otherness" whose work was such an important stimulus to the Romantic movement as a specific cultural historical phenomenon. The two central essays both deal more directly with figures and themes customarily associated with that movement; the first, a reading forward from the Romantic era, emphasizes the repression of the original Romantic impulse in the professional anthropological descendants of two of the founding figures of Romanticism; the second, a reading backward from the present, emphasizes the persisting influence of Romanticism in the *oeuvre* of the leading figure of modern structuralist anthropology. Reverting to a somewhat looser conception of "the romantic motif," the last two essays each treat manifestations of the primitivist yearning for unbroken community, which, deeply rooted in the European cultural tradition (cf. Baudet 1965; Friedman 1983), has been an essential component of the modern anthropological tradition—returning, at the end, to the implications of that yearning for the possibility of anthropological knowledge. Clearly, however one defines "the romantic motif," there are many relevant themes that might have been treated which are only touched upon or quite neglected here (cf. the note on how volumes are put together, *HOA* 4:10). The most that we would claim to have done is open up a topic that has been relatively underemphasized in the historiography of anthropology.

To reflect the diversity of the six contributions that are included in this volume, it has seemed appropriate for the title to adopt the plural "motives"— which also has the virtue of a somewhat broader connotational resonance. On the other hand, a certain degree of singularity seemed desirable in the volume's subtitle, in order to capture the sense of recurrence/perdurance which is an important attribute of the "sensibility" these essays are intended to evoke. Romanticism in the literary sense has been viewed not only as an historically specific movement (albeit differentiated by phase and national tradition) and as a "complex of literary phenomena associated with a change occurring in

European sensibility toward the end of the eighteenth century, and extending into the present," but also as "one of the poles between which Occidental art in all places and periods oscillates" (Weinberg 1974:717). Similarly, in regard to the romantic sensibility in anthropology: while it would seem to be most strongly expressed in particular historical moments (e.g., the 1920s), it is not peculiar to any given historical moment, but is rather a recurrent and we may expect permanent tendency within the anthropological tradition. Hence the need for a degree of singularity.

But just as the romantic sensibility is not limited to particular historical moments, neither does it entirely pervade any one of them. And while it may be strongly manifest in particular individuals (e.g., Paul Radin), it may not color all of their work; thus, the sensibility of Malinowski's *Argonauts* (1922) is quite a different thing from that of *A Scientific Theory of Culture* (1944). If this is true of individual practitioners, it must, *a fortiori*, be true of the discipline as a whole. While we may expect the heirs of the Romantic and the Enlightenment traditions to continue to make imperial claims, and the strength of the corresponding sensibilities to wax and wane, it seems unlikely that the dualism they reflect will ever be eliminated from anthropology. Hence, the avoidance of the definite article in our subtitle: "Essays on Anthropological Sensibility."

Even so, it is clear that this volume is itself the product of a particular (postmodern?) moment in the history of anthropology, in which a number of tendencies expressive of a romantic sensibility ("reflexive," "hermeneutic," "interpretive," "deconstructive," etc.) are quite strongly manifest (cf. Marcus & Fischer 1986). Similarly, several of the essays included here are themselves clearly instantiations of the phenomenon the volume seeks to illuminate. From the historicist perspective animating *History of Anthropology* it seems likely (and appropriate) that anthropology will long continue to be informed by quite divergent motivational and methodological impulses. However, we do hope that by highlighting a tendency within the anthropological tradition whose history has been until now relatively neglected, *Romantic Motives* may be a contribution to discussions now going on as to the future of anthropology.

Acknowledgments

Aside from the editor, the editorial board (including especially James Boon, James Clifford, and Dell Hymes), the contributors, and the staff of the University of Wisconsin Press, several other individuals and organizations facilitated the preparation of this volume. During the academic year 1988–89, the editor's efforts were supported by the Getty Center for the History of Art and the Humanities in Santa Monica, California. The staff of the Getty Center assisted in a variety of ways. George Marcus and Bill Young offered helpful advice at several points in the editorial process. Our thanks to them all.

References Cited

Baudet, H. 1965. *Paradise on earth: Some thoughts on European images of non-European man,* Trans. E. Wentholt. New Haven.

Boas, F. 1887. The study of geography. In *Race, language, and culture,* 639–47. New York (1940).

Bloom, H. ed. 1970. *Romanticism and consciousness: Essays in criticism.* New York.

Bock, K. 1956. *The acceptance of histories.* Berkeley.

Boon, J. A. 1982. *Other tribes, other scribes: Symbolic anthropology in the comparative study of cultures, histories, religions, and texts.* New York.

Clifford, J. 1988. *The predicament of culture: Twentieth-century ethnography, literature and art.* Cambridge, Mass.

Clifford, J., & G. Marcus, eds. 1986. *Writing culture: The poetics and politics of ethnography.* Berkeley.

Duchet, M. 1971. *Anthropologie et histoire au siècle des lumières: Buffon, Voltaire, Rousseau, Helvétius, Diderot.* Paris.

Evans-Pritchard, E. E. 1950. Social anthropology. In *Social anthropology and other essays,* 1–134. Glencoe, Ill.

Friedman, J. 1983. Civilizational cycles and the history of primitivism. *Soc. Anal.* 14:31–52.

Geertz, C. 1973. Thick description: Toward an interpretive theory of culture. In *The interpretation of cultures,* 1–30. New York.

―――. 1988. *Works and lives: The anthropologist as author.* Stanford.

Harris, M. 1968. *The rise of anthropological theory: A history of theories of culture.* New York.

Horton, R. 1973. Lévi-Bruhl, Durkheim and the scientific revolution. In *Modes of thought: Essays on thinking in Western and Non-Western societies,* ed. R. Horton & R. Finnegan, 249–305. London.

Jarvie, I. M. 1964. *The revolution in anthropology.* London.

Jones, W. T. 1973. *The romantic syndrome: Toward a new method in cultural anthropology and the history of ideas.* The Hague.

Kluckhohn, C. M. 1961. *Anthropology and the classics.* Providence, R.I.

Lerner, L. D. 1974. Sensibility. In *The Princeton encyclopedia of poetry and poetics,* ed. A. Preminger, 761–63. Princeton.

Lovejoy, A. O. 1924. On the discrimination of romanticisms. *PMLA* 39:229–53.

Lucas, F. L. 1936. *The decline and fall of the romantic ideal.* New York.

Malinowski, B. 1922. *Argonauts of the western Pacific.* London.

―――. 1944. *A scientific theory of culture and other essays.* New Haven.

Marcus, G., & M. Fischer. 1986. *Anthropology as cultural critique: An experimental moment in the human sciences.* Chicago.

Penniman, T. K. 1935. *A hundred years of anthropology.* London.

Ruby, J., ed. 1982. *A crack in the mirror: Reflexive perspectives in anthropology.* Philadelphia.

Service, E. R. 1985. *A century of controversy: Ethnological issues from 1860 to 1960.* Orlando, Fla.

Shweder, R. A. 1984. Anthropology's romantic rebellion against the Enlightenment, or there's more to thinking than reason and evidence. In *Culture theory: Essays on mind, self, and emotion,* ed. R. A. Shweder & R. A. LeVine, 27–66. Cambridge.

Sontag, S. 1966. The anthropologist as hero. In *Claude Lévi-Strauss: The anthropologist as hero,* ed. E. N. & T. Hayes, 184–97. Cambridge.

Stocking, G. W., Jr. 1968. *Race, culture, and evolution: Essays in the history of anthropology.* New York.

———. 1974. The basic assumptions of Boasian anthropology. In *The shaping of American anthropology, 1883–1911: A Franz Boas reader,* 1–20. New York.

———. 1988. The adhesions of customs and the alternations of sounds: two retrospective paradigmatic exemplars. Paper given at the meeting of the American Anthropological Association, Phoenix.

———. 1989. Paradigmatic traditions in the history of anthropology. In *Companion to the history of modern science,* ed. G. N. Cantor et al. London.

Tylor, E. B. 1871. *Primitive culture: Researches into the development of mythology, philosophy, religion, language, art and custom.* 2 vols. London.

Weinberg, K. 1974. Romanticism. In *The Princeton encyclopedia of poetry and poetics,* ed. A. Preminger, 717–21. Princeton.

Wolf, E. 1964. *Anthropology.* Englewood Cliffs, N.J.

ARISTOTLE'S OTHER SELF

On the Boundless Subject
of Anthropological Discourse

GREGORY SCHREMPP

Among the principles that have been suggested as capturing the essential character of Western thought, Aristotelian logic, or its founding principle, the law of contradiction, has proven particularly compelling. And certain other contenders—for example, "linearity" (as contrasted with "cyclicality") and even "rationality" itself—are sometimes thought to derive from the supposedly sequential and rigorous character of classical syllogistic reasoning. This special significance was recognized even before Lucien Lévy-Bruhl, in his classic formulation of 1910, *Les fonctions mentales dans les sociétés inférieures*, made the law of contradiction a specific focus for cross-cultural comparison and contrast. The notion of contradiction was, for example, implicitly addressed in the common nineteenth-century assumption that the evolution of thought was a matter of transition from confused images to clear concepts. The idea of such a transition can be found even in the Durkheimian tradition (e.g., Durkheim and Mauss 1903:5ff.), and is no doubt relevant to the interest that Durkheim and his descendants showed in Lévy-Bruhl.

Contradiction, and its significance in the comparative study of systems of thought, was carried toward more technical debates in the French tradition, particularly by Lévy-Bruhl and Emile Durkheim and his descendants. In a contrast that was initially sharply drawn, Lévy-Bruhl proposed that there were systems of representations that operated in terms of a law of participation rather than a law of contradiction. He presented the latter in several different formulations, most of which, however, center around supposed statements of "mystical" identities in which "the opposition between the one and

---

Gregory Schrempp is Assistant Professor of Folklore at Indiana University. His major previous publications include "The Re-education of Friedrich Max Müller." He is currently at work on Maori and Polynesian cosmology.

Aristotle Contemplating the Bust of Homer. Painting by Rembrandt van Rijn, 1653. (The Metropolitan Museum of Art, Purchased with special funds and gifts of friends of the Museum, 1961. [61.198].)

the many, the same and another, and so forth, does not impose . . . the necessity of affirming one of the terms if the other be denied, or vice versa" (1910:77).

Subsequent inquiries into the possibility of alternative logics have emphasized statements of seeming identity between humans and other entities of the natural world, notably an apparent claim of the Bororo that they are parrots. However, Lévy-Bruhl himself recurrently schematized "participations" as of three types: those between given individuals and their appurtenances (e.g., hair, nails, food, clothes, name, reflection, shadow); those between individuals and their social groups; and those between individuals and other entities of the natural world. These various kinds of participations will be considered in the course of this discussion.

It is well known that, in the posthumously published *Notebooks* of Lévy-Bruhl, there were some significant alterations in his formulation of the participation/logic contrast. Although many of these were matters of emphasis (cf. Horton 1973:257ff.), two are particularly important here. First, while there was still a general sense of an evolutionary transition from a preponderantly participatory to a predominantly logical mentality, there was a greater emphasis on *both* principles as fundamental to all humans, and an incipient interest in exploring the character and function of participation as a seemingly generic principle of human mentality (e.g., Lévy-Bruhl 1949:99–105). Secondly, the emphasis on the affective, noncognitive, character of participations was now accompanied by an uneasiness about pairing participation with logical thought (thus treating these two principles as comparable) (1949:61, 73, 99–106, 154).

Among subsequent scholars, debates about the law of contradiction developed into a fascinating set of variations, reflecting in part different questions brought to this discussion within changing intellectual contexts. In the dialogue between Durkheim and Lévy-Bruhl, the law of contradiction was involved in several momentous debates. Horton (1973:268ff.) has contrasted Lévy-Bruhl and Durkheim with respect to their views on the nature of the transition from traditional religious thought to scientific thought, suggesting that Lévy-Bruhl envisioned this in terms of contrast and inversion, while Durkheim saw it in terms of continuity and evolution. But the significance of participations to Durkheim was not limited to evolutionary issues. Durkheim's notion of effervescence and the arguments with which he surrounded it, such as the *pars pro toto* argument, suppose a kind of fusion that at least approaches the mystical participations that Lévy-Bruhl proposed. Though Durkheim's notion of contradiction is problematic (it will be considered below), it is important to note that ultimately Durkheim concluded that, with respect to contradiction, science and religion differ only in degree: both involve moments of contradiction and moments of noncontradiction, and necessarily so.

The polarity that Durkheim acknowledged as intrinsic to both religion and science was also played out between the perspectives adopted by some of his followers. The notion of a quasi-mystical force that is invoked by Marcel Mauss in *The Gift* can be seen as a further development of one side of Durkheim. In Lévi-Strauss, by contrast, a sense of "logic" prevails, though sometimes in a rather roundabout fashion. The logical thrust is manifested in a number of different ways, for example, in the theme of the scandalousness of contradiction as the propelling force in the development of mythologies (Lévi-Strauss 1955), or the argument that the seeming identities posed in totemic systems are essentially metaphorical and therefore really statements of likeness rather than of mystical identity (1962). It is no accident that, in his affectionate tribute to Mauss, Lévi-Strauss (1950:45ff.) singles out the "mystification" of *The Gift* as a major wrong turn.

The issues raised by Lévy-Bruhl still continue to arise in "rationality" debates. This is in part due to E. E. Evans-Pritchard's interest in Lévy-Bruhl, who was no doubt influential in leading him to place the analysis of contradictions, or apparent contradictions, at the center of analyses of the systems of thought he encountered in his own fieldwork (Evans-Pritchard 1937). And though the law of contradiction no longer forms the singular pivot of comparative analysis that it did for Lévy-Bruhl, there are many contemporary analyses in which this principle seems to linger on in the immediate background. The editors of a recent volume on "rationality," for example, comment on the notion of "relativism of reason," or the idea that

> what warrants belief depends on canons of reasoning, deductive or non-deductive, that should properly be seen as social norms, relative to culture and period. At its most ambitious, this thought reaches to deductive logic itself. (Hollis & Lukes 1982:10)

The law of contradiction is not specifically mentioned here. But since it is traditionally regarded as the founding principle of formal logic, the notion of the relativity of deductive logic as the most ambitious form of relativism would seem not far removed from the question of relativism posed specifically in terms of the law of contradiction.

Finally, Pierre Bourdieu has implicated Western logic, and indirectly the law of contradiction, in a reflexivist critique of anthropological representation. He suggests that ritual practice may in some instances be organized according to a "fuzzy" or "fluid" abstraction, which permits it an economy and flexibility grounded in and appropriate to the fact that it is a *lived* logic. Represented under the totalizing synopticism of the anthropological gaze, however, schemata generated through this logic can evince contradictions that do not appear as such in their primary context, since "it is unlikely that two contradictory applications of the same schemes will be brought face to face in what we must call a *universe of practice* (rather than a universe of discourse)" (Bourdieu 1972:110). This lived logic appears to be essentially the law of contradiction *minus* the "in the same sense" clause; in Bourdieu's words, the lived logic "excludes the Socratic question of the *respect in which* the referent is apprehended" (112). In one sense, the alignment here is the conventional one: the tighter logic belongs to the Western analyst and the looser logic to the indigenous system. The contrast that emerges, however, is not between different minds, but between minds engaged in different relationships to the matter at hand: living a given scheme vs. organizing it under the "fictitious" academic synopticism.

Bourdieu's conclusion might be seen as a kind of maximum statement of a principle that was given impetus by Evans-Pritchard: that analysis of systems of thought must be carried out within the context of social life and practice within which they operate. Bourdieu's work also exemplifies another tendency which stems largely from Evans-Pritchard: that is, the issues first formally posed by Lévy-Bruhl are now issues specifically taken to the field for investigation, rather than merely drawn out of standard ethnographic sources, as they had been by Lévy-Bruhl. Particularly noteworthy in this respect is Crocker's (1977) reinvestigation of theories that stem from Lévy-Bruhl's extrapolations about the Bororo.

In addition to these intellectual issues, some very weighty moral issues are involved in debates surrounding the law of contradiction. On the one hand, the denial of the cross-cultural applicability of this law can be seen as the attempt to deny fundamental humanity to "others"—Aristotle himself likened the person who would not accept such a principle to a vegetable. On the other hand, precisely because Aristotle announced the law of contradiction as the best established of all principles and as the principle necessary for all other knowledge, willingness to consider the possibility of the relativity of *even this* principle can be posed as the greatest test of humanistic pluralism. Whichever course is pursued, the moral extremes that come to focus in such debates are no doubt related to the significance of the law of contradiction within the Western quest for its own intellectual identity.

Given the many forms of interest that the law of contradiction has provoked, an overall assessment of this principle in relation to anthropology would be in order, and in fact is to some extent already underway. As part of this project there should be an assessment of the language of participations within the theoretical discourse of anthropology itself. My comments are in general in accord with the vision toward which Lévy-Bruhl's later work seems to have been moving, in which participations are seen not as a phase, present merely vestigially in advanced societies, but as a general phenomenon that forms a perennial complement to logic. The notion of a fundamental dualism of human consciousness is certainly nothing new in itself; the dualism at which Lévy-Bruhl arrived can be seen as a variation on a familiar theme of Western thought. Yet certain fundamental ways in which such a dualism has operated in the growth of a Western anthropological "self" have escaped attention, and my purpose here is to bring some of these into focus.

Before proceeding, it is necessary to inject an important clarification about the notion of "contradiction" as it will be used in the discussions that follow. The concept of contradiction has been formulated in more than one way. The tightest formulation would seem to be that of the formula: to hold p and *not-p* at the same time and in the same sense. But any statement that does not contain the "time" and "sense" phrases is susceptible to resolution into noncontradiction through further qualifications, either of the premises, or of the nature of the relation that is posited. From this point of view, the "contradictions" I am treating below may in fact be ultimately resolvable. The same is true of most if not all of the ethnographic "data" that are brought into these debates. But even assuming that all such statements are ultimately resolvable, there would be yet another, and not less interesting, problem. That is, apparently there are statements that are intended to seem, at least initially, contradictory, suggesting the possibility that the speaker feels that certain things can best be said in the form of an ostensible contradiction. Such statements often take the form of seeming to defy or destroy acknowledged borders, or at least to render them problematic. In the analyses that follow, the question of whether such statements are *really* contradictory or merely *ostensibly* contradictory, while not dismissed, is subordinated to the question: what is the place of such statements in anthropological discourse?

It is of course conceivable that if there is something like the language of participations in anthropological discourse, it crept in through the ethnographic data. In the opening pages of *The Gift* Mauss discussed the Maori term *hau*, which he took to signify a spiritual power inhering in the gift, and compelling its return. In commenting on the now illustrious *hau* of the gift, Lévi-Strauss asked, "Are we not dealing with a mystification, an effect quite often produced in the minds of ethnographers by indigenous people?" (1950:47). However, the Maori text that Mauss consulted is brief and obscure, and other interpreters have rendered it much less mystically; it is hardly fair to credit or blame the Maori for Mauss's mystical inclinations. Even if the Maori text may have been the proximate spur for Mauss's doctrine, it is important to realize that there is also an analogous doctrine, indigenous to the West, that formed a part of the theoretical milieu into which the Maori text fell. The mysticism of Western anthropology is a Western indigenous production; I will explore this claim by relating some central anthropological texts—from Durkheim, Mauss, and Boas—to a less well known, or perhaps merely less willingly acknowledged, side of the ultimate ancestral "totem" of Western thought. In contrast to the idea that Mauss's mystification came from the Maori, an at least equally compelling case can be made that it came from Aristotle.

Logic and the Definition of Humanity: A Founding Polarity

While the idea that Aristotle bequeathed formal logic to the West is not wrong, pursued exclusively it eventuates in the birth of an uninteresting ancestor. By way of alternative, one might find the paradigmatic character of Aristotle in a certain tension—between a form of discourse that centers around the law of contradiction, and one that acts as though it is seeking to subvert it.

Epitomizing instances of a tension within Aristotle can be found, on one hand, in the explication of the law of contradiction in the *Metaphysics*, and, on the other, in the explication of friendship in the *Nichomachaean Ethics*. Each of these analyses is concerned with the character of certain kinds of relationships, and each analysis attempts to transcend a particular kind of partialness and find the highest principles possible under its particular concern.

In the case of the *Metaphysics*, the partialness is that of the various particular sciences. But, in contrast to these, there is a science of "being *qua* being," which is the province of the philosopher:

> The philosopher must be able to state the best established of all principles, i.e. those about which one cannot be deceived, which are best known and rest on no hypothesis, and which must be known if one is to know anything. (Γ.3, 1005b11–17)

And then follows the venerable formula:

> The best established of all principles is that the same attribute cannot at the same time belong and not belong to the same subject in the same respect. (Γ.3, 1005b17–20)

The law of contradiction thus has a special status in a double sense: it belongs to the principles of being *qua* being, and of these principles, it is the best established.

The partialness in the case of the *Ethics* has to do with the nonfinal character of many ends:

> Now we call that which is in itself worthy of pursuit more final than that which is worthy of pursuit for the sake of something else, and that which is never desirable for the sake of something else more final than the things that are desirable both in themselves and for the sake of that other thing, and therefore we call final without qualification that which is always desirable in itself and never for the sake of something else.
>
> Now such a thing happiness, above all else, is held to be; for this we choose always for itself and never for the sake of something else. (1.7, 1097a30–1097b1)

There is then a sort of rough equivalence of stature between the law of contradiction in the *Metaphysics* and the end of happiness in the *Ethics*: each emerges as the highest unifying principle in its particular inquiry.

Of particular significance in the treatment of the law of contradiction is the way in which Aristotle attempts to demonstrate the necessity of this principle. The demonstrations are constructed around an admission that this kind of first principle—that which one must already know in order to know anything—must be axiomatic and not directly testable. The claim that the law of contradiction is necessary in order to know anything is made compelling though a consideration of the consequences of rejecting it. The first of these is the consequence for discourse: one cannot discount the law of contradiction and still argue; or, conversely, as soon as someone argues against this principle, his opponent can point out some way in which the argument rests on the nonequivalence of "to be" and "not to be." One important strain in Aristotle's discussion thus has to do with consistency of proposition and definition.

But the emphasis in Aristotle's demonstration shifts from the impossibility of discourse to the disarray in the order of the cosmos that would obtain if the law of contradiction did not hold: "All things will be one—the same thing will be man, god, ship, and the contradictories of these" (M Γ.4, 1008a24–25). Many of these arguments allege our dependence upon this principle in the negotiating of various prosaic life activities; for example,

> Why does one walk to Megara and not remain at rest, when one thinks one ought to walk there? Clearly we judge one thing, e.g. to see a man, to be better, another to be worse. And if so, we must judge one thing to be a man, another not to be a man, and so on. (Γ.4, 1008b14–27)

The fact that Aristotle passes from the law of contradiction as principle of intellectual coherence to the law of contradiction as statement about the order of the sensible world is significant. Two points are of particular interest to anthropology, and both can provide a point of contrast in turning to the other voice of Aristotle, that of the *Ethics*.

First of all, it should be noted that Aristotle's vision of metaphysics seems to have been clouded in anthropology, especially by nineteenth-century evolutionist writers, from Comte on, for whom "metaphysics" was disparaged as the realm of pure phantoms of the mind, devoid of any empirical character. It is true that Aristotle sets out the law of contradiction in the context of a search for the most encompassing and, hence, most abstract principles. But, in the absence of any higher principle, Aristotle in part turns his appeal to the opposite extreme, as it were, to immediate and prosaic life pursuits: getting to town, avoiding mistaking a man for a battleship, and so on. Such concerns form a central part of the context in which the law of contradiction is set out.

In pointing to the fact that conducting practical pursuits involves discriminations of better and worse, Aristotle does in a sense implicate values and ends. But the fact that we do make evaluations regarding relative desirability of alternatives is, in this discussion, simply assumed. The point is that he invokes this as a self-evident truth in order to support the larger argument: that we do make distinctions, and hence, Aristotle argues, rely upon the law of contradiction. Questions such as How should we determine what is desirable? and What is the nature of our associations with desirable people and things? remain peripheral. These issues belong to the *Ethics*.

Secondly, the fact of the several strategies for demonstrating our dependence upon the "law of contradiction" is of direct relevance to anthropology.
The movement between the several strategies—or at least what could readily
appear to a modern reader as several strategies—may have been unproblematic
in terms of Aristotle's overall vision of metaphysics. But in the present context of anthropological theory the implications of the different strategies are
critical. At one pole is the formula (*p* and *not-p*) characterization, which is
based on definitional consistency and which is not even necessarily "referential," at least in any obvious sense. At the other pole, there emerges a characterization in which "contradiction" is tantamount to failing to properly
perceive distinctions comprised in the given "essences" or "substances" of things;
at certain points at least it seems that Aristotle envisioned the law of contradiction and the notions of "substance" and "essence" as in some sort of
interdependent relationship.

Both of these ways of envisioning the notion of contradiction can also be
found in anthropological discussions. While the logical formula is sometimes
cited, the "contradictions" that are adduced are usually not *p/not-p* pairs of
propositions, but rather statements of seeming identity between objects that
Western observers consider to be "different" things, that is, distinctions such
that being one kind of thing (e.g., a "man") precludes being another kind of
thing (e.g., a "parrot"). Most of Lévy-Bruhl's characterizations of contradiction are of the latter type, as are those of Durkheim. Durkheim portrays the
contradictory character of religious thought not in terms of logically contradictory (*p/not-p*) statements, but in the claim that religious thought displays
an "aptitude for confusing things that seem to be obviously distinct" (1912:
268). He goes on to portray such confusions, however, as merely one form
of the uniting of the heterogeneous:

> Is not the statement that a man is a kangaroo or the sun a bird, equal to iden-
> tifying the two with each other? But our manner of thought is not different
> when we say of heat that it is a movement, or of light that it is a vibration
> of the ether, etc. Every time that we unite heterogeneous terms by an internal
> bond, we forcibly identify contraries. (271)

Durkheim thus invokes a fascinating but bizarre notion of contradiction: it
is apparently one segment of a spectrum of forms of mental copula, seemingly
distinguishable from the others only by the greater leaps that are involved.
And these leaps are not matters of definitional consistency, but of differences
in the "things" that religious thought seeks to unite.

Any full-scale history of the concept of contradiction will have to contend
with the fact of several possible characterizations whose interrelationship is
not obvious, though often treated as though it is. Some of the ambiguities
in the anthropological use of the concept have counterparts in the strategies

involved in Aristotle's demonstration of this principle. Yet, confronting the differences in formulation of the notion of contradiction also helps us to recognize the commonalities; the recurrent theme is the ideal of nonconfusable and discrete categories. And it is precisely in terms of this orienting spirit that we can place the discourse of logic in opposition to forms of discourse that seem to be at odds with the ideal of discrete categories, such as certain arguments that we find in the *Ethics*.

In the *Nichomachaean Ethics*, Aristotle constructs some arguments and definitions that appear to involve a discourse based on rules different from those advocated in the *Metaphysics* — those rules, that is, from which Western thought purportedly derives its linear/logical character. Perhaps most intriguing and puzzling is a formula that Aristotle invokes in characterizing a "friend," namely that a friend is a "second self" or "another self." The phrase occurs four times within the discussion of friendship in the *Nichomachaean Ethics* (Books 8 and 9), a number of times as well in Aristotle's other ethical writings (*Eudemian Ethics, Magna Moralia*). Furthermore, the phrase is pivotally situated: it operates as a conceptual vehicle by means of which Aristotle moves between self-love and love of another — a movement which is critical to his concept of human association. For example, of the virtuous man Aristotle says,

> Such a man wishes to live with himself; for he does so with pleasure, since the memories of his past acts are delightful and his hopes for the future are good, and therefore pleasant. His mind is well stored too with subjects of contemplation. And he grieves and rejoices, more than any other, with himself. . . .
>
> Therefore, since each of these characteristics belongs to the good man in relation to himself, and he is related to his friend as to himself (for his friend is another self), friendship too is thought to be one of these attributes, and those who have these attributes to be friends. (*NE* 9.4, 1166a23–33)

The "second self" argument cannot be dismissed as a mere aside, for the *Ethics* is a meticulously argued work. And Aristotle is obviously quite taken with this phrase. At the same time, the fit is awkward, in several different ways. The awkwardness may in part be a result of various sections of the *Ethics* being written on different occasions (e.g., see Jaeger 1923:201, 237–43, 376; Annas 1977:554). But other aspects of the awkward fit are more difficult to account for. Part of the difficulty lies in the style or strategy of presentation. It has been noticed that certain parts of the "second self" argument are constructed very logically, in such a way as to resemble syllogistic chains. In these the "second self" argument, however, sticks out as the "weak link" (Hardie 1968:332). In making the case that the good man would desire friends, for example, Aristotle argues,

> But if life itself is good and pleasant (which it seems to be, from the very fact that all men desire it . . .); and if he who sees perceives that he sees, and he

who hears, that he hears, and he who walks, that he walks, and in the case of all other activities similarly there is something which perceives that we are active . . . ; and if to perceive that we perceive or think is to perceive that we exist (for existence was defined as perceiving or thinking); and if perceiving that one lives is in itself one of the things that are pleasant (for life is by nature good and to perceive what is good present in oneself is pleasant); and if life is desirable, and particularly so for good men, because to them existence is good and pleasant (for they are pleased at the consciousness of the presence in them of what is in itself good); and if as the virtuous man is to himself, he is to his friend also (for his friend is another self):—if all this be true, as his own being is desirable for each man, so, or almost so, is that of his friend. (*NE* 9.9, 1170a25–1170b8)

But the discussion here is not limited merely to a given ego's circle of close acquaintances. Aristotle suggests that

friendship seems too to hold states together, and lawgivers to care more for it than for justice; for unanimity seems to be something like friendship, and this they aim at most of all, and expel faction as their worst enemy; and when men are friends they have no need of justice, while when they are just they need friendship as well, and the truest form of justice is thought to be a friendly quality. (*NE* 8.1, 1155a22–28; cf. *Politics* 3.9, 1280b38ff.)

Aristotle in fact develops an intricate characterization—something of a typology—of forms of government in terms of the kinds of friendship they involve. For example, kingship involves a kind of asymmetrical friendship, because among unequals, while the friendship of democracy is more equal. Tyranny is a form of government lacking in friendship. The distinguished Aristotle scholar Werner Jaeger commented that in these arguments the theory of friendship is "expanded into a general sociology of the manifold forms of human relationship," a "complex phenomenology of society" (1923:243). Indeed it seems part of Aristotle's point to review the various forms of human association or community, and to show that they all involve, or at least are facilitated in an essential way, by friendship among the associates. The "second self" concept is thus structurally pivotal, for it is invoked as a kind of epitomization of the character of friendship, and friendship, in turn, emerges as the common stratum of human association in general.

The significance for anthropology is this: the concept upon which Aristotle epitomizes human association in general is, from the standpoint of the law of contradiction, a catastrophe. It is as if the character of human association is epitomized in a perfect inversion of the rules laid out in the *Metaphysics*. While, as noted at the outset, any ostensible contradiction can potentially be resolved through further qualifications, this particular contradiction is not clearly resolved in the *Ethics*. And, in ostensible form, it is a very special contradiction—in a way, the most perfect contradiction possible. Unlike the examples that Aristotle cites in the *Metaphysics*, in which one can quibble about equivocation in predicates, the phrase here directly conflates "same" and "different," or "self" and "other." The "self" in Aristotle's phrases—"another self" (*allos autos*) or "different self" (*heteros autos*)—is, linguistically, the masculine form of "the same subject" or "a given thing" ("*to auto*") that is at the center of the law of contradiction, in the phrase, "the same attribute cannot at the same time belong and not belong to *the same subject* in the same respect" (emphasis added). If logical argument presupposes the law of contradiction, it can also be said that the law of contradiction presupposes—in fact, can be seen as a mere explication of—the concept of "the same subject" or "a given thing." A "*heteros autos*" is, more precisely, a meta-contradiction, for it conflates the very principles upon which the law of contradiction itself rests.

Having said all of that, one might argue that Aristotle is engaging in a sort of metaphor or hyperbole—that this phrase is not really contradictory because we recognize that it is not meant literally. After all, it is known that in the *Poetics* and elsewhere Aristotle recognizes legitimate uses of hyperbolic language; and the phrase itself is sometimes hedged ("a sort of," "or almost so," etc.). That the phrase is proffered as hyperbole in fact seems like the easiest and most natural solution, and I will simply accept it from here onward.

Yet, making this assumption does not render the passage less problematic or less interesting. The nature of the problem is merely altered—so that it consists no longer in the fact that we cannot understand this sort of talk, but in the fact that we can. And the question is raised of the significance—even necessity—of this kind of talk in the context of human affection and association. Granting the hyberbolic/metaphorical character of this language, the immediate lesson would be: the nature of human association is to be grasped through hyperbolic/metaphorical language. There are in fact some instances in which social theory has followed this paradigm—that is, has accepted the mandate that its fundamental propositions be oxymoronic in character. Some of these will be considered shortly.

In many other respects as well, contending that the phrase is a metaphor merely changes, rather than solves, the problem. For one thing, important aspects of Aristotle's overall vision work less well precisely to the extent that one accepts the phrase figuratively rather than literally. Consider, for example, the emphasis that Aristotle accords in the *Ethics* and *Politics* to the notion of humans as social beings, intrinsically political animals, on one hand; and, on the other, the exceptional value that is accorded to the ideal of the self-sufficient life—a tension that in fact may be of some antiquity in Greek culture (see Adkins 1963). The point here is that the more literally, and the less qualifiedly, the various selves could be the same self, the more successfully these values would be reconciled.

The metaphorical approach is further problematic insofar as many seeming clues to the "sense" of the metaphor are ultimately misleading. The phrase occurs for the first time in the context of a characterization of one type of friendship, that between kindred:

> Parents, then, love their children as themselves (for their issue are by virtue of their separate existence a sort of other selves). (*NE* 8.12, 1161b27–29)

This phrase suggests that the metaphor might be unpacked genealogically, for example, that the child is a "second self" to the parents *in the sense that* at one time the child was part of the form and substance of the parents, and is now is physically separated. But this interpretation does not help with some of the other incidences, which are clearly not restricted to friendship among kin.

There is yet another, entirely different, kind of solution possible. For many of the examples that Aristotle invokes in the context of the *Metaphysics* involve distinctions between *genera* of things (such as triremes vs. men), while the "second self" argument is developed in application to the relationship of different instances of the same (human) genus. That is, it might be claimed that Aristotle does not intend the law of contradiction to hold in intra-genus talk. Against this, however, it might be argued that while it is true that Aristotle's case relies heavily on inter-genus contrasts, not all of his examples are such; and it is thus doubtful that this is the solution. But it might be noted that if this were the solution, the significance for sociology would be momentous. The implication would be that within this concern—i.e., the relationship of the members of a given genus, such as sets of humans—the law of contradiction is not intended to apply; thus seemingly most of sociology would be exempt.

There is one more important point to be considered in thinking about the attitude we should bring to the "second self" formula, and this has to do with the larger context of the argument. At issue here is the final book of the *Ethics*, Book 10, which deals with the person who would be "dearest to the gods," a discussion which in many ways follows directly upon the chapters on friendship. Book 10 does nothing to restore a sense of logical clarity to Aristotle's vision of the nature of human associations. It offers no comfort for the view that "second self" could be restated in a logically nonproblematic form. The general tenor is, if anything, even more characterized by a sense of indeterminacy of borders.

The border at issue in Book 10 is one that Aristotle had considered in the *Metaphysics* (the fear that without the law of contradiction "the same thing will be man, god, ship"). The notion of humanity in Book 10 is subjected to a highly paradoxical treatment in which the life of the intellect is advocated as the highest possible human happiness:

But such a life would be too high for man; for it is not in so far as he is man that he will live so, but in so far as something divine is present in him. (NE 10.7, 1177b26–28).

This theme is subject to great elaboration, for example:

But we must not follow those who advise us, being men, to think of human things, and, being mortal, of mortal things, but must, so far as we can, make ourselves immortal, and strain every nerve to live in accordance with the best thing in us; for even if it be small in bulk, much more does it in power and worth surpass everything. This would seem, too, to be each man himself, since it is the authoritative and better part of him. It would be strange, then, if he were to choose not the life of his self but that of something else. (NE 10.7, 1177b.31–1178a7)

Whatever else he may be doing, Aristotle, in both the *Metaphysics* and the *Ethics*, is searching for a definition of humanity, and in both discussions his conception of man is posed, notably, over against the life of a "vegetable." In the *Metaphysics*, it is the person who would confuse "man" and "god" who is the vegetable. In the *Ethics*, by contrast, it is the one who would not activate the life of the divine within himself who would be the vegetable— humanity seeming to have as its essential defining character none other than just this possibility.

Thus the definition of humanity that emerges in the final part of the *Ethics* is one in which "humanity" is precariously devoid of its own specific content. One who would not be more than human will *ipso facto* be less than human, as if there are ultimately only these two possibilities. The notion turns on an indeterminateness that, while having something logically problematic about it—in the seeming claim that what is most essentially human is something that is not human at all—yet captures a sense of dislocation and striving that is certainly recurrent in the Western search for a definition of humanity.

The method of establishing a definition itself is of interest here. For early in the *Ethics* (*NE* 1.7) Aristotle argues that we should seek the definition of humanity not in that which humans share with other beings, as, for example, nutrition is shared with other plants and animals, but in that which is specific to humans. This method is in no way out of character with the discussion of the law of contradiction in the *Metaphysics*. But in the final chapter, what is *specific* to humans turns out to be something which they share, and in fact share as the lesser partners. Even in his method of definition, Aristotle is turned against himself (cf. Adkins 1970:204). He does not spell out the "logic" of the method of definition invoked in Book 10; but, borrowing from Lévy-Bruhl, we might refer to it as definition by "participation."

Persons and Things
in the Durkheimian Tradition

There are some basic affinities between Durkheim and Aristotle, and this quite apart from the mere fact that both are "giants" of Western thought. Aristotle gave us formal logic and, according to Durkheim and Mauss, a concept of "class" that is based on "the idea of a circumscription with fixed and definite outlines"–"one could almost say that this conception of classification does not go back before Aristotle" (1903:4–5). Durkheim brought us "socio-logic"– that is, a form of sociology that is centrally concerned with logic in its social manifestations and consequences, both in the sense of logical operations as implicated in the form of society (e.g., social classification), and also the social context or character of logical operations (e.g., the extent of its social construction and variation). But it may be possible to pursue the analogy between the Durkheimian and Aristotelian projects beyond the discourse of logic itself, into the kind of polarity that we have considered in the *Metaphysics* vis-à-vis the *Ethics*. If there is something analogous in the two giants, it may lie in the fact that both are masters of logic and illogic, as if the two poles activate and propel one another.

In the context of his discussion of the principles of his sociological epistemology, Durkheim, responding to Lévy-Bruhl, was led to consider the question of whether there might be systems of thought that operate without the law of contradiction (see Durkheim 1912:25ff.). He concluded that the difference between science and religion with respect to the law of contradiction was a matter of degree. Both religious and scientific thought followed the principle of contradiction in some instances and ignored it in others, though religion ignored it much more frequently (see Durkheim 1912:268ff.). While Lévy-Bruhl saw the polarity as lying in the contrast between science and religion, Durkheim saw both systems as internally polarized with respect to this principle.

Durkheim's own sociological perspective embodies, not surprisingly, the polarity that he attributed to both of these systems; and the polarity in Durkheim is additionally heightened by an ambiguous view of the relation of sociology to these two systems. On one hand, sociology is a science; on the other, it lifts some of its central concepts, such as "effervescence," directly out of religious life, so that it is ultimately futile to attempt to distinguish religious forms as something merely talked about scientifically from religious forms absorbed as instruments into the theoretical perspective itself.

The polarity of Durkheim's perspective is perhaps most evident in his view of the nature of human consciousness. For he portrays two visions of the condition that consciousness would helplessly confront were it not for society: one in which consciousness would confront pure homogeneity (for which society provides a remedy in the form of a model of differentiation); and another in which consciousness would confront a kind of absolute discreteness (for which society provides a remedy in the form of a model for fusing disparate things). In the first case, socially/religiously generated categories form the condition for the possibility of organized experience; without these categories all that is possible is a scarcely imaginable homogeneity:

> For example, try to represent what the notion of time would be without the processes by which we divide it, measure it or express it with objective signs, a time which is not a succession of years, months, weeks, days and hours! This is something nearly unthinkable. We cannot conceive of time, except on condition of distinguishing its different moments. Now what is the origin of this differentiation? . . . observation proves that these indispensable guide lines, in relation to which all things are temporally located, are taken from social life. The divisions into days, weeks, months, years, etc., correspond to the periodical recurrence of rites, feasts, and public ceremonies. (Durkheim 1912:22–23)

In the latter case, all is argued to be, at the level of the senses, "different and disconnected" (Durkheim 1912:268). Religion, and specifically religious effervescence, creates the conditions in which the first fusion of sensory data takes place, though from the standpoint of science, it is an overfusion:

> So this remarkable aptitude for confusing things that seem to be obviously distinct comes from the fact that the first forces with which the human intellect has peopled the world were elaborated by religion. Since these were made up of elements taken from the different kingdoms, men conceived a principle common to the most heterogenous things, which thus became endowed with a sole and single essence. . . .
> So it was social necessity which brought about the fusion of notions appearing distinct at first, and social life has facilitated this fusion by the great mental effervescences it determines. (268–69)

As suggested by the reference to ritual in this passage, the double movement is not confined strictly to Durkheim's view of the nature of knowledge, but finds at least a limited expression in his functional sociological perspective. On one hand, society and religion are regarded, in an ongoing sense, as the source of conceptual distinctions through which the world is organized and experience given form (e.g., Durkheim & Mauss 1903:83ff.). But on the other hand, particularly in the analysis of the effervescence of ritual, we continue to encounter the difficult language of fusion, suggested in many different ways, but particularly in the birth of "this moral being, the group" (Durkheim 1912:254), which is immanent in but not reducible to individual consciousness, and whose contagious character can render the part equal to the whole.

The essential polarity in Durkheim's discourse takes on some intriguing new manifestations in Mauss's work, *The Gift*, which was a kind of necessary correlate of his earlier work with Durkheim on classification (1903). The latter emphasized the principles for distinguishing of clans and subclans, and such principles are presupposed in *The Gift*. However, to the discreteness of classification, the gift poses a counter-principle which consists of a sort of controlled interpenetration of borders through exchange.

Prominent and recurrent in Mauss's discourse is a distinction between "persons" and "things," a contrast no doubt given a new kind of impetus in late-nineteenth- and early-twentieth-century concerns about the mechanization and commoditization of human relations. In general, the term "thing," when used alone by Mauss, bears the connotation of determinateness or discreteness, while the notion of "person" seems more problematic with respect to borders. Personhood seems to imply an inherent potential for a sort of contagion—a spilling over onto things and perhaps onto other persons—as well as a kind of temporary alienability. Similar connotations are also attached to some other polarities that are aligned with this one. Most notable is an opposition of "matter" and "spirit," the former suggesting containability, the latter uncontainability. And there is also a recurrent contrast of animation and motion vs. inanimateness and inertness. In trying to establish the character of the gift, Mauss frequently joins the pairs of polar terms in oxymoronic phrases such as "perpetual interchange of what we may call spiritual matter" (1924:12). Or again,

> this bond created by things is in fact a bond between persons, since the thing itself is a person or pertains to a person. Hence it follows that to give something is to give a part of oneself. . . . It follows clearly from what we have seen that in this system of ideas one gives away what is in reality a part of one's nature and substance, while to receive something is to receive a part of someone's spiritual essence. (1924:10)

The language that is utilized here—a linking of terms which are presupposed to be irreconcilable principles—is not somehow incidental or embellishing, but systematic and strategic. It is precisely in such phrases that the essential character of the gift is most fully drawn. The very explanation of the gift lies in part in such phrases. Particularly noteworthy in this respect is the use of the Aristotelian concepts of "substance" and "essence" to denote specifically *what is transferred*, for the usual Aristotelian context of these terms is the attempt to grasp the ineradicable and defining properties of particular things.

One might almost derive the structure of Mauss's argument from his double attitude, this "use and abuse," of the concept of "essence." For the peculiar quality of the gift to unite what is separate is expressed as the transference of "essence," while Mauss's answer to his own opening question—what compels the gift's return?—lies, at least in part, in a sort of reassertion of a more traditional sense of "essence" as that which, removed from a given thing, would result in that thing no longer being what it is. The gift must be returned because it is composed of the inalienable character of the giver.

The positive mystical force of the gift is thus captured, at least in part, through a tortured use of the apparatus of the *Metaphysics*, and in this sense is implicitly set against the *Metaphysics*. Mauss could have done as well by directly lifting Aristotle's already tortured concept of self from the *Ethics*; Mauss might have remarked, for example, that the giver and recipient become, as Aristotle said, one another's other selves. We can only speculate about Mauss's reasons for taking the long route, but, whatever else it may accomplish, one consequence is obvious: by drawing from the *Metaphysics* and then adding torturings that are his own, Mauss leaves the customary anthropological image of Aristotle intact.

As merely reiterated in this peculiar implication of Aristotelian terminology, it would thus perhaps be too narrow to think of the analogy between the projects of Aristotle and Durkheim in terms of the fact that Aristotle brought us logic and Durkheim brought us socio-logic. For it seems to be those thinkers who have brought us the most refined logic who have also brought us a sort of elegant illogic, as if the two poles draw each other out. Durkheim closes his discussion of Lévy-Bruhl in *Elementary Forms* with a summary statement about the character of religious thought with respect to the law of contradiction:

> The special characteristic . . . seems to be its natural taste for immoderate confusions as well as sharp contrasts. It is voluntarily excessive in each direction. When it connects, it confounds; when it distinguishes, it opposes. It knows no shades and measures; it seeks extremes; it consequently employs logical mechanisms with a certain awkwardness, but it ignores none of them. (1912:271–72)

Might not this passage also be read as a statement about the general character of Durkheimian sociology?

Natural Science and Its Complement in the Boasian Tradition

The idea that science (like religion) encompasses both moments of contradiction and noncontradiction was important in Durkheim's assessment of the epistemological status of sociology, for it allowed sociology to include both moments without weakening its claim to be fully a science. In the American tradition of Franz Boas we find some of the same polarities we found within

Durkheimian science. But rather than as a polarity that belongs to all science, these opposed moments are embodied in the idea that there must be both science and some complement to it, or, in other words, that there are concerns that are necessarily a part of systematic human knowledge, but which are beyond the reach of science and require a separate epistemological grounding. Some of the issues involved in the Boasian polarity are reminiscent of those that are present in the Lévy-Bruhlian and Durkheimian debates about logic and contradiction. But the issues of logic and contradiction were never approached as directly or formally in the Boasian tradition as in the Durkheimian tradition. And partly for this reason the polarity is not as localized— it takes more the form of a general methodological tension, which the present excursus aims to draw out. This methodological tension in Boas was predominantly a matter of his inheritance of the traditional nineteenth-century German distinction between *Naturwissenschaften* and *Geisteswissenschaften*, a distinction largely inspired by Kantian philosophy (see Stocking 1974:10ff.). Because Kantian philosophy figured centrally in the perspectives of both Boas and Durkheim, it is important to delineate the main characteristics of this influence. Emphasis will be given first to ways in which Kantian philosophy exerted similar influences on Boas and Durkheim, and then to some important ways in which Kant affected Boas and Durkheim differently.

Insofar as Durkheim is the source of the French and British anthropological traditions and Boas of the American tradition, Immanuel Kant is the nearest thing to a common source for these two—at least as far as epistemological issues are concerned. The interest of Boas and Durkheim in Kant was motivated in part by the concern of both to explore the character of natural science and the relationship of social to natural science. Though Boas and Durkheim each developed his own notion of categories, they were united in the general idea that knowledge presupposes some kind of *a priori* categories. Boas carried this idea in the direction of linguistic categories as categories of knowledge. Durkheim's interests are marked by yet another internal polarity of perspective. In a number of passages of *Elementary Forms*, Durkheim was concerned with categories that are *a priori* in the sense that they are historically prior to any individual—any individual acquires them from his society. The perspective here was roughly similar to Boas'; Durkheim emphasized the variability and relativity of the categories handed down in different traditions, and commented on language as the locus of the categories of knowledge (1912:26ff.). But a number of other passages of *Elementary Forms* signal a somewhat different project, which is to ground specific Kantian categories in the nature of society thought of universally and generically (e.g., social rhythms are the origin of the concept of time, the social group that of totality, and so on) (1912:488ff.; cf. Collins 1985).

Though there is much that should yet be explored in more detail regarding the influence of Kant on these founding figures of modern anthropology, of particular relevance here is a matter that, in assessing this influence, is frequently passed over: that is, the enormous Aristotelian presence in Kantian epistemology. It is specifically the Aristotle who brought us logic. The most obvious indications of this presence are the general equating of the possibility of knowledge with the existence of categories and the fact that Kant's table of categories is put forward as a modification of one proposed by Aristotle. But there is a great deal that is more specific than this. Kant was thoroughly schooled in classical logic, and this is evident in many ways in the *Critique of Pure Reason*. Most notably, in defining his method for discovering the transcendental categories of the understanding, Kant asserted that logic is the source of a "sure path,"

> evidenced by the fact that since Aristotle it has not required to retrace a single step. . . . It is remarkable also that to the present day this logic has not been able to advance a single step, and is thus to all appearance a closed and completed body of doctrine. (1787:17)

Kant accords primacy to the classical logical syllogism, claiming that the "categories of the understanding" should be exhaustively derivable from this form. The argument is complex, but roughly the idea is that "general logic," in the form of the syllogism, embodies in the abstract the rules by which reason establishes necessary conclusions; and it is by virtue of the same powers of reason that "transcendental logic" is able to formulate necessary conclusions (in this case, the laws of nature) when synthesizing and judging empirical experience. Thus, for example, as there are three possible kinds of relations within syllogisms (categorical, hypothetical, and disjunctive) there are also three corresponding categories of relation that apply *a priori* to any possible empirical experience, i.e., inherence/subsistence, causality/dependence, and community/reciprocity (1787:111ff.). Kant held that the categories of transcendental logic were exhaustively derivable in similar fashion. And thus, even in the Kantian dualism that Boas inherited, one of the poles is ultimately traceable to Aristotelian logic.

But if the aim of the *Critique of Pure Reason* was to exhaustively delimit the forms that made natural science possible, it was with two complementary ends: to firmly ground natural science, and to protect from pseudoscientific claims those matters not attainable through it, and which belong to another capacity, which for Kant was epitomized in religious faith and the possibility of moral freedom.

Though Boas was by no means a strict Kantian (notably, the subjective/objective contrast that he invoked is somewhat different from that of Kant), some of the basic polarities of Kantian epistemology are deeply engrained in Boas. On the one hand there was a firm commitment to natural science, in essence a matter of categories, whose ultimate goals are classification and the establishing of the laws of nature. On the other hand, there was a defense of a realm of human concern beyond the scope of natural science and different in character. For Boas this other realm was similarly spiritual, though not religious. It took the form of a kind of romanticism, pictured as a perspective that intrinsically involves the subject's "feelings" about the object of his study. While the complements to science posited by Kant and Boas have less in common than do their respective characterizations of science itself, there are nevertheless some points of contact. Most notably, both Kant and Boas invoked the tradition of "cosmology" as the exemplary bearer of humanly significant concerns that were beyond the scope of science. Kant devoted a large part of the *Critique of Pure Reason* (the sections on "Transcendental Dialectic") to the demonstration that the cosmological/theological concerns of traditional metaphysics must be forsworn as matters about which reason is capable of making scientific claims; while Boas framed the polarity in a contrast of temperaments between the physical scientist and the "cosmographer."

While both Boas and Durkheim were heavily influenced by Kant, this sense of a polarity between science on one hand, and a realm of intellectual/spiritual concerns lying beyond it on the other, is an aspect of Kant that influenced Boas more than Durkheim. It in fact forms one of the major ways in which Boas' and Durkheim's perspectives diverge. Yet it is not the only way. Considered in terms of Lévy-Bruhl's tripartite classification of participations (see above), Durkheim's and Mauss's more mystical sides would have the most numerous affinities with those participations that accrue between the individual and the collectivity (though the close identification of giver and gift might also in some respects resemble the kind of participation that Lévy-Bruhl postulated between the individual and his appurtenances). This merely reflects the fact that Durkheim sets up his study around the analysis of the relationship between the individual and the collective. The American tradition of Franz Boas, though similarly concerned with that relationship, often pursued it indirectly, in part though the study of the process of historical growth of the "cultures" that would variably shape and determine human behavior. This study focussed upon various cultural "traits," many of them material, which mediated between humans and their natural environment, and which turned an earth of mere physical matter into a "home." And within this perspective, there appears a dualism, different from the Durkheimian dualism in terms of concrete focus, but analogous in terms of the polar values contained within it.

The dualism is set forth by Boas in his early work, "The Study of Geography." Boas's discussion in fact involves several polarities, including "historical" vs. "physical" methods; "understanding" vs. "deduction of laws;" and "individuality in the totality" vs. "totality in the individuality." Perhaps the most recurrent polarity revolves around the claim that

> the naturalist demands an objective connection between the phenomena he studies, which the geographical phenomena seem to lack. Their connection seems to be subjective, originating in the mind of the observer. (Boas 1887:642)

The discovery of the order of the world, in the form of abstract laws of classes of phenomena, is the goal of physical science. But while the study requires a human subject, and in fact finds its motive in a human impulse for order, the implication for the most part seems to be that the ideal espoused is the discovery of an order that lies beyond any human "feeling" about them.

As a complement to this perspective, Boas sought to reaffirm a kind of study which not only requires a human subject, but in which the object itself is in some way constituted through the affectivity of the investigator. He posed the special power that geography and cosmography had, in their character as disciplines, to hold together concerns that now threatened to be "disintegrated and swallowed up" (1887:639–40) by specialized sciences such as geology, botany, and zoology. He found the model for geography as an integrative perspective in the tradition of cosmography. But if geography and cosmography had such an integrative power, it was by virtue of the fact that their boundaries as disciplines were drawn according to an ultimately subjective concept, such as "earth, the home of mankind" (647). The affect that is intrinsically involved in this approach "has its source in the personal feeling of man towards the world" (644), and imparts a kind of unity to the phenomena that is not to be met with in the scientific perspective.

It should be noted that the difference between the physical scientist's and the geographer's perspectives seems to consist in something that is added to, not in something that necessarily contradicts, the quest for scientific laws. Also, Boas' characterization of the emotional component of the physicist vs. cosmographer is one of the more complex aspects of this text, and it should be noted that affect is not wholly on the side of the cosmographer. The difference is not that the cosmographer is impelled in his study by the love for his study, while the physicist is not, but rather that the physicist is moved by the ideal of a great order of things, where the affect is towards order in the abstract, while what moves the cosmographer is things in so far as they form the human habitat, and thus are directly, and from the start, objects of affection.

Boas ends on a note about the desire for "gratifying the love for the country we inhabit and the nature that surrounds us" (1887:647), and it could be that one source for this perspective is the traditional German regard for the fatherland and all of the complex affectivity that this notion implies. This could also suggest in a more practical sense the difference in character of the two perspectives. It might amount to the difference between trying to understand the Black Forest as a set of types of mineral, floral, and faunal conditions—the specializations proliferated by the sciences—on one hand, and trying to understand it as the Black Forest of life, legend, and national soul, on the other.

The geographer's perspective imparts to all of the things of the cosmos a form of unity and interrelation which itself originates in a subject's feelings and a kind of unity that Boas saw as a necessary complement to the abstracting, classifying, fragmenting character of the specialized sciences. The notion is not that far removed from certain moments in Lévy-Bruhl, particularly those in which the latter addresses participations "between the individual and his group and the country which it inhabits and what that country produces" (1949:91). The idea of the human subject as a focal point of the larger harmony of the universe is clearly one that Boas drew on from a longer tradition of romanticist geography; one hears in it particularly the voice of Herder:

> And since man is no independent substance, but is connected with all the elements of nature; living by inspiration of the air, and deriving nutriment from the most opposite productions of the Earth, in his meats and drinks; consuming fire, while he absorbs light, and contaminates the air he breathes; awake or asleep, in motion or at rest, contributing to the change of the universe; shall not he also be changed by it? It is far too little, to compare him to the absorbing sponge, the sparkling tinder: he is a multitudinous harmony, a living self, on whom the harmony of all the powers that surround him operates. (1791:293–94)

Of greatest significance here is the "self" that is portrayed; it is not discreteness that is emphasized, but rather permeability. This permeability is emphasized especially in the theme of the interconnection and interpenetration of the substances of the universe. The substances said to be intermixed are the most elemental qualities of the human habitat, the stuff that traditional cosmogonies are made of: man, air, light, fire, food, and drink. There is also, in this characterization, a parallelism and near identification of the great and the small, the universe and the self, in such a way that the self emerges as as a pointal focus and showcase for the larger harmony that surrounds and indeed constitutes it.

Although among some of Boas' students the focus of American anthropology shifted away from the study of growth of cultures (as reconstructed through trait distributions), it is important to note that something of the human subject of romanticist geography remained, even within new kinds of concerns. Most noteworthy in this respect was the influential "culture and personality" movement, in which the study of the historical growth of cultures was replaced by a largely synchronic analysis of the interrelationship of individual and culture. The spiritually harmonious whole of the earth or the cosmos gave way to the spiritually harmonious whole of a given cultural configuration. But the notion of the self as the focus and showcase of the larger harmony remained, and provided a potent model for approaching the relation of the individual and culture. This model is most popularly known in Ruth Benedict's (1934) concept of "pattern," a concept proferred as descriptive equally of the affective/cognitive "mainspring" of a particular culture and of the personality of the typical individual within it.

Boas' underlying interest in the spiritual, affective self provides a means through which to rejoin Mauss, for both perspectives in the end owe much of their effect to a kind of special potency held to be characteristic of and distinctive to the human subject. Though developed in different ways, both Boas' and Mauss's perspectives rely fundamentally on a particular trope for which we find an important prototypical statement in Aristotle, namely, the image of a potentially boundless subject, or a "self," that, as in Aristotle's figure, "is not a static thing but capable of indefinite extension" (Ross 1949:231). The boundless self is an affective self, and there is a kind of implicit notion that affection draws its own boundaries.

Certain other tendencies seem to be bound up with this image. One of these is the sexual/procreative nexus that is situated in many mythologies (see below) as a kind of natural symbol of the problematic character of identity and difference. Just as Aristotle's first "second self" is the parent/child dyad, so Boas pictures the cosmographic activity in a sexual metaphor:

> The cosmographer ... holds to the phenomenon which is the object of his study ... and lovingly tries to penetrate into its secrets until every feature is plain and clear. (1887:645)

But the tendency of greatest concern here is an inclination towards exoticism that is recurrently associated with the image of the boundless self. The association may be due in part merely to exoticism as a sort of inevitable expression and consequence of the idea of boundlessness. According to Boas, the geographer reached outward with a "desire of unveiling the secrets of regions enlivened by imagination with figures of unknown animals and peoples" (1887:639). In a curiously romanticized version of the standard move of the eighteenth-century "comparative method," Benedict transposed Nietzsche's vision of the contrasting spiritual harmonies (Apollonian and Dionysian) of the temporally distant ancient Greek world to the (Eurocentrically-speaking) spatially distant contemporary tribes of North America. The personalized form of exchange that Mauss was seeking to recapture was similarly to be found in the European past and the contemporary ethnographic distance.

The significance of the notion of the self for the founding figures of anthropology is reflected, in the present day, in a renewed emphasis on this concept in both the Boas/Benedict and Durkheim/Mauss lines (e.g., see Rosaldo 1980; Dumont 1983; Carrithers et al. 1985). Some of the analyses pose a strong Western/non-Western contrast:

> The Western conception of the person as a bounded, unique, more or less integrated motivational and cognitive universe, a dynamic center of awareness, emotion, judgment, and action organized into a distinctive whole and set contrastively both against other such wholes and against its social and natural background, is, however incorrigible it may seem to us, a rather peculiar idea within the context of the world's cultures. (Geertz 1974:126)

Though few would wish to challenge the reality of modern Western individualism, might not there yet be something of the exotic tendency in the very monolithism of the Western self that is portrayed here? The very fact of a major cultural institution, that of academic anthropology, which, among other things, seeks to represent the possibility of alternative notions of the self, itself belies this monolithism. The inclination to portray such alternatives is—whatever else it might be—a part of the self that is portraying them. And the process of setting up such a contrast could by its very nature lead in the direction of polarization, and hence, oversimplification of the terms compared.

Such is certainly the case at least in the construction of Aristotle as totem of the Western intellectual self. This construction manifests a form of exoticism in terms of a selection of aspects of Aristotle to leave unacknowledged, in order that they can be discovered elsewhere. The logically ambiguous Aristotle, as in the discussion of friendship, goes for the most part unacknowledged, even though it is permeated with contemporary anthropological concerns. The main defect in the discussion of friendship is that it does not give us Aristotle as we would have him.

The exotic tendency is found, finally, even in Aristotle's own intellectual constructions. The chapters on friendship in the *Ethics* lead into the final book on contemplation, where it turns out that the real human longing for fellowship is for fellowship with the gods—in relation to which human fellowship forms a kind of temporary and inferior, though necessary, expedient. Thus Aristotle places a cosmological distance between the lived human condition and the ultimate human craving. This vision leads us to one final set of considerations, those having to do with cosmology. For the problem of where to locate the boundless subject is ultimately a cosmological problem.

Aristotle's Other Self as Ancestral Totem

A recent commentator concludes his summary of the significance of the thought of Lévy-Bruhl:

> ... Before we dismiss these occult manifestations – to say nothing of the fundamental tenets of Christianity and other mainstream religions – as inherently absurd, it would be well to remember that at least one thoroughly rational scholar, the author of *How Natives Think*, found himself constrained to conclude that the "logic" underlying these belief systems, as well as their counterparts in primitive cultures, may ultimately prove to be as valid – or at least as legitimate – as the one promulgated by Aristotle. (Littleton 1985:xliv)

I cite this merely as an example – others could be found – of an image of Aristotle that is widespread within anthropology. Aristotle, in this image, is that to which "primitive," mystical, religious, and, in general, "other" systems of belief and thought are contrasted. The tendency toward univocality in this image stands out particularly in the context of a generally increasing sensitivity to the complexity of influences that converge in most other major figures, including Lévy-Bruhl. This image of Aristotle raises questions, and inquiry into its origin is warranted.

In the *Nichomachaean Ethics* there is much that could serve as the intellectual charter for recent social thought, particularly Durkheimian/Maussian concerns. There are the highly technical discussions regarding differences between symmetrical and asymmetrical forms of friendship, which are extended to the analysis of political forms more generally. Aristotle's rehearsal of the various forms of human association ranges from close acquaintanceship, to the state, with many intermediate types, such as the comradeship among workers. And his discussion is punctuated by a continual return to the principle that all of these associations depend upon, or, minimally, work better when, in addition to the rules of that particular association, there is a "friendship" among the associates. The discussion, in other words, is permeated by a spirit that would seem akin to that expressed in Durkheim's classic argument that "a contract is not sufficient unto itself" (1893:215), but presupposes a more fundamental sociality as the condition of its possibility. Amidst many references to the *Ethics* in *The Division of Labor*, Durkheim quotes a particularly key passage:

> Some define it [friendship] as a kind of likeness and say like people are friends, whence come the sayings "like to like," "birds of a feather flock together," and so on; others on the contrary say "two of a trade never agree." (*NE* 8.1, 1155a32–1155b1; see Durkheim 1893:54–55)

Durkheim goes on to employ the contrast of association based on likeness vs. association based on difference as the framing device for his analysis. If

Aristotle incipiently was, as Jaeger suggests, attempting to develop a theory of friendship into a broader "phenomenology of society," so was Durkheim, whose discussion of these opposing kinds of friendship (that based on likeness vs. that based on difference) in fact forms a terse preamble to his long delineation of the essential nature of two forms of solidarity—one based on similarity and the other on difference.

Analysis of the relationship between Aristotle's *Ethics* and Mauss's *The Gift* is also appropriate, and some of the similarities are revealed, in a roundabout way, in the analogous difficulties that scholars have expressed regarding these two texts. For example, an important and recurrent theme in scholarship on the *Ethics* is Aristotle's seeming ambiguity regarding the place of self-interest vs. altruism in friendship (e.g., Ross 1949:230; Cooper 1980:302ff., 332ff.); here, even Aristotle may be reflecting an older tension in Western ethical theory (see Annas 1977). Many anthropologists have felt an analogous difficulty in Mauss. On the one hand, there is in *The Gift* the expressed desire to find an alternative to the impersonal utilitarian "calculating machine" (Mauss 1924:74) that man has become by restoring the spirit of "archaic" exchange. But this archaic form consists of

> prestations which are in theory voluntary, disinterested and spontaneous, but are in fact obligatory and interested. The form usually taken is that of the gift generously offered; but the accompanying behaviour is formal pretense and social deception, while the transaction itself is based on obligation and economic self-interest. (1924:1)

Neither Aristotle's treatment of friendship nor Mauss's treatment of the gift can be taken as embodying the full social perspective of its author. But at least in these particular works, both of these thinkers are experimenting with a certain kind of directionality of social analysis, one which pictures some aspect of the character of larger social formations in terms of an outward extension of given selves. Lévi-Strauss's criticism of Mauss's use of the concept of *hau* might, at moments at least, be directed against Aristotle's use of the concept of *other self*:

> ... Mauss strives to reconstruct a whole out of parts; and as that is manifestly not possible, he has to add to the mixture an additional quantity which gives him the illusion of squaring his account. (1950:47)

There are thus numerous analogies to be discovered between Aristotelian and Durkheimian/Maussian social thought, both in terms of positive character and in terms of possible deficiencies.[1]

But above and beyond all such particular parallels, Aristotle might gen-

---

1. The relationship suggested here between Aristotle and later social thinkers should not be thought of as merely a nebulous heritage of "Western thought." For, particularly in the earlier Durkheimian tradition, we find a kind of social science, decreasingly influential today, with close

erally be regarded as ancestral totem for those forms of social science discourse that rest upon a seeming logical deviance—for example, the mystical part of Mauss—for those characterizations of society that, whether found in any indigenous representations or among social science theories, involve formulas that are "rebellious to intelligibility" (Lévy-Bruhl 1949:99). Aristotle's discussion of friendship and the incipient "phenomenology of society" that follows from it exhibit a problematic and paradoxical sense of boundaries that is at least as paradigmatic for the mystical side of Durkheimian sociology as Aristotelian logic is for the study of comparative classification. Though situated centrally, if awkwardly, in one of Aristotle's acknowledged masterpieces, this dimension has been for the most part ignored in the construction of his image for anthropology. Yet if complicating factors have been ignored in favor of a less ambiguous Aristotle, there is something of broader anthropological interest in just this fact. The question arises: Are there perhaps broader human concerns in terms of which it is possible to understand the favoring of the one side of Aristotle?

Certainly the achievement of "fixed and definite outlines" is a recurrent human ideal, one that is manifested in numerous cosmogonic mythologies. Since Lévy-Bruhl, Maori notions regarding identity and difference have been implicated in debates on the nature of logic and rationality—Mauss's and Lévi-Strauss's reflections on the *hau* of the gift are only one particular instance. Particularly since the Maori have already been implicated in these debates, an excursus into problems of identity and difference from the perspective of Maori cosmology would perhaps be of use in attempting to understand the mythic stature that has been achieved by Aristotle.

For the Maori and many other peoples, the relationship of sky and earth forms a recurrent and powerful symbolic focus of speculation about identity and difference in the cosmos. From Hesiod's *Theogony* we know that the Greeks had a cosmogony that was similarly focussed; and, more specifically, in assessing whether friendship consists more of similarity or difference, Aristotle himself notes that some theorists, in searching for the nature of friendship,

> . . . inquire for deeper and more physical causes, Euripides saying that "parched earth loves the rain, and stately heaven when filled with rain loves to fall to earth." (*NE* 8.1, 1155b1–4)

It is worth noting that these lines about sky and earth are among the relatively few passages that Durkheim actually quotes from the *Ethics* (see 1893:55).

In Maori cosmogony, the period prior to the separation of Sky and Earth

---

ties to Western philosophical classics. These classics are, on the one hand, a source of analytical perspectives, and, on the other, subjected to critique from the perspective of cross-cultural analysis. It is important to note that in Durkheim and his students there are not infrequent references to Aristotle's epistemological, political, and ethical writings. Though the specifics of the influence may never be known in detail, there are many points at which a direct influence is quite possible.

is characterized by several kinds of indeterminateness among the initial beings. The children of Sky and Earth are caught between them and enclosed in darkness, and have not yet taken on characteristics that will later distinguish them from one another. In one of the acounts, the relationship of Sky and Earth itself is treated paradoxically, in a statement that reads literally "One indeed is the ancestor of the Maori people, Sky standing here, and Earth lying here."[2] The relation between Sky and Earth itself thus instances a very widespread cosmological theme of a fundamental ambiguity regarding a primordial unity vs. duality for the cosmos.

In the Maori account, the children debate as to whether the parents should be killed or separated. They agree on separation, and ultimately succeed in propping Sky and Earth apart. The separation of Sky and Earth is followed by arguments among the children regarding possible life strategies. These result in various partings, such as that between fish and lizards, which has been immortalized in a proverb, "Us to the Land, Us to the Sea." The distinctive species characteristics of fish, lizards, trees, ferns, *kuumara* (a sweet potato staple), and humans follow upon the different life-strategy commitments that stem from such disputes. This process of speciation then forms a paradigmatic backdrop for the formation, at a later phase, of particular political entities in an analogous history of various partings of ways among the progenitors of the various human tribes.

The cosmogonic process depicted here, like many others, takes the general form of a transition from the indeterminate to the determinate, what Lévi-Strauss calls the "continuous" to the "discrete" (1964:51ff.). But while there is a temporal progression from one condition to the other, it is, among the Maori at least, by no means the case that the transition is regarded as an unambiguous good. The fact that a decision is made to separate rather than kill the parents is central to the cosmological outcome: Sky and Earth continue to strain to reunite, and must be continually propped apart. One account comments:

> Today, Sky is separated from his woman, Earth. The woman continually cries out her love for her man—this is the mist rising upwards. Likewise the tears of Sky above pour down on Earth—this is the dew.[3]

Numerous allusions in present-day ritual contexts among the Maori suggest a nostalgia for the original "duality-unity" (to borrow one of Lévy-Bruhl's

---

2. This line occurs in an account written by Arawa chief Te Rangikaheke in the mid-nineteenth century (GNZMMSS 43); the summary that follows is also based on it, though there are many other versions that are roughly similar. The translation and summary are mine, and I have written about this account elsewhere (Schrempp 1985), as has Curnow (1985). A loose translation was published by George Grey in *Polynesian Mythology* (1855).

3. This comment occurs in a text that is apparently of South Island provenience (GNZMMSS 55). It is discussed by Simmons (1976:368). The translation is mine.

favorite phrases) of Sky and Earth, and this image continues to form a pre-eminent symbol of unity in ritual/political contexts. The original state seems to be regarded *not* as a condition dispensed with, but as a condition displaced, yet recoverable, in time (since all genealogies link to this condition) and in space (the halves of the original unity must be held apart, as if their essential nature is a condition of unity).

Yet though an intense nostalgia is accorded to the primordial condition, the first separation—the one that ushers in all of the others—remains a necessary and heroic act, and the instigators of that division remain heroic figures, as they are in many mythologies. The ultimate cosmological condition might be described, loosely, as an ontological dualism. It is the discrete world that is put close at hand, while the paradoxical and indeterminate—or at least the exemplary cases of these conditions—tend to be located at the beginning of time and the outer borders of space.

But what is the nature of this asymmetry? Are there principles in terms of which we can account for this particular placement? An obvious point is that of functional immediacy—the brute necessity, so to speak, of being able to distinguish men from other kinds of things, even for the purpose of creating ritual effervescence. In a choice of one form of angst over another, one of the images most emotionally compelling in Maori symbolic life—Oneness—is, in its most potent symbol, removed in time and space to the borders of the cosmos. Mythologies in part deal with the practical negotiation of life, and, for this purpose, there must be more than one thing, and confusion or conflation of kinds is, as Lévi-Strauss has suggested, scandalous. But it is also the case that mythologies sometimes document the price paid for this stance.

But there is something else here. If one wishes to imagine a world of borders and clearly differentiated entities, including political units, then, in this commitment itself there could be an impetus to "pick out" and sacralize the principle of identity. What better symbol of the identity of a given group than the principle of identity itself? What better hero than an unambiguous champion and bringer of this principle, whether in the form of a culture-hero who sets things right, or a logician who sets out the rules for doing so? And though it does not lessen our obligation to realize the complexity of Aristotle, or any other historical figure, it must be admitted that since emblematization is intrinsically at least a quasi-logical function, the idea of an emblem for our less logical inclinations is a kind of absurdity anyway.

The Maori have been implicated in Lévy-Bruhlian debates in ways that can be related even more directly to the more ambiguous Aristotle. In his work on the individual/collectivity type of "participation," Lévy-Bruhl called particular attention to Maori expressions that were noted and discussed by Elsdon Best, a prolific compiler of Maori traditions in the early twentieth century. The expressions in question ostensibly equate the individual and collectivity. In Lévy-Bruhl's works, these Maori formulas have roughly the same status in the analysis of individual/group participations that the Bororo human/parrot equation has in the analysis of human/nonhuman participations. Lévy-Bruhl presents such data as suggesting a kind of thinking radically opposed to Western concepts of the relation of the individual to collectivity (1927:67ff.). At issue here is a Maori speech pattern, still in use by contemporary Maori, in which personal pronouns and tribal names or ancestral names are used as though interchangeable, often being placed in direct apposition. For example, a speaker from the Ngatiraukawa tribe says, "Warriors! Heretaunga will be conquered by *me*, by Ngatiraukawa" (cited in Johansen 1954:35). While the ostensible equating of a particular individual with his social group is perhaps the most common apposition, there are many variations on this pattern. The apposition can also be extended to ancestors. For example, there is a tradition among the Arawa people of Roto-rua that one of their ancestors, Hine-moa, swam to Mokoia Island, where she married Tuu-taanekai. An Arawa chief concluded his account of this feat,

> But the descendants of Hine-moa and Tuu-taanekai, those who live here in Roto-rua never stop talking about the beauty of Hine-moa and her swim across the lake. Hence the words of the song: "Mine was the ancestor who swam hither. Hine-moa is me." (Biggs, Lane, & Cullen 1980:49; Biggs, Hohepa, & Mead 1967:73)

Such formulas occur in the context of tribal association, sometimes with past ancestors, which are more limited versions of the genealogical tracing back to the primal unity of Sky and Earth. As moments in the genealogy of all beings that begins with Sky and Earth, they are sort of miniature versions of the prototype paradox of the initial condition.

Western readers have much to learn from non-Western societies and from these particular phenomena. Still, confronted with such phrases, there is no need for the Western reader to feign innocence. Such statements by the Maoris, while morally edifying and instructive regarding the social bond, are not more "alien" than those we can find in the great hero and bringer of the law of contradiction for Western thought.

This is not to deny that there might be some ways in which these ambiguous phrases reflect different kinds of imperatives. Cooper (1980:317ff.), for example, has emphasized an argument, most clearly laid out in Aristotle's *Magna moralia*, which suggests that the "second self" formula might be understood in relationship to the emphasis that Aristotle accords to the ideal of self-knowledge. The argument is essentially that one can more objectively contemplate one's own nature when it is experienced in another person of similar character than when it is experienced in one's self. By contrast to the ideal of self-knowledge, long regarded as a particularly Western pursuit, the Maori examples seem to be essentially representations of the character of a "tribal" bond.

But we should keep these matters in perspective. The self-knowledge theme does not exhaust Aristotle's formula, and it is by no means clear that there is not an ideal of self-knowledge in the Maori formula. And whatever else Aristotle might have had in mind, the first use of the "second self" formula in the *Ethics* is, like the Maori phrase, tribal—or at least "kin-based" (see above). And one can find many other statements in Aristotle's ethical writings that amplify the kinship theme, for example the claim in the *Magna moralia* that "of all the kinds of friendship we have mentioned, it is in the friendships between kindred that love is pre-eminently manifest" (II.12, 1211b18–19). Most important, whatever differences can be detected in the contexts that give rise to such logically problematic formulas, there is no significant difference in the extent to which these two formulas of human association *are*, at least in ostensible form, logically problematic.

There are, however, several reasons we might wish such statements to be more exotic than they actually are. There is of course the desire to increase ethnographic drama, but this in itself does not account for why such usages should be enticing. If such usages as "other self" are metaphorical, the very emotional forces that lead us to create such logical abominations might also lead us to want to regard them unqualifiedly and literally—or at least to believe that there are people in the world who are capable of doing so. More important, the process of establishing identity can include a displacing as part of the process of selecting. As suggested in the earlier excursus into Maori cosmogony, affirmation of identity can involve a cosmological peripheralization of a part of ourselves. In our overall scheme, we might wish this part to be recoverable—but only exotically.

Acknowledgments

I wish to thank George Stocking for ongoing encouragement and numerous helpful comments through the several drafts of this paper. Webb Keane also provided a helpful commentary.

References Cited

Adkins, A. W. H. 1963. 'Friendship' and 'self-sufficiency' in Homer and Aristotle. *Classical Quart.* 13:30–45.
———. 1970. *From the many to the one.* Ithaca, N.Y.

Annas, J. 1977. Plato and Aristotle on friendship and altruism. *Mind* 86:532–54.

Aristotle. *Magna moralia. Aristotle.* Vol. 18 (Loeb). Trans. G. Armstrong. Cambridge, 1935.

———. *Metaphysics. Aristotle's Metaphysics.* Trans. W. D. Ross. Oxford, 1924.

———. *Nichomachaean ethics. The works of Aristotle.* Vol. 9. Trans. W. D. Ross. Oxford, 1925.

———. *Politics.* Trans. B. Jowett. Oxford, 1908.

Benedict, R. 1934. *Patterns of culture.* Boston (1959).

Biggs, B., P. Hohepa, & S. M. Mead, eds. 1967. *Selected readings in Maori.* Wellington, N.Z.

Biggs, B., C. Lane, & H. Cullen, eds. 1980. *Readings from Maori literature.* Auckland, N.Z.

Boas, F. 1887. The study of geography. In *Race, language, and culture,* 639–47. New York (1966).

Bourdieu, P. 1972. *Outline of a theory of practice.* Trans. R. Nice. Cambridge (1977).

Carrithers, M., S. Collins, and S. Lukes, eds. 1985. *The category of the person.* Cambridge.

Collins, S. 1985. Categories, concepts or predicaments? Remarks on Mauss's use of philosophical terminology. In Carrithers et al. 1985:46–82.

Cooper, J. M. 1980. Aristotle on friendship. In *Essays on Aristotle's ethics,* ed. Amélie Oksenberg Rorty, 301–40. Berkeley.

Crocker, J. C. 1977. My brother the parrot. In *The social use of metaphor,* ed. J. D. Sapir & J. C. Crocker, 164–92. Philadelphia.

Curnow, J. 1985. Wiremu Maihi Te Rangikaheke: His life and work. *J. Polynesian Soc.* 94:97–147.

Dumont, L. 1983. *Essays on individualism: Modern ideology in anthropological perspective.* Trans. Paul Hockings *et al.* Chicago (1986).

Durkheim, E. 1893. *The division of labor in society.* Trans. G. Simpson. New York (1964).

———. 1912. *The elementary forms of the religious life.* Trans. J. W. Swain. New York (1965).

Durkheim, E., & M. Mauss. 1903. *Primitive Classification.* Trans. R. Needham. Chicago (1963).

Evans-Pritchard, E. E. 1937. *Witchcraft, oracles, and magic among the Azande.* Oxford.

Geertz, C. 1974. From the native's point of view. In *Culture theory,* ed. R. Shweder & R. LeVine, 123–36. Cambridge (1984).

GNZMMSS. See under Manuscript Sources.

Grey, G. 1855. *Polynesian mythology.* London.

Hardie, W. F. R. 1968. *Aristotle's ethical theory.* Oxford.

Herder, J. 1791. *Outlines of a philosophy of the history of man.* Vol. 1. Trans. T. Churchill. London (1803).

Hollis, M., and S. Lukes, eds. 1982. *Rationality and relativism.* Cambridge.

Horton, R. 1973. Lévy-Bruhl, Durkheim and the scientific revolution. In *Modes of thought,* ed. R. Horton & R. Finnegan, 249–305. London.

Jaeger, W. 1923. *Aristotle: fundamentals of the history of his development.* Trans. R. Robinson. Oxford (1962).

Johansen, J. P. 1954. *The Maori and his religion.* Copenhagen.

Kant, I. 1787. *Critique of pure reason.* Trans. N. K. Smith. New York (1965).

Lévi-Strauss, C. 1950. *Introduction to the work of Marcel Mauss.* Trans. F. Baker. London (1987).

————. 1955. The structural study of myth. Trans. C. Jacobson & B. G. Schoepf. In *Structural anthropology*, 202–28. Garden City, N.Y. (1967).

————. 1962. *Totemism.* Trans. R. Needham. Boston (1963).

————. 1964. *The raw and the cooked.* Trans. J. & D. Weightman. New York (1969).

Lévy-Bruhl, L. 1910. *How natives think.* Trans. L. Clare. Princeton (1985).

————. 1927. *The 'soul' of the primitive.* Trans. L. Clare. New York (1966).

————. 1949. *The notebooks on primitive mentality.* Trans. P. Revière. New York (1975).

Littleton, C. S. 1985. Lucien Lévy-Bruhl and the concept of cognitive relativity. In 1985 edition of Lévy-Bruhl 1910.

Mauss, M. 1924. *The gift.* Trans. I. Cunnison. New York (1967).

Rosaldo, M. 1980. *Knowledge and passion.* Cambridge.

Ross, W. D. 1949. *Aristotle.* London.

Schrempp, G. 1985. Tū alone was brave: Notes on Maori cosmogony. In *Transformations of Polynesian culture*, ed. A. Hooper & J. Huntsman, 17–37. Auckland, N.Z.

Simmons, D. R. 1976. *The great New Zealand myth.* Wellington, N.Z.

Stocking, G. W., Jr. 1974. *The shaping of American anthropology, 1883–1911: A Franz Boas reader.* New York.

Manuscript Sources

The manuscripts cited are from the Grey New Zealand Maori Manuscripts (GNZMMSS) of the Auckland Public Library.

ANTIPODAL EXPECTATIONS

Notes on the Formosan "Ethnography" of George Psalmanazar

SUSAN STEWART

Henceforth the problem of the Other is a false problem. The Other is no longer first a particular existence which I encounter in the world—and which could not be indispensable to my existence since I existed before encountering it. The Other is the ex-centric limit which contributes to the constitution of my being. He is the test of my being inasmuch as he throws me outside of myself toward structures which at once both escape and define me; it is this test which originally reveals the Other to me.

(Sartre, Being and Nothingness)

The next pain in the balls was anthropology and the other disciplines, such as psychiatry, that are connected with it, disconnected, then connected again, according to the latest discoveries. What I liked in anthropology was its inexhaustible faculty of negation, its relentless definition of man, as though he were no better than God, in terms of what he is not. But my ideas on this subject were always horribly confused, for my knowledge of men was scant and the meaning of being beyond me.

(Beckett, Molloy)

How is otherness always an imaginary and reciprocally self-inventing relation? How does the imagining of the Other take shape through language— language's very utterability the possibility of both bridging and defining the

---

Susan Stewart is the author of two books of literary theory, *Nonsense: Aspects of Intertextuality in Folklore and Literature* (Baltimore, 1979) and *On Longing: Narratives of the Miniature, the Gigantic, the Souvenir, the Collection* (Baltimore, 1984), and two books of poetry, *Yellow Stars and Ice* (Princeton, 1981) and *The Hive* (Athens, Ga., 1987). This study of Psalmanazar is part of a forthcoming book of essays on "Crimes of Writing."

particularities of time and space? These questions are clearly keys to the anthropological enterprise; they in fact anthropologize all of existence and all of historical understanding in their refusal of a reified and transcendent subjectivity. Following them, we are able to frame the problem of imagining the Other as a matter of reimagining the entire subject-object paradigm.

These questions therefore must hover as the thematic of the study I would propose here—a study that looks to the eighteenth century as a precedent for the human sciences' current experience of a shifting relation between subjectivity and writing. My particular topic will be the writings of the eighteenth-century forger, imposter, and friend of Samuel Johnson, "George Psalmanazar." We know no other name than this pseudonym which he took from 2 *Kings* 17:3, "Shalmanesar," one of a line of Assyrian kings by this name. From 1702 to 1708 Psalmanazar presented himself to the British intelligentsia as a Formosan pagan, converted to Christianity, and he wrote a widely accepted "Historical and Geographical Description" of his "native" country. I will claim that the aberration Psalmanazar poses in the description of otherness is an aberration that is nonetheless typical of a period in which the claims of writing— the claims of authorship, originality, genius, and documentation—were in tremendous flux. In looking at the historical conditions of Psalmanazar's writing we find a problematic of artifice and authenticity that speaks particularly to ethnography's current self-consciousness regarding its roots in rhetoric as well as its roots in ethnology. The historical evolution of representational forms and the emergence of the articulation of social practices *as practices* are bound up together in a dialectic that defines the place of the speaking subject as it enables the description of what is other to that subject. If we have an opportunity here to pursue "interdisciplinary" work beyond the "connections" and "disconnections" of Molloy's "latest discoveries," the point is not the reduction of anthropological writing to the operation of literary tropes, but rather an investigation of the historical emergence of a writing so necessarily separated from its referent that a scholarship of documentation and verifiability, a science of universal social laws, and conversely a cult of authorship, originality, and genius, were necessary as cures for its instability.

Imposter, Forger, Ethnographer

Rodney Needham (1985) has through a rich essay and diligent bibliography brought the curious case of George Psalmanazar to the attention of contemporary anthropologists. Psalmanazar's account of his Formosan origins presented to the British literary, religious, and scholarly communities an elaborate deception, thus concealing his true identity—an identity, as we shall see, which can itself be gathered only via his "confession" of his crime.

If we find in Psalmanazar an imposter who was also an ethnographer and a forger, we also find that each term of this triple identity has a complementary and reciprocally cancelling term. Like many recent ethnographers, Psalmanazar wrote two tandem texts: the first, an account of his travels and a description of a remote society, the second a personal memoir. But unlike other ethnographers, Psalmanazar invented this society of a piece, and then invented a character for himself to accompany it (here "going native" has its own ironic reflexivity as a return to an origin one has one's self fabricated). And since to do this was technically a crime, Psalmanazar later wrote his final text as a form of repentance—that is, a repentance effected by a particular rhetoric of conversion. Our terms must necessarily slide here, for Psalmanazar "invented" a Formosa in toto, and the exposed fictional nature of his purportedly real invention resulted in the fictionalization of his own personal status—the "turn of fate" awaiting all impostors. But if he was clearly a "liar," Psalmanazar must also be referred to, even anachronistically, as an ethnographer, for his project is a complete description of a culture—his Formosa—its language, customs, religion, architecture, costumes, and social organization. As might be expected, the fabulous narrative of his account of his own captivity and travels is separated in his ethnography from the present tense and indirect free style of his cultural descriptions. And yet this separation has the effect of foreclosing our questions regarding his "true story," and also of suggesting the infinite possibilities for detailing and describing all cultural forms, not only invented ones.

There is little "external history" regarding the career of Psalmanazar. Contemporary accounts rely on the information provided in Psalmanazar's own *Memoirs of ****, Commonly Known by the Name of George Psalmanazar; A Reputed Native of Formosa, written by himself, in order to be published after his Death* (1765; see also Boswell 1791; Clifford 1955:239–41; Curley 1976; Lee 1917; Winnet 1971). In a brief passage in her *Anecdotes* Hester Piozzi (Mrs. Thrale) wrote that "I have heard Mr. Johnson say Psalmanazar was the *best* Man he ever knew" (Ingrams ed. 1984:117); and Boswell, in fact, recorded a conversation in which Johnson, when asked whether he ever "contradicted" Psalmanazar, said that he "should as soon have thought of contradicting a Bishop" (Boswell 1791:III, 443). Sir John Hawkins quoted Johnson as saying how much he admired Psalmanazar's penitence (Davis ed. 1961:245). These reverential comments deserve particular attention since they come from the figure most suffused with authenticity during the period—we should remember here, for example, Johnson's offended attitude toward the hoaxes of Chatterton, Percy, and Macpherson.

From Psalmanazar's *Memoirs* we know that he was born somewhere between Avignon and Rome (he was said to have been from Languedoc and to have had a Gasçoin accent), that his parents were Roman Catholics, and that his father was from "an ancient but decayed" family. His parents were separated, his mother living in France and his father in Germany; his mother raised him. He successively attended a free school run by two Franciscan monks, a Jesuit college, a school taught by the rector of a small Dominican convent, and a university. He was fluent in Latin, with a general facility for languages. At sixteen he secured his first false passport, in which he had himself described as a young Irish theology student. Setting out for Rome, he decided instead to visit his father, five hundred miles away in Germany; but when his father was unable to support him, he set off again—through Germany and the Netherlands with a new forged passport in which he designated himself as a Japanese convert to Christianity. Soon, however, he modified this detail so that he appeared as a Japanese pagan. Living on raw flesh, roots, and herbs, he constructed a language with an alphabet and grammar, practiced an invented religion, and renamed himself "Psalmanazaar" (at some later point he dropped one of the final *a*'s). In this character he had many adventures: he was captured as a spy at Landau, was hired as a coffee-house waiter at Aix-la-Chapelle, and enlisted in the army of the Elector of Cologne. After a period of poor health, he reenlisted in the Duke of Mecklenberg's regiment, made up of Lutherans serving the Dutch.

In 1702, his regiment moved to Sluys, then under the governorship of Major General George Lauder. Here Psalmanazar's imposture was detected by the villainous William Innes, chaplain to the Scots regiment at Sluys. Threatening exposure of Psalmanazar's hoax, Innes suggested that they conduct a kind of publicity stunt in which he would baptize the "heathen" Psalmanazar as a Protestant, thereby commending themselves to Henry Compton, bishop of London. Innes made several refinements in Psalmanazar's story, declaring the heathen was from Formosa (less well known to Europeans than Japan) and that, when kidnapped from that country by Jesuits, he had resisted pressure to convert to Catholicism.

Bishop Compton was duly impressed, and at the end of 1703 Innes and Psalmanazar arrived in London. Psalmanazar presented the bishop with a Church of England catechism translated into "Formosan," and for the next four years, Psalmanazar's imposture was a complete success. Although Father Fountenay, a Jesuit missionary to China, criticized him at a public meeting of the Royal Society, Psalmanazar successfully rebutted the accusations. In 1704, at the expense of Bishop Compton and his friends, he spent six months at Oxford, where he studied a variety of subjects and gave popular lectures on "Formosan" practices, including human sacrifice. That same year, at the age of twenty, he published *An Historical and Geographical Description of Formosa, an Island Subject to the Emperor of Japan . . . illustrated with several Cuts.*

By 1707, Innes had abandoned him, taking an appointment as chaplain-general to the English forces in Portugal—a reward for his conversion of

Psalmanazar. After 1708, Psalmanazar's patrons drifted away, and he was generally ridiculed and led by poverty into a life of aimlessness and dissipation.
He did, however, make one more attempt at imposture. In 1712, a man named
Pattenden persuaded him to invent "a white sort of Japan" paint which Psalmanazar was to introduce as "white Formosa work" from his own country. When
this venture failed, he became a tutor and then a clerk of a regiment in Lan-
cashire involved in the suppression of the Jacobite rebellion. In 1717, he tried
fan painting for a while and did some literary work for a London printer.
In 1728, after a serious illness, he had a conversion experience. Denouncing
his past life, he wrote his *Memoirs*, designed to be published after his death.
In his remaining years, during which he regularly took opium for his "every
other day ague," he studied Hebrew assiduously and wrote hackwork, including *A General History of Printing* and contributions to the multivolume *Universal History* compiled by George Sale and others. Psalmanazar lived this life
in Ironmonger's Row until May 3, 1763, when he died at the age of approxi-
mately 84, enjoying the general esteem noted in Johnson's recollections of his
saintly character.

Psalmanazar and the Eighteenth-Century Crisis in Authenticity

Needham's reading of Psalmanazar's career focusses upon the question of ethnographic verification and the "intrinsic difficulty of inventing a society." Providing a close reading of Psalmanazar's spatial symbolism, Needham shows
how it maps onto a system of analogical classification that he has claimed
appears in world-wide distribution (1986:112). Needham argues that the hoax
was successful for a time because of a combination of Psalmanazar's personal
qualities—secrecy, consistency, effrontery, and an air of sincerity—and concludes with a testimony to Psalmanazar's extraordinary character: "Given the
opportunity, what a marvelous genuine ethnographer he could have been"
(114–15).

Yet here I would like to reopen the case of Psalmanazar, for his writings
can also be seen in light of a larger eighteenth-century crisis in authenticity—
a crisis which, far from being resolved by the later advent of a "scientific"
ethnography, still pursues us in the irreducible conditions of ethnography as
writing. The point of this account of Psalmanazar's work is to note that one
is only given such an "ethnographic" opportunity within one's own particular
moment in historical understanding. The crime of Psalmanazar should not
be considered that of a failed ethnographer who, overly eager to make his
reputation, traversed the boundaries of truth. Nor should we see Psalmana-

zar as simply one in a series of eighteenth-century literary fakirs. Rather we find here a "crime" tied up with the problem of authenticity in the eighteenth century. If our current sense of the ethnographer's heroism often relates to our cultural valorization of marginality, the eighteenth-century sense of the ethnographer's value relates to a quite different set of qualities and circumstances: the persistence of cultural tradition in the face of an onslaught of technical innovations; the charm of novelty so long as it is strictly confined to its own sphere; the clash of religious differences as a clash of practices manifesting a more elusive system of belief; and the sense of culture as specimen rather than as system.

Furthermore, the specific conditions of Psalmanazar's ethnographic writing can be connected to the specific conditions of writing in general during this period. The background to Psalmanazar's hoax was a social scene in which the rise of new forms of literary production were resulting in a commodification of literary discourse. And this commodification of writing gradually demanded an authenticating apparatus, for to separate cultural productions from their contexts of origin was also to separate them from their grounds of intelligibility and closure.

During this period, older scenes of literary production – the patronage system, the court, the world of the coffeehouse, and the practice of subscriptions – gave way to more entrepreneurial modes, particularly the emerging reign, in the first third of the century, of the booksellers (Eagleton 1984:29-43). Although we find Psalmanazar initially protected by the patronage of Bishop Compton, throughout his career as writer he was subject to the pressures and demands of printers and the need to generate income through the sale of his manuscripts and by literary hackwork. Consider this account from Psalmanazar's *Memoirs* of the process of writing his *Description*:

> And this I was left to hammer out of my own brain, without any other assistance than that of Varenius's description of Japan, which Dr. Innes put into my hands, to get what I could out of it. All this while, both he and the booksellers were so earnest for my dispatching it out of hand, whilst the town was hot in expectation of it, that I was scarcely allowed two months to write the whole. (1765:182–83)

Psalmanazar adds that "the person, who englished it from my Latin likewise was hurried on by the booksellers." Psalmanazar arrived on the London literary scene at a moment when the classical public sphere of letters was beginning to disintegrate under pressures from private commercial interest, from the dissemination of literacy, from the expansion of wealth and population, and from the rise of professional writing. (Eagleton 1984:30, 34; Eisenstein 1979:I, 132 *et passim*.) In genres ranging from ballad imitations to the novel, with its new and abstracted forms of publication, finding an immediate context for one's voice was becoming problematic, the relation of author to audience increasingly one of speculation. And in this gap between a context of production and a context of reception, a certain slippage was inevitable—a slippage of the referent, and a corresponding necessity of invention.

How, then, was the writer to authenticate the grounds of his or her authorial subjectivity outside of the worlds of patronage and literary community? The most obvious method was the generation of more discursiveness—the author must incorporate these grounds by writing them. Here we find the problem of the constantly self-inventing grounds of nostalgia, the already fallen status of a desire for a point of origin which is "merely" the product of that desire and not its originating cause. And here we find the relentless discursiveness of a history which must constantly authenticate its own foundations of intelligibility by the generation of more history, more contexts. Thus we find the basis for, on the one hand, a "realistic" fiction, based upon commonly held assumptions regarding the immediacy of first-hand experience (Watt 1957:9–34), and, on the other, a grandiose lie—that is, an often unattributed literature of imitation, conjecture, and fantasy. During this period, the "responsibilities" of authorship were undergoing a great upheaval; conventions of originality, genius, authenticity, documentation, and even genre itself remained subjects of speculation and interest rather than of either natural "rights" or formulated law.

Although the century began with an idealization of Augustan Rome, a more eclectic mix of historical styles emerged as it went forward; Greek classicism, medievalism, orientalism, and primitivism appealed in turn to eighteenth-century aesthetics. The concomitant taste for a literature of sensation and terror appeared as the logical consequence of such movements, simply as forays into an otherness of time or space. As early as 1692, Sir William Temple had claimed in his essay, *On Heroic Virtue,* that certain parts of the world had been neglected by historians. He surveyed China, Peru, the Gothic North, and Islam as his examples. By the close of the century each of these cultures had been culled for its moral, political, or artistic possibilities (Sambrook 1986:168–97).

An intense desire to repeat history is doomed, however, by its limitations as the *production* of history. That is, the status of history as a made product—a labor, rather than an imagined spontaneity—continually returns to haunt the ironic and, ultimately, inauthentic desire to simply be in time. Thus, on the one hand, we find the author looking for an authentic role for himself or herself within an imagined feudal hierarchy; the minstrel, the poet/monk, and the bard appeared here as authorial roles grounded in patronage and its perhaps less-mediated forms of production and reception. And, on the other hand, authors invented a subjectivity marked by a tautological return from a foray into otherness.

These "unnatural" labors, these self-conscious forays into otherness, inevitably resulted in a series of humiliations and, eventually, scandals: humiliations such as the Wits' derisive reception of the imitative "epic" works of Blackmore, Glover, Wilkie, Ogden, and Ogilvie early in the century, and scandals of imposture such as those of James Macpherson's Ossian poems, Joseph Ritson's and Lady Wardlaw's ballad forgeries and Thomas Chatterton's forgeries of the works of an imaginary medieval monk, Thomas Rowley, toward the middle and latter parts of the century.[1] These were all writers who attempted to invent imaginary and radically distant contexts for their writings. It is one of the more elegant ironies of Psalmanazar's ethnography that he claimed that many cultural practices of the Formosans, including the calendar, were established by a prophet named, appropriately enough, Psalmanazar. We can thus begin to see Psalmanazar's writing, with its self-invented grounds of authenticity, as a kind of typical aberration.

From the time that Chinese visitors had first arrived in Europe at the close of the seventeenth century, their appearance produced its own anamorphosis. In his *Memoirs and Observations* of 1699, the Jesuit emissary and (later) travel writer Louis Le Comte wrote of his encounter with a lady who assumed the role of a Chinese princess swept to Europe by a series of shipwrecks and captivities. When she audaciously attempted to "pass off a wild ridiculous gibberish" as Chinese, Le Comte exposed her imposture (Appleton 1951:129). But even actual visitors from China had little to do with the construction of the Orient in the literary culture. During the eighteenth century Chinese vogue, the cultural Other was an occasion for reflexivity in the form of satire, that literary form which above all others assumes a natural stance in its focus upon the critique of all artificiality (Appleton 1951; Sambrook 1986). But these singular foreign visitors, cast upon the shores of British literary culture, held up another kind of satirical mirror to the stranded authorial subjectivity of the period. Without a context, without a tangible social world, any visitor could be an imposter; any pauper a prince; any author a god, to put it positively, or a forger, to put it negatively. Moreover, such visitors—prototypical ethnological "informants"—had their corollary, as items for collection and consumption, in the various literary "discoveries" from among the lower classes often promoted by members of the aristocracy. Among these "untutored geniuses" we find Stephen Duck, the poetical thresherman, discovered by Lord

---

1. For an introduction to some of these issues, see the discussion of the neoclassical epic in Wesley 1697:4–45, and Hagin 1964. On the ballad, see Hustvedt 1916; Macpherson 1765; Meyerstein 1930; Taylor 1978; Clyne 1859; Scott 1802.

Macclesfield; Henry Jones, the poetical bricklayer, discovered by Chesterfield; James Woodhouse, the poetical shoemaker, urged on by Johnson; Ann Years-ley, the poetical pigwoman of Bristol, and James Hogg, Sir Walter Scott's Et-trick shepherd-bard.[2] Here the literary culture estranges itself from its own past as well as from the cultural Other in order to invent a myth of cul-tural origins.

Throughout the eighteenth century, a variety of individuals were set loose from their moorings in a cultural context and consequently aestheti-cized. The self-consciousness of this "natural" artifice was eventually to find its release in the transgressions and expressiveness of Romanticism; but ear-lier in the period a variety of "cross-dressing" appears—tangential, surrepti-tious, even coy in its anticipations of what we now call *le mode rètro*. Aristo-crats and bourgeois authors collaborated in the production of a "written folklore"; orientalism and feudalism were combined in the apotheosis of spa-tial and temporal "otherness"; colonialism developed a market based on the consumption of exotic and exoticized goods (Bunn 1980). And everywhere, as Henri Lefèbvre has noted in a more contemporary context, capitalism re-vealed its capacity for the reinscription of everything—including history—as novelty:

> Capitalism has not only subordinated exterior and anterior sectors to itself, it has produced new sectors, transforming what pre-existed and completely over-throwing the corresponding institutions and organizations. The same is true of "art," knowledge, "leisure," urban and everyday reality. It is a vast process which, as usual, is wrapped in appearances and ideological masks. For example, capitalist production loots previous oeuvres and styles, changes them into ob-jects of "cultural" production and consumption and thus recapitulates these styles in restituted and reconstituted form as "neo" this or that, elite fashions and high quality products. (1976:83)

The production of knowledge does not take place in some transcendent context. In Psalmanazar's strange case we see the gap between subjectivity and otherness as the enabling possibility of both understanding and, of course, its flip side, delusion. At a time when the self-consciousness of ethnography as a form of writing has reached a new, and no less enlightened, pitch, it would be wise to remind ourselves of this shifting historical relation to a referent. The anthropologist as imposter is involved in an ultimately tragic production of signifiers, and ironically, a collapse of writing into the referent will suffer no less from the same end, a simple reversal, should the tide turn to a pre-dominance of an ever-elusive "signified."

2. Hogg, of course, had a chance to actually "discover" a hitherto unknown Scott, and turned the tables by writing a memoir that exposed the pretensions of his discoverer (Hogg 1834).

Analogy and Difference:
Psalmanazar's Cultural Reasoning

In his *Memoirs* Psalmanazar explains his decision to change his pose as an itinerant Irish theology student to that of a native of Japan:

> I recollected, that whilst I was learning humanity, rhetoric, and geography with the Jesuits, I had heard them speak of the East-Indies, China, Japan, &c. and expatiate much in praise of those countries, and the ingenuity of the inhabitants. . . . I was rash enough to think that what I wanted of a right knowledge of them, I might make up by the strength of a pregnant invention, in which I flattered myself I might succeed the more easily, as I supposed they were as little known by the generality of Europeans, that they were only looked upon, in the lump, to be Antipodes to them in almost every respect, as religion, manners, dress, &c. (1765:113)

Thus it would be Psalmanazar's goal to differentiate the lump in line with these "antipodal" expectations. He eventually arrived at a perfect method for the generation of ethnographic information: "Alas, for me, my fancy was but too fertile and ready for all such things, when I set about them, and when any question has been started on a sudden, about matters I was ever so unprepared for, I seldom found myself at a loss for a quick answer, which, if satisfactory, I stored up in my retentive memory" (115). No supply of answers here without the demanding questions: the con man's rule, "give'em what they want," became, for Psalmanazar, a way of structuring an imaginary social whole—its closure loaned by the prior assumption of closure on the part of its audience. The content of that closure, its very remoteness, ensured by this isolated and figuratively inverted island, was on hand to help Psalmanazar even before he began, as was the fact that in England, as opposed to continental Europe, the Jesuit letterbooks with their rich accounts of Asia, were neither translated nor circulated widely (Lach 1977:II, 389).

Psalmanazar's presentation was convincing in part because of his complete invention of a "native" personality for himself. While he was attached to the Duke of Mecklenberg's regiment in Holland, he watched the Lutheran and Calvinist services.

> But as for me, after listening awhile to them, I was commonly driven by my rashness and vanity to turn my back to them, and turning my face to the rising or setting sun, to make some awkward shew of worship, or praying to it, and was no less pleased to be taken notice of for so doing. This vain fit grew up to such a height, that I made me a little book with figures of the sun, moon, and stars, and such other imagery as my phrensy suggested to me, and filled the rest with a kind of gibberish prose and verse, written in my invented character, and which I muttered or chanted as often as the humour took me. (1765: 144–45)

As he left with Innes for England, he invented another ruse:

> I fell upon one of the most whimsical expedients that could come into a crazed
> brain, viz. that of living upon raw flesh, roots, and herbs; and it is surprising
> how soon I habituated myself to this new, and till now, strange food, without
> receiving the least prejudice in my health; but I was blessed with a good con-
> stitution, and I took care to use a good deal of pepper, and other spices, for
> a concocter, whilst my vanity, and the people's surprize at my diet, served me
> for a relishing sauce. (163)

We can imagine the spectacle of Psalmanazar during this period: his "rude,
cast off clothing," donated by Innes, his little book of the sun, moon, and
stars, his diet of barbaric simplicity, and, not least of all, his prodigious classical learning. Here was a fusion of classicism and the exotic—and at the same
time a complete negation of any ordinary presentness—which was to become
the daydream of the more marginal developments of eighteenth-century literary culture.

What is the shape of Psalmanazar's *Historical and Geographical Description
of Formosa?* How does he go about inventing a social totality? There are two
aspects of this ethnography which immediately present themselves as para-
mount: first, the production of a system of differences—that is, an immediately apprehensible, and hence comparable, system of categories of the social:
manners, gestures, means of transport, architecture, costumes, ritual, etc. Such
categories in turn internalize the situation of difference as social rank enters
into them in a pervasive and equally systematic way. And, secondly, there is
an internal consistency whose cumulative effect is that of rational necessity.

The *Description* begins, as might be expected, with etiology—an account
of the relation of Formosa to other islands "in the remotest parts toward the
East," especially Japan. Then there is a brief, dramatic account of how Formosa "preserved its form of government independent of a Foreign Prince until Meryaandanoo [a Chinese] first ravished Japan by villany, and then conquered Formosa by a trick." All this is designed to explain why Formosa is
under the contemporary rule of a Japanese "superintendent King." The extensive account of the Emperor Meryaandanoo, like any myth, tells of the
origins of cultural practices, legitimating them by appearance in a narrative
rather than by some more abstract rationale. But we must not underestimate
another function well served by this initial narrative—that of entertainment.
For Psalmanazar's description was not simply a contribution to science, but
also a text designed for public consumption. Following his narrative introduction, the schematic contents of the *Description* are frequently enlivened
by anecdotal passages and long interpolations on Formosan religion with its
obvious allegorical relation to Western religions and Psalmanazar's own situation. Psalmanazar's tasks were to balance authority, originality, convention,

and idiosyncrasy for a public clamoring for novelty—a novelty which should remain, nonetheless, familiar.

The *Description's* outline of the social life of the Formosans clarifies the universality of a system of differences which must have been more than familiar to Psalmanazar's readers. Murderers, thieves, slanderers, robbers, traitors, adulterers, and other rebels against family and state meet appropriate, if often shockingly "barbarous," ends. The religion of the Formosans included a sacred text—the *Jarhabandiond* ("The Election of the Land"), a revelation of "one supreme god," a practice of child sacrifice, and a prophet named, in the "coincidence" noted above, Psalmanazar, that is, "the Author of Peace." It is Psalmanazar who orders the construction of a temple, who establishes the calendar as ten months, each named for a star, and who commands that every year the hearts of 18,000 young boys under the age of nine years should be sacrificed. But throughout the text, it is the Formosan religion which is most strongly delineated: festivals, fasting days, ceremonies, the procedures for sacrifices, the election of priests, the worship of the sun, moon, and stars, the postures of the body in adoring, the ceremonies observed on the birth of children, weddings, funerals, the state of souls after death, and the form of priestly garments, are all carefully described.

Following the establishment of the principles of religious order, there are chapters on manners and customs and physical characteristics. Perhaps because by this time Psalmanazar was having difficulty explaining his complexion and overall facial appearance to missionaries who had in fact been to the Orient, he describes "the men of Estates, but especially the Women, [as] very fair; for they during the hot season, live underground in places that are very cold." We are next given an outline of costume by gender and rank; a description of cities, houses, palaces, and castles; "those commodities they have, and some that they want"; weights and measures; superstitions; diseases; revenues of those in high places; "the Fruits of the Ground"; "Things which they Commonly Eat"; animals; the language; shipping; money; arms; musical instruments; education; the liberal and mechanical arts in Japan; "the splendid Retinue that attends the Vice-Roy of Formosa when he goes to Wait Upon the Emperor of Japan"; "the History of the Jesuits in Japan"; "the History of the Dutch in Japan"; "Of the new Devices of the Jesuits for getting into Japan."

Yet the table of contents here does not do justice to the careful blend of anecdote, detail, and evaluation making up Psalmanazar's *Description*. Religious practice and its relation to belief are woven as themes into nearly every part of his account. Psalmanazar carefully balances what the reader needs to know and what the author needs to tell, always portraying details via firsthand knowledge, but hedging his judgments by claiming the limits of his experience as a member of the culture, rather than a transcendent observer, and by reflecting upon his changed status as a convert away from the culture—a

Christian. The reader is thus constantly aware of a principle of differentiation as the basis for culture—a principle whose structure is linked to the West, but whose "Formosan" referents constantly emphasize a defining otherness. It is therefore not surprising that rank is the first principle of Formosan social order—the king; the queen; the viceroy; the viceroy's lady; the general; the general's lady; a gentleman; a gentlewoman; a burger; a country bumpkin. These categories are elaborated in the discussion of costume, which itself becomes reduced in both quantity and quality as one descends in rank: "The Country People who dwell in Villages and Desert-places, wear nothing but a Bears skin upon their shoulders, and a Plate to cover their Privy-parts made of Brass or the shells of Fish, or the bark of Trees" (1704:204). In contrast, figures of the upper ranks are clothed in silk, gold, silver, and precious stones. Thus rank is tied to proximity to nature—the upper ranks linked to elaboration, refinement, and detail, the lower ranks linked to simplicity and raw materials.

As is evident from the paired categories above, gender is elaborated as another important principle of order. There are differentiated habits for differentiated categories of women: infants, virgins, brides, married women, and widows. And, finally, in a category close to his own experience, Psalmanazar describes the military. Here rank is separated into the king's officers and guards; the viceroy's guards; the soldiers guarding the city; the drummers and the ensigns. Psalmanazar's emphasis on costume, like his emphasis on architecture, is a brilliant device for reifying appearances. Just as narrative forestalls the questions of founding principles, so does costume assign differences in

---

"The Tabernacle and the Altar."

"1. A Crown hanging from the Roof over the top of the Tabernacle. 2. The Head of an Oxe, or the Symbol of their God. 3. The top of the Tabernacle with 5 burning Lamps. 4. A little Pyramid upon which is the Figure of the Sun. 5. Another upon which is the Figure of the Moon. 6. A Lamp to the honour of the Moon. 7. A Lamp to the honour of the Sun. 8. 2 Courtins which cover the Concavity of the Tabernacle on the Ordinary days. 9. The Concavity of the Tabernacle adorned with a Sky-colour and Stars of Gold, representing the Firmament, in which God appears. 10. Their God showing himself to the People, in the shape of an Oxe. 11. Two Lamps burning to the honour of their God. 12. Two Pyramids upon which are the 10 Stars, which are Worshiped. And all these things are to be made of Gold or Silver. 13. The Gridiron upon which the hearts of the young Children are burnt. 14. The Furnace of Fire for burning them. 15. The Chimneys by which the Smoke goes out. 16. The Caldron in which the Flesh of the Sacrifice is boyled. 17. The Furnace of Fire for boyling them. 18. The Sanctuary, or the place in which the young Children are Slain. 19. The pit in which their Blood and Bodies are placed. 20. The holy place wherein the Beasts are Slain for Sacrifice. 21. A Marble-structure in which is a Gridiron. 22. A Stone-structure that encompasseth the Caldron in the form of an Altar. 23. The smoke of a Furnace. 24. The round part of the Roof; 25. the Wall." (From George Psalmanazar, *An Historical and Geographical Description of Formosa . . .* [2d ed., London, 1705], pp. 155–56.)

Drawings of "Formosans." (From George Psalmanazar, *An Historical and Geographical Description of Formosa . . .*)

fig: 11.
A Married Woman
A Gentlemans Nurse
A Widow
A Country Woman

rank to the already given realm of surfaces. Psalmanazar concludes his discussion of costume by writing, "This is all I thought worthy to be remark'd as to their Apparel, which altho it may appear ridiculous to the Europeans, yet is there accounted very Beautiful and Splendid" (1704:208).

In addition to the familiar categories of Western European rank—the aristocracy, the gentry, the peasantry, the clergy, and the military—we also find the familiar literary categories of historical difference, categories which would have been well known to Psalmanazar's audience from traveller's accounts and other literary forms. The emphasis upon cremation, rather than burial, of the body; the worship of the sun, moon, and stars; and the practice of animal sacrifice would have echoed to Christian perceptions of paganism. Similarly the practice of polygamy and Psalmanazar's account of a husband's varying loyalties to his various wives echoed the attack on Islam by medieval European writers who charged Muhammed with promiscuity for the practice of polygamy (Alloula 1986:xv). And Psalmanazar's repeated descriptions of the prostrate body in his accounts of ceremony and ritual would have reminded readers of the humiliating kowtow ceremonies which the Chinese had imposed upon seventeenth-century Dutch traders (Pritchard 1970:98; see also Appleton 1951:166 for later accounts). Finally, the paradisal commodities of Psalmanazar's Formosa—gold, silver, silk, and cotton—provide a familiar background for Psalmanazar's fantastic narrative of greed and colonization. From the works of Herodotus, Ctesias, and later writers, Europe had imagined the Orient as a land overflowing with precious stones and treasure (Lach 1970:114). Thus the strange is always allied to the familiar in this system of resonant allusions and "antipodal expectations." We are reminded of the tradition of "digging to China, where everything will be upside down," in passages such as: "The Tree is like a Wall-nut Tree, but in this differs from all other Trees, that whereas their Fruit stands downward, the Fruit of this stands upright"; "Chilak is a kind of powder made like Coffee, but in this it differs from Coffee, that is may be drunk cold, whereas Coffee is always drunk hot" (1704:231–32).

No detail affirms the difference of Psalmanazar's Formosa, its existence as irredeemably "other," more than his account of the practice of child sacrifice. But as the imaginative limit of cultural difference, this practice, too, appears often in eighteenth-century literature. We are reminded, of course, of Swift's *Modest Proposal*, where in fact Psalmanazar is mentioned: "the famous Sallmanaazar, a Native of the Island Formosa, who . . . told my friend, that in his Country when any young Person happened to be put to death, the Executioner sold the Carcass to Persons of Quality, as a prime Dainty, and that, in his Time, the Body of a plump Girl of fifteen, who was crucified for attempting to Poison the Emperor, was sold . . . in Joints from the Gibbet." (1729:10). In this shocking relation, we find, in fact, an entirely Western European specter: the crucifixion and the transubstantiation of Christ mapped onto an allegory of total commodification, as well as the memory of a "barbaric" legal code aimed at the rectification of the body, and only recently supplanted by a penal system designed to rectify the spirit.

But, perhaps even more strikingly (because an echo and not, as in Swift's case, a precedent), we find here the sentiments of that foundation statement of the underlying principle of cultural variability, Locke's *Essay Concerning Human Understanding*, and its dogmatic insistence on the impossibility of innate moral principles:

> Have there not been whole nations, and those of the most civilized people, amongst whom the exposing their children, and leaving them in the fields to perish by want or wild beasts has been the practice; as little condemned or scrupled as the begetting them? Do they not still, in some countries, put them into the same graves with their mothers, if they die in childbirth; or despatch them, if a pretended astrologer declares them to have unhappy stars? . . . There are places where they eat their own children. The Caribbees were wont to geld their children on purpose to fat and eat them. And Garcilasso de la Vega tells us of a people in Peru which were wont to fat and eat the children they got on their female captives, whom they kept as concubines for that purpose, and when they were past breeding, the mothers themselves were killed too and eaten. (1690: I, 72–73)

Locke goes on with his list of moral atrocities which nevertheless affirm the variable organization of human culture—practices of cannibalism, infanticide, parricide, and the special case of cannibalism of one's own progeny. "Anthropophagi," or man-eating, had been part of the Western European mythology of the cultural Other from Homer forward. Psalmanazar's account of Formosan sacrifice thus touched on several familiar notions, especially the linking of cannibalism, human sacrifice, and addiction to human flesh (Pagden 1982:81–89). It is therefore not so surprising that the eccentric Psalmanazar himself came to be accused of cannibalistic deeds. Thus a sham advertisement in *The Spectator* for March 16, 1711, announced the performance of an opera, "The Cruelty of Atreus," at the Haymarket, in which "the scene wherein Thyestes eats his own children is to be performed by the famous Mr. Psalmanazar, lately arrived from Formosa: The whole Supper being set to kettle-drums" (*Spectator*: 65). Later, such satire was recorded as fact; Needham notes the following passage from Boucher de la Richardie's 1808 *Bibliotheque universelle des Voyages*: "Psalmanazar himself, transported to London, had retained this depraved taste to such an extent that, excited to eat the flesh of a woman who had been hanged, he did so without repugnance" (Needham 1986:89).

Psalmanazar had described the practice of child sacrifice with a hyperbolic intensity which was likely to elicit such horrified responses, but which also elicited disbelief. In the preface to the second edition of the *Historical and Geographical Description* he answered twenty-five objections, including a number referring specifically to his account of sacrificial practices. Thus the seventeenth—Is it possible that any people can be so barbarously superstitious as to sacrifice so many thousand children every year?—was rebutted by arguing that the Formosans lacked the blessing of revealed religion and by pointing to numerous instances of such sacrifices in the Christian Bible. To the eighteenth objection, that George Candidius, the early seventeenth-century Dutch missionary to Formosa, did not mention this custom, Psalmanazar replied that Candidius—whose *Account of the Island of Formosa* was in fact the major literary source for his own account—was a forger, and that these sacrifices were not so strange as Candidius' own mention that women pregnant before their thirty-seventh year have their bellies stomped until they miscarry. And to the nineteenth objection, that "the sacrifice of 18,000 boys a year would soon depopulate the island," Psalmanazar offered four responses: this is what the law says, but they never sacrifice that many; polygamy produces many children; children are sacrificed at a very young age; and, finally, "just consider how many Englishmen emigrate; there are now four times as many women as men."

With his rhetoric of analogy and difference underwritten by the familiarity of hierarchy and the exoticism of cultural practices, Psalmanazar added an undercurrent of satire. He continually muttered comments against the priestly class, in a clear attempt to criticize all priests, particularly the Jesuits, who functioned as his enemies both in his account of his "kidnapping" and in his current debates with missionaries such as Father Fountenay. This anticlerical subtext is evident, for example, in comments on priestly greed:

> But after such a Beast dies of itself, or is offer'd in Sacrifice to our God, then they believe that the Soul which was in it, shall be transformed into a Star in Heaven, where it shall enjoy eternal happiness. But all this seems to me to be a fiction invented by our Priests, because they reap great profit and advantage by it, for when anyone dies, the Relations of the Deceased, are to pay them a great sum of Money, more or less, according to their ability. (1704:185–86)

The same theme also appears in comments on priestly hypocrisy. In a passage describing "a Notable story" regarding superstitions, Psalmanazar told how a countryman exposed a hoax by a priest. Consequently "the High Priest, or their Pope" condemned the priest to perpetual imprisonment and the countryman to death "for not yielding due Deference and Submission to the Priest; from whence everyone may clearly perceive, what Tyranny the Priests exercise over the common people, who are not permitted to declare Publickly any doubt they have even of those things they know to be false" (1704:223).

Once again we see Psalmanazar working to maintain a balance between the novel and the comprehensible. Yet if idiosyncrasy served the interests of a rhetoric of credibility here—the particular detail, in this early phase of the realist tradition, lending authenticity to the whole—only replicability could ensure the cohesion of such facts. Thus we find Psalmanazar, in his encounters with objections, scrambling to make analogies to the cultural practices of the Japanese as the Formosans' landlords and closest neighbors, to the polygamy of the Turks, and to the foodways of the Tartars. These are objections of function, relying upon assumptions that a culture is interested in its own perpetuation and that cultural practices have some purpose, some material end. But if Psalmanazar's British audience may have been willing to believe that God would sacrifice his only son for the life of humanity, common sense rebelled against the portrayal of a widespread cultural practice of child sacrifice. Psalmanazar had at one and the same time to manage a radical difference that would ensure his own authority and a system of analogies that would make his claims intelligible. Thus he often pointed to "aberrations" in English culture—the beheading of Charles I before his own palace; the emigration of the male population; the inadequacy of existing English histories; even the "chalk scores" milkwomen used instead of numbers. What metaphorically gets lost in translation here is in fact the surplus which ensures that "there is something there there," to paraphrase Gertrude Stein. Consider Psalmanazar's answer to the twenty-fifth objection in the second edition—If he's really a Christian, why does he talk about returning home, where he must renounce his religion or be crucified? Psalmanazar suggested that he could "answer this in private," a reserve thereby constituting "a reserve," a kind of treasure of the unsaid.

We must note here that rationality is not simply a matter of logic, or causality, or effect—it is also a matter of predictability and repetition. As any spy knows, one's ability to reproduce the culture is what gives integrity to the culture. But, because of the obvious fact that he had no referent, Psalmanazar could only produce a culture, he could not reproduce one. Thus we find a central tragic scene in Psalmanazar's biography: his "fall from language," the exposure of his forgery's singularity, brought about by the equally cunning con man, William Innes (Psalmanazar 1765:151n.). At the onset of his imposture, Psalmanazar had invented a Formosan alphabet, including "names for the letters" and a partial grammar (114–15). During his service with the Scots regiment at Sluys, Innes expressed interest in converting Psalmanazar, yet

he was so far from believing me to be what I pretended, that he had some time before taken a most effectual way to convince himself of the contrary, beyond all possibility of doubting. His stratagem, if I may so call it, was to make me translate a passage in Cicero *de natura deorum*, of some length, into my (pretended) Formosan language, and give it to him in writing; and this I easily did, by means of that unhappy readiness I had at inventing of characters, languages, &c. But, after he had made me construe it, and desired me to write another version of it on another paper, his proposal, and the manner of his exacting

The Formolan Alphabet

Name	Power			Figure			Name
Añ	A	a	ao		I	I	I
Mem	M	m̃	m				
Nen	N	ñ	n				
Taph	T	th	t				XI
Lamdo	L	ll	l				
Samdo	S	ch	s				
Vomera	V	w	u				IƆNƆI
Bagdo	B	b	b				
Hamno	H	kh	h				
Pedlo	P	pp	p				
Kaphi	K	k	x				ƆXI
Omda	O	o	œ				
Ilda	I	y	i				
Xatara	X	xh	x				IƐ̃ƆI
Dam	D	th	d				
Zamphi	Z	tl	z				ƆXII
Epsi	E	ε	η				Ɔbᵢ̃
Fandem	F	ph	f				ƆUI
Raw	R	rh	r				AI
Gomera	G	g	j				IƆUƆ

T. Slater sculp.

it, threw me into such visible confusion, having had so little time to excogitate the first, and less to commit it to memory, that there were not above one half of the words in the second that were in the first. His desiring me to construe this likewise, confused me still more; especially when he showed me the palpable difference. (155)

Far from being scandalized, Innes was, as we know from his consequent relation to Psalmanazar as the patron of his "imposture," pleased with Psalmanazar's "memory and readiness."[3] As if to forestall a repetition of this exposure, Psalmanazar armed his chapter on the language of the Formosans in his *Historical and Geographical Description* with the catechisms he had given to Bishop Compton, translations of the Lord's Prayer, the Apostles' Creed, and the Ten Commandments.

The issues here have multiple levels of reference. Psalmanazar's rejection and even vilification of the Jesuits throughout the *Description* stemmed from their presence as the only extant "counterintelligence" regarding Formosa. His ingenious questioning of the tenets of faith referred directly to the questions occupying the more sceptical members of his readership: how could "the wonderful works pretended to be done by Christ and his Apostles [be] true and real Miracles, such as could only be wrought by an Almighty Power and not done by the Tricks of Jugglers and Conjurers?" (1704:70–71); how could one distinguish between "Objects of Faith Only" [such as the Roman belief in transubstantiation] and "Objects of our senses"? (82); how could one be certain, "that what the Evangelists and Apostles assert is Truth; for they might impose upon us, and write things which never were performed?" (104); how can one "be sure that the Books we have of the New Testament are the same the Evangelists and the Apostles penn'd, and that in Succession of Time they have not been changed and altered?" (106); and, "If the sacrificing of Children by the Pagans seems so very unnatural, surely the Death and Passion of Christ shew much more Cruelty; it is harder therefore to believe, that God should require the Sacrifice of his only Son, than of some thousands of Infants" (119). Here once more Psalmanazar brilliantly "covered his tracks," making invisible a writing that referred only to its own making as writing, erasing the "source" of its assumption of power. For these questions point to a com-

3. We must note, as Psalmanazar does, that this was the ironic exposure of a forger by a plagiarist, an exposure based upon the forger's inability to copy his own "knowledge": "I soon perceived him [Innes] to be a man of no small ambition, though he was so far from having any of the generous disposition which is mostly known to accompany it, that he was no less a slave to avarice; witness his arrogating to himself the credit as well as the advantage of that excellent treatise, entitled, *A Modest Enquiry after Moral Virtue*, for which he obtained from the present bishop of London a very good living in Essex; but which the real and worthy author, a poor episcopal clergyman in Scotland, since obliged him publickly to disown and disclaim in print, as well as to comprise with him for the profit of the edition" (*Memoirs*, p. 151n. [1765]).

mon ground of questioning; they are, after all, the issues raised against
Psalmanazar by his critics. And, as well, they point to the ingenuous quality
of the cultural Other, whose very naiveté is evidence of his authenticity.

That authenticity was further guaranteed by the many specific and non-
contradictory details that fill his text; here was clearly a photographic imagination, if not a photographic "memory." Psalmanazar had truly drawn a world
from his reading and his imagination. Thus the *Description* fulfilled an ultimate Enlightenment dream—the dream of animation in which logical consistency can itself produce a referent, a world engendered by reason alone,
unencumbered by history, materiality, or nature. Psalmanazar, we must assume, in fact recognized the skill of this accomplishment. When in the second preface he answered the objection that he was too young to have such
a knowledge of his culture, he countered:

> You do me more Honour than you are aware of, for then you must think that
> I forg'd the whole story out of my own Brain. . . . he must be a Man of pro-
> digious parts who can invent the Description of a Country, contrive a Religion,
> frame Laws and Customs, make a Language, and Letters, etc. and these differ-
> ent from all other parts of the world; he must have also more than a humane
> memory that is always ready to vindicate so many feign'd particulars, and that
> without eer so much as once contradicting himself. (1705:A2)

Here we find the ethnography's ultimate integrity, its closure as a systematic description—and also its collapse, its dislocation as a kind of refusal of
common grounds of intelligibility. Psalmanazar's forgery could not long stand
up to the pressures of its own claims. By 1708 it burst at the seams, and he
himself played a primary role in its collapse. This is the vulnerability of all
forgeries—their incapacity to carry their appropriate contexts with them. And
thus we can in fact see forgery as the antithesis of plagiarism, for while
plagiarism's crime is an inappropriate repetition, forgery's crime is an inappropriate, and entirely invented, singularity. The forger is always an imposter
by his or her attempt to escape the social grounds of subjectivity and authorship. Psalmanazar's brilliant move was to forge an entire social world and
hence to provide such grounds simply by writing them. If this was the dream
of Enlightenment reason, it was also the dream of Enlightenment authorship—
to usher in whatever was necessary to make the world, as a textual world,
cohere.

The Figure of Conversion

Psalmanazar's *Description of Formosa* is flanked by conversions, real and fictional, of which he provided extensive accounts. What should therefore com-
mand our attention in considering his later writings is an interplay between

two rhetorical modes—the description-testimony and the confession-conversion. These two gestures—one reaching out to the world within a stance of distance and objectivity, the other reaching inward in a claim of transformation that in itself asserts or posits the very subjectivity which is its "motivating" cause—run in an obvious course from the halted narrative and ensuing lyricism of Augustine's "confessions" to the paired volumes of ethnographic description and personal memoirs produced by anthropologists up to the present.[4] In fact, we might hypothesize that we find in these later complementary rhetorics the ghost of anthropology's missionary connections—the rhetoric of transformation projected as a rhetoric of writing—the conversion of "experience" or "spectacle" into detail, the conversion of "the scene" into form, and the conversion, ultimately, of "other" into self, "self" into other.

It is clear that these are interconnected sets of rhetorical modes, constantly bolstering each other in an attempt at persuasiveness and credibility. The confession is the narrative of the convert's fall and redemption, which of course only achieves closure at the moment of that redemption and so is, like tragedy, a narrative finished before it is begun. Furthermore, the confession acquires its integrity and value in proportion to its degree of detail and specificity. For every detail speaks to the authenticity generated by the "first hand," testifying as to the reliability of the speaker, lending authority to the speaker's self and capacity for truth. Thus it is obvious that the function of description in the confessional mode is not the replication of an "outside," an objective world unaffected by authorial consciousness, but rather the invention of the speaking subject as the location of veracity.

But these general features of confessional testimony, these qualities of "eye-witnessing" as "I-witnessing," are given a very specific form in Psalmanazar's texts. For Psalmanazar's initial conversions—from his native Catholicism to his imaginary "Formosan" religious practices, and from "Formosan" to a feigned Anglicanism, and, finally, from a feigned Anglicanism to a true Anglicanism—must be read as conversions both from one set of cultural practices to another and from one set of subjectivities to another. Weaving in and out of doctrine,

4. Pratt (1986:27–50) discusses the relation of the narrative memoir to the ethnographic description. We should also note the vaunting ambition of the opening of Rousseau's *Confessions* here: "I am commencing an undertaking, hitherto without precedent, and which will never find an imitator. I desire to set before my fellows the likeness of a man in all the truth of nature, and that man myself." The project of the confession narrative, we should remind ourselves, is a self which is an effect of writing: the undertaking is the complete confession which produces the unique self and not the reverse. My understanding of the confessional mode is influenced by my reading of Augustine's stunning "collapse" from the temporality of third person narrative to the atemporality of dialogical lyricism at the juncture of Books IX and X in *The Confessions,* and among secondary texts, by Neil Hertz's reading of "Flaubert's Conversion" (1985); and of course by Foucault's discussion of confession in *The History of Sexuality* (1980) and *Discipline and Punish: The Birth of the Prison* (1979).

practice, appearance, and sincerity, these conversions effect a remarkable set of transformations even as surface changes. Yet it is only in Psalmanazar's final conversion—his conversion from a lie to "the truth" in the revelations of his memoirs and the habits of his later life—that he partakes of the religious, and often sexual, transformations of darkness and light, sin and salvation, familiar from Augustine's "break" with the world.[5] And here we must realize what tremendous power the feature of closure has on our acceptance of this rhetoric of "truth." There is no intrinsic reason to accept Psalmanazar's final account as being any more valid than his other accounts. But there are two features that lend it a powerful credibility: the testimony of witnesses to his consistent practices of piety in his last years and the power of death as the ultimate closure. Thus the corroboration of a "social" as the other to "self," the absolute otherness of death (its resistance to the manipulations of style and the frame), and the play on closure in the nonclosure of answerability and salvation which death assumes in Christian myth, all impress upon us the authenticity of the "final account" as more than mere version.

In his *Memoirs*, just as in his rebuttals of objections to the *Description*, Psalmanazar still questioned the validity of religious doctrines, especially the issues raised by Catholic transubstantiation and Calvinist predestination. The singling out of these doctrines is not arbitrary, but rather a matter of the relationship such issues of appearance, reality, and free will had to his own transgressions and to his situation amid Jesuit, Anglican, and Calvinist influences. Indeed the emphasis upon faith in miracles in his writings provides a repetitive clue to the problem of his own discourse—its failed referent and its insistent singularity. But in the *Memoirs*, religion's shifting grounds of argument are finally subdued by a general appeal for tolerance and, in a prescient "echo" of his own repentance, by a recognition of God as the "only true Author" of understanding: "the truth of a Christian doctrine is not founded on the opinion or authority of any men, but on the evidence of Holy Writ" (1765:44).

---

5. These transformations foreshadow the important function of testimony in the later "ethnology" of the Marquis de Sade. The closed world of the chateau at Silling, for example, with its costumes, manners, ceremonies, customs, and social ranks, presents us with a spectacle of narrative testimonies which refuse to realize themselves as "events." Psalmanazar in turn blames his forgery and imposture, in the preface to his *Memoirs*, on "various carnal considerations and the violent hurry of my passions" (1765:10). The imposter, of course, does not have the patience for either Nature or History to produce its more proper, and seemingly desireless, forms of subjectivity. While I have largely left aside the matter of Psalmanazar's motivation, it is worth noting that this adolescent forger (like his counterpart, the forger of history Thomas Chatterton) was stranded in the lower ranks of the middle classes. Each could claim a lack of inheritance from an "ancient, but decayed family," each suffered from an aberrant relation to the Oedipal situation (Chatterton's father died before his birth; Psalmanazar's parents were inexplicably separated and his father mysteriously incapacitated), and each experienced an imbalance between the qualities of his education and his fortune.

The specific form of Psalmanazar's final conversion is designed to counter-act the dispersed fiction of his *Description* by the substitution of an originary and encompassing scholarship of culture. The work of Psalmanazar's later life (after the fiasco of the "Japanning" paint, a final pun on the "covering" of the material grounds of his being) was all designed as a kind of cross-hatching, to use an eighteenth-century writing practice as the metaphor here, of his earlier texts. In 1747, Psalmanazar contributed anonymously to Bowen's *Complete System of Geography*, providing the entry on Formosa and using it as a forum to criticize both his own imposture and the earlier account of Candidius, as deserving "as little credit as that of our pretended Formosan." Thus, in the *Memoirs*, he explained, "Formosa, which part I chose, that I might take occasion publickly to acknowledge, as it were by a third hand, the falsehood and imposture of my former account of that island" (1765:287). Anonymity, the "third hand," is of course the best cure for infamy, the one which allows a continued production, just as forgetting is the analogous cure for memory.

A decade earlier, Psalmanazar had played an important part in the writing of the *Universal History*, to which he anonymously contributed chapters on the Jews, the Celts, the Scythians, the Greeks, the empires of Nice and Trebizon, the ancient Spaniards, Gauls, Germans, Thebans, and Corinthians. Psalmanazar's work for the *Universal History* replaced the self-aggrandizing particulars of his *Description* with self-effacing generalities. The goal of the *Universal History* was the integration of all historical cultures within a specifically Christian chronology. Thus the preface to the first volume, dedicated to the Duke of Marlborough, suggested that "works of this nature carry our knowledge, as Tally observes, beyond the vast and devouring Space of numberless years, triumph over Time and make us, though living at an immense Distance, in a Manner Eye-witness to all the Events and Revolutions which have occasioned astonishing changes in the World." This was a world, a history, already known and already redeemed—and thus an ideal counter to the wild details of his *Description*, just as his reimmersion in Hebrew was a counter to his earlier invention of Formosan characters.

Psalmanazar's five-hundred-page "History of the Jews," which formed the eleventh chapter of the *Universal History*, takes us from the "return to Jerusalem" to the death of Christ and the "total destruction of Jerusalem and dispersion of the Jewish nation." Yet this history's strongly narrative impulse is mixed with techniques and concerns deriving from Psalmanazar's ethnography. We find Psalmanazar constantly questioning the grounds of an authentic culture and such a culture's relation to its sacred writings. At the beginning of his history, Psalmanazar traced the split between "authentic Jews" and the Samaritans "who were a mongrel mixture, partly of the ten tribes, partly of revolted Jews." The former, he suggested, remained averse to idolatry, observant of the Sabbath, and "willing to suffer the most bloody persecutions, and horrid butcheries, with utmost courage and constancy, rather than violate their laws or fidelity" (1738–44:2).

As Psalmanazar's history unfolds, we see this antithesis between the Samaritans and the Jews as one defined by differing relations to textuality. The Samaritans, unlike the Jews, "were guilty of the most flagrant forgery in corrupting their pentateuch in many places." Psalmanazar excused those errors resulting from poor transcription and those resulting from explanatory interpolations, but concluded "there are certainly several notorious ones, which could not but be designedly made to support their cause against their Jewish antagonists" (1738–44:33). This was certainly a style of "doctored" argument familiar to Psalmanazar.

The hero of Psalmanazar's history is Ezra, who compiled the sacred books in order to restore the church's discipline and rites, "according to its ancient patterns, under its former prophets," to which end "his first care was to collect and set forth a correct edition to the sacred books" (1738:44:13). Ezra's followers, the "Caraim or Karraites," cited by Psalmanazar as the "scripturists or persons wholly addicted to the reading, and thoroughly versed in sacred writings," were singled out for discussion and shown to be completely faithful to the tenets of scripture. Psalmanazar suggested that those scripturists "look upon the canonical books of the old testament as the only rule for their faith," and "expound scripture by scripture" (174). Here, then, was a textual world that did cohere. But, of course, there is a tone of straining credibility and anticipation throughout the history–the anxiety of the *Description of Formosa* is still with Psalmanazar, if only in his frequent railings against textual corruption. At the start of his *History*, we find an elaborate digression on the incorrectness of Bishop Hare's edition of the Psalms (16). And, at its close, we find strong criticism of derivative histories of the Jews. Psalmanazar attacked "Bengorian," whose work is "stuffed with the most absurd falsehoods," and applauded Josephus, who "hath all the marks of a judicious and exact historian" (291–92). The qualification, "hath all the marks," has a particular resonance here to the tragic situation of this reformed forger, who must yet convince by the expounding of text by texts, a writing whose marks would ostensibly, but only ostensibly, bear an authentic relation to their referents.

At the end of his life, in a systematic rejection of the accouterments of his fictional project, Psalmanazar turned away from ornament and detail. The more particular, the more finely "worked," the fictional ethnography, the greater its claims to authenticity. But once the artificial grounds for those claims were exposed, Psalmanazar's project became a matter of stripping away–the stripping away of information and complexity, the stripping away of the identity he fabricated as an author. No one, even Johnson, presumably ever learned his "real name"–and hence we are never given his "proper" name, the name which would locate him in time, space, and genealogy. His autobiography was posthumous, closed before it could be opened. Here he included his last

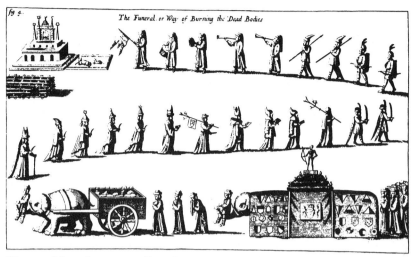

"Formosan" funeral procession. (From George Psalmanazar, *An Historical and Geographical Description of Formosa . . .*)

will and testament, prescribing: "I desire that my body . . . may be kept so long above ground as decency or conveniency will permit, and afterwards conveyed to the common burying-ground, and there interred in some obscure corner of it, without any further ceremony or formality than is used to the bodies of the deceased pensioners where I happen to die . . . and that the whole may be performed in the lowest and cheapest manner. And it is my earnest request that my body be not inclosed in any kind of coffin, but only decently laid in what is called a shell of lowest value, and without lid or other covering which may hinder the natural earth from covering it all round" (1765:3–4). In these requests—requests to strip away all ceremony, ornament, rank, architecture, and identity—to ultimately dissolve the figure into the ground, we see the final resolution of Psalmanazar's ethnographic dilemma. For this dissolution marks the end of articulation as well as the end of utterance—the mute and invisible narrative of the unmarked grave and its terrible threat to difference, as well as to identity.

Acknowledgments

The research for this essay was greatly aided by the staff at the Library Company of Philadelphia, the British Library, and by my colleague, Peter Tasch, who generously shared a set of references on Psalmanazar with me. The essay was written under the auspices of a grant from the John Simon Guggenheim Foundation. Finally, readings by George Stocking and Jim Clifford of initial drafts were of much help to me in completing this essay.

References Cited

Addison, J., & R. Steele. 1711 *The Spectator*. Ed. D. Bond. Vol. 1. Oxford (1965).

Alloula, M. 1986. *The colonial harem*. Trans. M. & W. Godzich. Minneapolis.

Appleton, W. 1951. *A cycle of Cathay: The Chinese vogue in England during the seventeenth and eighteenth centuries*. New York.

Augustine. *Confessions*. Trans. R. S. Pine-Coffin. Harmondsworth, Eng. (1961).

Beckett, S. 1965. *Three novels by Samuel Beckett*. New York.

Boswell, J. 1791. *Boswell's life of Johnson*. 6 vols. Ed. G. B. Hill, rev. L. F. Powell. Oxford (1934).

Bunn, J. H. 1980. The Aesthetics of British Mercantilism. *New Lit. Hist.* 11:303–21.

Clifford, J. L. 1955. *Young Sam Johnson*. New York.

Clyne, N. 1859. *The romantic Scottish ballads and the Lady Wardlaw heresy*. Aberdeen.

Curley, T. M. 1976. *Samuel Johnson and the age of travel*. Athens, Ga.

Davis, B., ed. 1961. Sir John Hawkins, *The life of Samuel Johnson LL.D*. New York.

Eagleton, T. 1984. *The function of criticism: From the Spectator to post-structuralism*. London.

Eisenstein, E. 1979. *The printing press as an agent of change: Communications and cultural transformations in early-modern Europe*. 2 vols. Cambridge.

Foucault, M. 1979. *Discipline and punish*. Trans. A. Sheridan. New York.

———. 1980. *The history of sexuality*. Vol. 1: *An introduction*. Trans. R. Hawley. New York.

Hagen, P. 1964. *The epic hero and the decline of heroic poetry*. Berne.

Hertz, N. 1985. *The end of the line*. New York.

Hill, G. B. 1934. Appendix A, George Psalmanazar. In 1934 edition of Boswell 1791: III, 443–49.

Hogg, J. 1834. *Domestic manners of Sir Walter Scott*. Stirling, Scotland (1909).

Hustvedt, S. 1916. *Ballad criticism in Scandinavia and Great Britain during the eighteenth century*. New York.

Ingrams, R., ed. 1984. *Dr. Johnson by Mrs. Thrale: the 'Anecdotes' of Mrs. Piozzi in their original form*. London

Lach, D. 1970. *Asia in the making of Europe*. Vol. II, Book 1: *The visual arts*. Chicago.

———. 1977. *Asia in the making of Europe*. Vol. II, Book 2: *The literary arts*. Chicago.

Lee, S. 1917. George Psalmanazar. *Dictionary of National Biography*. Vol. 16. London.

Lefèbvre, H. 1976. *The survival of capitalism: Reproduction of the relations of production*. Trans. F. Bryant. New York.

Locke, J. 1690. *An essay concerning human understanding*. 2 vols. New York (1959).

Macpherson, J. 1765. *The poems of Ossian*. 2 vols. London (1822).

Meyerstein, E. H. W. 1930. *A life of Thomas Chatterton*. New York.

Needham, R. 1985. *Exemplars*. Berkeley.

Pagden, A. 1982. *The fall of natural man: The American Indian and the origins of comparative ethnology*. Cambridge.

Pratt, M. L. 1986. Fieldwork in common places. In *Writing culture: The poetics and politics of ethnography*, ed. J. Clifford & G. Marcus, 27–50. Berkeley.

Pritchard, E. 1970. *Anglo-Chinese relations during the seventeenth and eighteenth centuries*. New York.

Psalmanazar, G. 1704. *An historical and geographical description of Formosa, an island subject to the emperor of Japan. Giving an account of the religion, customs, manners &c. of the inhabitants. Together with a relation of what happen'd to the author in his travels; particularly his conferences with the Jesuits, and others, in several parts of Europe. Also the history and reasons of his conversion to Christianity, with his objections against it (in defense of Paganism) and their answers. To which is prefix'd, a preface in vindication of himself from the reflections of a Jesuit lately come from China, with an account of what passed between them.* London.

————. 1705. *The second edition corrected, with many large and useful additions, particularly a new preface clearly answering every thing that has been objected against the author and the book. Illustrated with several cuts to which are added, a map, and the figure of an idol not in the former edition.* London.

————. 1765. *Memoirs of ****, commonly known by the name of George Psalmanazar; A Reputed native of Formosa. Written by himself, in order to be published after his death: containing an account of his education, travels, adventures, connections, literary productions, and pretended conversion from heathenism to Christianity; which last proved the occasion of his being brought over into this kingdom, and passing for a proselyte and a member of the church of England.* 2d ed. London.

————. 1738–44. *The history of the Jews.* Chapter XI of *An universal history, from the earliest accounts of time, compiled from original authors; and illustrated with maps, cuts, notes, ec.* 2d ed. London.

Rousseau, J. J. 1782. *Confessions.* Reprint, New York, n.d.

de Sade, The Marquis. c. 1800. *The 120 days of Sodom and other writings.* Trans. A. Wainhouse & R. Seaver. New York (1966).

Sambrook, J. 1986. *The eighteenth century: The intellectual and cultural context of English literature 1700–1789.* London.

Sartre, J. P. 1943. *Being and nothingness.* Trans. H. Barnes. New York (1971).

Scott, W. 1802. *Minstrelsy of the Scottish border.* 4 vols. Edinburgh (1932).

Swift, J. 1729. *A modest proposal.* Dublin.

Taylor, D. 1978. *Thomas Chatterton's art: Experiments in imagined history.* Princeton.

Watt, 1957. *The rise of the novel: Studies in Defoe, Richardson, and Fielding.* Berkeley.

Wesley, S. 1697. Essay on Heroic Poetry, *Series Two: Essays on Poetry,* No. 2. Augustan Reprint Society Los Angeles (1947).

Winnet, A. R. 1971. George Psalmanazar. *The New Rambler* 110:6–18.

SPEAKERS OF BEING

Romantic Refusion and Cultural Anthropology

THOMAS DE ZENGOTITA

What in your language is 'being' I should prefer to call the "word."
(Hamann to F. H. Jacobi, 1787, in O'Flaherty 1952)

So in the end when one is doing philosophy one gets to the point where one would like just to emit an inarticulate sound.
(Wittgenstein 1953)

With the history of anthropology in view, Meyer Fortes distinguished between the discipline's "sociological" and "cultural" traditions (Fortes 1953:11–14)—a distinction that corresponds roughly to the contending influences of the Enlightenment and Romantic movements in modern thought as a whole. Ironically, the ahistorical Enlightenment has had obvious effects on the history of a discipline recurrently inclined to emulate the natural sciences. But Romanticism, though explicitly historical, is more difficult to recover historically. It gets short shrift in general histories of anthropology (Lowie 1937; Harris 1968; Honigmann 1976; Evans-Pritchard 1981) even when they are written by its heirs (Boas 1904; Kroeber 1955).

Like Fortes' sociological tradition, academic anthropology is itself a manifestation of the Enlightenment project of rational progress, and its mere existence recalls the giant fact which must condition any account of modern thought: in obvious ways, that project has succeeded. Whiggish histories may

---

Thomas de Zengotita teaches at The Dalton School and The School for Continuing Education at New York University. His publications include "Systems of Kinship: The Historical Construction of Moral Orders" in *Noam Chomsky: Consensus and Controversy* (1987) and "On Wittgenstein's 'Remarks on Frazer's *Golden Bough*'" in *Cultural Anthropology* (1989). He is writing a book about Enlightenment social consciousness called *The Earthly Steward and his Flesh and Blood*.

distort but, insofar as our institutions have been whiggishly defined, they have a peculiar legitimacy: they have, in fact, legitimized. The Enlightenment influence in anthropology operates on the surface of things.

Not so Romanticism. It has always been the shadow of the modern positive—excessive, oppositional, holistic, emotional, intuitive, implicit, transitory, exalted, marginal, apocalyptic, elegaic and ineffable. Romanticism is a way of being and doing that eludes definition, for elusion is one aspect of the dialectic constituting its deepest purpose. When Romantics take history as ground for attacking the Enlightenment, they do not stand on it. Romanticism sacrifices all frozen postures to irruptions of genius and immanent spirit; to it belong the radiant moment, the noumenal touch.

Scholarly efforts to define Romanticism have nevertheless been legion. "History of ideas" distinctions are most familiar. To contrast with the Enlightenment, they come in pairs: transcendence vs. immanence, mechanical vs. organic, control vs. spontaneity, calculation vs. imagination/feeling, society vs. community, sincerity vs. authenticity, utility vs. inherent value, abstract vs. concrete, static vs. dynamic, liberty vs. self-determination (Lovejoy 1948; see also Peckham 1962; Frye 1963; Wellek 1963; Trilling 1971; Berlin 1980). Such contrasts have served various purposes well; but they fail us now because, as categories, they necessarily destroy elusion—and that necessity is today the issue, for the collapse of categories is quite general, and deconstructive reflection is eroding the substance of every humanist discipline. To be understood historically, today's reach for the postmodern must be Romantically situated.

Taken together, the traditional polarities can still evoke what they cannot define. Romanticism is the effort of the alienated modern mind to refuse itself, as alienated, and so re-fuse itself, as embodied in the world. In this essay, a dialectic of *refusion* will constitute an attitude of thought in motion rather than a concept, a pun rather than a category—a notion in the Hegelian sense (Findlay 1958:220-28). Actually, the pun recalls *the* Hegelian notion—for what was Hegel's project if not the refusion of Absolute Mind? Hegel repudiated Romanticism's excesses, but he was its ultimate philosopher (Abrams 1971:67, 173; Taylor 1979:5-13). And that not only in substance but also in genre; the *Phenomenology of Mind* was a manifestation of the development it described, a biography of spirit—which was what it was about (Abrams 1971:225-37). Hegel can also be read as the first anthropologist of modernity (Trilling 1971: 30-39). On all these counts, his example inspires this essay and suggests to anthropology an answer to the question "Why Hegel Now?" (Bernstein 1986).

Romantic ends can only be known by Romantic means. The translator of the *Phenomenology of Mind* defined its method this way: both generality and particularity "are satisfied at once if the experience considered . . . is treated as the experience of a generalized individual. . . . Without it we should merely have history alone, which is inexhaustible and so cannot be a whole; or a mere connexion of abstract ideas which cannot, as such, be experience" (Baille in Hegel 1807:55).

Fortes founded his structural-functionalism on the nineteenth-century comparative jurisprudence of Maine and McLennan. In an earlier paper on the Enlightenment tradition in anthropology, I extended those foundations to John Locke's *Second Treatise of Government* (1690) and the social historical matrix it articulated. In that paper, the Enlightenment was represented as a generalized individual, an ideal type of modern consciousness called the Earthly Steward. Locke proposed the Steward's calling: he was to take possession of the world—and of himself—through the labor of civilization. Institutions of improvement literally constituted modern minds as the forms of life of science, technology, administration, fine arts, etc. (as in Ryle and Wittgenstein). The *tabula rasa* invited Enlightened man to remake himself out of raw (rude) materials in the state of nature. The natural right of labor to its product undermined the claims of the Newtonian Maker, and He was replaced as the phenomenological subject of the world by the self-regarding and self-governing self we so often take ourselves to be and live to serve (de Zengotita 1984).

In this essay, Romanticism is represented in a complementary character, the alter ego of modern consciousness, the Speaker of Being. The "of" implies that the Speaker both expresses and creates being: he does not, like the Steward, govern a world of objects and instruments from a position of abstraction; he participates through utterance. Language is the principal locus of the Speaker's being because it is the archetype of mediation and the vessel of possibility. Part of being modern is wishing to be otherwise. The history of Romanticism's influence in anthropology is the history of the Speaker's effort to recover, for the future, the world the Steward lost.

Four representative thinkers take a turn in the Speaker's role, as four actors might play Hamlet. According to time and place and personality, each performance varies; but the role remains. The original trajectory of Romanticism is evoked by two eighteenth-century figures with established connections to anthropology—Rousseau and Herder. Two professional anthropologists, Sapir and Lévi-Strauss, show Romanticism under restraint in the modernist twentieth century. A row of portraits tells a tale of spiritual power domesticated, of totalizing vision reduced to "influence" in private minds.

The Speaker in a Vacuum: Rousseau (1712–1778)

Seeing that I am so little master of myself when I am alone, imagine what I am like in conversation, when in order to speak to the point one must think promptly of a dozen things at a time. The mere thought of all the conventions, of which I am sure to forget at least one, is enough to frighten me. I cannot understand how a man can have the confidence to speak in company. For not a word should be uttered without taking everyone present into account, without knowing their characters and histories, in order to be certain of not offending anyone. . . . In private conversation there is another difficulty, which I consider worse, the necessity of always talking. You have to reply each time you are spoken to, and if the conversation fails, to set it going again. This unbearable constraint would be enough in itself to disgust me with society. I can think of no greater torture than to be obliged to talk continually and without a moment for reflection. I do not know whether this is just an aspect of my mortal aversion to any sort of compulsion, but I have only to be absolutely required to speak and I invariably say something stupid. But what is even more fatal is that, instead of keeping quiet when I have nothing to say, it is just at those times when I have a furious desire to chatter. In my anxiety to fulfill my obligations as quickly as possible I hastily gabble a few ill-considered words, and am only too glad if they mean nothing at all. So anxious am I to conquer or hide my ineptitude that I rarely fail to make it apparent.

(Rousseau 1781:114)

Rousseau was the first Romantic. As such, he was a Speaker with no social being to articulate; language was so problematic for him that he barely realized it. He did not so much propose as body forth the contradictory essence of Romanticism. A vast literature reflects the indeterminacy of his position. He became the Rorschach test of modern culture history because he was the "odd man out" of the Enlightenment before there was a modern alternative to it (Rude 1972:155; see also Gay 1966:7; Cassirer 1970:1–18; Collingwood 1956:86; Martin 1954:111–15; Mornet 1929:195–221).

The politically inclined have often placed Rousseau in the Enlightenment because it "led to" the French Revolution and Rousseau figured so prominently in revolutionary minds. For reactionaries like Burke and Taine, Rousseau was estranged from other philosophes because he was so extremely what they all were—absolutist, abstract, selfish. For the corresponding left, Rousseau was the real thing: only *he* exalted manual labor, attacked private property and saw through democracy to community; only *he* truly hated injustice, while the rest of the philosophes, the drawing-room radicals, catered to their patrons. For both parties to political interpretation, *The Social Contract* and the *Discourse on Inequality* are the essential texts. Apolitical interpreters, emphasizing emotional style, are more likely to find a Romantic Rousseau in the *First Discourse*, the *Nouvelle Héloïse*, and *The Confessions*. No wonder that, like Solomon's baby, Rousseau has been divided; when he speaks of social contract, he is "enlightenment"; when he praises passion, he is "romantic"—and the categories themselves are suspect.

But if political distortion and literal-minded cataloging were the only difficulties, the best historians of culture would long since have settled matters.
The hard fact is that the emotional Rousseau was enormously popular before
the Revolution, among the same people of fashion who sustained the philosophes. The real problem is that a proto-Romantic cult of sensibility was
as much a part of the Enlightenment as Newtonian abstraction and medical
pragmatism. And this problem—of Romantic and Enlightenment coexistence
in the popular mind—is reproduced throughout the whole career of modernity.

The passage cited above from *The Confessions* provides the interpretive key.
It tells us that Rousseau himself could not function in the salons that made
him a darling; he was not a successful Steward; he was not self-possessed and
self-governing, and his misery was the proof. Like so many Romantics since,
Rousseau celebrated that misery as a token of authenticity in an artificial world.
More flexible spirits, with a fashionable taste for the natural, made Rousseau
the first victim of radical chic.

Rousseau's Romantic visions can look like Enlightenment abstractions because they were necessarily cast in the idiom of Locke and Condillac. The
first Speaker's true world was imaginary—and difficult to imagine, let alone
to describe. In the false real world of high society, *faux pas* was the only real
freedom. In disrupted floods of words based on nothing but reaching, Romantic self-determination occurred to Rousseau. In the hollow settings of salon
life, the Lockean Steward's tawdry liberty was to calculate convenience and
pleasure; there, self-governing reason produced only manners, the appearance
of virtue. In such contexts, ineptitude was a manifestation of genuine virtue
—and of genius, for the passage cited was in fact part of Rousseau's description of his own creativity. Like ineptitude, he said, illumination washed over
and through him, taking him as its vessel. Only later, in Wordsworthian tranquility of recollection, could he articulate the spontaneous overflow.

The price of community in the original void was high. Impaled by con-
temptuous and pitying eyes, Rousseau discovered himself through the other
in humiliation. Complacent before his suffering, masters of self and society
imagined themselves superior when, in glorious agony of fact, they were contained in his ravished openness. As the original annihilated self, Rousseau
gave puppets of Enlightened artifice the only real being they ever knew. Hence
the undertone of self-glorification throughout *The Confessions*, the boast of
the shamed and the shameless: "Let the last trump sound when it will and
I shall come forward with this work in my hand" (1781:17).

No wonder Rousseau inclined so often to imagine omnipotent self-
sufficiency, the independence of Robinson Crusoe. That inclination motivated
the aspect of his anthropology in which the earliest savages were isolated and
barely conscious engines of survival. He envied the "savage man" who "lives
within himself"; he pitied "social man, always outside himself," who "can live
only in the opinions of others, and . . . only from their judgment . . . draws,

so to speak, the feeling of his own existence" (1755:200). But Rousseau fell back on a Romanticism of solitude in his work as he retreated from company in his life—because he could not realize an alternative. Above all, he longed to feel his existence in others, and that longing motivated the other aspect of his anthropology, the effort of imagine authentic moral consciousness in society. But his images of true community were necessarily as ephemeral as his experience—and they were few and far between. The orphaned wanderer turned his children over to the foundling home and clung to his illiterate Thérèse, "who at least never mocked me." For Rousseau, apotheosis in description and action succumbed immediately to the fundamental contradiction in the impulse to refusion. Can being be full *and* be known—intended, articulated? Or is consciousness by its nature a wound in being and "meditating man . . . a perverted animal" (150)? The original Speaker had to utter refusion out of and into nothing. Hence, the notorious "paradoxes of Rousseau."

In the *Discourse on Inequality* (1755), modernity turned seriously to savage minds in its first moment of self-doubt—and there was literally a moment. On the way to visit to an imprisoned Diderot in 1749, Rousseau was blasted by a vision which left him exhausted and weeping at the foot of a tree in the park at Vincennes. That vision was first expressed in the *Discourse on the Arts and Sciences* (1750), and was dryly summarized in a quote from Aristotle's *Politics* on the title page of the second *Discourse*: "We must look for the intentions of nature in things which retain their nature, and not in things which are corrupted." But the modern Speaker was inspired to lift that ancient truth to urgency and universality:

> O man, whatever may be your country, and whatever opinions you may hold, listen to me: Here is your history as I believe I have read it, not in books by your fellow men, who are liars, but in nature, who never lies. Everything that comes from her will be true; if there is falsehood, it will be mine, added unintentionally. The times of which I am going to speak are very remote: How greatly you have changed from what you once were! It is, so to speak, the life of your species that I shall describe to you, on the basis of the qualities that you have received. Your upbringing, education, and habits may have corrupted those qualities, but they have not been able to destroy them. There is, I feel, an age at which each individual man would like to stop; you will seek the age at which you would have liked your species to stop. Dissatisfied with your present state, for reasons that portend even greater dissatisfaction for your unfortunate descendants, you may wish that you could go backward in time; that feeling must be interpreted as praise of your early ancestors, criticism of your contemporaries, and a fearful omen for those who will have the misfortune of living after you. (1755:145)

Romanticism has been characterized as a naturalization of the fundamental forms of Christianity and the great Romantics as the seers and prophets of that transformation (Abrams 1953, 1971). Rousseau may have been uncer-

"Il retourne chez ses egaux." Frontispiece to the first edition of Rousseau's *Discours sur l'origine et les fondemens de l'inégalité parmi les hommes* (Amsterdam, 1755).

tain of his voice but he was sure of his mission in a fallen world. In quest of refusion "midway between the indolence of the original state and the irrepressible activity of our own egotism" (Rousseau 1755:179), he turned to the moment in which knowing had first emerged from being. Speakers to come would turn to that moment as well and, in so doing, they would shape the imperative to anthropology.

A description of a fulfilled state of being and knowing became the ever-receding goal of Rousseau's life's work. In the whole *Discourse on Inequality*, not more than a few paragraphs substantiated its possibility—and even then a tragic flaw was immediately apparent. Like an evil seed, the perception of superiority was planted at the moment of transition from animal awareness to the bare consciousness of "certain relations" ("strong," "weak," "large," "small") between living things—and between them all and the only creature capable of perceiving and exploiting such relations; thus, man's "first contemplation of himself gave him his first surge of pride" (Rousseau 1755:174). Then, over "multitudes of centuries," people came into association—at first occasionally, out of convenience or lust, but later habitually. Technical and economic innovations multiplied and with them the fatal notion of property emerged, a cause of conflict from the beginning. But somewhere along this line the precious balance was struck. It coincided with the "first developments of the heart," as families were distinguished and bonded by "the sweetest feelings known to man: conjugal love and paternal love" (174–76). The "torpor" and "vigor" of savagery lay immediately behind; invidious self-consciousness ahead. Then the balance broke, it seems inevitably. "Conveniences" were no sooner contrived than they "lost all their charm and degenerated into real needs, so that the pain of being deprived of them was much greater than the pleasure of having them" (177). With the multiplication of needs and conveniences went elaborations of reflection. People together in consciousness could not help making comparisons—as they had when they contrasted themselves with nature to become conscious in the first place:

> Connections were extended, ties became closer. People acquired the habit of gathering in front of their huts or around a large tree; singing and dancing, true children of love and leisure, became the amusement or rather the occupation, of idle men and women who had formed themselves into groups. Each began looking at the others and wanting them to look at him; public esteem came to be valued, and it went to those who were the best singers or dancers, the most beautiful or handsome, the strongest, the most dexterous or the most eloquent. This was the first step towards inequality and also toward vice. (Rousseau 1755:178)

So Rousseau in salon society recovered the original sin of society itself. In life, in humiliation, he atoned. But try as he might, he could not endow alternatives with positive content, even in writing. Out of context, language failed him. The first Speaker lacked an idiom; refusion began as pure contradiction.

Rousseau sensed that his problem involved language. In the *Discourse on Inequality*, he tried to confront it as a whole, at a distance—again in anthropological speculation about origins. But the contradictions embedded in all his assertions were only intensified in considerations of the "origin of conventional signs." He began by contrasting his own confusion with the easy confidence of the Abbé de Condillac's treatment. The reason for the difference was that the Abbé "assumes what I question, namely, the existence of a kind of society already established among the inventors of language." For Rousseau, imagining his solitary creatures and his herds of families, that assumption was entirely unjustified. A "vagabond life" would engender few communicative needs and little opportunity for language to "solidify," even assuming its pointless invention. If we "suppose that this first difficulty has been overcome" and "the immense space that must have separated the pure state of nature from the need for languages" has been crossed, "we encounter a new difficulty, worse than the first one, for if men needed speech in order to learn to think they had a still greater need to be able to think in order to acquire the ability to speak." One could imagine the gradual conventionalization of instinctive cries and the assignment of particular noises to particular objects. But how to specify by convention a word for "oak" out of a language in which "one oak was called A" and "another oak was called B?" How to inflect, by agreement, for a future tense? How to abstract adjectival properties from things and define them as a part of speech? And what of "purely abstract ideas" with no substantive exemplars? In all these cases, the thoughts would have to exist before the meanings of words could be stipulated. At the same time, without the "aid of discourse" the thoughts themselves seemed impossible. In the end, Rousseau announced himself "so appalled by endless difficulties" for an understanding of the establishment of language "by human means" that he left only "this difficult question to anyone who may undertake to discuss it: Which is the more necessary assumption: that language could not have been invented if society had not already been established or that society could not have been established if language had not already been invented?" (1755:157–62).

Itself containing Rousseau's purpose, the Enlightenment idiom allowed no more than a half-conscious struggle with the assumption that language was invented. That assumption was in fact coextensive with the limits of Enlightenment consciousness, a condition on the very existence of a reason which stipulated human conventions to accord with natural law—with the prior stipulations of a Newtonian Maker. But, in daring to fail, Rousseau again succeeded in framing the future of Romanticism. Unable to distinguish language,

reason, and society in prehistory, he produced instead a consciousness of alienation within the alienating categories. Unable to refuse in words or thoughts
or in social action, he posed dilemmas for a dialectic not yet conceived. What
Rousseau experienced as defeat, a developed Romantic tradition would one
day affirm, and language, thought, and society would be united as indissoluble
aspects of humanity's being, as a reunion of the moral and the mental with
nature—indeed, as *a* nature, and eventually, as the anthropological concept
of culture.

The posthumously published *Essay on the Origin of Language* (1852) was
written between 1749 and 1755. Rousseau's remarks on language in the *Discourse on Inequality* may be summaries of the frustrations which attended that
more extended effort. But there are interesting differences. In the unpublished
essay, he attempted explicitly to oppose the idea of language as reason's instrument, and so came much closer to the Romantic idea of it. The "language
of the first men," he said, was not like "the tongues of geometers," but like
the "tongues of poets" (11). The specific implications were: first, that sound
was not an accidental but an essential constituent of language; and, second,
that metaphor was prior to the naming of objects. With that, Rousseau proposed an outline of the whole Romantic tradition of primitivist poetics. It
is worth emphasizing that it came to him in a comparison of language with
music:

> With the first voices came the first articulations or sounds formed according
> to the respective passions that dictated them. . . . Thus verse, singing, and speech
> have a common origin. Around the fountains of which I spoke, the first dis-
> courses were the first songs. The periodic recurrences and measures of rhythm,
> the melodious modulations of accent, gave birth to poetry and music along
> with language. . . . The first tales, the first speeches, the first laws, were in verse.
> Poetry was devised before prose. That was bound to be, since feelings speak
> before reason. And so it was bound to be with music. (1852:50–51)

The musicality of emotional speech was a promise of healing for the wound
of reflection. Sound itself was being. Like feeling, it was continuous with things.
If the first expressions of anger and pity were frightening and consoling sounds,
then those sounds were part of their meaning, and language did not have
to be a loss. So it was that the first tongue "in its mechanical part . . . would
have to correspond to its initial object, presenting to the senses as well as
to the understanding the almost inevitable impression of the feeling that it
seeks to communicate" (15). The priority of unintended metaphor reinforced
the same promise: conceptual life emerged in figured things; words did not
refer, but created situations in which meaning existed:

> But for moving a young heart or repelling an unjust aggressor, nature dictates
> accents, cries, lamentations. There we have the invention of the most ancient

words. . . . As man's first motives for speaking were of the passions, his first expressions were tropes. Figurative language was the first to be born. Proper meaning was discovered last. One calls things by their true name only when one
sees them in their true form. At first only poetry was spoken. Upon meeting
others a savage man will initially be frightened. Because of his fear he sees the
others as bigger and stronger than himself. He calls them "giants" . . . [later] . . .
he invents another name . . . such as the name "man" . . . and leaves "giants"
to the fictitious object. (1852:12–13)

Impelled by emotion, the first expressions were events, not inventions. The
figurative name of man as "giant" was a cry from the heart. The true and
proper name of man as "man" was a later discrimination of thought. Excesses
of emotion would one day appear to be virtually synonymous with Romanticism because the original appeal of feeling was too simple and too serious
to be recovered by modernists steeped in psychology. But for the first Romantics, emotion overcame the mind's alienation as a matter of experienced fact;
in it, the promise of refusion was immediately kept; emotion just *was* a continuity of consciousness beyond stipulation, the soul's life in the world. When
the soul was shriveled to private psyche under modernist restraint, what was
left over, in public, was—excess.

Feeling guaranteed the possibility of refusion, but it was not sufficient in
itself. Like all real Romantics, Rousseau wanted refusion; and that meant some
kind of reason—hence, his ambivalence toward the operatic primitives. He
could not call for a return to a world of fearful giants but he could not avoid
the outcome of reason's history either. Its distancing effect was coincident with
its first inventions and, as its articulations developed, so did its divisions;
Rousseau was forced back to the aim of the *Second Discourse*—tracing the developmental line, looking for the balance, the moment of both being and
knowing.

It was as Lévi-Strauss puts it: for Rousseau, the history of language "repro-
duces, in its own way and on its own plane, the process of humanity" (1962a:
38). In the end, the process of distinguishing and abstracting yielded writing—
and that destroyed the life of language in the world (Derrida 1974:97–140).
Promising to "crystallize," it merely reduced. For it changed "not the words but
the spirit, substituting exactitude for expressiveness" (Rousseau 1852:21) until
finally singing and speech, which had a common origin, were irretrievably
separated. In his time, Rousseau was witness to what seemed the ultimate mutilation; articulation in music was sacrificing the moral sensations of melody
to formalized harmonies (1852:68–72). He would never hear Beethoven.

In *The Social Contract*, Rousseau made his final attempt to realize refusion
in a description of a modern *polis*. From its conceptual outset, in the very
title, the work was beset by contradictions internal to Enlightenment categories. Reaching, as always, for a dialectic that was not there, Rousseau ad-

mitted his dilemmas as he wrote (1762:36, 56, 71, 84, 110). But they led him at last to disavowal, not synthesis: *The Social Contract* would come to look like "squaring the circle" (Lowith 1967:235). All the dilemmas it raised pointed back to the one he most required and most notably failed to make intelligible: what did it mean to be "forced to be free" (Rousseau 1762:20)?

To a Steward concerned with self-government, the phrase was and remains incomprehensible nonsense. But this was not an administrative proposal; it was another call for a resolution of Romanticism's fundamental paradox: the meditating animal was to be redeemed from perversions of reflection through community. If every mind were open to the ravishing world then natural compassion would yield social virtue as directly as each joyous voice sings out Beethoven's "Freude!" in its choral form. And who, listening to the whole, would dare deny the freedom of each singer? Was human being ever more truly uttered? "Why is the general will always well meaning, and why does everyone constantly will the happiness of each individual, if not because everyone applies the word 'each' to himself and thinks of himself when he votes for the good of all" (Rousseau 1762:28).

"Each" means what it meant to Hegel when, as a young student, Rousseau's vision first claimed him. As one word, it combines its varying referents in a deictic unity—as all uses of "that" or "I" have a single sense. In reciprocal containment, what does it mean to say that "anyone who refuses to obey the general will shall be compelled to do so by the whole body" and so "forced to be free" (Rousseau 1762:20)? It means that a true self-determination occurs as chorus rather than a flood of *faux pas*, that the symphony of authentic social life is the home of the mind, and that the individuated self, like a runaway child, must sometimes be reminded of its place if it is to be realized. Perhaps the notion is impossible; perhaps no description can convey it; certainly, the Enlightenment language of contract could not, and Rousseau was the victim of that language as well as of its project. But he spoke on, torturing the only words and things he knew until they yielded the irresistible promise of refusion. The only mockery Rousseau really dreaded was the mockery of the façade.

In that way, the fundamental Romantic situation was established and, in spite of incidental triumphs of community, that situation has persisted. It has been the doom of Romantics to contradict perpetually and reach endlessly. Unrealized in the real world, Romantic vision would elaborate the private mind as a sensational refuge, an aesthetic sanctuary of yearning and fulfillment. On beaches and mountains, in theaters and concert halls, in novels and poems, in therapies and bedrooms, the cult of sensibility's descendant institutions has been maintained. Elsewhere, the descendants of Rousseau have prolonged the trajectory of self-annihilation long enough to produce the art and thought we call Romantic.

Like the hero of *Rameau's Nephew*, Rousseau was "self-estranged spirit," a "disintegrated consciousness" held together by sheer will (Trilling 1971:33–47). He embodied what Hegel meant when he said that the "principle of negation" is the pure "activity of Self" (1807:99); that activity was and remains the limit of the life of the mind for the Speaker of Being. In emptiness, refusion cannot fail and cannot succeed.

The Speaker Overflowing: Herder (1744–1803)

> The earliest poets of all nations generally wrote from passion excited by real events; they wrote naturally, and as men: feeling powerfully as they did, their language was daring, and figurative.
>
> (Wordsworth 1800)

Plucked by Providence from a dark corner of a non-nation, Johann Herder made his way into the world as he would make his way out of it – translating. Providence's instrument was a surgeon in the Russian army who brought young Herder to Koenigsberg in 1762 to enroll him in medical school in exchange for translating a medical treatise into Latin (Clark 1955:40). No boy from Mohrungen would ever get anywhere in the world, warned Herder's master when he left – and Voltaire had said as much about all Germany, notwithstanding Pangloss/Leibniz and the aspiring Frederick's court. When he died in 1803, Herder was exhausted and bitter, alienated from Goethe and the glittering Hellenes of Weimar, supported only by his devoted Caroline; but he was still translating – *El Cid* into German. Master of half a dozen languages, Herder was always faithful to his own. He had found it as Shakespeare – crude and vigorous enough for life, yet refined enough for literature; he proposed to leave it as a mediating tongue for the languages of mankind. Into German, through himself, Herder tried to pour the *volk*-streams, the songs of Humanity (for the "inmost destiny" of German in translation see Steiner 1975:266, 380–82).

Herder's medical studies did not go well. The first dissected cadaver induced a vertigo; his soul divided in disgust as the scalpel split the body's flesh on an Enlightened doctor's slab (Clark 1955:41). Just so did the fabricated analytic of Stewardly philosophies vivisect the unity of Creation with "schooldust" lists of laws and faculties and rights – or such, we may imagine, were the revelations of the wizard Hamann explicating that dissection as hellish poiesis for his pupil's Pietist mind. And so young Herder, like other German Romantics who "spilt religion" into literature (Hulme 1924), turned to theology. From there he moved, through literature, to language – and from there to everything. For Speakers were now in community, assured of a reality to which each and all gave composing utterance. In Germany, at the end of the eighteenth century, there was no limit to containment or expression, no gap between the word and the world. Language was an ample "house of being" then (Heidegger 1971:63), because being united the actual — already vast beyond the dreams of ancestors — with an even vaster possible. Articulate refusion was not *only* a possibility. It was, immanently, already real: "Anything that can happen, does and everything that can live upon our earth, lives upon it," declared Herder — and he exulted in the knowledge, for his universe was filled with meaning. For Herder, being was forever housed in the Divine Word, and that Word was intelligible. It was contained in both Holy Books, in the Bible and in Nature; and the mystery of its hermeneutic had been passed to him through Hamann from Boehme and the German Gnostics (Steiner 1975:58-63). Reutterance of Divine Poiesis would be refusion of the spirit, and that reutterance was the aim of Johann Herder's philosophical anthropology.

In earliest *Fragments* (1767), in *Critical Forests* (1769), in the *Scattered Leaves* of the 1780s and 90s, Herder ransacked the genres of the world. He wrote and read his way through everything, and if his works are fragments scattered through forests, that is a fact too easily understood in an age which assumes fragmentation. Herder's fragments were real pieces — of a whole; they were scattered — but not willingly. To his biographer, Herder's is an *oeuvre* of unfinished "torsos," surrounded by scaffolds which outlined a purpose "incapable of execution by any ordinary mortal" (Clark 1955:365). But Clark's account of Herder's life shows that this impracticality was not a character flaw, not an indulgence of pride or laziness: the scaffolding represented authentic aspiration, authentically disappointed. Another scholar has suggested that "argumention about the essence of Herder's thought is analogous to a dispute about which brilliant flower in a luxuriant tropical garden is its most characteristic expression" (Manuel 1968:x). But it was a *garden* that Herder cultivated — and *there* is the essence of his thought.

Pastor Herder preached his sermon in a community of spirits coming to consciousness as a community. To protect their precious German from French accents of contempt and the inimitable purity of Winckelmann's Greek, he opened its house to other scorned languages and discovered Homers and Ossians in them all. Through those ancient and forgotten Speakers, Herder summoned to utterance the binding and dividing and rebinding forces of nature and history as they actually were, as they actually felt. Forces of the tides, gravity, electricity, magnetism, and of von Haller's vital fluids; forces of economies, moralities, religions, and politics — he called them all to confluence in the "genetic power" of the universe, and at that confluence he proposed to speak. "Word idols" of Enlightenment abstraction could not hope to perform such a synthesis. Only poetry might articulate such power into mind; only poetry, the art in which all senses fuse and experience reforms

as the Word of God formed Creation to begin with; and so not just any poetry but, for a minister of Luther's gospel, the *Ur*-poem, the Book of Genesis.
There was

> . . . the first dawning of the illumination of the world, while our race was yet
> in its infancy. We see in it the earliest perceptions, the simplest forms, by which
> the human soul expressed its thoughts, the most uncorrupted affections that
> bound and guided it. . . . In it the earliest Logick of the senses, the simplest
> analysis of ideas and the primary principles of morals, in short, the most an-
> cient history of the human mind and heart, are brought before our eyes. Were
> it even the poetry of cannibals, would it not be worthy of attention for these
> purposes? (1782:45–46)

From the "Oldest Document" (1774), from *The Spirit of Hebrew Poetry* (1782),
Herder recovered Creation. He recast its Testament for the nineteenth century, for Arnold and Whitman and the brethren of art. He reframed icons
and rituals abandoned long ago and returned communion to lapsing Prot-
estants in aesthetic experience. The familiar verses became, like Platonic
recollections, known again for the first time. In Herder's rereading, they were
mytho-philosophic presentations of the elements, of Earth, Fire, Water, and
Air; they were natural historical half-truths—made whole in beauty. Herder's
Romantic Bible was the world's greatest poetry and, through him, it became
for many moderns what it was for Blake—the "Great Code of Art" (Abrams
1971:33).
   In their ancient tongue, the Tribes of Israel had aimed—as Herder himself
did now—"to say the whole at once" (Herder 1782:35). Because their language
was "animated with a living spirit," (29) it was dominated by verbs. Even nouns
were verbal in feeling and function and could therefore body "forth the forms
of things" (35). Like Whorf's Hopi, those "Eastern Hurons" (27) of Eden lived
in a world where "all is present time" and the soul "feels itself in the midst
of the objects described" (37, 93). At the "first dawning of the illumination
of the world," being and knowing necessarily coincided as Creation occurred
in the first Words spoken to the first men—and by them. New bodies just
were absolutely Below what was absolutely Above; knowing, once and (therefore) for all, what was truly High, they raised naive eyes to the first Light
and glad voices in the first Song. In that *Ur*-dawn, surely, world and word
were one.
   Similarly with latter-day tributaries of that first spring—for there had been
many beginnings. It was for Herder's Germans as it had been for Rousseau;
indigenous victims of modern culture took the anthropological turn to civilization's other (Berlin 1976:173). In *Folk Songs* (1778), Herder did for Germans
and Celts and Slavs what he did for Judeo-Christians—and he did it also
for Incas and Iroquois and Hottentots. He raised the voice of the unlettered

to be heard—and the living Word was revealed again. Called the "Silver Book" when begun as a scrap-collecting hobby for family and friends, *Folk Songs* eventually inspired Bopp, the Brothers Grimm, and the whole folkloric tradition in the nineteenth century. Long before anthropologists went to the field to invalidate an image of humanity's origins, and long before later anthropologists cast all images into doubt, this Romantic Speaker conceived the anthropological enterprise as translation. As Wordsworth turned to the rustic "speech of men," so Herder turned to folk songs for what all poetic language provided: being—articulated, known. He pursued a synthesis of poetries, a "metaphysic of translation," an "ontology of language" (Steiner 1975:64, 322). As his God roared "with the lion after his prey" and looked down "from the mountain eyry with the glance of an eagle," so Herder "listened with attention to the ideas of the most ancient of the infant world" (1782:77, 83). And he heard them perfectly well—for he too spoke at dawn. Ordinary-language philosophy, like ordinary-language poetry, was once sublime:

> While still an animal, man already has language. All violent sensations of his body, and among the violent the most violent, those which cause him pain and all strong passions of the soul express themselves directly in screams, in sounds, in wild inarticulate tones. . . . It is as though it could breathe more freely as it vents its burning, frightened spirit. It is as though it could sigh out part of its pain and at least draw in from the empty air space new strength of endurance as it fills the unhearing winds with its moans. So little did nature create us as severed blocks of rock, as egotistic monads! Even the most delicate chords of animal feeling . . . whose sound and strain do not arise from choice and slow deliberation, whose very nature the probing of reason has not as yet been able to fathom . . . are aligned in their entire performance for a going out toward other creatures. The plucked chord performs its natural duty: it sounds! It calls for an echo from one who feels alike, even if none is there. (Herder 1769:87)

Herder's biographers, Haym in the nineteenth century and Clark in the twentieth, agree: the "Essay on the Origin of Language" (1769) is the most representative work (Clark 1955:135). It is Herder's Book of Genesis, his effort to "sing Spinoza." The original resounding only set the stage; Herder was not celebrating unconscious immediacy, he was after real refusion, and he believed he had found the way to it. The Romantic spiral (Abrams 1971:183–90) dictates that "the hand that inflicts the wound" must be "the hand which heals it" (Hegel 1827:55) and, for Herder, language was that hand; it would heal Rousseau's perverted animal without loss of consciousness because it constituted consciousness in the first place. To reutter that constitutive utterance would be to refuse historically, in deeds of speech. In Herder's "Essay," the fundamental paradox of Romanticism would literally announce itself and its own resolution simultaneously.

To begin with, the automatic joinings of audition were the "sap," not the "roots" of language (Herder 1769:91). A voluntary dimension, the blessing-curse of reason, had to be added in order for true language to become. But how to add it and save wholeness? How could a contingency, a freedom, a voluntary reason, be added without loss of place and necessity? In Herder's dialectic, freedom began as a natural disadvantage which, once realized, constituted its own order, its own place and necessity. Man was not obliged to look at or listen to or want just this or that; the spider's web, the beaver's dam, the cities of the ants were all denied to this derelict of nature. But the spider's glory was also his limit; the aimless diffusion of man's instincts was, in its other aspect, the boundless sphere of his activity. Only man was "in need of the entire universe" (103–5, 134).

This reversal of fortune was no incidental aftereffect, as in Mandeville and the Victorian natural historians. It was positive and glorious, an "active totality" which was simultaneously created as, and creating, the "sphere of self-reflection." The "tempering of all . . . powers in subservience to this major orientation" was man's "destiny at the first moments of his life," in "the first state in which he is a man." For that total orientation of reflective activity just *was* "the total undivided soul at work." At this point in the "Essay," Herder addressed the reader directly, almost pleading. He had recovered Rousseau's failure to distinguish between language and thought as an affirmation: you can "call this entire disposition of man's forces rationality, reason, reflection, call it what you will," he said, but don't call it a thing, a faculty (cf. Ryle 1949). Away with the "hollow sound" of philosophy's "verbal delusions," "mere concepts," and "scholastic abstraction" (Herder 1769:109–14). To succeed, the discussion of such objects and subjects must partake of them. If the discourse of moderns were a total orientation of being, then alienated reflection would simply *be* refused.

But the possibility of that saving closure had to be in the first and innocent utterance. It had to be present at the beginning of the Romantic spiral, at the creation of consciousness. The first words had to be binding, not dividing—and yet they had to be *words*. The deepest question became: how were certain features selected from the "ocean of sensations . . . the vast hovering dream of images"? How did the total creature, submerged in that ocean, come to "single out one wave, arrest it" and (fatal moment) "concentrate its attention on it and be conscious of being attentive"? How could that happen without (too much) abstraction? How did we (could we) become free and conscious without being separate (Herder 1769:115)? If language were identical to the "state of reflection" in which man became man and if language could avoid the dangers of fixation and division, then Herder might achieve his aim. How could language enter the ocean of sensation and constitute consciousness without division? If being was to be found rather than lost in the word, then the word could not be invented, stipulated by an imperial Enlightenment consciousness—that assumption had led Rousseau to his dead end in the *Discourse on Inequality*. The first words had simply to occur and Herder had to recover the seamless flow:

> Let that lamb there, as an image, pass by under his [proto-man's] eyes; it is to him, as it is to no other animal . . . the hungry, scenting wolf . . . the blood-lapping lion . . . the rutting ram. . . . Not so with man! As soon as he feels the need to come to know the sheep, no instinct gets in his way; no one sense pulls him too close to it or too far away from it. It stands there, entirely as it manifests itself in his senses. White, soft, woolly—his soul in reflective exercise seeks a distinguishing mark—the sheep bleats! His soul has found the distinguishing mark. The inner sense is at work. This bleating, which makes upon a man's soul the strongest impression, which broke away from all the other qualities of vision and of touch, which sprang out and penetrated most deeply, the soul retains it. The sheep comes again. White, soft, woolly—the soul sees, touches, remembers, seeks a distinguishing mark—the sheep bleats and the soul recognizes it. And it feels inside, "Yes, you are that which bleats." (1769:116-17)

A generalized attention was *weak* enough simply to register the bleat. The necessary disinterest was built in. The lion and the ram covered the woolly sheep flesh in immediate fusional ways and so remained unconscious. Their intensity was enviable but unmediated; they knew not what they did.

But Herder had not yet reached language-reason. He hid from himself the poisonous *a priori*, the "need to know," in rutting and blood-lapping exclamation marks and went to the questions he was prepared for: first, why the *bleat*? Why did *it* become the "third," the mediator, the thought-word binding a reflective soul to the world, the pivot and center of the total orientation that man was becoming? And second, how could such an origin for *some* words guarantee that language *in general* would heal the wound in being that wave-fixing consciousness threatened to become? The sheep's announcement of its own name obviously retained connection with the being of sheep. But how did other first words, not spoken by their referents, retain the world?

Here was Herder's inspiration, "the precise point of genesis," the nativity scene of Romanticism. For the "genius of language" was no sooner articulated than it returned to its fusional "sap," to the way sound runs through the totality of human dispositions. The foundation of Herder's linguistics was the natural position of sound in the phenomenological sensorium. Hearing was the "central and unifying sense" of humanity. Through it, other senses became "language-apt" and men became "creatures of language." How was hearing "central"? Was this another system's fiat from some Cartesian axiom grinder? Not for those willing to listen. For them, and for them only, the music of sound guaranteed that refusion would not merely be assigned to language but would occur *in* it (1769:143).

Sounds just *were* mediate. Most obviously, they moved between subject and object, and between subjects, penetrating; nature did not merely "ring it out," she "rang it in, deep into the soul." No self-regarding pride moved Adam to this fruit; *it* came to him (Herder 1769:129). The deed of the word made us free and would keep us connected, inwardly, soul to soul. There was no original sin of abstraction. Sound/hearing was middle/central in all of its aspects: in its "range," between the sighted distance and the immediate touch; likewise in "distinctness and clarity" it fell between the outlines of the carving eye and the blur of prehended textures; in "vividness" also, for touch "overwhelms" and "cuts into us too deeply," while vision was "cold and aloof" and "too quiet." But also "with respect to the time interval of its effect": touch is "simultaneous but brief and abrupt," while vision is constant, all at once, all encompassing. Only sound, the gentle teacher, "counts out the tones and pours them into the soul one at a time . . . keeps giving and does not tire." And sound was obviously made for expression, more public than "ineffably dark" touch, more private than visual objects exposing themselves shamelessly to separated pointings. And finally, in development, sound/hearing was also mediate: the "dark sleep of tactile feeling" formed the "trunk of nature from which sprout the more delicate branches of sensuousness" that were "awakened to distinction and abstraction" (but not too much) by sound (1769:142–46). The deployment of the human head among the dispositions of the world secured the mind's unfolding in Creation.

But resolution was not yet at hand. The question remained: how do we have words for silent objects, for ideas and relations, for all the things we talk about which do not name themselves? The apotheosis of mind's unity, the "total orientation," was still to be recovered.

The problem had only to be posed to be resolved. Was it not obvious that, in real experience, sensations and their objects "commingle into one," that we "are a single thinking *sensorium commune*, touched from various sides" without division into sense-parts? Only the advance of philosophy could have deceived us; in our natural consciousness we were already synthesized, we were "as though slumbering by a brook where to be sure we still hear the rustling of every wave, but so darkly," and "the darker the senses the more they commingle." Even vision was "no more than feeling" in that flow, and colors were as intimate as textures. All "analysis of sensation," even the distinctions between the senses as such, was falsifying abstraction: "at a certain depth [Herder here referred to mental patients] all the threads are one single tissue." In that "throng of sensations," the soul, "needing to create a word, reached out and grasped *possibly* the word of an adjacent sense whose feeling flowed together with the first" (Herder 1769:139–41; italics mine).

Schooled by self-christening things and given the inherent centrality of sound, the mind was prepared to borrow from sound its words for silent objects. The first word for lightning gave the ear "the feeling of suddenness and rapidity which the eye had." The root words of ancient languages made "the analogy of the senses noticeable"—as in glorious Hebrew, words related to anger "*snort* out their origin," and the very name of life respires. Likewise in the poetry-languages of the Hurons and Hottentots, Finns and Laplanders: "feelings intertwine" in the "bold metaphors" of word-roots. In those jungles of meaning there was less logic, less grammar, and, above all, less abstraction. But the languages were not therefore strictly comparable, no more than particular leaves or snowflakes; each was unique, "each in its own way" was "in conformity with the manner of thinking and seeing of the people," each was "specifically national" as well as wild (Herder 1769:147–58).

So much for Sussmilch's Newtonian thesis, which Herder was explicitly opposing in the "Essay"—so much for language designed and delivered *in toto* by God. The very richness of the field, its marvelous imperfections and individualities, displayed the history of its growth. In that growth, wild languages had retained the living connections to the world which refined languages had lost through formal stipulations. Herder's God, like Herder himself, disdained prefabrication (for the influence of Herder's "linguistic turn" see Kieffer 1986).

But why "*possibly* the word of an adjacent sense"? What tickle of doubt interrupted the flow of Herder's pen? Reuttering the origin of language, did he anticipate the vacuum that would embrace all utterance in the Godless world to come? Did he hear the whisper of arbitrariness at the heart of the sign?

"The earth is a star among stars" began the most ambitious of Herder's projects. The *Ideen* (in four parts: 1784, '85, '87, '91) proposed a history of the human species, but only gathered some "stones for a building which . . . the centuries can finish" (in Clark 1955:308). And, as the trail of dates suggests, even the stones were beyond quarrying. Yet another torso, the most colossal ever framed, a ruin of time not past but passing—and running out. The mortal Speaker could only say so much.

But the ruin provided direction; it was the first work of cultural anthropology. In Herder's mind, genetic power met Montesquieu's climate and yielded a world-spanning variety of "folk genius"—with "genius" understood as a way of life, a manifold of weather-settings, subsistence modes, myths, values, customs, and sensibilities, next to which Gregory Bateson's organicism looks tentative. No twentieth-century celebration of particular holisms could match this vision of myriad *Geister*, just as no anthropological synthesis—not Tylor's psychic unity, White's cosmic energetics, Kroeber's Superorganic, or the patient convergence of Boas' four fields—could propose unity in diversity as wantonly as Herder did here. For Herder was not after the Hegelian concrete, although his voracious attempt may well have conditioned it (Clark 1955:330). As the "stupendous documentation of the anthropological Books VI–VIII" shows, Herder wanted nothing less than the *ethnographic* concrete, all of it, contained in him and uttered for a united Humanity as a matter of historical fact (ibid.: 322–26).

If Romanticism was a secularization of the fundamental forms of Christianity, the point of view of the "generalized individual" now brings out the most essential substitution. The overall characterization of Herder's "ideal philosopher" as "the cultural anthropologist" (Clark 1955:322) comes down to this: Klopstock and Goethe expressed the genius of Germany; in Ossian, Homer, and the Old Testament, other geniuses spoke. The genius of all the peoples, to be articulated, had to be embodied in a person, in a "voice of genius"; Romantic awe for the genius was engendered at the intersection of these meanings. The artist or thinker as prophet and seer embodied and expressed the spirit of a particular age as Christ incarnated the universal spirit — and Herder's cosmic aspiration bears that comparison, if any does. The position of the first cultural anthropologist, what Herder called the "historian of mankind," was comparable to "the Creator of our race or the Genius of Earth" (in Clark 1955:322–26). That astounding imperative must be remembered when the Speaker of Being is recovered simply as "influence" in twentieth-century academic anthropology. Modernist scholars sought discipline for good reason.

At the end of his career, the *Ideen* gradually abandoned, Herder seemed to lose faith in his omnivorous particularism. The capacity of the Genius of Earth was tragically limited and he was forced to reconsider reason and system. He wrote a scathing *Metacritique* (1799) of Kant — but a personal grudge was involved; it may be that he was fending off a concession in himself as well. It is certain that he turned decisively away from the aestheticism of the Weimar circle. All the glamour and gesture began to look "selfish" to Pastor Herder. Perhaps he came to envy his old friend Goethe — the "true creator" — and to resent the beautiful Schiller who had replaced him as the second of the "divine twins" (Clark 1955:366). But with Hegel's repudiation of Romantic individualism and irrationalism in mind, Herder's insistence that real art was a social and moral construction takes on larger value. The claim was consistent with Herder's project and with his dedication to pastoral and administrative duties. Ever since his (then unpublished) "Travel Diary" of 1769, he had favored action over criticism; his philosophy of history was an aspect of praxis, of the education of humanity toward Humanity (Burkhardt 1940:9; Clark 1955:100–102).

In any case, in *God, Some Conversations* (1787), Herder turned seriously to philosophy. He consolidated the Spinozaist movement in German thought which led Hegel to say: ". . . either Spinozaism or no philosophy" (Hegel in Burkhardt 1940:9). In *God*, a continued resistance to the abstractions of Kant was balanced by Spinoza's promise of a generality that might remain concrete and alive. That promise drew Herder in the direction Hegel would take. Under pressure of the infinity of particulars, the mortal Speaker had overflowed – at first joyously, but not indefinitely. For affirmative Romantics like Herder and Hegel, refusion had to be an achieved and experienced state. To welcome, like Schiller and Fichte, the endless quest was to strike a pose on the brink of decadence. If the world was too much for the Genius of Earth, his song would inevitably decline into cacophony unless refusion was found in the only Speaker who could truly utter total Being:

> The more life and reality, that is, the more rational, powerful, and perfect energy a being has for the maintenance of a whole which it feels belongs to itself, to which it imparts itself inwardly and entirely, the more it is an individual, a self. . . . And so instead of struggling with empty words let us awaken to our true self and strengthen the principle of individuality in us. The more spirit and truth, that is, the more active reality, knowledge, and love of the all there is in us, the more we possess and enjoy God, as active individuals, immortal and indivisible. He alone in whom all is, who comprehends and sustains all, can say: 'I am the Self. There is none apart from me.' (1787:213)

The Speaker under Discipline: Sapir (1884–1939)

> . . . the sounds and marks used therein obviously have no meaning in themselves and can have significance only for those who know how to interpret them in terms of that to which they refer.
>
> (Sapir 1934:564)

In 1907, at the age of twenty-three, Edward Sapir published a review of Herder's "Essay on the Origin of Language" in *Modern Philology*. This early work shows Sapir preparing himself for his profession in an encounter with a Romantic ancestor who was both an embarrassment and a temptation. He was guided throughout by the criterial distance of intellectual modernism, the sense of proportion and limitation which came to mean, if not sanity, at least maturity. But what the article reveals is a Sapir not yet mature, not yet at home with those limits. To read this review is to follow one of the finest minds of twentieth-century anthropology submitting to modernist restraint because nothing else could be trusted.

Sapir was a poet as well as an academic, and he would practice his art under a corresponding constraint. "The Grammarian and his Language" (1924a) knew a "profoundly serene and satisfying quality which inheres in mathematics and in music and may be described as the creation out of the simple elements of a self-contained universe of forms" (124). That is, modernist linguistics conferred upon its communicants the same neoclassical "hardness" commended by Eliot and Pound and pursued by Sapir in his poetry. Both disciplines involved a "dry" rejection of Romantic "slush," an effort to rescue a debased language in rigorously defined and self-contained domains (Handler 1986:128–31). Sapir was determined by the divisions of his disciplines; in them he found a "freedom in restraint" which was "antagonistic to the romanticism . . . which debauches so much of our science with its frenetic desire" (1924a:159). Modernism was not so much a repudiation of the impulse to refusion as an effort to subdue it to realizable dimensions and degrees. Sapir could not approach Herder as he would an anthropological other; his own life and work were at issue.

Sapir showed some grasp of Herder's context but little interest in it. In an introductory paragraph, he explained that the Francophile Berlin Academy had posed "the only question" about language's origin that made sense to the Enlightenment: was the "human mind intelligent and resourceful enough to invent so fine a machine, or did the latter require the master-hand of the Deity"? With a flourish of dismissal for such simple-mindedness, he concluded –"Voila tout" (1907:1).

The point of the review was not Herder in his time and place. The point was that the "chief progress from the older to the modern view of the question lies [in] doing away with the conception of divine interference, and the introduction of the idea of slow, but gradual and necessary, development from rude beginnings." Sapir wanted, first of all, to recognize Herder's "inestimable service" to the development of the modern view–but there was more on his mind than a just distribution of recognition. There was also a hard lesson for beneficiaries of that progress who, in considering Herder's arguments, were reminded that "we cannot today make bold to assert that this problem is satisfactorily answered, or apparently in a way to be." Sapir was writing to show that, in spite of the "vast accumulation of linguistic material" and the "immense clarification that has been attained in linguistic conception," the ultimate question remained unanswered–and perhaps unanswerable (1924a:2). The problem Sapir was really working through in his review of Herder was this: in such a situation, what were the valid satisfactions of the mind?

His various aims more and less consciously established, young Sapir moved through old Herder's "Essay": he forgave ("We should never forget that . . . Herder was still compelled to operate with the less than six thousand years that orthodoxy stingily doled out" [1924a:9]); he approved ("It is truly refreshing to find Herder, in the age of neatly pigeon-holed faculties, boldly asserting them to be but more or less convenient abstractions" [12]); he corrected ("It is somewhat strange to find as keen a mind as Herder's occupying itself with so useless and at bottom so meaningless a problem as the priority of parts of speech" [15]); he sneered ("As to the finished art works of ancient Greece being survivals from Herder's hypothetical period of spontaneous poesy, *that* needs no comment here" [16]); and he applauded ("Herder seeks the solution of this puzzling question [of how auditory impressions can express those of other senses] in a psychological truth, which one is somewhat surprised to see grasped so clearly in the eighteenth century. His remarks are so illuminating that I cannot do better than quote from them" [17]). Sapir summed up his assessment of Herder this way:

> That much of the work is quite antiquated, both in subject matter and general attitude, is, of course, self-evident; it is rather to be wondered how much in the "Essay" is still valid, and with what remarkable intuitive power Herder grasped some of the most vital points both in psychology and language. One wishes that we today could be so cocksure of the solution of certain linguistic problems as Herder seems to have been; but, then . . . philosophers of the eighteenth century, relying very heavily on pure reason unfettered by hard facts, proceeded, with admirable courage, to attack and solve some of the most obscure and intricate problems in the history of human culture – problems to the solution of which we have now learned to proceed quite timidly. (1924a:28)

A closer reading of Herder's "Essay," on the one hand, a reminder of a melancholy "intellectual emptiness" in Sapir's mature reflections, on the other (Silverstein 1986), together frame this remarkable passage as it deserves.

Herder's aspiration turned out to be preposterous; with its religious dimension fully recovered, it was even more so than Sapir realized. But "cocksure" is not the word. It was Sapir at twenty-three who was cocksure – patting a figure of world historical importance on the back. Was he chafing at the "timidity" of an age which left his own talents so little scope? He could not hope to be Speaker of a great moment, but the last sentence of his review shows how hard it was to give up Herder's question: "Perhaps the ends of the two series [animal cries and language development] can be bridged over?" were Sapir's last words. What was hidden under the condescension of his praise for Herder's "intuitive power"? It could not have been a lack of confidence; Sapir's gifts are legend in the discipline (Darnell 1986:178–80). Is a Genius of Earth reconciling himself to knowing-better-than-that? If so, what the manner obscured was also divided and transformed; Sapir's quest for refusion was channeled into a passion for music, a vocation for poetry, and a constant and ironic influence on his view of linguistic anthropology. In his whiggish reading of Herder, Sapir systematically embraced the constraints implied by his criticisms; contemplating a great mind made foolish by Romantic excess, he tempered his own determinations.

Consider the series of quotations in parentheses above. Was Herder "compelled" by a stingy "orthodoxy"? No, he was the willing minister of a living God's Creation. It was Sapir who was compelled by a very different and much stingier orthodoxy, and it was Sapir, the grammatical pragmatist for whom being was unutterable, who took "pigeon-holed faculties" as a matter of "convenience." To Herder, striving for total utterance, they had been an abomina-

tion, a mutilation of spirit. The "priority of parts of speech" was not a "problem" to Herder. The priority of verbs just *was* the presence of the living world
in language. The bleat of sheep, the snort of anger; those sounds were themselves the first words—and they were verbs. At the base of the spiral ascent
of Romantic Reason, they promised the apotheosis of refusion. Herder's object was a state of mind to be redeemed in an experience of total truth, not
a linguist's puzzle with a solution. Of Sapir's italicized *that*, it might be said
that needs no comment here. But it does. There is a measure of our distance
from Sapir in the fact that the precise object of his contempt is not clear.
Is it the "finished" nature of Greek art (compared to primitive art) that makes
the idea so absurd? Or is it the idea of survivals from a "hypothetical period"?
Or the notion of "spontaneous poesy"? Or all of them?

What was the "psychological truth" which precocious Herder grasped so
well that Sapir could do no better than quote him? It was that unity of mind,
that *sensorium commune* that made it possible to express soundless objects and
signify the world in a total orientation. As it turned out, Sapir *could* do a
little better after all. Where Herder had said impressions of color and sound
"directly combine by some rapid mutation," Sapir noted: "we should say 'association' nowadays" (1907:17). But in that rendering Herder's united mind becomes a Lockean mirror of nature—the cardinal foe of Romantic epistemology. The psychological law of association carries just the sense of contingent
separateness that Herder was bent on overcoming. The point was not to link
pieces of experience under the cover of a principle but to actually put into
words the unity of experience that was and is language/reflection. For Herder,
uttering this unity was the whole point of the "Essay," of his life's work. It
was not really a theoretical claim or argument, valid or otherwise.

No wonder Sapir missed the significance of the "supposedly middle sense."
To him, it was a product of "Herder's antiquated and subjectively confused
psychology," and rather than "bother with an unprofitable critique of it," he
proposed to "consider it proved" (i.e., "that all intense outward stimuli . . .
find their natural response in vocal expression") and then move on to more
"of those wonderfully intuitive bits of insight that one meets with frequently
enough in Herder's writing" (1907:20). The sense of "natural response" in Sapir's
context is entirely contingent, post-Hartley, Darwinian: objective psychology describing observed regularities. But there was no such thing as a psychology distinct from philosophy—or from reflected experience itself—when
Herder wrote. The absence of just these academic distinctions, among others,
made Herder's philosophical poiesis subjectively confusing *for Sapir*. Such
distinctions—say, between psychology and poetry—just were the institutionalized disciplines which constituted validity and objectivity in Sapir's life and
mind.

"And so on indefinitely," said Sapir of Herder when he got off on the wrong

track (1907:19). Irony breeds its own, and the temptation is to say the same
of his treatment of Herder. But, irony of ironies, there is today a doubled constraint which offers itself as liberation. The temptation now is to identify instead with the sheer temptation of representing Sapir as a misrepresentation
of Herder. That is, the temptation now is to admit misrepresentation to presentation on purpose. In misrepresenting Herder, Sapir submitted to a development of modern thought without knowing it. Does it follow that, if our presentations are subjunctive, we submit to development *and* know it? Do we
thereby elude the trap of the positive and the fate of all moderns at the hands
of ambitious successors? Is that the way to refusion?

Introducing a "little book" called *Language* (1921), Sapir addresses an audience he wanted to create. He hopes that the "outside public" might find more
than "private pedantries" in his account of linguistic science, and that "professional students" might be saved by it from a "sterile and purely technical
attitude" (v). That immediate aim is the most obvious of the many attenuated
refusional gestures in this now-classic text. Its ultimate source comes into focus in the transition to the last chapter, "Language and Literature." Sapir says:
"When it comes to linguistic form, Plato walks with the Macedonian swine-
herd, Confucius with the head-hunting savage of Assam" (219); elsewhere,
he says that every word in a language is "a miniature bit of art" (35); and,
as a whole, language "is the most massive and inclusive art we know, a moun-
tainous and anonymous work of unconscious generations" (220). Like Herder,
like Wordsworth, Sapir construes natural language as the art of humanity—
with a small *h*, now, but to the same Rousseauian purpose. The influence
of Romanticism in twentieth-century anthropology characteristically appears
as an emanation of grace from the ordinary furniture of experience.

In his Introduction, Sapir touches on the same theme; the "unconscious
and unrationalized nature" of language, he says, gives access to "the life of
the human spirit *which we call* history or progress or evolution" (1921:vi; italics
mine). But in the text itself, "spirit" is more likely to get the nominalizing marks
while categories like history and psychology go free (10). This familiar rhetorical structure is a manifestation of Romanticism as influence in modernist
scholarship in general. What the responsible scholar cannot admit to his work,
to validity's realm, he may express in concluding paragraphs and prefatory
remarks. The convention itself testifies quite openly to discipline, and to the
embarrassment that made it necessary. One has earned the right to strike
a "personal note" in public; at the same time, the personal note is a grand
old theme, for that is where grand old themes belong now—in the privacies
of life, in love and art and the struggle to work. Within us, the convention
implies, great forces still stir, value is not lost and aspiration is still pure. Or
maybe it is just that the tomb of grand illusions is the only altar left—and

one does it homage in its own tongue. In any case, a hint of refusional lift and historic drive is permitted at the boundaries of modernist provisionality, at the moment when the scholar claims a modest place in an institutional legacy no single Speaker will ever again contain.

But the text itself tells the institutional story, at least on the surface. Even in this quasi-popular treatment, professional responsibility is everywhere and, instead of the human spirit, the reader meets the "historical and psychological foundations" of language. For language itself a "serviceable definition" is provided: "Language is a purely human and noninstinctive method of communicating ideas, emotions, and desires by means of a system of voluntarily produced symbols" (Sapir 1921:8). If such definitions seem designed for the Magic Markers of cramming students, it is because, in a sense, they are. The institutional obligation to improve and increase knowledge of a subject matter—and to teach it—shapes Sapir's book, as it does the university department. That obligation is fundamental to the academic form of life. In Sapir's book, however, as in so many of the best of its kind, the obligation is subtly opposed even as it is sincerely accepted. The longing for beauty and meaning, Sapir's real (personal?) motivation, causes suggestive decorations to be sprinkled upon technical descriptions, and these embellishments lure the reader into an ironic undertow running steadily beneath the superb scholarship. The grammarian's technical taxonomy bears refinements like this: an uninflected form (e.g., "sing") is a "twilight word, trembling between the status of a true radical element and that of a modified word of the type of *singing*," and so "we do feel there hangs about it a variable mist of added value" (27, 28). The Speaker no longer hopes to utter mists of added value, but he has not lost his sense of such things; if anything, they have become all the more precious just as they are—out of reach.

The central chapters converge on summaries of the technical apparatus of linguistics, on scientific "schemes of grammatical concepts," basic "types of languages," "laws" of "phonetic and morphological drift" and "formulas" which "cover" kinds of words and other analytic fabrications which would have horrified Herder (Sapir 1921:25-32, 88, 101, 142-43, 174-79). But a close reading shows that this is not Enlightenment positivism; the schemes turn out to be devices of a special kind, devices which serve a seditious aim as well as the improvement of knowledge. The tell-tale sign is in the tone, offhand and exquisite at once; a master artisan's easy care is combined with a fugitive delight in the inadequacy of all formulas and schemes, no matter how finely wrought. Sapir realizes the muted refusion of the academic ironist who commits himself to his abstractions and then commits his abstractions to life—in peripheral and gestural admissions of the failure of abstraction itself. Again and again, Sapir betrays his private identification with the living world his public self analyzes and fails, finally, to capture. No matter what the linguist's categories, the facts of language "will need trimming before they fit" because "speech is too variable and too elusive to be quite safely ticketed" (121).

Elusion again—and surrender to it; in this elusion, Sapir notes, language is like "all human institutions" (1921:121). But on this vital point the situation of the student of language differs profoundly from that of his modernist colleagues in other fields of meaning: *the limitations of theory about language correspond in kind to limitations of language itself.* In Sapir's words: "Were a language ever completely 'grammatical,' it would be a perfect engine of conceptual expression. Unfortunately, or luckily, no language is tyrannically consistent. All grammars leak" (38). There is no doubt how Sapir evaluates fortune here. The life of language depends upon the leakiness of grammars; the imperfections of scholarly categories, participating directly in the imperfections of language, share that life. The profile of the Romantic Speaker is thus preserved in the modernist linguist—or philosopher of language—and so is his mission. The enormous and still-gathering momentum of the linguistic turn in the twentieth century derives from the preservation of that possibility, developing dialectically with positivist approaches to language from Carnap and Bloomfield to Chomsky and generative semantics. In the process, modernism has yielded more and more of the world to language, and twentieth-century cultural history may someday appear as the attempt to refuse in a linguification of reality.

So the art of humanity (of the "outside public") escapes the grasp of science while linguists are consoled in the knowledge that, in their very limitations, a kind of refusion is theirs. From that beginning, Sapir moves carefully toward more substantial reunions—most notably, toward one between thought and language, sometimes even between experience and language. Sapir is more cautious than the undisciplined Whorf in promoting the hypothesis that bears their names. In 1921 Sapir says: "Language and our thought grooves are inextricably interrelated, are, *in a sense*, one and the same" (217; italics mine); and a sentence is the "esthetically satisfying embodiment *of* a unified thought" (32; italics mine); and we "*feel* relieved" to provide the kind of word the grammar calls for in a sentence (85; italics mine). Language seems to its speakers to be complete, to be capable of saying anything because there is a "*felt* unity" at every linguistic level. Are these unities of language, so reminiscent of Herder in spirit, a repudiation of Sapir's earlier associationism? Not at all—and the italicized qualifiers suggest the crucial difference. For Sapir, the unity he proposes is not metaphysical; it is a "psychological unity" (82). The question that makes sense is whether, as a matter of psychological fact, "speech and thought be not two facets of the same psychic process" (13). The refusion of the modernist linguist is not *realized in* poiesis—it is *described by* psychology. As a private person, the modernist linguist of course experiences the unities psychology describes. He may even be a poet. But those are other subjects.

Still, the Romantic assimilation of being to language has been proposed, if only as a description. The "psychological validity" of grammars is empirical fact. The "realities of speech" and "realities of experience" are united at the level "of history, of art," in billions upon billions of actually uttered words and sentences. The coherence of things is maintained in the psychological processes of humanity's anonymous speakers. Thousands of languages take up, in grammatical deposits, the "powerful drifts" of history and so move "to balanced pattern" (Sapir 1921:122). The elements and categories of linguistic analysis only "respond to the conceptual world of science"; they have a "merely logical and abstracted existence" (32–35, 122). But at the psychological and historical level (the real level), "grammar" is "a generalized expression of the feeling that analogous concepts and relations are most conveniently symbolized in analogous forms" (38). Such forms just are the "habitual associations" of psychology which, when multiplied in the contingencies of history, constitute "tradition" (37). Even universals, like the subject-predicate form of sentences (119), derive in this way from the "immensely ancient heritage of the human race" (23). *The Spirit of Hebrew Poetry* still animates the Speaker's heir, but the world is too vast for utterance. He speaks now *of* being only in the sense of "about," not in the sense of "constitute" or even "for." He imitates in abstract description what he still longs for in reality, and occasionally recovers in the sanctuaries of the private mind.

Sapir valued great art above all. He believed that the greatest writers were capable of genuine refusion, of ontological utterance. On this point, he read seriously in philosophy, in Benedetto Croce, the Hegelian aesthetician who brought "History . . . Under the General Concept of Art" (1893). But of his several disciplines, it was linguistics, not poetry, which commanded Sapir's best efforts. Was it simply that his particular gift was intellectual, that he lacked a great poetic talent (Handler 1986:151–52)? Was Sapir resigned to science because he was not a Goethe? A veneration for great art and artists is unquestionably a deep source of Romanticism's influence in modernist scholarship. Creative genius speaks the living world while poorer speakers respond— and write commentaries. Analogues in political and social studies are easy to discern. Is that the posture underlying Sapir's self-effacement and irony?

Not quite. Some inherent value lingers in the neighborhood of reason, some half-forgotten promise still pursued in the twentieth-century academy. In Sapir, that promise lives between the lines on "Language and Literature" (1921:221–31). The greatest poets, he says, are also the translatable ones because they operate on a "generalized linguistic layer." The Shakespeares and Heines had access to a kind of "literary algebra," an "unknown original," an "absolute language." Their art consisted in their realized ability to "fit" that original language "to the provincial accents of their daily speech" (224–25).

That absolute language was, in itself, unuttered and unknown—an eerie counterpoint to the ideal language of science the positivists never managed to construct. Was there an excess of mystery in art, a residue of the inarticulate in its fusions? Is there not a trace of reason's pride in remarks like these: "any classification that starts with preconceived values or that works up to sentimental satisfactions is self-condemned as unscientific" (Sapir 1921:124); or "on the whole, it must be admitted that ideation reigns supreme in language, that volition and emotion come in as distinctly secondary factors"; or "objective reality is the unavoidable subject matter of human communication," and "desire, purpose, emotion are the personal color of the objective world; they are applied privately by the individual soul" (38, 39). This is unquestionably a modernist reaction to debauches of Romantic art and personality; does it also recall the original claims of Romantic reason?

If so, there are revealing parallels in some of Sapir's formulations of the Sapir-Whorf hypothesis. The insulation of psychology, of descriptions of *habits* of language and thought, could not entirely contain the ontological issue. A more complete identification seemed to be, at least in principle, possible. In 1921, Sapir compared the everyday use of language to

> . . . a dynamo capable of generating enough power to run an elevator [being] operated almost exclusively to feed an electric doorbell. . . . From the point of view of langauge, thought may be defined as the highest latent or potential content of speech, the content that is obtained by interpreting each of the elements in the flow of language as possessed of its very fullest conceptual value. From this it follows at once that language and thought are not strictly coterminous. At best, language can *but* be the outward facet of thought on the highest, most generalized level of symbolic expression. . . . Language is primarily a pre-rational function. It humbly works up to the thought that is latent in, that may eventually *be read into* its classifications and its forms. . . . Language is an instrument originally put to uses lower than the conceptual plane and . . . thought arises as a refined interpretation of its content. (14, 15; italics mine)

What is the implication of "but"? Are we to understand that thought on that "highest, most generalized level" cannot actually be uttered—as opposed to "be read into"? Is the assumption that it is impossible to speak language possessed of the "fullest conceptual value"? Psychologically impossible, perhaps?

If so, then Romantic reason's central mission is evoked—and then declined—in this extraordinary rumination on the relation between thought and language. Sapir placed that reason just beyond the (not quite reflective) art of language because he could not drive home a larger claim for it—or for himself. He could not, for example, draw the inspiring conclusion that such a reason could be the fulfillment of the "ancient heritage" of all linguistic forms. He certainly could not make the attempt Hegel made to actually speak in language possessed of its fullest conceptual value, to actually realize the fulfillment of reason. But as soon as that is said, the restraint is understandable. No responsible twentieth-century intellectual would attempt to lift natural language up into rational perfection in actual practice. Confronted by his own supreme talent, with Romantic reason as immanent relic, Sapir took the only course available to him—he kicked it upstairs. Perhaps this is why, in spite of his perception of the "ultimate need" for a "humble" psychological approach to "large-scale patterning," he never undertook it himself (Silverstein 1986:73). The gap between what he called his "verses" and great poetry was only one limit Sapir had to live with—and there he could blame an absence of talent. But the gap between the Speaker of Being and his disciplined heir could not be accounted for in that way. If Edward Sapir could only read reason into language, then there was nothing more to say.

One reduction of the Romantic notion of language was sufficient in itself to install psychology in reason's place. Recall Herder's disposition of the senses constituting mind and compare this from Sapir: the tongue and larynx are "no more to be thought of as the primary organs of speech than are the fingers to be considered as essentially organs of piano playing." The body's organs are "incidentally useful" to language and "there are, properly speaking, no organs of speech" (1921:9, 10). Why could the "organic and psychological mechanisms" of language "be taken for granted" in this way? Because, in themselves, languages are "arbitrary systems of symbolization." In the vast manifold of events, meanings are "automatically associated" with the symbols of language as they "ticket off" and "tag off" experience (11–13). Where once there was a total orientation of minds-in-the-world, modernist linguists found the arbitrariness of the sign.

That was so, once again, at both levels of the discipline. For Sapir also spoke of "ticketing" when exposing the inevitable inadequacy of linguistic categories: he said that theoretical "abstraction is justifiable" precisely because of the arbitrariness of meaningful relations in language itself (1921:11). The nineteenth-century idea of natural history had reconstituted a vast subject matter for study. Under reduced readings of Romantic historical organicism, the arbitrariness of Enlightenment stipulation (Rousseau's "invention") was transformed into the arbitrariness of psychological association at the level of natural historical processes. At the level of study, stipulations of Enlightenment consciousness retained authority within modernist disciplines. At both levels, meaning was constituted by the tag. The centrality of hearing in Herder seemed entirely unmotivated to Sapir because it was lodged in a transpsychological structure of significance inclusive of all reflection. When Sapir substituted psychological "association" for "mutation" in the *sensorium commune*, he acknowledged the death of God and human reason's limited sovereignty under its own discipline. By contrast, Herder's pious and participating mind had wanted "a reason, some reason for everything"—but arbitrary language was conceivable to him. The essence of the Romantic Speaker's vantage point in modern culture history is displayed in Herder's response to that possibility.

For him, the idea of an arbitrary language seemed "no less of a torture" for the mind "than it is for the body to be caressed to death" (1769:139).

The particular image tells the tale. The modernist learned to experience the torture/caress of arbitrariness as a kind of freedom, a *frisson* of release. Sapir must have felt it when he realized for the first time the implications of saying that the larynx is to speech as the fingers are to piano playing. In the moment of that torture/caress, all meaning is simultaneously a loss and a gain—a loss of the world and a gain for the private mind. The world, had, in any case, made its irrationality all too obvious and the individual needed what leverage circumstances allowed. At bottom, the modernist is preoccupied with form (Davis 1986:11-14), out of the conviction that all form is arbitrary, that the only mind there is hovers about the skulls of biological accidents.

In anthropology, a last vestige of the Romantic idea of culture as objective mind was threatened by Sapir's influential critique of Kroeber: hard modernists said "no" when asked "Do We Need a Superorganic?" (1917). In the private practice of his art, Sapir had experienced the psychological foundation of culture, and he proposed to describe it publicly in culture and personality theory. But if psychological individuals alone were real and culture a product of anthropological analysis (Handler 1983:226-27), then was *all* culture spurious (1924b)? That was Sapir's secret question; the ultimate issue of the arbitrary tag was arbitrary culture, arbitrary art and arbitrary morals—and that was more than Sapir could bear. But where else was a mind to turn? In reflections on the enterprise of reason, Sapir's turned again and again to the muted redemptions of irony:

> The relations between elements of experience which serve to give them their form and significance are more powerfully "felt" or "intuited" than consciously perceived. . . . It would seem that we act all the more securely for our *unawareness* of the patterns that control us. It may well be that, owing to the limitation of the conscious life, any attempt to subject even the higher forms of social behavior to conscious control must result in disaster. Perhaps there is a far reaching moral in the fact that a child may speak the most difficult language with idiomatic ease but that it takes an unusually analytical type of mind to define the mere elements of that incredibly subtle linguistic mechanism. . . . Is it not possible that the contemporary mind, in its restless attempt to drag all the forms of behavior into consciousness, and apply the results of its fragmentary or experimental analysis to the guidance of conduct, is really throwing away a greater wealth for a lesser and more dazzling one? It is almost as though a misguided enthusiast exchanged his thousands of dollars of accumulated credit at the bank for a few glittering coins of manifest, though little, worth. (1927b:548-49)

In another venue, Sapir recovered some of that accumulated credit in the modernist "aesthetic of glimpses" (Kenner in Handler 1986:132). In glimpses, he was reconciled—for as long as the aesthetic rush lasted—to the "limitation of the conscious life." Apart from the disciplines of institutions, where words made sense of personal tragedy, Sapir could even hear the centrality of sound:

> For silence is but air and emptiness
> Wherein I hear you neither curse nor bless,
> But when you twist wild words of pain for me
> I know that rage may but a loving be.
> However you point the tongue and shoot the arrow,
> Your voice is love in my most inward marrow.
>   (1927a:195)

The Speaker in Disguise: Lévi-Strauss (1908–   )

> . . . we feel the anguish of living together weighing on each of us . . .
>   (Lévi-Strauss on Rousseau 1962a:40)

With characteristic tenderness, Lévi-Strauss embraced Rousseau; upon the orphan of the Enlightenment he conferred the title "founder of the sciences of man" (1962a:33). Addressing an audience gathered in Geneva for the 250th anniversary of Rousseau's birthday, Lévi-Strauss began by citing a few passages which seemed vaguely to justify his large and ahistorical claim. At first reading, his speech seems an occasional gesture, an ironic salute across the centuries from one of history's waifs to another.

For example, Lévi-Strauss plucks from Rousseau's context a remark about seeing human differences before universals and promotes it immediately to the rank of "methodological rule" for all ethnology. But then he explains:

> To study man, one must first learn to look into the distance; one must first see differences in order to study characteristics. . . . [This] . . . makes it possible to overcome what, at first glance, one would take for a double paradox; that Rousseau could have, simultaneously, advocated the study of the most remote men, while mostly giving himself to the study of that particular man who seems the closest — himself; and secondly that, throughout his work, the systematic will to identify with the other goes hand in hand with an obstinate refusal to identify with the self. These two apparent contradictions, which resolve themselves into a single reciprocal implication, must be resolved, at one time or another, in every ethnological career. (1962a:35)

The first absurd impression (Durkheim pondering Rousseau's remark as he writes the *Rules for Sociological Method*) is replaced by something more plausible. A (rhetorical?) *pas de deux* of resolved contradictions transforms a courtesy into genuine insight. Lévi-Strauss on Rousseau turns out to be a revelation of the Romantic spirit in anthropology.

In his original alienation, Rousseau really could be said to have discovered the "principle . . . on which to base the sciences of man"–if allowance is made for the continental use of the term "science," and for "principle" as that which guides a life. That principle, says Lévi-Strauss, echoing Rimbaud, is "I is an other"–and it would "remain inaccessible and incomprehensible so long as there reigned a philosophy which, taking the *cogito* as its point of departure, was imprisoned by the hypothetical evidences of the self" (1962a:36). And that also makes culture-historical sense. For what is any object of Enlightened explanation and description if not hypothetical? That is precisely the view positivist philosophers like Popper and Hempel would eventually commend. At a broader and more practical level, are not moderns compelled to live with assumed identities in order to function progressively? Must not one assume one is this if one would be that? Such an assumption is the basis of Stewardship, of self-government in association–of *Gesellschaft* as Tönnies described it. And what would Rousseau and Romanticism overcome if not the hypothetical self to which the *cogito* removed us when it instrumentalized the world and exiled the mind?

Whether Lévi-Strauss would embrace the heritage of Romanticism or not, his tribute to Rousseau invites assessment in those terms. There is no denying that he grasps Rousseau's principle, not as a hard-bitten modernist would, but in Rousseau's own manner; he feels its truth and, in spite of his alleged indifference to emotion, he places that feeling at the foundation of anthropology. He realizes that Rousseau's principle was not really the tacitly contractual "I is an other" but the compassionate "I am not 'me' but the weakest and most humble of 'others'." That is "the discovery of the *Confessions*" and what does "the ethnologist write but confessions? In his own name first" and then "in the name of his society which," through its anthropological representative, "chooses for itself other societies . . . which appear to it the weakest and most humble . . . in order to verify how 'inacceptable' it is itself." For Lévi-Strauss, anthropology is an institutionalization of the purpose of Rousseau, the first modern victim to utter the loss; it aims to utter the losses of all modernity's victims and locate the instrumental success of the West in a realm of pure significance where it "is not at all a privileged form" (1962a:39). The *Discourse on Inequality* shaped that purpose in a "conception of man which places the other before the self, and . . . a conception of mankind which places life before men" (ibid.: 37). The latter placement is crucial; for Rousseau, the first inequality was between man and nature.

Lévi-Strauss begins with the same distinction. Does he believe that nature, in principle, "transcends itself" perpetually in the savage *bricolage* which fuses "man's biological existence and his social existence" (1969a:24, 25)? Or was the mind's alienation inevitable when the first "systems of denotation" were "borrowed from the realm of nature" (1962b:14)? Structuralism's sign seems to promise the "death of dualism" (Boon 1972:70) but an ominous latitude

"Il retourne chez ses egaux." Lévi-Strauss in Amazonia, c. 1937. (Courtesy of the photographer, Claude Lévi-Strauss.)

stirs in its arbitrary heart. Does Lévi-Strauss, like Rousseau, feel the impulse to "set above" in "set apart"?

In Rousseau's "imperious preoccupations" with "linguistics, music and botany," Lévi-Strauss finds an "underlying unity" in the effort to disrupt a "philosophical tradition" through anthropology (1962a:38). In fact, these are the characteristic preoccupations of Romanticism—rich sources for figures of refusion—and they are Lévi-Strauss' preoccupations as well. Every *thing* is positive, the correlative of a stable and separate subject. Romantics, inclined to relations and polarities at the margins of things, especially value whatever inclines to margins on its own accord. Plants are classifiable but, in blending profusion, they invite the mind to join. For Lévi-Strauss, myths are like plants and of them both he says, with Goethe: "Their chorus points to a hidden law" (1981:693).

And "chorus" is the word—for no medium of refusion compares to music. Music is the purest pleasure because, in it, the listener loses

> his individuality and his being; he has become the place or space of the music in whom normally incompatible principles (incompatible, at least, according to what he has been taught) are reconciled . . . and, in the process, arrive at a sort of organic unanimity. This organizing function . . . was made most clearly manifest in Romantic music, from the time of Beethoven, who raised it to incomparable heights. . . . The joy of music is, then, the soul's delight in being invited, for once, to recognize itself in the body. (Lévi-Struass 1981:656–57)

Lévi-Strauss says that he founded a science of mythology to "make up for my congenital inability to compose a musical work" (1981:649). He locates his science within a Structuralism which "includes four major families of occupants: mathematical entities, the natural languages, musical works, and myths." Math and language are in vertical opposition on a dimension of embodiment; that is, mathematical entities have no bodies and linguistic entities are doubly embodied in Saussure's sign. Music and myth are opposed on a horizontal axis; music is all sound and myth is all sense; that is, both are less embodied than language but more embodied than math. Why section titles like "Fugue of the Five Senses," "Opossum's Cantata," and "Birdnester's Aria" (1969b)? Because the *Mythologiques* are a symphony of sense—*the* symphony of sense, the human mind composing itself in a reutterance of the "the great anonymous voice whose utterance comes from the beginning of time and the depths of the mind" (1981:640). The *Mythologiques* are offered to the twentieth century as nothing less than a realization of Sapir's absolute language and Herder's Poiesis of Creation.

Is it possible? How could a Speaker overcome his mortal limitations? Lévi-Strauss says he discovered something that made it possible; he did not have to translate the folk-poems of the world into his own tongue because the meaning of myth is "not within language but above it." Since "every myth is by its very nature a translation" already, the "mythologist who is apprehending it through translation does not feel himself to be in an essentially different position from that of the native" (1981:645–47). Herder was too literal in his ambition, too positive about sound; he did not listen, along the horizontal axis of Structure, to music's opposite, to the chorus of soundless sense. Sapir was too modest, too committed to restraint; he would not make his art and science one. Neither brought language as a kind of structure to the world as the whole of experience. By doing so, the Speaker of the "myth of mythology" (Boon 1972:136), native to all tribes, linguified realities far beyond the domains of mythology as discipline defined it.

In Lévi-Strauss's articulations, the sign suffuses the world and everything is music in the wild mind. Women signify social orders in an aboriginal mathematics of marriage. Like Baudelaire's cat, synesthesiac totems unite the "sensory-concrete and the intellectual-abstract" (Boon 1972:117, 121–23; 131–32). Distinctions maintained by ghostly phonemes breed analogues throughout the *sensorium commune,* and the alienated subject is refused by sheer diffusion. In the prose of daily life—in ornaments, in table manners, in dispositions of the home and hearth—the universe is bound to mind. Four volumes of a hemisphere's mythology converge as

> . . . we come to understand how the modest account of a family quarrel that I took as my starting point, contains the whole system in embryo, and how the, for us, insignificant act of striking a match to kindle a flame perpetuates, in the very midst of our mechanized civilization, an experience which . . . was [once] invested with great solemnity, since it is a symbolic gesture holding in balance the most profoundly meaningful oppositions that it is given to the mind of man to conceive: between the sky and the earth on the level of the physical world, between man and woman on the level of the natural world, and between relations by marriage on the level of the social world. (Lévi-Strauss 1981:624)

The "Oldest Document" rewritten; the furniture of ordinary experience returned to sanctity in redemptive imagination; the raw world cooked to meaning in the play of signs—and, in the utterance of this Speaker, the play goes on.

No modernist judgment of validity could possibly contain such a production. But Lévi-Strauss did not defy that containment in open rebellion; he confounded it from within. He disguised his enterprise, professing it as an extension of linguistics, offering formal devices derived from unimpeachable sources along with examples of their innovative application. His overall manner suggested to qualified professional colleagues that he awaited their judicious consideration. But what did he actually present? Doubled arrows in bold relief etched across dotted lines linking overlapping circles and revolving triangles "based" (who could say how?) on data drawn from every corner of the ethnographic archive; diagrams of cattle bodies mapped onto constellations (in the winter sky) and then (by mediation of the solstice) onto inverse images of the floor plan of the men's house as seen from above, from the point of view of the such-and-such a moth mediating between night and day and the sky and the underworld and the woodpecker's crest. It was all delivered with absolute seriousness and precision, each skeptical question answered with scrupulous care—as if the whole towering architectonic were tuned . . . (to what?) . . . so finely that decades of patient labor might stand or fall with a distinction between a detail of kinship terminology recorded by the Salesian fathers in 1656 and a variation recorded by Wagley two centuries later on the *north* side of the valley. For those who wished to try their hand, it was patiently explained, as to a slow but willing child, that the (somehow vital, if one could just get clear on this) distinction between the axis and the level of the underlying structure was in the *model.*

Was it a giant spoof? Was it arrogance, or plain foolishness, on a massive scale? Was it a new art form—Kandinsky in another medium? Or was it sheer genius? What could be grasped was plausible, original, powerful, even thrilling. The unrecorded wanderings of primitive mind *would* range broadly across the cosmos and into the crannies of life; and that wandering would yield an overtly nonrational but articulated whole that would have to hang together somehow. And language was obviously real—structured by grammars so complex that they had operated unnoticed in the stuff of mind for millennia. And some of the middle-level principles had fieldwork applications: exchange structures had been missed by static Britishisms; marriage was, very often, exchange; "totemism" did look silly now. At the same time, Lévi-Strauss articulated broader tendencies; he gave focus to the increasing significance of linguistics in anthropology and, in the context of positivism's decline, he enhanced the Americanist tradition, bringing new meaning to the idea of culture (Hymes 1983:191–94). Up to a point and in part, Lévi-Strauss made sense to modernist scholars. But at the end of the day what and where were these "structures" and "models"? In the brain-minds of natives? Some of the natives? The ethnographer? Both? Were these structures theories or heuristic devices or creations with their own rights?

These were the questions modernist scholars asked of structuralism—and they were never satisfactorily answered. The most complete Romantic in academic anthropology was conditioned also by the twentieth century—but he made wings of its restraints, and the one that served him best was privacy. Technical form and professional manner were recast to serve the oracular mode.

Other constraints of academic modernism were similarly used. Consider an example of how Lévi-Strauss transforms provisionality into liberty without fetish. He presents a particular myth as a template for the entire cycle of American mythology. He baptizes it the "Oregonian singularity" and holds out the possibility that this is the "umbilical cord," the original "One Myth Only" from across the Bering Sea—a dream of Romanticism fulfilled. Then he airily remarks that the whole situation can be "interpreted differently"; it might just as well be a late synthesis, a convergence of the traditions of the continent. There is no way of knowing; Lévi-Strauss, the responsible scholar, submits to his limits (1981:605). But the second interpretation is as magnificent as the first. Modernist modesty on the face of it, while a gigantic transcendence of history by meaning is performed in a minor key.

Similarly with the appeal to the brain and the binary processes of neurophysiology. The materialism seems reassuring, empirical. But what constraints actually follow from that basis? Is there only analogy of form between the neural on/off and the diagrammatic +/−? And, if that is all there is, is he saying *that* is all there *is*? Or consider the awesome grasp of ethnography, the obvious respect for it; Lévi-Strauss is a certifiable authority of some kind—but not as a fieldworker. Is this the expertise of *The Golden Bough?* Underlying the whole enigma is a peculiar appropriation of the arbitrary sign. In modernist scholarship, in Sapir's linguistics for example, arbitrariness yielded technical analyses in well-defined domains. The whole point was to submit to explicit standards of validity. But Lévi-Strauss made of arbitrariness a license for his intuition.

Interviewed by the *New York Times*, Lévi-Strauss sighed for the nineteenth century "when someone like Victor Hugo could imagine applying his reflections to all the problems of humanity" (12/21/87:4). Under the discipline of his profession, he dismisses that "unrealizable dream" and calls himself an "artisan." But we need not be fooled by this restraint; Lévi-Strauss is indeed "the truest" of the "author-writers" in anthropology (Geertz 1988:27). His has been the boldest move—through the Romantic dialectic of elusion and affirmation into fusion which knows itself as Speaking Being. He is bound, in the end, to admit the "absolute superiority" of Western science as a "mode of knowledge" and to denounce the "phoney activities" of the current "philosophico-literary scene" (Lévi-Strauss 1981:636, 640–41). After replacing a stagnant philosophy with the social sciences, he must subordinate them, in turn, to the exact and natural sciences. They are a "shadow theater," symbols of symbols of phenomena offering only a "prefiguration, on the walls of the cave, of the operations . . . [of] . . . the real objects of which we are examining the reflections" (641–43). The complete Romantic Speaker strives to utter universal being—not relativist fabrications.

But not in a positivist reduction to physics; like Hegel, Lévi-Strauss finds reason in being: "Thought, and the world which encompasses it and which it encompasses, are two correlative manifestations of the same reality" (678). If he returns to Hegel's ontology, and not to his history (Murphy 1963), it is because to deny history in the twentieth century is only to admit manifest irrationality. Lévi-Strauss was obliged by events to seek reason deeper in being:

> Structuralism, unlike the kind of philosophy which restricts the dialectic to human history and bans it from the natural order, readily admits that the ideas it formulates in psychological terms may be no more than fumbling approximations to organic or even physical truth. One of the trends of contemporary science . . . validating the intuitions of savage thought, already occasionally succeeds in reconciling the sensory with the intelligible and the qualitative with the geometrical, and gives us a glimpse of the natural order as a huge semantic field. . . . It is not the type of reality irreducible to language but, as the poet [Baudelaire] says, "a temple in which living pillars from time to time emit confused words"; except that, since the discovery of the genetic code, we know that the words are neither confused or intermittent. (1981:689–90)

The exception of Baudelaire is criterial. This is not a retreat from the world to a modernist aesthetic of struggle and play in the independent work of art. Lévi-Strauss means to be nature "automythologizing" (Boon 1982:214). At the end of the last volume of the *Mythologiques*, the Speaker casts off his modernist disguise and refuses alienated mind in a language now "given a natural and objective status through the discovery and the cracking of the genetic code; the universal language used by all forms of life . . . As can be seen, when Nature, several thousand million years ago, was looking for a model she borrowed in advance, and without hesitation, from the human sciences; this is the model which, for us, is associated with the names of Trubetskoy and Jakobson" (Lévi-Strauss 1981:684, 685). The "borrowing" is, of course, a tribute to discoveries of linguistic science which accomplish an objectification of consciousness embracing the universe:

> If an explosion, a phenomenon that sensory experience allows us to perceive only during a fraction of a second and without being able to distinguish any of the details . . . can be the same thing as cosmic expansion, which appears infinitely slowed down in comparison with the scale of the phenomena in which we live our daily lives, and which we cannot imagine but only translate into the abstract formulae of mathematics, then it does not seem so incredible that a project conceived in a flash by a lucid consciousness . . . might be of the same kind, on an infinitely reduced scale, as that obscure drive which, over millions of years and with the aid of torturous and complicated devices, has insured the pollenization of orchids [by] insects . . . intoxicated . . . with secretions of the flower. (688–89)

We know the vessel of that lucid flash of consciousness; the scale may be "infinitely reduced" but that does not make the project small: "with the death of religion" at the "beginning of the modern age," works of art became "sacred." Having "taken over the structures of myth" at that time, the art of music was later obliged by a new "assumption of consciousness" after Wagner to "rid itself" of those structures—which then became available to music's intimate opposite, to myth. That is, they became available *again* to myth and so could "assume a self-consciousness in the form of a discourse on itself" (Lévi-Strauss: 1981:653–54). In uttering the discourse of myth returned to itself, Lévi-Strauss was refusing eternal mind. He concludes the *Mythologiques* by moving from the "twilight of the Gods" to the "twilight of man" to the twilight of life itself. Confronting the choice of Hamlet, he (arbitrarily) affirms the whole against the ultimate "reality of non-being":

> My analysis, by proving the rigorous patterning of myths and thus conferring on them the status of objects, has thereby brought out the mythic character of those objective realities: the universe, nature and man, which, over thou-

sands and, millions or billions of years, will, when all is said and done, have simply demonstrated the resources of their combinatory systems, in the manner of some great mythology, before collapsing in upon themselves and vanishing, through the self-evidence of their own decay. (693–94)

To those who have suspected him of playing "a gratuitous and decadent game" he offers simple testimony. Structuralism "can only appear in the mind because its model is already present in the body." It "brings to the surface of the consciousness . . . profound organic truths. Only its practitioners can know, from inner experience, what a sensation of fulfillment it can bring, through making the mind feel itself to be truly in communion with the body" (Lévi-Strauss 1981:692).

In the Speaker of Being, body and universe come to mind—but, in the twentieth century, the last affirmation of Hegel is withheld. Rather than a *polis* of the Absolute, we are offered its elegy. The arbitrariness of the sign, pushed back as far as the age allows, evokes Wittgenstein's experience of absolute value and yields the only religious question remaining to us: why is there anything at all? With Claude Lévi-Strauss, the Romantic influence in cultural anthropology returned to power in a Speaker unashamed to utter the genius of earth. Among the Bororo and the Gé, the spirit of Jean-Jacques came home at last, forced to be free in more hospitable salons:

For if the final aim of anthropology is to contribute to a better knowledge of objectified thought and its mechanisms, it is in the last resort immaterial whether in this book the thought processes of the South American Indians take shape through the medium of my thought or, whether mine take place through the medium of theirs. What matters is that the human mind, regardless of the identity of those who happen to be giving it expression, should display an increasingly intelligible structure as a result of the doubly reflexive forward movement of two thought processes acting one upon the other, either of which can in turn provide the spark or tinder whose conjunction will shed light on both. (Lévi-Strauss 1969:13)

The Postmodern Move

". . . there is no longer anything but writing . . ."
(Barthes 1987:64)

Modernity is most itself as it embraces the new. From Bacon's Great Instauration to the *Encyclopedie*, the new appeared in progressive trajectory interrupted only by reaction. Hiding from the Terror, Condorcet looked for more triumphs of Enlightenment in the epoch initiated by the French Revolution. With the rise of Romanticism-Idealism, however, modernity produced an opposition

internal to itself. The past was revalued—to be included spiralwise, in the dialectic of refusion. Since then, the history of modern culture has been punctuated by a succession of apocalyptic pronouncements that have, in their turn,
failed refusion; that fact alone has done much to motivate the restraints of
modernism. Only Romanticism itself did not have to reckon with this history
of disappointment, and thus it remains the original of modern opposition.
As such, it anticipated all struggles of alien subject and positive form; it was
the first avant-garde (Chase 1957:146–47; see also Trilling 1967:72; Howe
1963:3–34; Raymond 1967; Abrams 1971:146; Karl 1985:22–24). Any would-
be postmodern anthropology must begin with and in this historical situation.

The comprehensive promise of anthropology has always emerged in modernity's moments of self-doubt—for that is when we look elsewhere. Herder's
project was conceived during the original dissolution along lines anticipated
by Rousseau, the indigenous alien. Half a century later, as religion retreated
before the Darwinian tide, the first anthropologists tried to place it in a new
master narrative, in a natural history of humanity (Stocking 1987:149–60).
Wilhelm Dilthey expected anthropology to replace the philosophy Nietzsche
deconstructed under "*das Gleitende* [the moving, the slipping, the sliding],"
in an era of "multiplicity and indeterminacy" when "nothing allowed itself
to be embraced by concepts any more" (Hofmannsthal in Schorske 1981:19).
He proposed an "anthropological reflection" on the "objective mind" of culture which would be "akin to poetry" and evoke a living and factual universality after metaphysics and beyond psychology (in Ermarth 1978:227–33).
In today's slipping moment, however, anthropology is not promising synthesis. From the culture historical point of view, the first question is: why not?

The answer is obvious in outline. Anthropology is no longer a possibility
on the horizon of philosophy and history. In the twentieth century it became
an academic institution, to be undone by institutional crisis. With an identity to sustain and programs to administer, what can a discipline founded to
comprehend *Homo sapiens* make of *Local Knowledge* and "Partial Truths" (Geertz
1983; Clifford 1986)? Is ". . . Being Out of Words" (Tyler 1986) release or decay—
and what are the consequences for disciplinary practice? A "Crisis of Representation" (Marcus & Fischer 1986:7–16) in the humanities generally becomes
the more pointed, weighted, and urgent as it bears on the anthropological
concreta of food, work, sex, and death. Are poetry and prayer and ordinary
language as close as we get to truth, and is that truth as lost as it is found
in translation? The prospect suggested by its very name makes anthropology
the discipline most threatened by the dissolving questions of the day, and
the crisis of modernism in anthropology is correspondingly significant.

As aspirations of Enlightenment and Romanticism succumbed to events
and the nineteenth century unraveled into world war, modernity looked at
itself in embarrassment, betrayed by its ways. Like an adolescent's body under

scrutiny, forms of culture lost their unquestionable familiarity and became objects of study and experiment in themselves. Even the most inclusive form, consciousness itself, was suspect—undermined by the unconscious in Freud and Nietzsche, Conrad and the Symbolists (Schorske 1981:85–86). Plastic arts abandoned representation; literature, especially poetry, struggled with "the lacking word" trying to invent new language or avoid the "necessary defeat" of the old by the private "radiance of the inexpressible" (Steiner 1975:176–83). Modernism is a "world rejecting" retreat into the "self-limited and self-sufficing work of art," a "cutting off" of the Romantic object from the "ordinary world" where Romantics discovered it (Abrams 1971:418, 445). In a way, modernism actually "intensifies the Romantic revolt" in retreat from reality; in aesthetic realms it reigns supreme—uncommitted to any form, author of them all. In effect, modernism finally succeeds in uttering a world as it exercises arbitrariness under failsafe restraints of its own devising. By displaying the provisionality of all form, modernism can "make us at home with indecision" and "humanize the state of doubt" (Burke 1931:267). We may suffer and vacillate; we may live divided lives; but we are nobody's fool.

In the same context, under the same pressures, the social sciences turned to nominalist rigor and the humanities as a whole turned to specialization. Philosophy became a legislature of validity. Like all professionals, academics have governed public lives as Stewards of their portion of the world. In private realms, where tastes and convictions form, Romanticism has retained its limited sway. That division of labor between Enlightenment and Romantic traditions has been the dominant adjustment of liberal culture since the nineteenth century (Williams 1958; Sennett 1974; Taylor 1979:71); from Boas to Geertz, Romanticism in anthropology exercised its influence under that arrangement. Private commitments of the spirit have been publicly expressed in courts of validity—as arguments for the particular against the reductions of scientism, as descriptions of pattern and meaning in humanity's ways.

Jacques Barzun characterized modernism in general as a "crippled state" of will. Hopes dashed once too often yielded a "recoil from risk, not out of cowardice but out of self-knowledge." The modernist is compelled to "forestall derision by someone else or one's later self"; at bottom is the "fear of being duped." Barzun established his point in comparisons like this: Franz Liszt, gliding across Lake Como, reading with natural passion to his lady from Tasso and Victor Hugo; Ezra Pound dedicating a book of poems to "Mary Moore of Trenton, if she wants it" (Barzun 1961:115–21). This essay began with a pair of quotes making the same point less exquisitely, more comprehensively. For Hamann, Herder's teacher, the identity of the world and the word was Divine Utterance—which Hamann understood and expressed. For Wittgenstein, the same identification was a groan of frustration. Returned to sound as being, he uttered, not Ur-poems, but white noise. Postmodernism in general is out to recover Wittgenstein's condition—and celebrate it.

Variety thrives; let all the flowers bloom and no category will secure them (Marcus & Fischer 1986:45–76). But there is a garden, as there was for Herder, and Rousseau would have grasped its essence immediately: what is at stake is knowledge as representation and the hegemony of Western rationality (Clifford 1986:10). The postmodern "move" (the word rings with Romantic aspiration) foils modernism by turning ironic provisionality back on itself and exploding. Postmodernism collaborates with the failure of representation in order to escape it entirely and return to being. The question is: can it be done? Can *willing* dupes refuse?

In concluding *Works and Lives* (1988), Clifford Geertz assesses the interpretive turn he did so much to authorize. All in all he is glad that the "inadequacy of words to experience" is no longer "covered over with a professional mystique." With just a hint of apology, he deflects "back-to-the-facts table thumping in the establishment"; with more than a hint of paternal impatience, he admonishes "will-to-power gauntlet throwing" from the postmodernists (138). He will not disown the brood—but he lectures them, in the name of a discipline he does not, on the other hand, actually believe in.

Geertz knows his junior colleagues work in difficult circumstances; he sympathizes with the temptation of "rhetorical artifice designed to move intellectual goods in a competitive market" in "the increasingly desperate scramble to be noticed" (1988:142–43). But the phrasing conveys the hard note of modernist restraint. "Moral hypochondria" and "authorial self-doubt" in an "academy beset with paradigms, epistemes, language games," lead to "half-convinced writers trying to half-convince readers of their (the writers') half convictions." While this is not an "especially favorable situation for the production of works of very much power," it is what "must happen if the business is to continue." With the business threatened, "the burden of authorship cannot be evaded, however heavy it may have grown; there is no possibility of displacing it onto 'method' or 'language' or (an especially popular maneuver at the moment) 'the people themselves' redescribed ('appropriated' is probably the better term) as co-authors. . . . The responsibility for ethnography, or the credit, can be placed at no other door than that of the romancers who have dreamt it up" (137–40).

Calling an institution to order, Geertz asks: What is "the next necessary thing?" But at that critical juncture he returns to the radical provisionality which placed him at the door of dissolution to begin with. He will not speak of necessity; it is beyond him. "Anthropological authors" must "actually author" the future and find some way "to enlarge the possibility of intelligible discourse between people quite different from each other . . . tumbled as they are in endless connection" (1988:147). As a matter of personal taste, he points to a space of writing somewhere between "author-saturated texts like *David Copperfield*" and "author-evacuated texts like 'On the Electrodynamics of Moving Bodies'." He hopes for a new genre of "factions" to keep the discipline alive (141). But, in the end, he accepts the risk to anthropology's identity. It was the right time for a "thoroughgoing revision" of "our understanding of what it is to open (a bit) the consciousness of one group of people to (something of) the life form of another, and in that way to (something of) their own. What it is (a task at which no one ever does more than not utterly fail) is to inscribe a present—to convey in words 'what it is like' to be somewhere specific in the lifeline of the world" (143).

Sapir would have understood the parenthetical caveats; in certain moods, he might have have smiled wry agreement. Might he also have found them a touch overdrawn, one parenthesis too many, the "utterly" a shade too soft? Maybe so; but, in general, Geertz's voice would have been familiar to Sapir. He would have admired the erudition, the pragmatic constraint, the grace of modulation under the pressure of an indifferent reality. For Geertz's attitude is still essentially modernist, still innocently ironic. Nevertheless, it is modernism *in extremis*; Sapir would have been less sanguine at the prospect of anthropology's demise; imagine him reading this:

> Like any cultural institution, anthropology—which is a rather minor one com-
> pared with law, physics, music, or cost accounting—is of a place and time,
> perpetually perishing, not so perpetually renewing. (Geertz 1988:146)

In his melancholy, Sapir often allowed irony to bear upon the "conscious life"—but he would not have allowed private feelings to converge in public with a specific threat to Dr. Boas' legacy, to his profound and serene discipline, to the only institution in the world speaking for the victims of history. The cost-accounting comparison would have seemed to him gratuitous, an insult to music and physics as well as anthropology. But for postmodernists Geertz's insouciant diagnosis is just the beginning. They embrace a dissolution of institutions on a grander scale.

> Orality and literacy are contemporary reflexes of an ancient argument between
> the ear/mouth and the eye, between "saying" and "seeing," between *kinesis* and
> *mimesis*. Ever since the Greeks learned to write, the eye has dominated the
> ear/mouth in the west. The argument reemerges now because writing, the in-
> strument of domination, has undermined itself and is being challenged by new
> technologies of representation. The whole idea of writing and literacy, at the
> very moment when this hegemony seemed most assured, is now suspect in a
> way that it has not been for many centuries in the West. There is no need here
> to reiterate all the formidable cliches that intone the futuristic possibilities of
> computerization and literacy's key notions of "book," "word," "reading," and
> "writing," except to note that these further triumphs of the eye portend the end
> of the domination of the eye, for they imply a logographic writing that will
> entail a pattern of sensorial integration different from that of the alphabet.
> They will engender a new struggle for domination, not just between the eye
> and the ear/mouth but between the eye and the hand that will finally end the

hegemony of mimesis over kinesis in a consciousness that does not overcome orality but recovers, without repetition, the miraculous, the mutable, the chance, and the passion of speech. (Tyler 1986:136)

To a late modernist like Geertz, Stephen Tyler's prose is "pumped up" and "febrile"—though he has a point to be admitted (Geertz 1988:138). Sapir would have dismissed "On Being Out of Words" as a debauch and would probably have lacked the patience to take any point from it at all. And that is not surprising, for in the larger context of modern culture history, Tyler recalls aspects of Romanticism that the original modernists scorned.

Tyler appears as a prophet—no question about that; and he is out to redeem the past and the everyday, not in art but in life, and spiralwise, "without repetition." The "pattern of sensorial integration" to come and the *sensorium commune* at Herder's Creation resemble each other because "the idea of a dialogical anthropology" is the idea of a "'re-oralization' of writing" (Tyler 1986:135). The dialectic is there, in writing's self-destruction—but the call to a positivist Marx in "technologies of representation" is declined in "formidable cliches." The point is not to rewrite *Capital* for the computer age or to organize history better than communists did—all that belongs to the "'letterized' epistemology of being, knowing, and representation" (136). The point is in the becoming of things, in a realized relocation of the eye and the ear/mouth (and the hand, of course, for this is a "move," not a description). Most striking is the tone and the scope—*Sturm und Drang* and a return to hugeness. The end of anthropology, or even of cost accounting, is barely perceptible on the scale invoked; it is the Greeks, the whole project of Western Reason, which are crumbling unmourned into oblivion. And the sheer size of the thing permits the release of feeling from its private bondage; once again, the "miraculous" can be publicly uttered in the "passion of speech" and the would-be postmodern appears as a Speaker of Being becoming—in the refusion of Writing:

> But this age of ours, the one just before the age of the new writing, is a stage in which not even the eye can long survive. In order for the new writing to be born, it must first be disconnected not only from the voice, but from the eye as well. It must break the whole spell of representation and project *a world of pure arbitrariness without representation*. It must be disconnected from any world that is not built into its own circuitry and programs. The new writing will be preceded by this writing that closes upon itself. . . . For us, "orality" is the name of the resistance to this algebraism—this soundless shuffling of meaningless signs. Our redemption in/from this tale of loss and liberation is not in sight, nor at hand. Could it be just on the tips of our tongues? (Tyler 1986:137; italics mine)

What, exactly, is this new age which is to be—and the one we are in, the one just before it? What, for example, is "writing that closes upon itself?" What, exactly, is "logographic writing" and the "sensorial reintegration" it entails?

Once asked, such questions are immediately beside the fundamental point—which is to elude dependence on anything like quantificational studies of cross-references in TV commercials between 1958 and 1988. Not that a postmodern sensibility would find such studies uninteresting—but they would not be, could not be, in any way conclusive. Studies *of* anything, per se, take place under the spell of representation and the willing dupe is never there.

So it cannot be clear what the "next necessary thing" is—for that would be to represent it. But it is not to be shrugged off in the manner of Geertz, still burdened with authority and a modernist's respect for truth, however partial. On the contrary, the "next necessary thing" is proposed ecstatically, without any restraint at all. For modernist provisionality, turned against itself, yields freedom from all authorship, absolute elusion—one aspect of the Romantic dialectic brought to apogee. Arbitrariness of meaningful form confounded Rousseau at every turn; it was a torture/caress to Herder; it gave Sapir the only freedom he could trust and to Lévi-Strauss the camouflage he needed. But to Tyler, the willing dupe, it is all caress. His is not the age of the new writing in which the Eden of orality returns. His is the age just before the millennium, "a world of pure arbitrariness without representation," a "soundless shuffling of meaningless signs" which will, somehow, engender a "new kind of natural sign to parallel a new kind of nature" (Tyler 1986:133). There is no burden of authorship, for that new nature will not depend upon the truth or falsity of any utterance. Apotheosis is pragmatically secured, and the self in praxis falls away in the pure deed. There will always be the difference of another reading, and the new writing, like orality itself, will sustain

> a reality that constantly remakes itself, a reality whose total structure is never realized and cannot be known, yet can be participated in as if it were known or as if participation grounded itself. Our understanding, growing within participation, is autotelic; it develops its own standards of rightness and interpretation from within itself [and] relativizes knowledge and representation to communication, to the purposes, interests, and agreements of the communis. (136)

Succeeding sections of "On Being Out of Words" are titled "Yes, I know but . . . ," "On the other hand . . . ," "How Can You . . . ," "Really . . . ," "Tell?" And there's the rub. The refusal to tell, the pure deed, the autotelic communis—elusion unto fusion, not refusion, is proffered. The "principle of negation" has returned with the tone inverted; the estranged self is not, like Rousseau, suffering in the vacuum; it gambols in the void, exulting in arbitrariness, preparing the way for events beyond reason. The willing dupe declines the second moment of Romanticism, the Speaker's fate—which is, precisely, to *tell*; to bring the world in reverence to the mind; to utter truly.

Of course, it may not matter; there may be nothing but white noise and mutant skulls. But if the dialectic is real, if there is reason in being, then form is not arbitrary and refusion is the authentic aspiration of conscious-ness. If the dialectic is real, the deconstructive gesture will grow arch with repetition and Nietzsche's decadence of fragmentation will be its only issue. If the dialectic is real, the life of the mind will show itself again as the desire for the world as a whole—as it was for Hegel, the last of the "giant race be-fore the flood" (Lichtheim 1967:xxxii). His penultimate position made him the greatest dupe of all but, if the dialectic of Romantic Reason is real, the nobility of Hegel's risk will be recovered at elusion's apogee and minds will once again make claims which do not "fail" beforehand, but reach for com-pletion with their whole being and if they fail, *fail*.

References Cited

Abrams, M. 1953. *The mirror and the lamp: Romantic theory and the critical tradition.* New York.

——. 1971. *Natural supernaturalism.* New York.

Barthes, R. 1987. *Criticism and truth.* Minneapolis.

Barzun, J. 1961. *Classic, romantic, and modern.* Chicago.

Berlin, I. 1976. *Vico and Herder: Two studies in the history of ideas.* London.

——. 1980. *Against the current: Essays in the history of ideas.* New York.

Bernstein, R. 1986. Why Hegel now? in *Philosophical profiles.* Cambridge.

Boas, F. 1904. The history of anthropology. *Science* 20:513–24.

Boon, J. A. 1972. *From symbolism to structuralism.* Oxford.

——. 1982. *Other tribes, other scribes: Symbolic anthropology in the comparative study of cultures, histories, religions, and texts.* New York.

Burke, K. 1931. Thomas Mann and André Gide. In *The idea of the modern*, ed. I. Howe, 257–68. New York (1966).

Burkhardt, F. H. 1940. Herder's development and the place of the "Conversations" in it. In 1940 edition of Herder 1787.

Cassirer, E. 1970. *Rousseau, Kant, Goethe.* Princeton.

Chase, R. 1957. The fate of the avant-garde. *Partisan Rev.* 24:363–75.

Clark, R. 1955. *Herder: His life and thought.* Berkeley.

Clifford, J. 1986. Introduction: Partial truths. In *Writing culture*, ed J. Clifford & G. Marcus, 1–26. Berkeley.

Collingwood, R. 1956. *The idea of history.* Oxford.

Davis, R. 1986. *Contemporary literary criticism.* White Plains, N.Y.

Derrida, J. 1974. *Of grammatology.* Trans. Gayatri Chakravorty Spivak. Baltimore, Md.

Darnell, R. 1986. Personality and culture: The fate of the Sapirian alternative. *HOA* 4:156–83.

Ermarth, M. 1978. *Wilhelm Dilthey: The critique of historical reason.* Chicago.

Evans-Pritchard, E. E. 1981. *A history of anthropological thought.* New York.

Findlay, J. 1958. *Hegel: A re-examination.* New York.

Fortes, M. 1953. *Social anthropology at Cambridge since 1900.* Cambridge.

Frye, N. 1963. *Romanticism reconsidered*. New York.

Gay, P. 1966. *The rise of modern paganism*. New York.

Geertz, C. 1983. *Local knowledge*. New York.

———. 1988. *Works and lives*. Stanford.

Handler, R. 1983. The dainty and the hungry man: Literature and anthropology in the work of Edward Sapir. *HOA* 1:208–31.

———. 1986. Vigorous male and aspiring female: Poetry, personality. and culture in Edward Sapir and Ruth Benedict. *HOA* 4:127–55.

Harris, M. 1968. *The rise of anthropological theory*. New York.

Hegel, G. 1807. *The phenomenology of mind*. Trans. J. B. Baillie. New York (1967).

———. 1827. *The logic of Hegel*. Trans. William Wallace. Oxford (1892).

Heidegger, M. 1971. *On the way to language*. Trans. P. Hertz. New York.

Herder, J. 1769. Essay on the origin of language. In *On the origin of language: Two essays by Jean-Jacques Rousseau and Johann Gottfried Herder*. Trans. Alexander Gode. New York (1966).

———. 1782. *The spirit of Hebrew poetry*. Trans. James Marsh. London (1833).

———. 1784–91. *Reflections on the philosophy of the history of mankind*. Trans. T. O. Churchill. Chicago (1968).

———. 1787. *God, some conversations*. Trans. F. W. Burkhardt. New York (1940).

Honigmann, J. 1976. *The development of anthropological ideas*. Homewood, Ill.

Hough, G. 1966. Symbolism. In *The idea of the modern*, ed. I. Howe, 183–89. New York.

Howe, I. 1963. *Decline of the new*. New York.

Hulme, T. 1924. *Speculations: Essays on humanism and the philosophy of art*. New York.

Hymes, D. 1983. Linguistic method in ethnography: Its development in the United States. In *Essays in the history of linguistic anthropology*. Amsterdam/Philadelphia.

Karl, F. 1985. *Modern and modernism*. New York.

Kieffer, B. 1986. *The storm and stress of language*. University Park, Pa.

Kroeber, A. 1955. History of anthropological thought. *Yearbook of anthropology*, ed. W. L. Thomas, Jr., 293–311. New York.

Lévi-Strauss, C. 1962a. Jean-Jacques Rousseau, founder of the sciences of man. In *Structural anthropology II*. Trans. Monique Leyton. New York (1976).

———. 1962b. *Totemism*. Trans. R. Needham. Boston (1963).

———. 1969a. *The elementary structures of kinship*. Trans. J. H. Bell & J. R. von Sturmer. Ed. R. Needham. Boston.

———. 1969b. *The raw and the cooked*. Trans. J. & D. Weightman. New York.

———. 1981. *The naked man*. Trans. J. & D. Weightman. New York.

Lichtheim, G. 1967. Introduction to the Torchbook edition. In 1967 edition of Hegel 1807.

Locke, J. 1690. *Two treatises of government*. Cambridge (1967).

Lovejoy, A. O. 1948. *Essays in the history of ideas*. Baltimore.

Lowie, R. 1937. *History of ethnological theory*. New York.

Lowith, K. 1967. *From Hegel to Nietzsche*. Garden City, N.J.

Manuel, F. 1968. Editor's introduction. In 1968 edition of Herder 1784–91.

Marcus, G., & Fischer, M. 1986. *Anthropology as cultural critique*. Chicago.

Martin, K. 1954. *The rise of French liberal thought*. New York.

Mornet, D. 1929. *French thought in the 18th century*. Englewood Cliffs, N.J.

Murphy, R. 1963. On Zen Marxism: Filiation and alliance. *Man* 63:17–19.

O'Flaherty, J. 1952. *Unity and language: A study in the philosophy of Johann Georg Hamann.* Chapel Hill, N.C.

Peckham, M. 1962. *Beyond the tragic vision.* New York.

Raymond, M. 1967. Considerations on symbolism. In *The idea of the modern,* ed. I. Howe, 194–201. New York.

Rousseau, J. 1755. Discourse on the origin and basis of inequality among men. In *The essential Rousseau.* Trans. Lowell Bair. New York (1974).

———. 1762. The social contract. In *The essential Rousseau.* Trans. Lowell Bair. New York (1974).

———. 1781. *The confessions.* Trans. J. M. Cohen. Harmondsworth, Eng. (1953).

———. 1852. Essay on the origin of language which treats of melody and musical imitation. In *On the origin of language: Two essays by Jean-Jacques Rousseau and Johann Gottfried Herder.* Trans. J. H. Moran. New York (1966).

Rude, G. 1972. *Europe in the 18th century: Aristocracy and the bourgeois challenge.* New York.

Ryle, G. 1949. *The concept of mind.* New York.

Sapir, E. 1907. Herder's "Ursprung der Sprache." *Mod. Philol.* 5:109–42.

———. 1917. Do we need a "Superorganic"? *Am. Anth.* 19:441–47.

———. 1921. *Language.* New York.

———. 1924a. The grammarian and his language. *Am. Mercury* 1:149–55.

———. 1924b. Culture, genuine and spurious. *Am. J. Soc.* 29:401–29.

———. 1928a. He implores his beloved. *Poetry* 30:194–95.

———. 1927a. The unconscious patterning of behavior in society. In *Selected writings of Edward Sapir,* ed. D. Mandelbaum, 544–59. Berkeley (1949).

———. 1934. Symbolism. In *Selected writings of Edward Sapir,* ed. D. Mandelbaum, 564–68. Berkeley (1949).

Sennett, R. 1974. *The fall of public man.* New York.

Schorske, C. 1981. *Fin-de-siècle Vienna.*

Silverstein, M. 1986. The diachrony of Sapir's synchronic linguistic description; or, Sapir's "cosmographical" linguistics. *Stud. Hist. Lang. Sci.* 41:67–99.

Steiner, G. 1975. *After Babel.* Oxford.

Stocking, G. W., Jr., 1987. *Victorian anthropology.* New York.

Taylor, C. 1979. *Hegel and modern society.* Cambridge.

Trilling, L. 1967. On the modern element in modern literature. In *The idea of the modern,* ed. I. Howe, 59–82. New York.

———. 1971. *Sincerity and authenticity.* Cambridge, Mass.

Tyler, S. 1986. On being out of words. *Cult. Anth.* 1:131–37.

Wellek, R. 1963. The concept of romanticism in literary history. In *Concepts of criticism.* New Haven.

Wittgenstein, L. 1953. *Philosophical investigations.* New York.

Williams, R. 1958. *Culture and society: 1780–1950.* New York.

Wordsworth, W. 1800. Preface to the *Lyrical ballads.* New York (1958).

de Zengotita, T. 1984. The functional reduction of kinship in the social thought of John Locke. *HOA* 2:10–29.

LÉVI-STRAUSS, WAGNER, ROMANTICISM

A Reading-back . . .

JAMES A. BOON

Nothing is more absurd than ownership claimed for ideas.
(Heinrich Heine)

One fact is certain: That most influential and controversial corpus of twentieth-century anthropology—Lévi-Strauss's—contains a complicated dialogue with that most influential and controversial corpus of nineteenth-century hybrid arts—Richard Wagner's. This fact's certainty has recently been intensified by Lévi-Strauss's elaborations of earlier references to Wagner as the "undeniable originator" of the structural analysis of myths and folktales, who discovered "that the structure of myths can be revealed through a musical score" (Lévi-Strauss 1969a:15). These references, subsequent augmentations, and earlier allusions serve as the present essay's points of departure, and arrival.

Lévi-Strauss's concerted studies of marriage systems and New World mythology have been accompanied by fragmentary forays through the library of anthropological evidence about symbolic classifications, ritual exchange, and social arrangements not governed by agencies of centralized control. He has interwoven a body of work that is simultaneously many kinds of text echoing many forebears. Prominent among these are Wagner's aesthetics of unending transition and his musical devices of multiple transpositions, now gathering, now dispersing. Lévi-Strauss's corpus inscribes a way of reading

---

James A. Boon is Professor in the Department of Anthropology at Princeton University. His major publications include *The Anthropological Romance of Bali, 1597–1972*, and the forthcoming *Affinities and Extremes*, with comparative essays about the East Indies, Hindu-Bali, and Indo-Europe. He is currently at work on links between music and cultural theory and the anthropology and history of Protestant colonialisms.

variant mythologies and social structures, a way that has come increasingly to resemble the ordering interrelationships advanced in and as Wagner's music drama.

This dimension of Lévi-Strauss's anthropology recalls many predecessors engaged or enraged by Wagner who have either embraced or decried different aspects of "Wagnerism." They include literary and philosophical symbolists: Baudelaire, Mallarmé, later Eliot; novelistic modernists after them: Proust, Mann, Virginia Woolf; and savants then and since: Nietzsche, Shaw, Adorno. (These lists of examples could be much longer, as resplendent, and somehow *tristes*.) His affinity to Wagner and previous Wagnerians and anti-Wagnerians does not make Lévi-Strauss's work any less empirical or anthropological in the disciplinary sense. His corpus remains a transforming response to particular ethnographic and comparative pursuits: Boasian studies of Northwest Coast myths and contexts; Lowie's approach in *Primitive Society* to a range of kinship organizations; analyses of "primitive and archaic" ritual practice, economic exchange, and social logic advanced by Durkheim, Mauss, and associates of *L'année sociologique*; Radcliffe-Brown's too-abstract formulations of social structure. (This list, too, is longer, resplendent enough, only partly outmoded, and perhaps encouraging.) Both explicitly and indirectly, Lévi-Strauss has wedded and divorced his work, sometimes winkingly, to and from figures as varied as Bergson, Proust, Goethe, D'Arcy Wentworth Thompson, Ruth Benedict, Saussure, *Playboy*, Marx-Freud-Archaeology, *Hamlet*, and at least three faces of Rousseau: Rousseau; Jean-Jacques; and Rousseau, Juge de Jean-Jacques. (This list too is longer, dazzling even by today's interdisciplinary standards, and somehow comic, or tragicomic.)[1]

This is the list, moreover, that includes Wagner, slyly invoked as the "first authentic structuralist," at a pivotal "point of return" in a musical cycle listed by Lévi-Strauss as Bach-Beethoven-Wagner/Debussy-Ravel-Stravinsky (1969a: 28). Lévi-Strauss's score or so of books — manifoldly linked to French, American, British, and Dutch anthropology plus many strands of semiology — resonates as well with Wagnerian methods of musical-textual composition and, I shall argue, reading, or reading-back. This essay's second half reads back

---

1. These names are drawn from different moments in Lévi-Strauss's work, particularly from *Tristes tropiques* (1955), *Le totemisme aujourd'hui* (1962b), *L'homme nu* (1971). Benedict enters into the Introduction to *Sociologie et anthropologie* (1950), and Freud is most recently reconsidered in *La potière jalouse* (1985). On Rousseau and Rousseau/Chateaubriand in Lévi-Strauss, see Boon (1972, 1982a) and de Zengotita, "Speakers of Being," in this volume. Rousseau enters Lévi-Strauss (1962a) after a discussion of different constructions that signify relations with predecessors, including totemic codes, ancestral panoplies, and narratives of substantive legacy. Lévi-Strauss's construction of Rousseau as a "founder" (1973: ch. 2) accentuates one such construction. Positions on marriage and kinship, ritual and literature, myth and music, and the history of ideas are developed in Boon (1972, 1973, 1982a, 1982b, 1984, 1985, 1986a, 1986b, and forthcoming) with extensive discussion of the literature on so-called structuralism.

over Lévi-Strauss reading back over Wagner. Preparatory to that reading, I revisit select moments in the contrastive construction of Romanticisms, a construction that continues. I enlist—citing, paraphrasing, sometimes pastiching—distinctive scholars inclined to beg differences (such as Romanticism) and both to subvert and to sustain demarcations. *This* list includes Heinrich Heine, Vladimir Nabokov, Hugh Kenner, Lévi-Strauss himself, and others. I favor coincidences of reading-back that both cancel and harness distinctions such as Romantic and Structuralist. Assembled from the ironies of chronology and corpus making, my essay is *motificly* constructed, its overlappings studied. Parallels between mythic processes and reading-back should emerge. But first, a few words about Wagner.

Preliminaries

Whatever Wagner was, he was not a Romantic, whatever that was, or is, or wasn't (see below). Yet, together with Cosima Wagner after 1869, Wagner kept reading the writings of early Romantics and later ones, inspired by their cross-cultural and historical translations. Richard and Cosima together read copiously, always with an eye toward Wagner's own emerging works. Details of their reading registered in Cosima's diaries can be added to the outpourings of Wagner scholarship during the years on either side of 1983 and 1982—centenaries of Wagner's death and of *Parsifal*'s first performance, respectively. This scholarship figures importantly in my own departing-returning reading between Lévi-Strauss's anthropology and Wagner's all.[2]

Wagner directly influenced the school in France later designated Symbolists who, following Baudelaire, developed counterbourgeois canons of transgressive poetry and politics unhitched from state sponsorship. Symbolists in turn were harbingers of *L'art pour l'art*, Aestheticism, and ensuing contraventions of bourgeois propriety. At the same time, the cult of Wagner enshrined at Bayreuth between Wagner's death in 1883 and Cosima's death in 1930 could be leashed to opposite, totalitarian ends.

Wagner's storied hatreds included the French *état* and musical establishment; operatic conventions he would thwart (e.g., isolated arias); Jewish influence in music and certain Jewish roles in German history; Prussian regi-

---

2. A ready point of entry into the overpowering scholarship on Wagner and Wagnerism is *Opera Quarterly* (1983). Interpretations and translations have not diminished since. I read both Wagnerites and anti-Wagnerians with the music uppermost in mind. Recent sources most helpful for background relevant to this essay are Large & Weber (1984), Burbidge & Sutton (1979), Cooke (1979), and Ewans (1983). Cosima Wagner's diaries can be seen as a daily-memory variation in prose of Wagner's mythic-historical dramas in music and text. As in the case of Lévi-Strauss, one must compare prose to music-text.

"I myself [Moi-même], in considering my work from within [du dedans] as I have lived it, or from without [du dehors] which is my present relationship to it as it drifts away into my past [s'éloigne pour se perdre dans mon passé], see more clearly that this tetralogy of mine, now that it has been composed, must, like Wagner's, end with a twilight of the gods [elle doive s'achever sur un crépuscule des dieux comme l'autre]; or, to be more accurate, that having been completed a century later and in harsher times, it foresees the twilight of man, after that of the gods which was supposed to ensure the advent of a happy and liberated humanity. At this late hour [soir] in my career . . ."

(Claude Lévi-Strauss, *L'homme nu* [Paris, 1971], p. 620; translated by John and Doreen Weightmann, *The Naked Man* [New York, 1981], p. 619; the translators have replaced his allusion [comme l'autre] with a reference to Wagner's name, diminishing into clarity the passage's evocation of the crepuscular and its sense of *soir*.)

(Photograph courtesy of Claude Lévi-Strauss.)

mentation and dominance over his or anyone else's art; and more, and more. This list is long, perhaps endless. His notorious views and prejudices reflected desires for a newly spiritualized German nationalism after the failure of reforms in 1848 when Wagner had been a revolutionary at Bakunin's side. I can imagine nothing to say briefly of Wagner's anathemas and loves except that they portended both the most dire and the loftiest excesses of the twentieth century: its politics, its violence, its chromatics, its arts, its aspirations.

Wagner's relation to Romanticism is similar. At his death in 1883, his work portended the extremes—left-wing Bohemians, right-wing nationalists—of everything in the "Modernist" century to come. Again, at his death, his work recapitulated the extremes, and even the many medians, of everything in the "Romantic" century past. Wagner, moreover, was pivotal in the development from Romanticism to Symbolism, one neatly formulated by polymath critic Hugh Kenner:

> In the Symbolist poem the Romantic effect has become a structural principle, and we may say that Symbolism is scientific Romanticism, thus an effort to anticipate the work of time by aiming directly at the kind of existence a poem may have when a thousand years have deprived it of its dandelions and its mythologies, an existence purely linguistic, determined by the molecular bonds of half-understood words. . . . Certain poems of Mallarmé . . . (1971:130)

Wagner, at whose altar Mallarmé worshiped, and Lévi-Strauss after him, (1969a:15), both recapitulated Romantic effects and anticipated Symbolism's purging of referential "dandelions" in the name of purely linguistic and/or musical resonance. The wealth of anticipation and recapitulation in Wagner's music is very like Lévi-Strauss's anthropology. Or so, I suspect, it will increasingly appear as the years to come roll past.

Wagner's music, libretti, treatises, and unstoppable reading retrace, like a parodic coda, the Romantic era, converting its tonalities, tenets, and narrative values to the wherewithal of music-drama. Does this make him ultra-Romantic, post-Romantic, anti-Romantic, anti-anti-Romantic, first-Symbolist, proto-structuralist? Regardless, Romantic indeed were major musical precedents that Wagner esteemed and engulfed: Weber's *Freischutz*, Beethoven's *Fidelio*, and Mozart's *Magic Flute* (well, Classical verging on Romantic). Romantic, too, were many authors that he prized: E. T. A. Hoffmann, Carlyle, and Goethe (well, Romantic trailing Classical). Above all, Romantic were Wagner's enthusiasms for transpositions of medieval works, folktales, and Indological sources. Upon these world-translations Wagner based his music dramas: those he achieved, those he but hoped, those he dreamed.

With Cosima Wagner (*née* Lizst, Catholic, and illegitimately), Richard Wagner (*né* Protestant, *genitor* in doubt) scanned books representing other cultures, mythic pasts, and comparative religions. There they sought grist for his libretti and politico-aesthetic theories alike, reading their own and Germany's present circumstances into and across a deuniversalized history—*Geschichte* championed by such *Frühromantiker* as Friedrich and Wilhelm Schlegel, the Brothers Grimm, Novalis, Wilhelm von Humboldt, and Herder (Enlightenment beckoning Romantic) and Heine (Romantic regretting Enlightenment). This much longer list included Schopenhauer: harder to tag even as an alloyed Romantic—although he lectured, little noticed, in Berlin on the other side of Hegel's classroom wall. Schopenhauer's impact, delayed until shortly before his death in 1860, accelerated when his un-Romantic, Buddha-invoking pessimism (anticipating Modernism?) helped Nietzsche attain after-Romantic transvaluations. Wagner fished in all these Romance-books—including Schopenhauer and the early Nietzsche, when Nietzsche, too, still worshipped at Wagner's altar and did not yet write that he despised him and his work. Yes, Wagner combed history's myths, pasts, and renunciations (Christian, Buddhist), for motives of and for his unique libretto-music, a kind of wordsong.[3]

Later, after history since 1883 had often tragically increased the store of anthropological evidence, Lévi-Strauss began returning upon Wagner; upon the Wagner/Debussy difference; upon that Dreyfusard Wagnerian, Proust; and upon others too numerous to list. Lévi-Strauss's corpus, moreover, came to be regarded as a centerpiece of Structuralism, whatever that is, or was, or wasn't—such as Romanticism. To which we now turn.

Part I. What Isn't Romanticism?

Pondering *isms*, I recall Kenneth Burke's reminder that "whereas 'isms' *look* positive, they are all negatively infused, taking their form antithetically to other 'isms' (some elements of which, paradoxically, they often end by incorporating" (Burke 1970:24).[4] Any *ism* echoes aspects of "totemism," placed per-

---

3. This paragraph alludes to questions about Wagner's paternity and facts about Cosima's birth that have figured in their "biographies," which grow more mythic the more details are known. For example, that Cosima's birthplace was until recently mistakenly commemorated as Bellagio (not Como) is made much of in Walker (1983). That we will never know what Nietzsche made of *Parsifal*, or why (see Newman 1968:IV, chs. 15–16), becomes clearer the more we learn. I am convinced that the Nietzsche/Wagner issue cannot escape the sane formulation that Nietzsche coined for the relationship: "we antipodes." (On the fleeting evidence that Malinowski was alert to Nietzsche/Wagner, see Stocking [1986].)

Schopenhauer is pivotal—yet out-of-chronology—both because Wagner only eventually engulfed his pessimism (see Magee 1983; Simmel 1986; Feldman & Richardson 1972) and because Schopenhauer embraced Indological sources in a distinctive way (Sedlar 1982; Willson 1964).

4. I have argued this point for structuralism and French symbolism, for functionalism and Romanticism, and for various constructions of Hinduism, hermeticism, and Tantrisms (Boon 1972, 1982a, and forthcoming). One might brush any ism, or culture, with an aphoristic judg-

manently in quotation marks and prefixed with "so-called" by Lévi-Strauss (1963b:16). He likened the phantom-category of totemism to Charcot's contemporary scientific model of diagnostic "hysteria": both convert fragmentary bits of evidence into whole-types and falsely mark off unified symptoms from the investigator's universe. Nor was Lévi-Strauss content simply to correct errors of reifying totemism; rather he investigated how the "vogue of hysteria and that of totemism" were mediated by and contingent upon cultural and historical conditions.

Burke's and Lévi-Strauss's counter-positivist sense of isms holds for *cultures* as well. Any so-called culture is also "negatively infused, taking form antithetically to other such units, yet paradoxically resembling what it opposes" (Boon 1982a:9, 1973). Thus, neither cultures nor isms necessarily cohere doctrinally. Cultures are not things possessed—like so much property or even intellection—by their "members," as consensualist theory suggests, or by their perpetrators, as conspiracy theory implies. Nor are their "members" beings possessed by the creeds of their cultures or isms, as theories of idealist "infusion" assert.

The dialectical or apophantic quality of isms may be masked when they flag a founder—Marxism (!), Freudianism, Wagnerism—to whose touchstone tenets disciples presumably could be true. (We can thank the label "Structuralism," and Lévi-Strauss himself, for helping avoid the hero-worshipping pitfalls of "Lévi-Straussism.") In the cross-cultural and historical discourse of disciplines, Romanticism seems conspicuous for its self-consciousness of "negative infusion," ongoing antithetical play, and quality of resistance. "Romantic" moves have resisted political absolutism, epistemological logicalism, Enlightenment universalism, encyclopedic knowledge, legal and linguistic standardization, rhetorical authoritarianism, and philosophical *esprit simpliste* (Boon 1982a: ch. 2). Of course, whatever Romanticism resists, including the Enlightenment, is as dialectic and contrastively-constituted as Romanticism itself. Moreover, the other side of resistance is collusion, absorption, and, frequently, capitulation.

Hugh Kenner has phrased Romanticism's paradoxical legacy as follows:

> The Enlightenment lingers in our intellectual histories as a puzzling phenomenon, puzzling because it is so hard to say briefly what it was. It lacks chronology, it lacks locality, it lacks identity. It is personified by no convenient heroes, being by definition antiheroic. Diderot and d'Alembert are rather examples than exemplars. It perhaps hardly knew that it was happening, or not much more than the Middle Ages knew that they were happening, and we may perhaps speculate that the Romantic Movement was the first such event that did know that

---

ment attributed to Oscar Wilde concerning his preferred ism: "For Wilde aestheticism was not a creed but a problem" (Ellmann 1988:310; see Boon 1972:28).

it was happening, and that this was where the romanticism lay. The Enlightenment seems in retrospect a sort of mystical experience through which the mind
of Europe passed, and by which the memory of Europe remains haunted. (1962:1)

Kenner's ultra-modernist sensibilities lead him to a salutary, puckish reversal
of conventions: Enlightenment reason is placed under the sign of the haunt-
ingly mystical or cultic. Attuned to Walter Ong's literary history of printing
praxis, Kenner retrospectively stresses the Enlightenment's distinctive genre
and publishing industry:

> We carry with us still one piece of baggage from those far-off days, and that
> is the book which nobody wrote and nobody is expected to read, and which
> is marketed as The Encyclopedia: Britannica, Americana, Antarctica or other.
>   The Encyclopedia, like its cousin the Dictionary, takes all that we know apart
> into little pieces, and then arranges those pieces so that they can be found one
> at a time. It is produced by a feat of organizing, not a feat of understanding.
> No Bacon, no Aquinas, is tracing the hierarchies of a human knowledge which
> he has assumed the responsibility of grasping. If the Encyclopedia means any-
> thing as a whole, no one connected with the enterprise can be assumed to know
> what that meaning is. (1962:2)

Kenner is alluding to Romanticism's rejection of universal knowledge from
the later vantage of Flaubert's modernist ironizing (in *Bouvard et Pecuchet*) of
any Romantic return to a dispersed authority of understanding coupled with
encyclopedic nullity. The present essay adopts Kenner's tactic of considering
the Enlightenment/Romantic distinction from a subsequent such distinction.[5]

Aimed against encyclopedias and dictionaries (while yet preserving and
expanding them into the world of diverse languages), Romanticism dispar-
ages mere organizing and heralds whole understanding. Analytics thereby declines and hermeneutics looms, or relooms; Romantic doubts becloud the
certainties of any alphabetic or visual-grid ordering. Aimed against a State's
status quo, Romanticism becomes Revolution. Aimed against unitary narrative, Romanticism becomes ironic fragments—not alphabetic ones in the fashion of encyclopedias but self-authorized ones following Friedrich Schlegel's
Lucinde. Aimed against regimented controls and bureaucratic writing, Romanticism becomes vernacular voice, following Herder. Aimed against anonymous omnipotence, Romanticism becomes Rousseau-esque confessionals that
invite or beseech readers' empathies (see Darnton 1984:215ff). Aimed against
conventions of propriety and court-approved or Academy-enforced *bienséance*,
Romanticism becomes colloquial usage, local color, peasant carnival, *enjambre-*
ment, relative (and theatricized) licentiousness, and more.

5. Again, this policy of scholars selected to guide this essay suggests an affinity with Lévi-
Strauss, who returns (secondarily?) on Wagner's ever-returning. Thus, my list of Heine, Kenner,
Nabokov, Lévi-Strauss, Wagner, etc., is not random.

Aimed last and perhaps most enduringly against what Thomas Carlyle
decried as anonymous "steam-engine Utilitarianism" or the "*eyeless* Heroism"
of Benthamism, Romanticism becomes Hero-Worship or the championing of
History's seers and Prophets (Carlyle 1841:400). Indeed, Carlyle promoted the
outsized proportions of not just Cromwell, Napoleon, modern Revolutionism,
Writers of Books (Johnson, Rousseau, . . .), Knox, Luther, Dante, Shakespeare,
Odin, Paganism, and Scandinavian Mythology, but also Mahomet. Invoking
Mahomet, or his "Sacred Book, which they name Koran, or Reading," Carlyle
advanced a direct attack on Benthamism (but not on Bentham himself, as
he stipulated):

> What is the chief end of man here below? Mahomet has answered this ques-
> tion, in a way that might put some of us to shame! He does not, like a Bentham,
> a Paley, take Right and Wrong, and calculate the profit and loss. . . . Benthamee
> Utility, virtue by Profit and Loss; reducing this God's-world to a dead brute
> Steam-engine, the infinite celestial Soul of Man to a kind of Hay-balance for
> weighing hay and thistles on, pleasures and pains on:—If you ask me which
> gives, Mahomet or they, the beggallier and falser view of Man and his Destinies
> in the Universe, I will answer, It is not Mahomet! (310)

Needless to say, Carlyle's intricate judgments imply no siding with Islam.
Moreover, dissatisfaction with Utilitarian dreams of level moral scales could
fuel other parochialisms in a history too familiar to bear much repeating: localized folk, evoked to withstand Napoleonic codes imposed from outside,
transform later into exclusivistic abstract Folk, invoked to purge long-term
resident "outsiders" from sacral turf. Romantic resistance, like any other, contains seeds of the reactionary.

Finally, to signal Kenner's contrast with the Enlightenment or Carlyle's
contrast with Utilitarianism is not to deny that Romanticism shared aspects
of earlier and later times. For example, Romanticism sustained and expanded
Renaissance and Reformation questioning of Vulgate Latin's and Rome's
primacy. To humanists' Greek, used at times to parry or up-end Church learning and authority, Romantics added freshly historicized senses of India and
Egypt. By the high Victorian era Greek art and life headed the tally of time's
exemplars. This cross-cultural, world-historical expansion in Romanticism coincided with Europe's accelerated appropriation of history's translated pasts
and of the globe's ennobled and enslaved others. A counterpoint of transforming motives for denigrating racial others accompanied this trend. On the
idealizing side, additional languages became candidate fonts of hermetic wisdom, enshrined transgressions against logical order or conventional propriety. After a grudging primitivism appeared during the eighteenth century, a
greater abandon in embracing exotic traditions proliferated.[6] One possible

---

6. This condensed discussion alludes to major issues in the history of Enlightenment versus

metaphor for characterizing the relation between these Romantic developments and the subsequent anthropological appreciation of "other" tribes and civilizations that endures to our own day is "continuity." But that metaphor underestimates both how Romanticism remained different and was invented contrastively, repeatedly, and increasingly—the subject of the present fragmentary sketch.

Romanticism Made Contrastive

Wrinkles in Romanticism's (or any ism's) heritage, ironed out in chronologies of influence, may perhaps be recaptured by readingback through history's motives (of reading). Toward that end I offer an episode—drastically truncated—from Cosima Wagner's convoluted diaries, not as a digression but as profoundest evidence of ambivalences in the Wagners' daily readings of Heine and so many others:

Thursday, July 1, 1869. Another sleepless, thought-laden night! . . . At breakfast R[ichard] spoke of the inestimable boon which would come from a real fusion of the French and the Germans—though certainly the French should not go to Heine, Meyerbeer, and Kaulbach to find out about the German character. . . . The joyful moment of the day was the arrival of Beethoven's portrait, which R. has had copied.

Tuesday, December 7 . . . Tuesday, December 14, 1869. Letter from Prof. Nietzsche, he is coming to us at Christmas. In the evening R. reads me *Tristram Shandy*, in which diatribes against solemnity give me much enjoyment, reminding me of those bigots the Schumannians. Spoke with R. about Mendelssohn . . . ; such an enormous talent as Mendelssohn's is frightening, it has no place in the development of our music. . . . Very nice letter to R. from Prof. N[ietzsche] . . . Children, my children, hold firm to one another—brotherly love, sisterly love, nothing else can make up for it.—Richard completes the pencil sketch of the Prelude to *Götterdämmerung*. . . . After tea continued with *Tristram Shandy*. . . . In the evening R. reads to me out of a volume of Heine (posthumous things). As always things of incomparable genius, but also very repulsive pieces. "He is the bad conscience of our whole era," R. says, "the most unedifying and demoralizing matters one can possibly imagine, and yet one feels closer to him than to the whole clique he is so naively exposing."

Sunday, February 12, 1871. The Frenchman Michelet has written a splendid book, *La France devant l'Europe* . . . —R's astonishment that *Kladderadatsch* is

---

Romantic representations of cultural and historical differences. For some contrary appraisals of how standardized and uniform eighteenth-century schemes of reason became and how diverse nineteenth-century "histories" could be, see for example Feldman & Richardson (1972), Foucault (1970), Aarsleff (1982), Manuel (1979), Steiner (1975), Eksteins (1985), Gossman (1984). Much is at stake in such sweeping works, including distinctions between myth and logic and tenets of proper historiography (see Boon 1982a, and forthcoming).

edited by Jews, since the Jews have no wit of their own; though they are excellent subjects for witty observations, they themselves, he says, have no powers
of observation. Heine an exception – the *daimon familiaris* of the evil conditions
in the Germany of his time. – In the evening Richter brings the conversation
around to Gounod, and that sets us off on a dreadful musical tour, *Faust, Le
Prophète, Les Huguenots*, Bellini, Donizetti, Rossini, Verdi, one after another, I
feel physically sick. I pick up and seek refuge in a volume of Goethe (*Parali-
pomena zu "Faust"*). But nothing helps, I suffer and suffer. . . . At last, God knows
how, we come to Bach's organ fugues . . . Bach always extraordinarily beautiful . . . in all this to-ing and fro-ing, as steadfast as the Protestant faith itself
[N.B., Cosima was Catholic]. . . . Mozart gives us a picture of this juxtaposition
of the two things in *Die Zauberflöte* . . . –Thus R. continues for a long time
to speak, and the Italian and Jewish ghosts are dispersed – but the feelings of
nausea remained! (C. Wagner 1980:I, 117, 170–72, 336)

Whoever wishes seriously to engage the nineteenth century or Romanticism
across its aftermaths must confront the seaflow and slippery tone of such
reading-records as Cosima Wagner's diaries: generally pious, even sanctimo-
nious; sometimes sarcastic, occasionally even self-sarcastic, and always un-
imaginably twisting even when not twisted. An opus in their own right,[7] they
twist us here back to a precocious essay that Heine published in 1836, four
years after Goethe's death.

Occasioned by Madame de Staël's French work *De l'Allemagne* (1814) (itself perhaps prompted by the coaching of August Wilhelm Schlegel, tutor
to De Staël's children), and written during Heine's Parisian exile, "*Zur Geschichte der neuren schöne Literatur in Deutschland*" (only later called "The Romantic School") was among the earliest consolidated yet intimate analyses
of German Romanticism. But it depicted less a school or a doctrinal movement than a set of differences from tendencies of the French Romanticists.
Like many after it, Heine's construction was contrastive and doubly from the
outside (Holub 1985).

Like Herder, Heine was partly sympathetic to the Enlightenment; he was
also "a quasi member of the Young Germany movement, as well as a some-
time Romantic" (Firchow 1971:5). Accordingly, he sometimes elaborated Germany's Romantic School:

---

7. It is tempting to call each interlude drawn from Cosima's diaries "Fidelity and Playfulness,"
taking a title from Schlegel's fragmentary *Lucinde*. The rhythm of the diaries' unending 2,000
pages may call to mind Nabokov's (parodic) schoolboy memories of reading Hegel and discovering the "essential spirality" of all things in their relation to time: "The spiral is a spiritualized
circle. In the spiral form the circle, uncoiled, unwound, has ceased to be vicious; it has been
set free. . . . Twirl follows twirl . . ." (1960:275). Nabokov also mentions triadic dialectics (compare Lévi-Strauss [1964–1971] on interminably spiraling mythological analysis; and Lévi-Strauss
[1963b] on dialectics).

It was nothing other than the revival of the poetry of the Middle Ages as manifested in the songs, sculpture, and architecture, in the art and life of that time. This poetry, however, had had its origin in Christianity; it was a passion flower rising from the blood of Christ. I do not know whether the melancholy flower that we call passion flower in Germany also bears this name in France and whether that mystical origin is likewise attributed to it by folk legend. (Heine 1836:3)

Heine here tokens the different fates of Catholicism in the respective histories of France and Germany, a contrast prolonged in their two styles of Romanticism. The German passion flower (later set resonating with the Indic lotus in Novalis' *blaue Blume*) suggests the uncanny ecstasy-suffering that Heine found representative of this Romantic school:

It is a strange flower of unpleasing color, in whose chalice can be seen depicted the instruments of torture used at the Crucifixion of Christ, namely, hammer, tongs, nails, etc., a flower that is by no means ugly, only eery, indeed the sight of which even arouses in us an uncanny pleasure like the convulsively sweet sensations which result even from suffering itself. (Heine 1836:3)

Heine next celebrated medieval literary works: *Barlaam* and *Josaphat* (whose Buddhist *Jataka* sources became evident only later), the *Nibelungenlied*, *Lohengrin*, Wolfram's *Parzifal*, and Gottfried's *Tristan und Isolde*. Like Wagner after him, Heine lumped these cycles with the *Eddas*, the *Ramayana*, and the *Mahabharata* (portions of which were then newly translated into English and German)—a form of expression that "strove to represent the infinite and consequently produced monstrous abortions of imagination, for example, in Scandinavia and India, . . . works that we also consider romantic and are accustomed to call romantic" (Heine 1836:9).

From medieval grail cycles Heine slips quickly past the rich, transitional case of Goethe to a comparison between August Schlegel and Osiris. This odd, allusive digression is later converted to Heine's most pregnant, comparative anecdote. Producing such anecdotes is, I propose, what Heine's essay is for, or about:

This is what I too had imagined a German poet to be [a man who wore a shabby, tattered coat, and who fabricated baptismal and wedding poems for a taler apiece . . .]. How pleasantly surprised I was, therefore, in 1819, when, as a very young man, I attended the University of Bonn and there had the honor of seeing the poet A. W. Schlegel, the poetic genius, face to face. With the exception of Napoleon he was the first great man I had seen, and I shall never forget this sublime sight. . . . Mr. A. W. Schlegel . . . wore kid gloves and still dressed completely in the latest Paris fashion . . . when he spoke about the Lord High Chancellor of England, he added "my friend," . . . his body was so thin, so emaciated, so transparent, that he appeared to be all spirit and looked almost like a symbol of spirituality. (Heine 1836:57)

Again, I propose that such essayed anecdotes (worthy of pastiche in any essay on Romanticism) achieve in and of themselves Heine's critical reflections on Romantics. Heine's ostensible anecdote about first encountering in person the lofty ideal of a Romantic poet who had achieved worldly renown for his otherworldliness turns suddenly into allegory. Heine's anecdote-become-allegory then apologizes for its obscurity by kicking the allegory up a meta-phorical and mythic notch:

> Despite this [Schlegel] got married at that time, and he, the chief of the Romanticists, married the daughter of Parish Councillor Paulus in Heidelberg, the chief of the German Rationalists. It was a symbolic marriage. Romanticism was wedded, so to speak, to Rationalism, but the marriage bore no fruit. On the contrary . . . the very morning after the wedding night Rationalism ran back home and would have nothing more to do with Romanticism. . . . I know I am speaking obscurely and will try to express myself as clearly as possible:
>
> Typhon, wicked Typhon, hated Osiris (who, as you know, is an Egyptian god), and when he got him in his power, he tore him to pieces. Isis, poor Isis, Osiris' wife, laboriously collected the pieces, patched them together, and succeeded in repairing her mutilated husband completely. Completely? Alas, no, one important piece was missing, which the poor goddess could not find, poor Isis! She had to content herself with a replacement made of wood, but wood is only wood, poor Isis! Thus there arose in Egypt a scandalous myth and in Heidelberg a mystical scandal.
>
> After this Mr. A. W. Schlegel disappeared from sight entirely. He was forgotten. (Heine 1836:57–58)

This oscillation between anecdote and allegory, too, invites pastiche today and was perhaps offered as such by Heine, who remained half outside the Romantic School even when discovering its self-critical potential.

Before digressing, Heine had offered a brief disquisition on Friedrich Schlegel's fragmentary *Lucinde*, enthusiastically reviewed by Schleiermacher (Heine 1836:47). Heine's half-outsider's eye for paradox was unfailing: "A similar novel [to *Lucinde*] called *Florentin* is mistakenly attributed to the late Schlegel. They say this book is by his wife, a daughter of the famous Moses Mendelssohn, whom he took away from her first husband and who went over with him to the Roman Catholic Church" (48). Heine assumes that Friedrich Schlegel's Catholicism, before his disenchantment, was serious, although such matters are difficult to ascertain because "religion and hypocrisy are twin sisters" (48). Again, Heine himself prefers Herder's universalism: "For Herder did not sit in judgment on the various nations like a literary grand inquisitor, condemning or absolving them, according to the degree of their faith. No, Herder viewed all mankind as a mighty harp in the hand of the great master, each nation seemed to him one string of this giant harp tuned to its special note, and he understood the universal harmony of the harp's various tones" (49). Yet Heine respects Schlegel's *Wisdom and Language of India*, his passion for Indian epic meter (*slokas*), and his introduction of Sanskrit studies into Germany, becoming there the equivalent of England's William Jones. Heine only questioned Schlegel's ulterior motive: "It was written in the interests of Catholicism . . . had rediscovered in the Indian poems not merely the mysteries of Catholicism, but the whole Catholic hierarchy as well and its struggles with secular authority. In the *Mahabharata* and in the *Ramayana* they saw, as it were, an elephantine Middle Ages" (49).

Heine's judgments shifted, and they deflected doctrinal constructions, even as he refurbished such distinctions as Enlightenment and Romantic. Heine doubted any "origins" explanation, any "genetic" teleology, and any "influence" story of ideas' history. At one point he ironically rescued Spinoza from untoward obscurity:

> Nothing is more absurd than ownership claimed for ideas. Hegel did, to be sure, use many of Schelling's ideas for his philosophy, but Mr. Schelling would never have known what to do with these ideas anyway. He always just philosophized, but was never able to produce a philosophy. And besides, one could certainly maintain that Mr. Schelling borrowed more from Spinoza than Hegel borrowed from Schelling. If Spinoza is one day liberated from his rigid, antiquated Cartesian, mathematical form and made accessible to a large public, we shall perhaps see that he, more than any other, might complain about the theft of ideas. All our present-day-philosophers, possibly without knowing it, look through glasses that [optician] Baruch Spinoza ground. (Heine 1836:70)

Heine's trope of the hidden source undermines any manifest legacy of philosophical ideas. He skillfully introduces differences that erode a pat persuasion attributed to the school his essay portrays. For example, Heine likens the distinction between Novalis and Hoffmann to one between real (Indian) mystics and Arabian magicians (see Boon 1982a: ch. 7). His contrast could hardly be more spirited:

> Novalis saw everywhere only marvels, lovely marvels. He listened to the plants conversing with each other, he knew the secret of every young rose, in the end he identified himself with all of nature, and when autumn came and the leaves fell, he died. Hoffmann, on the other hand, saw everywhere only ghosts; they nodded at him from every Chinese teapot and every Berlin wig. . . . This he felt; he felt that he himself had become a ghost; . . . his works are nothing but a terrible cry of anguish in twenty volumes.
>
> Hoffmann does not belong to the Romantic School. He had no contact with the Schlegels, still less with their views. I mentioned him here only as a contrast to Novalis, who is quite strictly a poet of that School. Novalis is less well-known in France than Hoffmann. (Heine 1836:77)

Unrelentingly, unremittingly—Heine turns these remarks and contrasts toward his own reading of Novalis/Hoffmann:

> The great similarity between the two poets probably lies in the fact that their poetry was in reality a disease. . . . The rosy light in the works of Novalis is not the color of health but of tuberculosis, and the fiery glow in Hoffmann's *Fantastic Tales* is not the flame of genius but of fever.
>
> But do we have a right to such remarks, we who are not all too blessed with health ourselves? Especially now, when literature looks like a huge hospital? (77)

To these self-turned queries he adds examples presented as if purely incidental, matters of happenstance rather than systematically ordered, cumulative knowledge. Consider, per chance, Heine's discussion of Novalis, whose *Heinrich van Ofterdingen* emblemizes a medieval-Indic lily-lotus that blends Gnostic passion and floral suffering in the *blaue Blume*—a compounded alliteration of *hoch Deutsch* becoming a Sanskritlike *sloka*. Heine elides Novalis' symbol and muse, bringing (coyly, I suspect) the latter down to earth and actuality:

> Novalis' muse was a pale slender girl with serious blue eyes, golden jacinth hair, smiling lips, and a little red birth-mark on the left side of her chin. For I imagine as muse of Novalis' poetry the very same girl who first made me acquainted with him when I saw in her lovely hands the red morocco volume with gilt edges, which contained *Ofterdingen*. She always wore a blue dress, and her name was Sophia. (80)[8]

Heine's essay, then, anecdotally and allegorically traced a double movement toward a medieval past and Indic texts that fueled early Romantic enthusiasms. Wagner would repeat in his music-drama and political-aesthetic treatises such a double movement. And later Lévi-Strauss would return upon this variety of return with much of New World mythology and many of the world's marriage systems in tow. Heine's sense of contrast, then, can be made pivotal, something of an "original" in this historical perspective. That he proceeded by distinguishing German Romanticism from Madame de Staël's French view of it and from French Romanticists, without himself aspiring to either brand, suggests a "tradition" of construing Romanticism that the present essay seeks to enter.

Romanticism Consolidated, Deconstructed, Cancelled, and Returned

M. H. Abrams' now-canonical studies of the history of Romanticism, *The Mirror and the Lamp* (1953) and *Natural Supernaturalism* (1971), stress the impact of German thought and genres on Wordsworth and Coleridge. Abrams

8. Details of Novalis' image and inspiration, and its actual reference, are too intricate to pursue; for some suggestions and thoughts on other Romantic responses to Indic sources, see Will-

explores predispositions, symptoms, and proclivities to detect a doctrine tucked under texts that presumably screen it, a history of ideas in A. O. Lovejoy's sense. Abrams discovers and explicates diverse views worth enumerating, particularly insofar as they provide parallels with anthropology. I telegraph and extend Abrams' commentary on key themes in Romantic theory:

> 1) . . . Neoplatonic figure of the soul as a fountain . . . frequent in romantic poetry . . . usually reformed to imply a bilateral transaction, a give-and-take, between mind and external object. (Abrams 1953:61)

Here Abrams incisively begs the very distinction generating his book's history: theme of mirror (Augustan, Enlightenment reflection) becoming theme of lamp (Romantic, interior illumination). Ambiguities about objective/subjective and outsider/insider associated with Romanticism will later resonate with anthropological issues of the ethnographer's calling and contradictory stance vis-à-vis inside/outside.

> 2) . . . A few writers of [eighteenth] century . . . deliberately . . . revise the bases of the neo-classic theory of poetry. Sir William Jones . . . in 1772 published . . . translations and "imitations" of Arabic, Indian, and Persian poems . . . [and] an important "Essay on the Arts Called Imitative" . . . a conjunction of . . . : the ideas drawn from Longinus, the old doctrine of poetic inspiration . . . major emphasis on the lyric form and on the supposedly primitive and spontaneous poetry of Oriental nations . . . reformulation of the nature and criteria of poetry and of the poetic genres. (Abrams 1953:87)

The conjunction represented by Jones's theory of historical connections among Indic and European languages sets the course for comparative studies, including anthropology, through the nineteenth century and beyond.[9]

> 3) The *Frühromantiker* pressed these ideas of Herder to an extreme . . . music as . . . the very essence and form of the spirit made patent—a play of pure feeling in time, unaltered by its physical medium. . . . Tieck, Wackenroder, and E. T. A. Hoffmann (following the lead of Herder) praised symphonic music as the art of arts . . . indefinite, innocent of reference to the external world . . . the attempt to make literature aspire to the condition of music . . . furthered that general synesthetic abandon which Irving Babbitt was to interpret as a symp-

---

son (1964) and Boon (1982a). On a deconstructive turn taken by scholars of Romanticism, see Rajan (1980) and its sources. That Heine converts Novalis' muse to the concrete Sophia who provided the book that let Heine depict her is one of Heine's characteristic anecdotal allegories, used to conclude Book Two of his essay. I have deleted an echo of this device.

9. Some sense of Jones's importance is conveyed by Feldman & Richardson (1972), Willson (1964), Mojumdar (1976), and Freemantle (1974). Other sources are discussed in Boon (1982a, and forthcoming), including the impact of Jones's frameworks on Melville's parodic-Romantic prose, styled partly after Carlyle.

tom of the dissolution of all the boundaries and distinctions on which a rational civilization depends. (Abrams 1953:93–94)

This Romantic concern with music-like interminglings of sensory orders anticipates principles of symbolist aesthetics, modernist aestheticism, and aspects of symbolic classification alike. Lévi-Strauss is one anthropological figure who consolidated these issues in his readings of linguistics, poetics, and
evidence of *pensée sauvage* and mythic-logics (Boon 1972, 1984).

> 4) Wordsworth remained within a well-defined tradition . . . a basic standard
> for establishing validity, . . . – the common nature of men, always and every-
> where . . . to which A. O. Lovejoy has given the name "Uniformitarianism,"
> . . . a leading principle in normative provinces of thought – moral, theological,
> and political, as well as aesthetic – in the seventeenth century and through most
> of the eighteenth century. (Abrams 1953:104)

Recent studies dispute Abrams' claim that Wordsworth retained the *ésprit
simpliste* of Uniformitarianism. Regardless, subsequent Romantics resisted low-
grade conformity, anticipating cultural anthropology's questioning of a lowest
common denominator, universal "reason." In 1965 Clifford Geertz posed what
he would later call interpretive anthropology against "Uniformitarianism," the
local reason of the Enlightenment, mistakenly universalized by certain *philosophes* (Boon 1982a: ch. 2).

In *Natural Supernaturalism* Abrams added important refinements to his
account of Romantic resistance to what Lovejoy called "Uniformitarianism":

> A. O. Lovejoy has said that the shift from "uniformitarianism" to "diversitarian-
> ism" – the preference for maximum diversity, for the fullness of individuality,
> and for particularity, as against the earlier preference for the uniform, the sim-
> ple, and the general – emerged in "the generation of German writers who came
> to maturity between the [seventeen] seventies and the nineties and that this
> diversitarianism constitutes "the most significant and distinctive feature of the
> Romantic revolution." This is true, but it is not the whole truth; . . . what was
> most distinctive in Romantic thought was the normative emphasis not on pleni-
> tude as such, but on an organized unity in which all individuation and diver-
> sity survive, in Coleridge's terms, as distinctions without division. . . . The norm
> of the highest good was thus transferred from simple unity, not to sheer diver-
> sity [?] as such but to the most inclusive integration. (Abrams 1971:186)

Recent critical readings of Romantic texts have questioned whether the in-
tegral actually and inevitably won out over the fragmentary and whether desires and norms were so patently exalted. Similar questions have been raised
concerning anthropology's various styles of resisting so-called Uniformitarianism and championing a diversitarian cause.[10]

___

10. I am thinking of several issues current in anthropology's critical reflections: preferences

Finally, even Abrams' earlier *The Mirror and the Lamp* glimpsed the potential for a Romantic corpus to contain its own undoing. Abrams anticipated a possibility later insisted on by de Man: the critique of Romanticism is not afterwards and outside it, but internally, erodingly co-present. But Abrams learned this lesson from the parodies of Thomas Love Peacock:

> The doctrine of the overflow of powerful feeling has its derisory counterpart too. The highest inspirations of poetry are resolvable into three ingredients; the rant of unregulated passion, the whine of exaggerated feeling, and the cant of factitious sentiment . . . [Peacock]. It is idle to inquire about the exact boundaries between the serious and the playful in this witty essay. Peacock cannot be pinned down. He had the eye of the born parodist, before which everything pretentious writhes into caricature. If he was a poet who mocked at poets from a Utilitarian frame of satirical reference, he was a Utilitarian who turned into ridicule the belief in utility and the march of intellect, as well as a critic who derided the contemners of poetry, after having himself derided the poetry they contemned. (Abrams 1953:126)

Despite the idealist predilections in Abrams' style of history (a style, among others, with merits), here he almost invites a deconstructive assessment of Romanticism to happen. And it did.

Cynthia Chase's recent "rhetorical readings in the Romantic tradition" join *au courant* scholars engaged in challenging any doctrine of origins, whether sacred or secular. Phrased quasi-positively, the task has become "a deconstruction of the genetic model that has been at the heart of the concept of history" (Chase 1986:1). Written in the wake of Derrida, Lacoue-Labarthe, and similar figures, Chase's study at one point depicts Romanticism as run-of-the-mill logocentrism, standard foe of poststructuralists:

> For Romanticism has been most tellingly identified, beyond considerations of style and theme, precisely with the full emergence and elaboration of the genetic model, whereby we imagine the intelligibility of the cosmos in terms of an ultimate adequation between origins and ends. This would seem to be the Romantic tradition to which we inevitably still belong, a teleological orientation that is the lasting heritage of Romanticism, transmitting ultimately an orientation of Western thought or philosophy "from its beginnings." (1986:1)

Yet this uncharacteristic moment quickly passes when Chase pursues the late Paul de Man's own readings of Rousseau, Hegel, Nietzsche, and Wordsworth. By de Man's lights these authors' writtenness itself contained, or resembled, a critique of what their critics (his predecessors) claimed these authors be-

for fragmentariness versus totalization, charges that "culture" is consensualist and/or aestheticized, questions of the political effectiveness of so-called relativism, and stylistic projects in/as description. A recent clearing-house for these and related concerns is Clifford & Marcus (1986) and Clifford (1987).

lieved. Under de Man's scrutiny of Romantic rhetoric, Romanticism "would then be the movement that challenges the genetic principle which necessarily underlies all historical narrative" (de Man 1979:82). Romanticism, then, turns out to have slipped out from underneath the very fallacies its critics assume it committed. Many Romantic figures once thought credulous are now shown difficult to pin down. Convictions of distinctions between belief and doubt, originality and return, causality and palimpsest, history and rationalization, have been shaken, not just for "now" but for "then." yet this de Manian school of reassessing Romantic rhetoric seeks urgently itself not to be accused of revisionism.

For our purposes it is immaterial, or inconsequential, whether Romanticism is or was auto-deconstructive, as de Man, Chase, and many more would have it, or dialectically undone by opponent isms. What does matter is this: the ism of Romantic movements can be multiplied to include both Romanticism as naive, credulous, and logocentric *and* Romanticism as self-negating and always already resistant. Of consequence for the present essay is this proliferation of Romanticisms.[11]

Another scholar mindful of that proliferation was Vladimir Nabokov, the arch, perhaps history's last, utter modernist. In a study aiming to debunk all isms, he must foil his own ambition, if only because the label "Romanticism" pertains to, and was embraced by, the text which Nabokov was introducing (his translation) and which he was adoring: *Eugene Onegin.* Nabokov's "number" on academic categorizations by ism ends, perhaps parodically, by capitulating to a—yea, *the*—primary conceit of romanticism:

> . . . so, in literary history the vague terms "classicism," "sentimentalism," "romanticism," "realism," and the like straggle on and on, from textbook to textbook. There are teachers and students with square minds who are by nature meant to undergo the fascination of categories. For them, "school" and "movements" are everything; by painting a group symbol on the brow of mediocrity, they condone their own incomprehension of true genius. (Nabokov 1968:281)

---

11. An earlier version of this essay introduced Abrams' works as a matter of "local knowledge" at Cornell (his home-base), to sustain a Romantic-ironic questioning of any generalized approach, even to Romanticism. In that version Abrams was discussed after the positions of Chase and de Man, from which vantage Abrams' reading of Peacock could appear to anticipate deconstruction. The chronology from Abrams to deconstruction is, from the perspective of ism-formation and reading-back, a "secondary chronology," not unlike a "secondary diatonics" (see below, "The Reticulated Corpus").

Nabokov may be seen both as a giant among critics of Romanticisms and as a local, anecdotal coincidence with Abrams. (This kind of coincidence is often called Nabokovian; although Nabokov coincided with Abrams in time and at Cornell, they are separated in this essay.) Nabokov's constructive scepticism about isms (plus Kenneth Burke's) and Clifford Geertz's counteruniversalist accentuation of "local knowledge" underlie this section.

Concluding romantically his note defaming the likes of "romanticism," Nabokov adds a characteristically luminous list of different types (coined to play
with and toward Pushkin), pegged and pinned like so many butterflies. Nabokov, the *littérateur*-lepidopterist, itemizes eleven (count them, eleven) brands
or species of "romanticism," committing, at least momentarily, a spree of classification that he has just avowed "true appreciation of genius" should pre-
clude. It all serves as prelude to Pushkin's 1825 testimony to the "origin of
romanticism"—saluted at the end of the scheme whose surface ridicules the
concept.

The modernist finds beauty even in classifications he disavows and aesthetic
pleasure in the scepticism that overcomes itself into admiration of a play of
features, even of "movements" and "schools." Nabokov's divisions of eleven
little "romantics" include Johnson's *Dictionary*; military fables and pastorals
of the Middle Ages; Pater's strangeness added to beauty (building on a tradition of enchantment through distance); Highland grotesques, eerie gloom,
and melancholy; romanesque landscapes, lakescapes, mountainscapes, and
emotionscapes; German sentimentalism, with its apparitions and moonshine;
the post-1810 wedding of Ossianic poetry and Renaissance vigor produced by
the brothers Schlegel; minglings of tragic/comic, lofty/lowly, sacred/profane;
local color, exoticism, nationalism; Chateaubriand, Hugo, Lamartine; relaxa-
tion of classic constraints; new literary genres (he names not the novel); modern, not ancient. . . .

Finally, Nabokov serves up Pushkin's own cross-cultural model of Romanticism's causes: "The invasion of the Moors, 'who inspired it with frenzy and
tenderness, a leaning toward the marvelous and rich Oriental eloquence,'
and the Crusades, which imbued it 'with piety and naiveté, a new code of
heroism, and the loose morals of camp life'" (Nabokov 1968:285). But this
apparently historical view really enabled Pushkin to oppose French "'pseudo-
classicism' as personified by Boileau" (285). Thus, even where Romanticism
appears causally-historically shaped, its representation, as we saw in Heine,
is still coined contrastively, framed against whatever it isn't. By this point in
the present essay, what Romanticism isn't is beginning to seem less and less.

Again, something like this proliferation of Romanticism's negatives had
earlier been recapitulated in the corpus of Wagner before the alternatives
became critical positions in writing designed to contest history, the genetic
principle, and related teleologies. Something like this proliferation would later
become a bridge, of sorts, between the twentieth century (in the form of Lévi-
Strauss's anthropological corpus) and the nineteenth (in the form of Wagner's
operatic corpus). Lévi-Strauss's Structuralism bridges back not to Romanticism but to a corpus that recapitulates a proliferation of Romanticisms, which
anticipated many moves in the times and isms to come.

Part II. "Like a Solved Riddle, Incest . . ."

Il fallait qu'un contrepoint entre le poème et la musique rendît cette formulation explicite. Sinon, comment comprendrait-on que Siegmund ar-
rachât l'epée de l'arbre et conquît l'amour de Sieglinde sur le thème de
la renonciation?

Lévi-Strauss, "Notes sur la tetralogie"[12]

Tuesday, the fifth of January, 1960, was one hundred years to the month after
Hans von Bülow's Paris performances of *The Flying Dutchman* Overture, selections from *Tannhäuser* and *Lohengrin*, and the *Tristan* Prelude. Bülow had hoped
to help Wagner win "a success with Tristan that would force the German
theaters to take up the *Ring*," or so Wagner told Otto Wesendonk (Newman
1941:III, 28). The strategy resulted instead in the 1861 Paris failure of *Tannhäuser*, a flop with its own complex, endless aftermath, including Baudelaire's
Richard Wagner et Tannhäuser à Paris.

The Sketch

On that Tuesday, one hundred years later, Claude Lévi-Strauss assumed
the College de France's new chair of social anthropology and delivered a *leçon
inaugurale* that stands to his subsequent quarter century of ethnological *opera*
very much as Wagner's renowned First Sketch of 1848 anticipated the even-
tual, backwards-written *Ring*. In 1960 Lévi-Strauss offered a framework of and
for comparative mythological analysis that recalled his earlier work in *The
Elementary Structures of Kinship* [first edition 1949; see 1969b] about systems
of proper marriage exchange and their imagined antitheses: the nonexchange
of incest, the nonexchange of sexual renunciation, the nonexchange of ran-
domly dispersed couplings. Lévi-Strauss's address hearkens back as well to *Tristes
tropiques* (1955), whose prose fashions a variational-retrospective method of
remembering across cultures and times, a method inspired by Wagner and
by Proust (who was also inspired by Wagner), among many, many others. And
Lévi-Strauss's address, again, anticipates his *oeuvre*'s future, dialectically.

Here is an extract cited neither from the original *leçon* nor from the first,
flawed English translation that spread its news, but from a subsequent French
revision published in 1973 as the first chapter of "Vues perspectives" in *L'anthropologie structurale II*:

> Among populations separated by history, geography, language and culture, the
> same correlation between riddle and incest [l'enigme et l'inceste] appears, then,
> to exist. To facilitate comparison, let us construct a model of *l'enigme* . . . and

---

12. "It was necessary that a counterpoint between poem and music render explicit this formulation. If not, how could one understand that Siegmund wrested the sword from the tree

define it as "a question that one assumes will not have any answer. Without broaching here all the possible transformations of this formulation, let us by way of experiment inverse its terms, yielding: an answer for which there has been no question. (Lévi-Strauss 1973:33; my trans.)

At this pivotal moment in his career, Lévi-Strauss allusively relates an "apparently nonsensical formula" to myths and fragments of myths where this "symmetric and inversed" structure comprises the dramatistic motive ("le ressort dramatique"). Lacking time for American Indian examples that were his primary concern, he evokes instead a suggestive parallel:

> the death of the Buddha, made inevitable because a disciple fails to pose the awaited question; and, nearer ourselves, the old myths reworked into the Grail cycle where action is suspended upon the hero's timidity in the presence of the magical vessel, of which he dares not ask "what's it for." (33)

In the same breath Lévi-Strauss conjoins Buddha and Grail as variants of non-question-posing renunciation: one kind of antithesis to proper and regular periodicity, exchange, and alternation.

At this juncture Lévi-Strauss turned not to *Parsifal* but to Chrétien's *Percival*. (Remember: this was Paris. For Lévi-Strauss, Wolfram's *Parzival* [with a z] and Wagner's *Parsifal* [with an s] would come later, elsewhere, in 1975 at Bayreuth.) Yet Wagnerites, perfect and otherwise, might understandably leap from Lévi-Strauss's juxtaposition of Grail and Buddha to Wagner's *Parsifal* and *Die Sieger* ("The Victors"), that almost-composed Buddha opera in Schopenhauerian pessimism once intended to precede, and later to succeed, *Parsifal*. Indeed, *Parsifal* was not always conceived of as the end of Wagner's corpus, much less as a nostalgic vault forward-back (*Aufhebung*) into the victory of Christianity or something like it (the reading fueled by Nietzsche's powerful, devious, and profoundly untrustworthy *Nietzsche Contra Wagner* and *The Case of Wagner*). As evidence, consider a page for November 23, 1873, from the 2,000 in Cosima's diaries covering 1869 to 1883:

> In the evening R[ichard] reads to us the little sketch of *die Sieger*. How splendid! I hope to God, who protects me, that he will complete this work—God will hear me, and I want, mean to force him to it through this prayer! . . . Read the original legend in Burnouf. R. says he will write *Parcival* when he is 70 and *Die Sieger* when he is 80, I say when he is 65 and 70. He says yes, if I do not hold him back through my timidity, but allow him to get the house [Wahnfried] finished quickly. We laugh; but I always restraining my tears. (C. Wagner 1977: I, 701)

---

and made a conquest of [sister] Sieglinde's love accompanied by the renunciation theme?" (Lévi-Strauss 1983:321).

To appreciate convolutions in Wagner's reception of additional Indological studies from the early Romantics on through Wilhelm von Humboldt's *Kawi-sprache*, I linger over several more sentences of November 23, 1873, where Cosima inscribed their longings about Buddhism versus various Hindu extremes, never straying far from home:

> Talk about the pedantic elaborations of the Indians, their divisions, circles, etc: it looks pedantic, but if one examines it more closely, one sees it is always profoundly meaningful – as, for example, that the Chandalas stem from the marriage of a Sudra with a Brahman woman, bad seed in a noble soil produces dreadful things. The Greeks also possessed this pedantry, it seems to me; it is like the arithmetic of music; in Christianity, in the mystics, it is not present to the same degree. It is as if this aid is required, like the apparatus of a diver, to plumb the depths. – R. has the feeling that the Kshatriyas, who were overcome by the Brahmans, were the ancient Germans – the warrior caste. (I, 701)

Whatever else these ideas were, they were not naive: the "pedantry" of marriage and descent regulations and "bad seed" status distinctions suggesting that an arithmetic of music (in social structural terms?) is required in certain lands – India, Greece – in order to plumb the depths, like a diver. Such ideas resonate.[13]

The Reticulated Corpus

Five years after his 1955 article on myth, where Oedipus tokens incest, Lévi-Strauss hinted at an intricate formula of incest/riddles governing his work from the start: another antithesis (along with renunciation) to regularized exchanges in on-going direct or indirect cycles. Lévi-Strauss's corpus represents a vast empirical meditation upon various communication "relays": cultures' answers to a base injunction against any solo-category's self-reproduction. This base injunction (call it "incest taboo") evokes a danger of consanguineous unions (a danger, by the way, that may be idealized where higher forms of human marriage are likened to divine unions). For Lévi-Strauss the resistance to consanguineous unions must be combined with a sense of positive "social benefit" (1969b:480). This "essence of reciprocity" takes the form of an inclination, however slight or strong, *towards* others (an empathy called *pitié* by Lévi-Strauss, following Rousseau's figure of "language's origins"). We might call the formulaic contradiction: alone/inclined-otherwards (towards alters, critters, gods); or incest/exogamy-myth. Such was the gist of Lévi-Strauss's program in 1960, both retrospectively and prospectively.

In 1955, *Tristes tropiques*'s concluding chapters had narratively saluted Rous-

---

13. For suggestions about marriage-descent regulations and ideals of an arithmetic of music in various scholars and societies, see Boon (1982a, and forthcoming). Such resonances through-

seau and Buddhist monks, among others, who in their solitudes retain *pitié*, contrasted by Lévi-Strauss to existentialists' arrogant self-isolation. Even this Rousseau-Buddhist conjunction echoes back to Wagner, whose music's impact is acknowledged in *Tristes tropiques*, but whose interests in conjoining Buddhism (beyond Schopenhauerian pessimism) and Rousseau were probably then unknown to Lévi-Strauss. Again, Cosima on October 1, 1882, reveals the range and engagedness of their reading; notice the sweep, the synapses:

> At lunch much chatter in all languages; we go out for a ride around 4 o'clock; because of my bad foot I remain in the gondola. . . . In the evening the children go for another walk in Saint Mark's Square; R. then talks to Stein and me about the book on Buddha . . . more significant than Koppen's. Buddhism itself he declares to be a flowering of the human spirit, against which everything that followed was decadence, but also against which Christianity arose by a process of compression. Buddhism shows evidence of an extraordinarily youthful power in the human spirit, he says, not unlike the time when language was first invented. It exerts no compulsion of any sort, in consequence it has no church; the monk could return to the world if he no longer cared for the monastic life; no divine service, just atonement and good works. But it was this happy lack of organization which made it so easy for such a highly organized power as Brahmanism to oust it. . . . At lunch the English travelers had been referred to as "shopkeepers"; in this connection R. reflects that in England the most useful segment of society is regarded with contempt. . . . And he frequently invokes Buddha and Rousseau; the first, who never said what he knew about the beginning and end of things, the second, who could not say what had been his inner vision.—Then he talks about an article he intends to write on Italian church music and German military music, finding it utterly wrong that our army organization should be presented as something positively good. (C. Wagner 1980:II, 920)

Recall that Lévi-Strauss's corpus of writing divides into two major phases—the opus on marriage structures (1969b) and his "own tetralogy" (*Mythologiques*) sustained in subsequent studies (*La voie des masques*, 1979; *La potière jalouse*, 1985) in a career that happily did not end as soon as his prose feared when intoning "the twilight of man" in *L'homme nu* (1971). Between these monumental thrusts fell overlapping transitions (called just that by Lévi-Strauss—see Boon 1972): the fragmentary *Tristes tropiques* (1955) and *La pensée sauvage* (1962a), plus that book's alternative "history of ideas" prelude, *Le totemisme aujourd'hui* (1962b). Along the way related tentatives, professional pronouncements, methodological essays were collected in *Anthropologie structurale I* and *II* (1963a, 1973) and *Le regard éloigné* (1983). The overlappings of this ethnological corpus suggest a musicological analogy (recalling that *pensée*

---

out the corpus of Lévi-Strauss are best appreciated in Backès-Clément (1970) and Bellour & Clément (1979).

sauvage is "analogical thought"–1966:263). *Mythologiques* is Lévi-Strauss's *Ring*–that much he has stipulated; and its compressed, prolonged aftermath perhaps his *Parsifal(/Victors)*. *The Elementary Structures of Kinship* (1969b) then represents Lévi-Strauss's earlier, more conventional opera–his *Lohengrin, Tannhäuser, Flying Dutchman* (let's recede no further). This positioning perfectly clarifies–and here is the force of the analogy–that major interlude of *Tristes tropiques* and *La pensée sauvage-totemisme aujourd' hui*, equivalent to *Tristan* and *Die Meistersinger*, respectively.

I offer this analogy seriously. Lévi-Strauss's "*Ring*" (*Mythologiques* 1964–71) was indirectly announced in the "Structural Study of Myth" (1955) and even anticipated in the concluding chapters of *The Elementary Structures of Kinship* (1969b), which shift toward linguistic messages. With *Mythologiques* being gradually composed, he twice pulled back–once to engage in an exercise of nearly pure chromaticism (*Tristes tropiques*) and then to construct an "as-if" analytics, a work that seemed to "restore" analytic logic after the articles on dialectics collected in *Structural Anthropology* (1963a). But *Pensée sauvage* actually placed analytics in the quotation marks implied by the analytic/dialectic opposition. *La pensée sauvage*–become *The Savage Mind* (1966)–was divested of its key cover illustration, its appendices from medieval heraldry, and the play between illustrations (aboriginal drawings and pseudo-graphs) and the prose that glossed them. Among all Lévi-Strauss's works this one was most domesticated, neutered, and sanitized in its translation and repackaging. Distracted by the famous dispute with Sartre, readers generally neglected to situate *La pensée sauvage* in the corpus of which it is an episode. When engaged with its self-transposings in mind, this book's "analytics" enter the play of (mythic) variations, tying it even more intimately to *Totemism* (1963b:16).[14]

La pensée sauvage stands, then, to analytic reason much as Wagner's *Die Meistersinger* stands to diatonic music: both represent an ironic return. Indeed the *New Grove Dictionary of Music* finds the diatonicism of *Die Meistersinger* somehow dreamlike, not quite real in the 1860s, calling it a "secondary Diatonicism" like Hegel's "secondary nature" (Dahlhaus 1980:134). A rare insight from Adorno's *Versuch über Wagner* stresses a paradox in his chromati-

---

14. Distortions introduced into reading Lévi-Strauss's corpus by the "domesticated" translation of *The Savage Mind* continue today. The original's exercise in analytic reason opens from a term *pensée sauvage* (defined as "analogical thought") for the tricolored violet. The bloom illustrated on the book's cover is the subject of diverse traditional allegories, including a story of its springing from a brother-sister incest (Backès-Clément 1970:20–22). In *La pensée sauvage* logic and analytics remained embedded in allegory. The book's contents are a delay-relay of codes, literally a text of transformations between representations of incest (one pictorial, one narrative), just as *Tristes tropiques* is a text of transformations between identified *je* and *chat*, its opening and closing words.

cism that "never quite loses a certain reserve towards modulation, apart from *Tristan*":

> Without the counterweight provided by diatonic passages like that of the ante-cedent, the variety of chords and the chromatic part-writing would lead to that esotericism which Wagner feared like the plague. To pour scorn precisely on that was not the least of the polemical intentions of the *Mastersingers*, where the over-sophisticated Meistergesang is contrasted with the unrestrained healthy instincts of the people: the idea of retracting his own innermost beliefs reaches right into the history of Wagner's own work, which stands in something of the same relation to its productive centre, *Tristan*, as the Rider over Lake Constance. (Adorno 1952:53)

Again, *Tristes tropiques*—that "productive center" of Lévi-Strauss's work (see Geertz 1973, 1987; Boon 1972) is its *Tristan*, but just as surely *La pensée sauvage*—a concerted exercise in "secondary analytics"—is its *Meistersinger* (Boon 1972, 1982a).

Lévi-Strauss à Bayreuth

Fifteen years after 1960, our turning point, Lévi-Strauss published a commentary in the "Programmhefte der Bayreuther Festspiele" for that season's *Parsifal*. The piece was later expanded into "De Chretien de Troyes à Richard Wagner" and included in *Le regard éloigné* (1983), the book Lévi-Strauss tells us he opted not to call *Structural Anthropology III*. The essay briefly reviews versions of the resurrection legends of Osiris, Attis, Adonis, and Demeter. Lévi-Strauss suggests that visits to the grail castle illustrate vestiges of "une initiation manquée à un rite de fertilité" (1983:301), and he accentuates the protagonist's not daring to ask whom the grail serves ("qui l'on en sert"). This question, the hideous maiden later reveals, would have ended the king's suffering and the kingdom's sterility (antithesis of fertile, periodic cycles).

Readers who failed to acquire a genuine copy of the original text in 1975 could shortly have sampled Lévi-Strauss's views on *Percival-Parzival-Parsifal* from the *Royal Anthropological Institute News* which contained a handy summary of Lévi-Strauss's 1973 lecture at the Institut français in London (*RAIN*, Jan.–Feb., 1976). Lévi-Strauss valued this synopsis (eventually attributed to the Institut's then-director André Zavriew) enough to add it to *Paroles données* (1984, summaries of his 1973-74 College de France lectures): "Le graal en Amerique" covered New World myths plus farflung parallels of what might aptly be deemed "Pearcszivfal" codes.

Again, the lecture stresses peripheral European examples more familiar to his audience than the Algonkian and Mandan evidence that is Lévi-Strauss's major empirical concern. I telegraph *RAIN*'s message, "squaring," so to speak, the artful synopsis composed by creative editor Jonathan Benthall:

... Percival myth of interrupted communication ... opposed to Oedipus myths [of] excessive communication characterized by resolution of a riddle, rankness, and the explosion of natural cycles. By contrast ... Percival ... questions without answer or questions that are not asked, the virginity of the hero, an earth without fertility, the "waste land" of the Grail ... a systematic opposition. . . . Wagner's transformation ... consisted in his seizing the dualism of the Percival story [after Wolfram's "confusion"] ... Instead of the opposition between here-below and beyond, Wagner substitutes an opposition between the Percival myth and the Oedipus myth ... the Grail [and] the magician Klingsor's castle ... non-communication ... king Amfortas stricken ... the earth ... stricken by steril-ity, and a question is not asked by the hero. By contrast, at Klingsor's castle in the second act ... an Oedipus world ... of [too] instantaneous communica-tion ... the climate of incest between the enigmatic Kundry and Parsifal ... re-call the rankness of Thebes. (Benthall 1976)

Let me add that although Kundry is rank, she is also chromatic: that is her meaning, like Isolde's and New World mythological opossums (*sarigues*) (see Lévi-Strauss 1964–71, *passim* under "opossum"). Scholars suspicious of synopses —although Lévi-Strauss apparently approves the original of this one—might check it back against Lévi-Strauss's 1960 *leçon*, his sketch, which had not yet bent from *Percival* through *Parzival* to *Parsifal*. There, again, he traced New World mythic oppositions of incestuous, raunchy heroes who know all the answers versus chaste innocents who cannot even pose the questions. The latter Percival-type is an inverse Oedipus-type; but this handy formulation— obviously easy to parody, as Lévi-Strauss himself has done—is less important than the complex affinity of contradictions found pulsating between incest imagined and riddles solved, and cultures' doubled reluctance for and resis-tance to either. The formula I am stressing is one linking Lévi-Strauss, Wag-ner, and world-translating Romantics:

> Comme l'énigme résolue, l'inceste rapproche des termes voués à demeurer séparés: le fils s'unit à la mère, le frère à la soeur, *ainsi que fait la réponse en réussissant, contre toute attente, à rejoindre sa question.* (Lévi-Strauss 1973:34)[15]

In this earlier formulation, however, son-mother incest and brother-sister in-cest are amalgamated. Part of the tale I have to tell about Lévi-Strauss is that brother-sister incest later assumes a primacy, echoingly Romantic or Wag-

15. "Like a solved riddle, incest draws together components destined to remain separated: son is united with mother, brother with sister, *just like the response that, succeeding against all ex-pectations, rejoins* (becomes a rejoinder to) *its question*" (Lévi-Strauss 1973:34, my trans.).

On the primacy of sibling incest, or sibling-like incest, see Boon (1982 a, 1982b, and forthcoming). I must reserve for another time discussion of Romantics' concern with sibling incest as it paradox-ically bridged extremes of social difference. For some suggestions on related topics, see Irwin (1975), and Finney (1983). Far-reaching work on incest, exchange, and political economy and philosophy is being pursued by Marc Schell, who has, however, cultivated something of a blind spot to Lévi-Strauss.

nerian, that displaces the Oedipus theme proper and links *Mythologiques* more precisely to *The Elementary Structures of Kinship*.

But before that development, still back in 1960, Lévi-Strauss's sketch outlines seductive extremes that myths imagine: either eternal summer (too-ripe corruption) or eternal winter (sterility). Against these extremes myths pose terms for periodicities of seasonal rhythms. They conceptualize the social realm as regular marriage exchanges and equilibriated communications—exchanges of words or translations—rising above ruse, *perversité*, or *arrière-pensée* (Lévi-Strauss 1973:35). Although that remarkable sketched-score would continue constraining the writing of *Mythologiques* (plus aftermaths), the tetralogy altered as it emerged during the years of publication (1964–1971). After *Le cru et le cuit* (1964), the volumes evolve toward pessimism, or rather back toward the resignation of *Tristes tropiques*. Similarly, Wagner's *Ring* sketch of 1848 stood to the ultimate work as both what it would be and what it would supersede. Between the sketch and the *Ring* fell Wagner's disillusion following the failed Revolution of 1848, a change that scholars often link to Wagner's taking up Schopenhauer's *World as Will and Representation* thirty years after its publication. Between Lévi-Strauss's sketch and his achieved tetralogy (indeed, between the first three and the final volume of the tetralogy) falls Lévi-Strauss's disillusion after 1968, a change that possibly resonates with his renewed embrace of Wagnerian pessimism in the *Ring*, or even in *Parsifal*, where, we remember, "The Victors" had been compressed.

Returning Twilights

Wagner appears only fleetingly in *L'homme nu*: three references (two of them epigraphs among the book's meta-epigraphs: epigraphs about the nature of epigraphs) and the concluding parallel between myth and Proust's recurring musical "little phrase of Vinteuil," the most Wagnerian (*leitmotivic*) component of *À la recherche du temps perdu*. Strikingly, *L'homme nu*'s prolonged musicological analysis pertains not to Wagner's music or myth but to the pure musical message of Ravel's *Boléro*. Nor does *L'homme nu* reenlist the code of baroque fugues that orchestrated *Le cru et le cuit*.

My terms code/message/myth derive from a crucial comment and a footnote (omitted when the "Overture" was first translated into English in the *Yale French Review*—Boon 1986a). Lévi-Strauss draws the history of Western tonal music into a closed cycle of development and subsequent exhaustion. This structure remains submerged in the cycle of the *Mythologiques* volumes themselves, the cycles of mythic genres they catalogue, and distinct episodes of myths evolving. The composers Lévi-Strauss names form a chronological sequence: Bach-Beethoven-Wagner/Debussy-Ravel-Stravinsky. They also form a cycle of musical forms (or communication) he tags as code-message-myth/ myth-message-code. The latter half can be seen as secondary returns on earlier conventions. Standard musicological labels, of course, would be the permutations and combinations of Bach's baroque (later revisited in the quotations of Stravinsky); the classical style (with movement to cadence and closure) of Mozart-Haydn-Beethoven (revisited/parodied in Ravel), and the multiple chromatic transpositions of Wagner's music-drama soon echoed, indeed parodied in a way, in Debussy, particularly "Les jeux" (see Austin 1982).

I would emphasize that *Mythologiques*'s elaborations conclude with neither a point of the closed cycle (back at code) nor at the pivotal myth/myth reversal (Wagner/Debussy), but half way back along the cycle at Ravel. Moreover, this realm of message (with its closure toward cadence over time—one made ironic in the repeating crescendo that is *Bolero*) resembles narrative plot, the very mode of meaning most challenged and/or neglected in Lévi-Strauss's stress on code and myth. Yet this device is consistent with his reluctance to reach closure. Announcing a code-message-myth/myth-message-code cycle as the music-like format of myth (and *Mythologiques*), his tetralogy ends not by closing the circle but implying or anticipating closure only at other levels, at another time, or in another work. By ending his "*Ring*" with Ravel rather than Wagner, Lévi-Strauss manages a kind of multiple ending of chromatic juxtapositions like the conclusion of *Tristes tropiques*'s ostensible adventures, to whose "Sunset" chapter *Mythologiques* finally returns, indeed which it confesses never having left (1971:620; Boon 1982a).

Where does this leave Wagner? Kept relatively offstage in 1971, but there all along, he reenters in 1975 and 1983. Lévi-Strauss stresses Wagner's transformation of Chrétien's motive (motif) of the *question non posée* into an inverse motive devoted to affect. He argues that Wagner's new device advances us beyond communications between substantively separated worlds (e.g., licentious/moral realms with Tannhäuser as go-between), whose linking resembles musical diatonics rather than chromatics. Through chromaticism, Wagner achieves instead a resonating single world of mediation and only mediation. Lévi-Strauss puts it this way:

> Actually in Wagner's poem it is not a matter of Arthur's court nor, therefore, of a communication to be reestablished between the terrestrial world (represented by this court) and the beyond [l'au-delà]. In fact the Wagnerian drama unfolds exclusively between the kingdom of the Grail and that of Klingsor: two worlds, one of which had been and would become again endowed with every virtue and the other destroyed for its infamy [dont l'autre, infâme, doit être détruit]. Thus it was not a question of reestablishing or inaugurating a mediation between them. By the annihilation [l'anéantissement] of one and the refurbishment [redressement] of the other, the latter alone subsists and is constituted as the world of mediation [monde de la médiation] (1983:316; my trans.).

This shift from "communication" between two separate spheres to the world of mediation recalls Lévi-Strauss's own move from kinship structures to *Mythologiques*. *The Elementary Structures of Kinship* still posed social organization as "communications" between two sides of any marriage transaction, effected by codes connecting ideas/practice (separable spheres). In place of transactions between substantively separate worlds, or categories, or social sides, the subject of *Mythologiques* became the very terms of mediation that allow any such spheres, or sides, or separations to be posited: the differences constituting various possibilities of "spheredness," so to speak (Boon & Schneider 1974).

Lévi-Strauss's evocation of *Parsifal*'s "monde de la mediation" has retrospective implications for his work on incest as well. The summary cited earlier shifts his pole of incest to Klingsor and Kundry's unbridled exchange (*communication sans frein*) in utter contrast to inert Amfortas's congealed condition (*communication figée*). The ethnologist here begins reconfessing, via Wagner's last work, humanity's unconscious (and his personal) renunciation of too-near exchange in order to espouse societies' balanced separation and distance by harnessing the potential of *pitié: durch Mitleid wissend* (1983:318). Lévi-Strauss thus refines his theme of incest as an antithesis to proper exchange, one way among others of negating or valuing-by-contrast balanced reciprocity. In shifting toward the incestuous tonalities of Klingsor and Kundry, the mother-son incest tokened by Oedipus in Lévi-Strauss's single most influential article can be seen as at most a second-order incest, one that harbors the trace of a previous generation's exchange: a mother from another (as wife). The incest "purely" antithetical to exchange or longer cycles of reciprocity is sibling incest at a moment of profound *oubli*. Although Klingsor and Kundry's incestuous tonalities are not restricted to this register (and indeed *Parsifal* possibly alludes to son-mother transgression as well), musically they hearken back to this incest-without-residue-of-exchange: the *Ring*'s incestuous twins, Siegmund and Sieglinde, the most familiar transgressors in all Wagner. Even if Wagner had not continually reread the history of early-Romantic through high-Romantic speculations and translations, his somewhat hackneyed theme of sibling incest would tie him to these predecessors. This incest generates links across extremes (between gods and men, between opposed castes, between opposed races, etc.).

Lévi-Strauss's view of incest as anti-exchange is most powerfully conveyed by sibling incest, which is forgetful of any prior spouse-exchange. Against the imagined transgression of sibling incest stands the compound ambiguity of incest taboos: anti-isolationist, yet not quite social, taboos to which cultures add something positive (*pitié*, an inclination toward) whether expressed in positive marriage rules or alternative mode of communication (see Boon 1982b:xi).

Augmented Analysis

It was only in 1983 that Lévi-Strauss abruptly published a condensed re-reading of the *Ring*, making it into a virtual palimpsest of the *Ganzgesamt-*

"Wotan: In eigner Fessel
fing ich mich,
ich Unfreister aller!
Wotan: I forged the fetters;
now I'm bound.
I, least free of all living!"
(*The Valkyrie*, II, 2; translated by Andrew Porter [New York, 1977], p. 105; the translator, striving
to preserve alliteration and assonance, is powerless not to eliminate the *ich-mich* internal rhyme.)
    (Portrait reproduced from the frontispiece to H. A. Guerber, *Stories of the Wagner Operas* [New
York, 1895]).

werk of his own life's corpus-making. His ostensible motive was to correct an error: he had transposed the names Gunther and Hagen (from *Götterdämmerung*) during a radio interview in Canada which was published as his book *Myth and Meaning* (1978). Much to his chagrin, that book presented his responses to questions as if they were continuous prose and retained the error to boot.[16]

Yet, his CBC Hagen/Gunther gaffe was later converted to advantage, joining the many comic moments also recouped and confessed as parts of *Tristes tropiques*, if readers will only to take this extraordinary narrative for what it is: a form of myth-making (truthful, I'm convinced), playing on the full keyboard of memory's distinctions and experience's multiple modes (Boon 1986b). That endearing blooper becomes the pretext for his "note sur la tetralogie" in *Le regard éloigné* (1983), where, his error corrected, Lévi-Strauss launches an allegorical analysis of the *Ring* vis-à-vis his own work. Characteristic highlights continue questioning the authority of sequence, what one might call chrono-logics (Boon 1984):

1. Lévi-Strauss tallies twenty or so occurrences of the "Love renounced" musical motif and mentions the weave of semantic and phonetic oscillations, contradictions, antitheses, and contrasts that constitute the invariant element of Wagner's *stabrimes* and text: Minne/Liebe, Heiligste/Not, sehnende/ sehrende, Tat/Tod . . . (1983:319, 322).

2. He suggests the play of pre- and postfiguration around Siegfried: Siegmund is his earlier *essai manqué* and Hagen his later *pâle reflet*.

3. He places *Das Rheingold* under the sign of "reciprocity" valued against and through transgression. The three subsequent evenings seek to resolve the problem posed by *L'Or du Rhin*: "a conflict among contradictory exigencies that constituted the social order," which "in every imaginable community forbids receiving without giving" (Lévi-Strauss 1983:321, my trans.). Wotan thus engraves "l'esprit des lois" on his lance. Moreover, even among the gods, and more so among men, "on n'a jamais rien pour rien." (Here the lexical play

---

16. I learned this fact in a chat with Lévi-Strauss when we happened to be riding in a limousine to Dulles Airport, to tape him reading his works for a National Public Radio program I authored introducing his anthropology to listeners. Not then having read Heine, I can only now echo Heine's reaction to A. W. Schlegel (his Osiris—see above): Lévi-Strauss "was not what I had imagined [a French *savant*] to be . . . he appeared to be all spirit [*esprit*]. . . . I know that I am speaking obscurely and will try to express myself as clearly as possible" (Heine 1836:57). Lévi-Strauss, gentle Lévi-Strauss, hated travel and travel-tellers in *Tristes tropiques*'s travel-tales ("Je haïs les voyages . . ." [1955:13]) and doubtless continued disliking travels and interviews.

With this last footnote, the present essay now merges subtextual details into the text— overlapping, transitioning—to intensify questions of whether detail, theme, anecdote, allegory, or repetition looms largest or means most. Unpolarized between text/footnote, such an essay would seek to transform itself into a "monde de la médiation." That movement, however, must remain incomplete; earlier schisms linger to return.

of negatives by means of repetition—*rien/rien*—is too perfect to translate; the last word of *L'homme nu*—its "sesame term" [Boon 1982a:143]—is likewise *rien*, not yet doubled into an explicit positive/negative.)

Lévi-Strauss stresses an identity between the tetralogy's first term (the ring itself) and its closing term (Brunhilde herself) (1983:322). (Readers might compare *Mythologiques*'s closed circle of the rhyme between its first title-term, *cru*, and final title-term, *nu*.) In Wagner the ring recycles to the Rhine, which floods the site of Brunhilde (and Siegfried, and the horse Grane) aflame, consumed in a spiral of fire and water. Might this Indo-European style of heroic death and transition (gods-succumbing) imply an aftermath outside the music-drama's frame? Does Wagner suggest an extension of the Gibichung variations into ultimately nonheroic humanity, routinely speaking-not-singing, resigned and limited to exchange cycles—a proper "exogamous vocation" in Lévi-Strauss's terms (1983:322)?

One might also extend Lévi-Strauss's suggestions about incest versus proper alliance, assuming that before the *Dämmerung* the Gibichungs adumbrate possibilities of humanity's fate of regularized exchanges. This fate is foreshadowed in *Das Rheingold* by Fricka's sense of domestic propriety, which, if respected, would have precluded her spouse Wotan's mating either with Erde (begetting Brunhilde and her sister Walkyries) or with a human (begetting Siegmund and Sieglinde, whose incest produced Siegfried). The Gibichungs attempt a near equivalent of proper sister-exchange between one pair of siblings (Gunther and Gutrune) and another consanguineal pair (Siegfried-Brunhilde are half-nephew–aunt: Wotan is her father and his grandfather). But the propriety of Gutrune and Brunhilde being exchanged for each other between Gunther and Siegfried is a false one, given previous evenings' incest and Wotan's philanderings that produced Brunhilde and Siegfried. Only with the eclipse of the gods and heroes is mundane regularity conceivable.

Lévi-Strauss concentrates less on these relationships than on the path of the ring: from the watery Rhine, to subterranean Alberich, to celestial Wotan, to earthly giants, to the hero Siegfried, plus a round of giving/back-snatching between Siegfried and Brunhilde during the complex episode of Siegfried's disguise as Gunther under the influence of the potion of *oubli*. The ring's final return to the Rhine suggests that in the gods' world of word-song, there is no escaping the circle of incest.

Ever richer grow the resonances with Lévi-Strauss's own *The Elementary Structures of Kinship*. In the *Ring* gods try out transgressions against proper exchange, including "le code de la parenté et du mariage." Moreover, as attentive readers of the concluding pages of *The Elementary Structures of Kinship* know, for Lévi-Strauss, regulated orders never quite escape resonances of transgression, called a "mystery" of relations between the sexes at the book's ending (1983:469; see Boon 1982a: ch. 7; forthcoming: chs. 5–6). Lévi-Strauss now poses these human marriage systems as actualized grapplings with the same problem that Wagner's *Ring* performs. His summary deserves direct quotation:

> Respectively brother and sister, twins to boot, Siegmund and Sieglind are united [s'unissent] by an incestuous act [un inceste]. They thus form a pair of cousins [germains] in correlation and opposition with another: the pair formed by Gunther and Gutrune, themselves also brother and sister, but with a calling to exogamy [à vocation exogame]; their entire problem consists in discovering elsewhere whom to marry [avec qui se marier]. (Lévi-Strauss 1983:322; my trans.)

Like a pendant to Wagner's *Ring*, Lévi-Strauss's empirical studies of variant solutions to finding elsewhere "avec qui se marier"—so to effect a balanced "social economy" of credit/debt relations—became transformed into a tetralogy (*Mythologiques*) that assembles codes of categorical relations attuned to transgressions kept in abeyance only for propriety's mysterious sake.

Further Surges

In 1983 did Lévi-Strauss at last still, like a closing cadence, the on-going controversies of interpreting *Mythologiques* and *The Elementary Structures of Kinship*, plus their interludes and aftermaths? Has he committed a roundly allegorical analogy between his efforts and Wagner's? No serious reader of Lévi-Strauss, gifted multiplier of endings, could suspect so. Rather, Lévi-Strauss's account takes its place on the shelf of other allegorical readings of Wagner's own allegorical returns upon the *Oresteia*. This list (which includes brief entries by E. M. Forster and Kenneth Burke) is long and, pending cataclysm, unstoppable. Lévi-Strauss's angle on the *Ring* seems to me more compelling than Robert Donington's elaborate Jungian analysis, which, although recognizing the importance of marital exchanges, sees sibling incest as secondary and parent-child incest as archetypal (Donington 1969:102ff). Lévi-Strauss's entry is perhaps on a par with Shaw's famous construal of Siegfried as a Protestant-style harbinger of dawning religio-economic transformations:

> The most inevitable dramatic conception, then, of the nineteenth century, is that of a perfectly naive hero upsetting religion, law and order in all directions, and establishing in their place the unfettered action of Humanity doing exactly what it likes, and producing order instead of confusion thereby because it likes to do what is necessary for the good of the race. This conception, already incipient in Adam Smith's *Wealth of Nations*, was certain at last to reach some great artist and be embodied by him in a masterpiece. It was also certain that if that master happened to be a German, he should take delight in describing his hero as the Freewiller of Necessity, thereby beyond measure exasperating Englishmen with a congenital incapacity for metaphysics. (Shaw 1923:60)

Shaw's *Perfect Wagnerite* went through four editions, each with a new preface and key additions, between 1898 and 1922. Yet Shaw, good Shavian that he was, tempered his influential championing of Wagner with a disclaimer that undercuts not just the tawdry side of Wagner's politics, hates, and aesthetic prejudices but the "decidability," *au courant* critics might say (or the appropriateness), of any allegorical reading: "In short, Wagner can be quoted against himself almost without limit, much as Beethoven's adagios could be quoted against his scherzos if a dispute arose between two fools as to whether he was a melancholy man or a merry one" (1923:102).

Is this the moment again to recall that Lévi-Strauss culminated his *Mythologiques* variations not with Wagner but with Ravel, one step ahead/back of the completed Bach-Beethoven-Wagner/Debussy-Ravel-Stravinsky cycle? Moreover, Lévi-Strauss's analogical thought ("pensée sauvage") between his own work and Wagner's indirectly admonishes readers not to plumb for a bottom-line allegory or extramusical (extramythical)·paraphrase. For even when he engaged more in musical cadences, Wagner resisted mythical-musical alignments or simple correlations. In *Lohengrin* Wagner excluded key lines he had pondered that risked synthesizing its strands of love/renunciation. *Tannhäuser* was rewritten towards the indeterminacies and unsettling displacements in the more chromatic version we experience today, a product of Wagner's compositional techniques developed after 1843. And later Wagner never let Brunhilde utter "I saw the world end," words so powerful and paradoxical that they might have wrapped the *Ring* up into tight closure. Rather he left an open, ambiguous ending (three strands, at least, unresolved), often since declared an imperfection, a residue of Wagner's indecisiveness, or a flaw lingering from the work's backwards composition. Wagner converted the originally intended "Death of Siegfried" into the trilogy plus fore-evening that ends with *Götterdämmerung*, structurally and "operatically" more traditional than the three evenings that precede it. Many scholars attribute this "incoherence" of the *Ring* to Wagner's conversion from the optimism of redemptive love to the Schopenhauerian pessimism of Wotan's end. At least since Shaw, critics have disputed *Götterdämmerung*'s traces of chorus, plot tensions, hints of older aria/recitative phasings (recalling Wagner's pre-*Tristan* works), and failure to be radically reworked into uninterrupted, unchaptered, ideally undemarcated, endless transitionings—like the other evenings.

This "neglect" to make *Götterdämmerung* of a piece with the rest of the *Ring* may complement implications of a human phase when exchanges would be proper and devoid of incest. We can imagine after the *Ring* a fully human-historical condition of those very opera conventions that Wagner had gradually thwarted. His revolutionary music becomes in the *Ring* the communicating condition of gods-heroes of the mythical past implicitly superseded (as the Gibichungs anticipate) in actuality by the opera that his music-drama was designed to surmount, overthrow, cancel out. Again, Wagner's fully realized music of the future is depicted in the *Ring* as the music of the gods past, leaving the music of the past as the presumed mytho-historical future, adumbrated in those conventional components that *Götterdämmerung* retained. This *Zukunft* consists in the operatic conventions that its listeners once took for granted yet see utterly denied in the *Ring*, at least in its first three portions.

Is, then, the cyclic *Ring* moving forwards or back? Yes. Wagner manages to convert the writing backwards of the *Ring* (from a conventional "Death of Siegfried" into a radical tetralogy that ends with that residue of conventionality) into part of the thematics of the work's performance. Moreover, all the work's components occur as if they were already being recalled: initial premonitions seem repetitions or echoes. Relations of preludes and acts are upset—the first evening is a prelude to the subsequent three; some evenings begin with anticipations and/or recapitulations woven through elaborate retellings of what has already been presented. The narrative flow, such that it is, proceeds through so-called leitmotivic fracturing and chromatic transitions in ambiguous tonalities. All of this is echoed in Lévi-Strauss.

Moreover, *Götterdämmerung*'s throwbacks and fast-forwards underscore the *Ring*'s catalogue of everything "Word-Tone-Speech" can be. Peter Conrad summarizes this dimension, adroitly reading backwards through the *Ring*, across the genres it encapsulates in and as music-drama:

> [The dynastic ambition of] *Götterdämmerung*, both the end and the beginning, is epic, because epic, while the beginning of literature, has as its subject the end—the fall of civilizations. . . . Beyond *Götterdämmerung*, Siegfried belongs to the genres of pastoral, which treats not the politician or soldier but his apprenticeship in private life, and of romance, which describes the hero's journey through the world towards self-discovery. The next part to be unfolded in Wagner's backward movement, *Die Walküre*, approximates to the form which emerges next in the evolution of literature, the novel. . . . This opera is a series of dialogues in which errant individuals are constrained by the loyalties and contractual obligations which comprise their society. Beyond this is *Das Rheingold*, musically the beginning, as literary form the conclusion . . . concerned with the war of ideas. It abstracts the novel into philosophical debate . . . and hence, in Shaw's sense, it is less an opera than an oratorio—a conversion of oratorio from religion to economics, for it dramatizes not the operation of grace through nature but the corrosion of money in society. (Conrad 1977:35–36)

There are, of course, alternative ways to construe the *Ring*'s compendium of "major forms through which modern literature has developed," (36) but a compendium it surely is, and reversible.

The parallel with Lévi-Strauss's tetralogy is resonant. His endlessly transitional decodings inscribe simultaneously a compendium of mythic forms, alluded to in the volumes' titles: (1) polar, alliterative contrasts ordering multiply differential features (*Le cru et le cuit*'s culinary triangle and fugal play of sensory correspondences); (2) transformations (*Du miel aux cendres*) entailing transpositions across social/environmental realms to surmount the previous opposition (honey is more than raw, ashes more than cooked); (3) a just-so tale of beginnings (*L'origine des mannières de table*), ostensibly about codes of propriety, concretely about menstrual regulation, celestial cycles, etc.; (4) a universal-sounding epithet of and for human experience (*L'homme nu*), the quest to modify *the* generalized noun of Western humanist arrogance. A continual oscillation between advance and recapitulation (*pour l'accord*) coupled with leitmotivic proliferations of oppositionings make Lévi-Strauss's work literally and lushly Wagnerian.

Secondary Surge

That striking sense of sustained tension, even dialectics, between lawlessness and regulation (e.g., incest/regulated exchange) highlighted in Wagner (and Lévi-Strauss after him) struck Theodor Adorno negatively, to put it mildly. In paragraphs as ardent and convoluted as Wagner's plots, Adorno proclaimed Wagner's "phantasmagoria" the *summa* of things bourgeois. Here is one of Adorno's more muted moments:

> In Wagner, law is unmasked as the equivalent of lawlessness. The *Ring* could have as its motto the statements by Anaximander [quoting Nietzsche's translation] recently analysed by Heidegger, who as a mythologist of language is not unlike Wagner: "Wherever existing things have their origin, there too they must of necessity perish, for they must pay the penalty and be condemned for their iniquity, in accordance with the order of time." . . . The archaic idea of Fate presides over the seamless web of universal immanence in the *Gesamtkunstwerk*, and . . . provides the foundation for the musical principle enshrined in the notion of "the art of transition," of universal mediation. Wagner's music conforms to the law that tension and resolution should, in the main, correspond to one another, that nothing should be left unbalanced or allowed to stand out aloof and isolated; in his eyes all musical being is Being-for-another, it is "socialized" in the process of composition itself. . . . This establishes the primacy of exchange over the organization and internal progression of the work of art: it becomes the incarnation of the processes of exchange in society as a whole. (1952:117–119)

Adorno then accelerates to a fortissimo of Marxist prose that winds up (recalling Kenneth Burke) incorporating components of isms it critiques:

> With this regression to myth, bourgeois society salutes itself by name in Wagner: all novel events in music measure themselves against their predecessors and by cancelling them out the new is itself constantly cancelled out. The origin is reached with the liquidation of the whole. The realization that late bourgeois society possesses these anarchist features decodes the totality as a prehistoric anarchy. This anarchy is still repudiated by Wagner the bourgeois, but it is already desired by Wagner the musician. If in the *Ring* mythic violence and legal contract are confounded, this not only confirms an intuition about the origins of legality, it also articulates the experience of the lawlessness of a society dominated in the name of law by contract and property. (1952:118–19)

Adorno felt obliged to brand Wagner's work the ultimate bourgeois phantasmagoria. Yet Adorno's prose, phantasmagoric in its own excess, achieves a vituperation so extreme, and so informed by knowledge of Wagner's works, that it begins to look like praise, a livid laud, a Nietzschean transvaluation of yea/nea, of course in a negative register or rather dialectics.

Were one to follow through in Adorno's vein, Lévi-Strauss's extension of such mediations to the endless variations of nonliterate myth and stateless social arrangements could be declared the furthest expansion of that "bourgeois society" saluting itself by name in Wagner, constantly cancelling out the new. Yet mulling over what anarchy or nonanarchy Adorno might have been urging that we transcend towards, I wonder whether even he escapes the cycles. I begin to suspect Adorno's rhetoric of resuscitating certain modes of Romanticism and indeed of being indebted to Wagner's consolidation of aesthetics and politics. Will they never cease, these out-cancellings of the new?

At a far more pedestrian level than Adorno's, I suggest that Lévi-Strauss cancels out the cancelling-out of Wagner's *Ring* by concluding *Mythologiques* with the "twilight of man." Throughout these achievements—Lévi-Strauss's or Wagner's or Adorno's—it would be difficult to argue that Romanticism had been left behind. These out-cancellings, nevertheless, set in question hopes of a future uncontaminated by a past, of any new work previously unwritten on or under, of any sequence that could leave prior positions behind. Palimpsests are here to stay and have been. And *tristes* lists continue.

This view too would doubtless have sounded "bourgeois" to Adorno (what position other than his own did not?). Yet a nuance appears that may render this charge quizzical. If Lévi-Strauss has declared *Mythologiques* his tetralogy (his *Ring*), he later makes the reciprocal gesture of declaring the *Ring* Wagner's *Elementary Structures of Kinship*. Totalizing indeed, and reciprocally. To avoid any directionality, or tyranny of sequence, might we readers, moietylike, "split the difference"? Would this have been Heine's way, were he here, to read not just from Romantics back to Enlightenment but from structuralists and their aftermath back to Romanticism? Might we make Lévi-Strauss and Wagner stand as palimpsests, each to each, in the rereading of them, just as Wagner stood to the Romanticisms he revisited, absorbed, and wished to wear out?

Concluding Modulations

Lévi-Strauss's "notes on the tetralogy" (1983), help distance his anthropological writings from the methodological and standard logical pegs nailed to them in conventional disciplinary assessments. Years before the 1983 "notes," soon after completing *Mythologiques* (1964–1971), Lévi-Strauss described to Raymond Bellour the complexities of reading myths. He repeated his frequent contrast between his style of reading across myths and between languages versus the saturated reading of a given myth, poem, or novel in its particular language. Yet Lévi-Strauss qualifies the difference by stipulating a resemblance between the two activities: any poem or novel is a variant of the author's others. At that point he returns to Baudelaire's "Les chats": "a variant of all the other sonnets of the 'Flowers of Evil'" (1979:169; see Boon 1972: chs. 2–3). And he invokes Wagner, or rather Wagner/Debussy. Lévi-Strauss's theory of reading back/forward towards variations—intensifying, relaying, connecting, and subverting boundaries and works—can almost sound Romantic, or early Romantic, or post-Romantic (Wagnerian?). Listen:

> To take another example, true both at the level of the poem and of the music, who could deny [comment douter] that the third act of *Parsifal* is a variant of the same act of the *Maitres chanteurs?* In the latter and the former an aged, experienced man (Gurnemanz or Sachs) withdraws [s'efface] before another, younger and exceptionally gifted, whom he enthrones. In the latter and the former their long encounter precedes *la marche au sacre* with, between these two phases, an intermediary moment of appeasement and of unanimity recaptured [retrouvée]— "Enchantment of Good Friday" or "quintette." No satisfactory analysis of one could be made without knowing and bringing in [faire intervenir] the other. Thus, the analysis of the *Maitres* had to await *Parsifal*'s being written, and that of *Parsifal* will remain incomplete because we will never know the opera that Wagner would have written next, had he not died (just as we will never know the variants of *Pelléas* that would have been revealed by "The Fall of the House of Usher." (In Bellour & Clément 1979:169; my trans.)

Who too would deny (*comment douter*) that similar differences and difficulties pertain to reading Lévi-Strauss as pertain to reading/hearing the works of Wagner (and the works of Debussy, who, parenthetically, parodied Wagner) and to reading/hearing myths-as-variants. Throughout *Mythologiques*, Lévi-Strauss insisted on an epistemological limit: variations, insofar as they can be communicated, are interminable. Yet even without knowing what would have followed *Parsifal* or *Pelléas* (or Lévi-Strauss), we know what was collapsed into the first (*The Victors*), and we can keep exploring variants among the constituents of each corpus and among it and other works it reread and invited. That Debussy never wrote "The Fall of the House of Usher" in turn can return us upon previous Symbolists turning upon Poe, and the complex aftermath of that as well. Those who reduce Lévi-Strauss to a logician, rather than seeing him as a reader-writer alert to the palimpsest-nature of myths and works, might as well imagine that *Parsifal* (not *The Victors*; son of Lohengrin) had no bearing on *Meistersingers*, or that *Meistersingers* was not *both* the as-if diatonic companion-opposite to chromatic *Tristan* and the sequel to *Tannhäuser*'s tale of minnesingers, *and* a work whose characters authored some of Wagner's sources (characters likened to Wagner himself as well). Endlessly extend these links and winks. Adorno, perhaps understanding their power better than anyone, gets fed up, but intermittently (so must we all; it's only human):

The fact that [Wagner] is an allegorist shows itself not least in the way . . . forms and symbols become intermingled until Sachs becomes Mark, the Grail becomes the Nibelungs hoard and Nibelungs become Wibelungs . . . the jettisoning of everything unequivocal, . . . the negation of everything with an individual stamp. . . . The Wagnerian totality is the enemy of genre art. Like Baudelaire's, his reading of bourgeois high capitalism discerned an anti-bourgeois, heroic message in the destruction of *Biedermeier*. (1952:101)

Peter Conrad, more unambiguously tolerant of Wagner's "oddly overlapping romance narratives" adapted from medieval tales, condenses details tirelessly mapped in Ernest Newman's unsurpassed *Wagner Nights*:

Parsifal, whom Lohengrin claims as his father, was in one project for the third act of *Tristan und Isolde* to stray into Tristan's Breton estate of Kareol; the author of the medieval *Parzival*, which Wagner used as a source both for *Lohengrin* and his own *Parsifal*, is a character in *Tannhäuser*; in *Die Meistersinger* Walther acknowledges the influence of another of the contestants at the Wartburg, Walther von der Vogelweide, and Sachs quotes the cautionary example of Isolde and Marke. (Conrad 1977:10)

Denying Lévi-Strauss's way of reading, one might as well deny that Richard and Cosima kept rereading E. T. A. Hoffmann (source, with Heine, *Tannhäuser* and other tales) or all those early Romantics and the medieval and Indological translations and transpositions they championed. Cosima's diaries recount the exploration of world mythology and epic for motives of cremation, seeking to overcome the dilemma presented by her Catholicism versus her Richard's Protestantism, a schism that *then* would have prevented burial together. Near-parody bourgeoises in their outsized domestic trappings, the twosome accumulated an array of personal favorites in comparative studies, world drama, and literature. These they wove transfiguringly into what Borchmeyer has called a contaminated *synkretistische Mythologie* (what mythology isn't?) of Wagner's compositions always in progress (1982:299). Or perhaps it was a postsyncretist mythology, given earlier Romantics' embrace of mixtures.

Final Strains, Full Circle, No Closure

The degree of rereading entailed in Romanticism-become-Wagnerism-become-Lévi-Strauss (or an aspect of his corpus) qualifies metaphors of begetting, legacy, and ownership in the history of ideas — whether anthropological, literary, or operatic. Hence my homage to Heine. Lévi-Strauss accentuates variants, always variants, even after a composer ceases living (an author is "dead" anyway, if we follow Foucault). Lévi-Strauss, moreover, calls us to scrutinize Wagner's poem and music together and contrapuntally — "il faillait qu'un contrepoint entre le poème et la musique . . ." (1983:321). The case of Wagner (and of Nietzsche) underscores the advisability of tracing sketches, sources, libretti, omissions, insertions, interventions, and correspondences over fuller ranges of variations: telescopically and microscopically, before and since; back to the *Eddas*, through lateral readings, and onward to the works prein- scribed or invited, including Lévi-Strauss's. Like Lévi-Strauss's *Werke*, Wagner's *livrets* unfold in a way that alters how subsequently to hear or to read them. Wagner's obsessive mingling, moreover, doubtless echoes an inability to com- pose sequentially and without self-interruption. Consider this nexus described by Newman, drawing heavily on Wagner's somewhat fictionalized autobiog- raphy, *Mein Leben*:

> . . . while at work on the score of one opera a theme would suddenly spring up within him which had nothing to do with the subject in hand but, as he would soon realise, belonged of right to some other work that had not been consciously occupying his thoughts at the time. One day in 1876 when he was writing the American Centennial March [commissioned by Philadelphia, ac- cepted for profit] the idea flashed across him for the ensemble of the Flower Maidens in *Parsifal*; and in 1859, while engaged on the third act of *Tristan*, the joyous melody of the Herdsman took, without his willing it, a turn which, as he soon saw, was more appropriate to his forgotten young hero Siegfried [the work he had set aside, therapeutically, to compose *Tristan*]: it became later the "Love's Resolution" motive of the *Ring*. [In 1856 he wrote] ". . . while I was once more working at *Siegfried* I could get no peace from *Tristan*. I actually worked simultaneously at them both . . . the double labor was a perfect torment to me." (1949:I, 193–94)

With Wagner it was ever so: his compositional devices and throes reveal the inadequacies of chrono-logics for mapping an *oeuvre*, tracing an influence, or attributing ideas' ownership.

Indeed, Wagner's explicit and indirect critique of chrono-logics anticipates the heart of Lévi-Strauss's challenge to both historical consciousness and the value of sequence and plot as ordering devices. These points were advanced methodologically in *Structural Anthropology I, II* (and *"III"–Le regard éloigné*). They were posed epistemologically in *La pensée sauvage*, including its parodic challenge to how one can "know" through dates, and its penultimate chapter- title borrowed from Wagnerian Proust, "The Past Recaptured" ("*Le temps retrouvé*")–an achievement attributed to myth and ritual, related dialectically. This challenge to chrono-logics is clinched in *Mythologiques*, which parallels mythical selections and combinations and its own process of composition (and, I have added, reading) to musical ordering.

Through leading-motives that reecho and transpose–both musical (*sons*) and semantic (*sens*)–Wagner's synaesthesic *Gesamtwerk* devices incrementally eroded boundaries, sequence, and the sway of serial order in a combined sub- versiveness and recuperation. It is this motion–decried by Adorno, but search- ingly and in defiance of partisan expectations–that prefigures Lévi-Strauss and that I have explored, as often as not, through pastiche. It is the same motion that made Wagner "mythic" in the concrete (Symbolist-to-Modernist) sense rather than the idealistic (Romantic) sense—"mythic" in the sense of *Le cru et le cuit*. After *The Elementary Structures of Kinship* (1969b), Lévi-Strauss's controversial anthropology became, increasingly and simultaneously, many things. Among these becomings are an augmented rereading of Wagner's *opera*, themselves rereadings of just about everything Romantic, themselves included. Many works—operas and anthropologies and myths and social structures—require reading both from and toward the futures they promise. Lévi-Strauss's corpus, too, developed in a manner which cancelled the way its preceding installments had been read. Is, *pace* Adorno, reading-back the only way there is? *Zurück vom Ring!*

Acknowledgments

This exploratory essay is part of a continuing project on comparative discourse (including fieldwork) and musical form that I began in 1966, when Lévi-Strauss's *Du miel aux cendres* could first be read. Part I continues my work on constructions of cultures, isms, and eras. A sketch of Part II was delivered at Cornell's conference on "Reading Opera" in 1986; I thank the organizers and participants for their encouragement upon hearing something different done with music, even with musicology.

George Stocking provided many helpful editorial suggestions. For crucial conversations I am grateful to Olivian Boon, Sander Gilman, Robert Smith, Walter Lippincott, Caryl Emerson, Arthur Groos, Cynthia Chase, Carolyn Abbate, David Schneider, Ivan Brady, Carol Greenhouse, and Clifford Geertz, among others. And I thank Claude Lévi-Strauss, who keeps writing.

Finally, gratitude goes to Princeton and Cornell colleagues and students in anthropology and related disciplines who are willing to engage hybrid arts, even at certain peril.

References Cited

Aarsleff, H. 1982. *From Locke to Saussure*. Minneapolis.

Abrams, M. H. 1953. *The mirror and the lamp*. New York (1974).

———. 1971. *Natural supernaturalism*. New York.

Adorno, T. 1952. *In search of Wagner*. Trans. R. Livingstone. New York (1981).

Austin, W. W. 1982. Debussy, Wagner, and some others (review article on R. Hollway, *Debussy and Wagner*). *Nineteenth century music*: 82–91.

Backès-Clément, C. 1970. *Claude Lévi-Strauss, ou le structure et le malheur*. Paris.

Bellour, R., & C. Clément, eds. 1979. *Claude Lévi-Strauss*. Paris.

Benthall, J., ed. 1976. *Roy. Anth. Inst. News*, Jan.–Feb.

Boon, J. A. 1972. *From symbolism to structuralism: Lévi-Strauss in a literary tradition*. New York.

————. 1973. Further operations of "culture" in anthropology. In *The idea of culture in the social sciences*, ed. L. Schneider & C. Bonjean. Cambridge.

————. 1977. *The anthropological romance of Bali, 1597–1972*. New York.

————. 1982a. *Other tribes, other scribes: Symbolic anthropology in the comparative study of cultures, histories, religions, and texts*. New York.

————. 1982b. Introduction. In *Between belief and transgression*, ed. M. Izard & P. Smith, v–xx. Chicago.

————. 1984. Structuralism routinized, structuralism fractured. *Am. Ethnol.* 11:807–12.

————. 1985. Mead's mediations: Some semiotics from the Sepik, by way of Bateson, on to Bali. In *Semiotic mediations*, ed. E. Mertz & R. Parmentier, 333–57. New York.

————. 1986a. Claude Lévi-Strauss. In *The return of grand theory*, ed. Q. Skinner, 159–76. Cambridge.

————. 1986b. Between-the-wars Bali: Rereading the relics. *HOA* 4:218–47.

————. 1987. Anthropology, ethnology, and religion. In *Encyclopedia of religion*, ed. M. Eliade. New York.

————. Forthcoming. *Affinities and extremes: Crisscrossing the bittersweet ethnology of East Indies history, Hindu-Balinese culture, and Indo-European allure*. Chicago.

Boon, J., & D. M. Schneider. 1974. Kinship vis-à-vis myth. *Am. Anth.* 76(9):799–817.

Borchmeyer, D. 1982. *Das Theater Richard Wagners*. Stuttgart.

Burbidge, P., & R. Sutton, eds. 1979. *The Wagner companion*. New York.

Burke, K. 1970. *The rhetoric of religion*. Berkeley.

Carlyle, T. 1831. *Sartor resartus*. New York (1975).

————. 1841. *Heroes and hero-worship*. New York (1975).

Clifford, J. 1987. *The predicament of culture*. Cambridge, Mass.

Clifford, J., & G. Marcus, eds. 1986. *Writing culture: The poetics and politics of ethnography*. Berkeley.

Chase, C. 1986. *Decomposing figures: Rhetorical readings in the Romantic tradition*. Baltimore.

Conrad, P. 1977. *Romantic opera and literary form*. Berkeley.

Cooke, D. 1979. *I saw the world end: A study of Wagner's Ring*. New York.

Dahlhaus, C. 1980. Wagner, Richard: Music dramas. *The new Grove dictionary of music*.

Darnton, R. 1984. *The great cat massacre, and other episodes in French cultural history*. New York.

de Man, P. 1979. *Allegories of reading: Figural language in Rousseau, Nietzsche, Rilke, and Proust*. New Haven.

Donington, R. 1969. *Wagner's "Ring" and its symbols: The music and the Myth*. New York.

Eksteins, M. 1985. History and degeneration: Of birds and cages. In *Degeneration: The dark side of progress*, ed. J. Chamberlin & S. Gilman, 1–23. New York.

Ellman, R. 1988. *Oscar Wilde*. New York.

Ewans, M. 1983. *Wagner and Aeschylus: The "Ring" and the "Oresteia."* New York.

Feldman, B., & R. D. Richardson, eds. 1972. *The rise of modern mythology*. Bloomington, Ind.

Finney, G. 1983. Self-reflexive siblings: Incest as narcissism in Tieck, Wagner, and Thomas Mann. *Ger. Quart.* 56:243–56.

Firchow, P. 1971. Introduction. Lucinde *and the* Fragments, by F. Schlegel. Trans. P. Firchow. Minneapolis.

Foucault, M. 1970. *The order of things.* New York.

Freemantle, A. 1974. *A primer of linguistics.* New York.

Geertz, C. 1973. *Interpretation of cultures.* New York.

————. 1983. *Local knowledge.* New York.

————. 1987. *Works and lives: The anthropologist as author.* Stanford.

Gossman, L. 1984. Basle and Bachofen. *J. Warburg & Courtauld Inst.* 47:136–85.

Graham, J. 1986. *Difference and translation.* Ithaca, N.Y.

Heine, H. 1836. The Romantic school. Trans. H. Mustard. In *The Romantic school and other essays,* ed. J. Hermand & R. C. Holub. New York (1985).

Holub, R. C. 1985. Introduction. *The Romantic school and other essays,* ed. J. Hermand & R. C. Holub.

Hopkins, P. 1977. The homology of music and myth. *Ethnomusicology* 21:247–61.

Erwin, J. T. 1975. *Doubling and incest, repetition and revenge.* Baltimore.

Kenner, H. 1962. *The Stoic comedians.* Baltimore.

————. 1971. *The Pound era.* Berkeley.

Large, D. C., & W. Weber, eds. 1984. *Wagnerism in European culture and politics.* Ithaca, N.Y.

Lévi-Strauss, C. 1950. Introduction. In *Sociologie et anthropologie,* by M. Mauss. Paris.

————. 1955. *Tristes tropiques.* Paris.

————. 1962a. *La pensée sauvage.* Paris.

————. 1962b. *Le totemisme aujourd'hui.* Paris.

————. 1963a. *Structural anthropology.* Trans. C. Jacobson & B. G. Schoepf. New York.

————. 1963b. *Totemism.* Trans. R. Needham. Boston.

————. 1964–71. *Mythologiques.* 4 vols. 1964: *Le cru et le cuit;* 1966: *Du miel aux cendres;* 1968: *L'origine des manières de table;* 1971: *L'homme nu.* Paris.

————. 1966. *The savage mind.* Chicago.

————. 1969a. *The raw and the cooked.* Trans. J. & D. Weightman. New York.

————. 1969b. *The elementary structures of kinship.* Trans. J. H. Bell & J. R. von Sturmer. Ed. R. Needham. Boston.

————. 1971. *L'homme nu.* Paris.

————. 1973. *L'anthropologie structurale II.* Paris.

————. 1978. *Myth and meaning.* Toronto.

————. 1979. *La voie des masques.* Paris.

————. 1983. *Le regard éloigné.* Paris.

————. 1984. *Paroles données.* Paris.

————. 1985. *La potière jalouse.* Paris.

Lockspeiser, E. 1962. *Debussy: His life and mind.* 2 vols. Cambridge.

Magee, B. 1983. *The philosophy of Schopenhauer.* Oxford.

Manuel, F., & F. 1979. *Utopian thought in the Western world.* New York.

Mojumdar, A. T. 1976. *Sir William Jones: The Romantic and the Victorian.* Bangladesh.

Nabokov, V. 1968. *The portable Nabokov,* ed. P. Stegner, New York.

————. 1970. *Speak memory, An autobiography revisited.* New York.

Nattiez, J. J. 1973. Rencontre avec Lévi-Strauss: Le plaisir et le structure. *Musique en Jeu* no. 12.

————. 1983. How can one be Wagnerian? *Opera Quart.* 1(3):3–10.

Newman, E. 1941. *The life of Richard Wagner.* 4 vols. Cambridge (1968).

————. 1949. *The Wagner operas.* 2 vols. New York (1983).

Opera Quarterly. 1983. Commemorative Issue on Wagner. Vol. 1(3), ed. S. & I. Sloan. Chapel Hill, N.C.

Poizat, M. 1986. *L'opéra ou le cri de l'ange.* Paris.

Rajan, T. 1980. *Dark interpreter: The discourse of Romanticism.* Ithaca, N.Y.

Robinson, P. 1985. *Opera and ideas.* Ithaca, N.Y.

Sedlar, J. W. 1982. *India in the mind of Germany: Schelling, Schopenhauer, and their times.* Washington.

Shaw, G. B. 1923. *The perfect Wagnerite.* New York (1967).

Simmel, G. 1907. *Schopenhauer and Nietzsche.* Trans. H. Loiskandl and D. & M. Weinstein. Amherst, Mass. (1986).

Steiner, G. 1975. *After Babel.* New York.

Stocking, G. W., Jr. 1986. Anthropology and the science of the irrational: Malinowski's encounter with Freudian psychoanalysis. *HOA* 4:13–49.

Wagner, C. 1980. *Diaries.* 2 vols. Trans. G. Skelton. New York.

Wagner, R. 1977. *The Ring of the Nibelung.* Trans. Andrew Porter. New York.

Walker, A. 1983. *Franz Liszt: The virtuoso years, 1811–1847.* Rev. ed., Ithaca, N.Y.

Willson, A. L. 1964. *A mythical image: The ideal of India in German Romanticism.* Durham, N.C.

ZUNIS AND BRAHMINS

Cultural Ambivalence in the Gilded Age

CURTIS M. HINSLEY

Wretched men! to suffer themselves to be deluded with desire of novelty, and to leave their own serene sky to come and gaze at ours.
(Michel de Montaigne, "Of Cannibals," 1580)

God help my poor doomed Zunis!
(Frank H. Cushing, diary entry, July 15, 1892)

For five hundred years the New World Indian has served as the object and mirror of Western ambivalence toward the exercise of power and the direction of progress. It has been an instrumental ambivalence, abetting the very progress that it doubts. On Indian persons, real and constructed, have been played out both the first impulses and the second thoughts of American culture: God had hardened their hearts to the task and deafened their ears to the children's screams, explained the Puritan soldiers after the slaughter of the Pequot tribe in the swamps of Mystic in 1637 (Ziff 1973:91). Two centuries later, the insistent romantic motif of the noble savage that ran through Irving, Cooper, Schoolcraft, and Longfellow coexisted in complex, antidotal relation to the murderous frontier policies and Indian-hating metaphysics of Jackson, Harrison, and Crockett. A few, such as Melville, recognized this at the time for what it was: the inescapable counterpoint of self-ambivalence

---

Curtis Hinsley is chair of the History Department at Northern Arizona University. His major previous publications include *Savages and Scientists: The Smithsonian Institution and the Development of American Anthropology, 1846–1910* and (with Melissa Banta) *From Site to Sight: Anthropology, Photography and the Power of Imagery.* He is currently at work on studies of the Hemenway Southwestern Archaeological Expedition of 1886–89 and the Peabody Museum of Harvard.

in American history. As if in compensatory balance, political and military destruction brought forth imaginative reconstruction of the American's shadow Other, the Indian.

After the Civil War, as the venue of destruction shifted to the trans-Mississippi West, a new cultural phenomenon emerged to help resolve the long-standing ambivalence: the museum process. The resolution was achieved by announcing and then demonstrating the end of Indian history. The museum process constructed a meaning of Indian demise within the teleology of manifest destiny; it indirectly addressed the insistent doubts of Gilded Age Americans over the import of industrial capitalism; and it did so by encasing, in time and space, the American Indian. Dehistoricization was the essence of the process. Anthropologists, journalists, politicians, and philanthropists collaborated to bring about what they assumed to have already arrived: the final stage of the transition of Native Americans from living communities to "life groups," from autonomous historical agents to market commodities and museum pieces. The museum process took many forms: World's Fairs, Wild West shows, anthropology museums and publications, on-site tourist attractions, curio shops and Indian markets. All provided public spaces for safe consumption of a newly dehistoricized Indian; in most of them, there was an element of theater.

One of the more revealingly theatrical forms of the museum process was the Indian tour which, since Montaigne's Tupinamba, had provided standard tropes for Euroamerican cultural critique, as occasionally it still does (e.g., Janowitz 1987). Nineteenth-century Americans became used to hearing of a steady stream of Indian delegations to the East Coast, primarily to the seat of government in Washington, D.C. While they customarily provided theater—dancing, singing, oratory—increasingly, visiting Indians occasioned little in the way of reflective commentary (Viola 1981:140–41), and, by 1830, little in the way of serious politics. By the post–Civil War period, a tradition that had begun a century before as a political act—a form of state visit for purposes of treaty negotiation—had devolved to a photo opportunity. In the last quarter of the century, Indian history itself was rapidly becoming theater, and the Indian visit, even when otherwise intended, became yet another form of the museum process.

On February 22, 1882, anthropologist Frank Hamilton Cushing left Zuni pueblo with six Indians who had been selected to make a pilgrimage to the Atlantic Ocean: Palowaihtiwa, governor of Zuni and political chief of the Macaw clan; his father, Pedro Piño, or Laiiuahtsaila, former governor of Zuni; Naiiuhtchi, senior priest of the order of the bow; Kiasi, junior bow priest; Laiiuahtsailunkia, priest of the temple; and Nanahe, or Cornflower, a Hopi who had been adopted as a member of the little fire order in Zuni. Boarding the Atcheson, Topeka & Santa Fe railroad at Gallup, New Mexico, they ar-

Frank Hamilton Cushing, seated with Native American pilgrims to the Atlantic Ocean. Left to right: Laiiuahtsailunkia, Naiiuhtchi, Palowaihtiwa, Kiasi (all Zuni); Nanahe (a Hopi); Laiiuahtsaila (Pedro Piño) was in Washington, D.C., when the photograph was made during the group's visit to Worcester, Mass. (Courtesy of the Peabody Museum, Harvard University; photographed by H. Burger.)

rived in Chicago on March 2. Here they attended their first theater performance: "My Sweetheart," starring Minnie Palmer, at the Grand Opera House.

Travelling on to Washington, the Zunis called on President Chester A. Arthur, studied collections at the Smithsonian, climbed the Washington Monument, and performed planting ceremonies in Rock Creek Park. Pedro Piño, the aging former governor, fell sick and was left behind to recuperate while the group continued on to New York and Boston in late March. In Boston, the Zunis became the center of social attention in churches, schools, theaters, and private homes. They also visited Salem, Wellesley, and Worcester. On Tuesday, March 28, the pilgrimage culminated with seaside services on Deer Island in Boston harbor, where they gathered water from "The Ocean of Sunrise" for retrieval to Zuni.

Fatigued and sick, Cushing and the Zunis recovered for three days in Brooklyn before visiting Zuni children at the Indian school in Carlisle, Pennsylvania. They then returned to Washington, whence Pedro Piño and three others of the group returned via Chicago to Zuni. Palowaihtiwa and Naiiutchi remained in Washington for informant work with Cushing through the summer. After (probably) attending Cushing's wedding to Emily Magill in July, they travelled with him to the Cushing family homestead and the Seneca reservation in upstate New York (in August and September) en route to New Mexico. On September 17, the party arrived at Fort Wingate, and eleven days later, after an absence of nearly eight months, Cushing and the Zunis re-entered the pueblo amid great celebration.

Warriors and City-Builders in the Southwest, 1876–1881

Between the Mexican-American War of the mid-1840s and the end of Southern Reconstruction in 1876, American society stood at war with itself on many levels. Since Miles Standish and George Washington, the contrasting, balanced images of the American as agriculturalist/artisan and as soldier—as city-builder and warrior—had alternated deeply within the American historical imagination. In the immediate pre–Civil War years, the first evidences of urban squalor appeared, the first antimodern, Concord-based voices arose, and a fragile political structure began to fracture over slavery and economics. It was in this period that military and commercial reconnaissance reports (Sitgreaves' *Report* of 1853, Simpson's *Journal* of 1852, Whipple's *Pacific Railroad Reports* of 1853–54) first introduced the new southwestern acquisitions to the national public. Predictably, since the concerns of the occupiers largely set the terms of colonial confrontation, the language of these reports presented southwestern Indians in the familiar binary categories of the military campaign: peaceful/warlike, defensive/aggressive, agricultural/nomadic, city-builders/raiders. The terms proved to be resonant and persistent. Americans' search for an integration and balance between their own divided selves—North and South, pastoral and urban, nostalgic and progressive—readily found expression through all those observers who would write of the new landscapes and peoples of Arizona Territory for the remainder of the century.

When Hubert Howe Bancroft sat down in 1875 to summarize for the public the present state of knowledge regarding *The Native Races of the Pacific States*, the "wild tribes" of Arizona and New Mexico presented conveniently meaningful contrasts. In the arid regions one found, on one hand, the southern Athaspascans (Apache and Navajo): nomadic, roving peoples—Bancroft called them "American Arabs" or "American Bedouins" (cf. Hunt 1882:108)—who swept down from craggy heights to rob and murder unwary travelers and, "then fleeing to their strongholds, bid defiance to pursuers." On the other hand, the desert was also home to the peaceful Pueblo peoples: "In the midst of all this, we find another phenomenon in the semi-civilized townspeople of New Mexico and Arizona; a spontaneous awakening from the ruder phases of savagism" (Bancroft 1875:I, 472–73). The initially striking physical feature of the pueblos—their terraced house structures—was interpreted by Bancroft and other Anglo observers in this light; they were presumed to be clever defensive units designed by a peaceful but wary people: "To wall out black barbarism was what the Pueblos wanted, and to be let alone; under these conditions time was giving them civilization" (536). Bancroft saw evidence of potential for civilized success: "Industrious, honest, and peace-loving, the people of this division are at the same time brave and determined, when necessity compels them to repel the thieving Apache" (555).

Contemporary speculation over the prehistory of the Southwest established a similar narrative of pacific but vigilant gardeners under constant threat of savage raid. Exploring the San Juan valley cliff-dwellings in the summer of 1875, for instance, William Henry Holmes mused imaginatively on past scenes of war and siege:

> From the top of the wall we looked out and down; there was the deep Canoma Valley. The cliffs above the trees slope below, and the winding thread of the Mancos in the green strip [at] the bottom. How secure; how impregnate [sic]; one man with loose rocks at his command could keep off the world. . . . We admired the skill with which these fortresses were built and the hardihood, and were amazed that means of defense could have been conceived and carried out with the nearest water far below, and only these great jars to contain a supply. With their fields and flocks and the supply of water within the hands of an enemy . . . [they] must have perished or have crept down the cliffs to fight or yield to the foe. (WHHP 4:30)

A year later, when the mysterious "cliff-dwellers" were first presented publicly at the Philadelphia Centennial in the form of W. H. Jackson's plaster model of cliffhouse structures, Holmes and Jackson's visionary history achieved a wider currency.

"Industrious, honest, peace-loving"—Bancroft's terms for the Pueblos, living or prehistoric, stood in clear relief against the fearsome Comanche-Apache type. The terms reflected the preferred Anglo self-image of pioneering and settlement: at heart Americans, too, were gardeners in a trackless wasteland, proto-agents of civilization. They struck, accordingly, deep resonance in American national political mythology, stirring approved cultural memories: of long-suffering Pilgrim communities, of Cincinnatus figures called reluctantly to arms, of Minutemen slow to anger but invincible once aroused. On the other hand, the alternate southwestern Other, the Apaches, received no such cultural latitude or military mercy, as General Miles's relentless campaign of the next decade demonstrated. But here, as throughout Southwestern commentary, ambivalence predominated, for the warrior also demanded respect. Helen Hunt Jackson, attending "A Midsummer Fête in San Juan Pueblo" in 1881, was struck by the contrast between "the mounted Apaches—splendid, dashing creatures, with scarlet cheek-bones and scarlet blankets"—and the "gentler Pueblos," basking "as content as lizards" in the hot sun, their children "with heads lifted like turtles" as they watched the dancing in the plaza (Hunt 1882:105–8). Through such representation Pueblo peoples stood to a certain advantage both by virtue of association with cherished Anglo self-identity and folk history, and by distinction from neighboring tribes judged truly hostile.

The key term in this early construction of the discourse regarding the Pueblos was "semi-civilized." "Semi-civilized" connoted a desirable, though probably not historically sustainable position of balance, a middle landscape. It named a prescriptive category that contained an attitude or emotional posture for Anglos toward the Indians, not any specific anthropological knowledge. Lewis Henry Morgan, it is true, tried more precise definitions. He called the Pueblos the "Village Indians of New Mexico" and grouped them with the "Village Indians" to the south (Aztec, Maya, Inca) as examples of the middle state of barbarism. Morgan's "middle barbarism" in the western hemisphere was characterized by irrigation cultivation and the use of adobe or stone masonry. But the specific index of evolutionary status was ultimately less important for the general reader than the stance that was called forth. The state of knowledge was, after all, still low: "Notwithstanding their apparent accessibility we know in reality but little concerning their mode of life or their domestic institutions. No systematic investigation has ever been made. What little information has found its way into print is general and accidental" (Morgan 1877:183).

Neither savage nor civilized, the Pueblos' in-betweenness inspired a vigorous debate between Bancroft and Morgan over their historical and ethnological status in the decade after 1875. The controversy, which burned intensely until Morgan's death in 1881, initially focussed public and ethnographic attention on the Southwest. The essential point of the dispute was methodological and epistemological: How are we to know the history of this hemisphere? Following the model of William Prescott and other Romantic historians of New Spain, Bancroft presented the Aztec empire at contact as a politically sophisticated, socially advanced, hierarchical and monarchical civilization, brought to its knees by avaricious but technologically superior *conquistadores*. Citing architecture, patterns of land tenure, and calendrical-astronomical accomplishments, Bancroft concluded that "the Nahuas, the Mayas, and the subordinate and lesser civilizations surrounding them, [were] but little lower than the contemporaneous civilizations of Europe and Asia and not nearly as low as we have been led to believe" (quoted in Keen 1971: 390). While Bancroft, a staunch evolutionist, firmly believed in the steady rise from savagery to civilized practice—which he interpreted as the triumph of good over evil through history—he also questioned the rigidity of all schemes of social evolution, such as Morgan's multiple-stage series, that presumed to set forth specific criteria of progress.

Morgan, writing with the confidence of one who has found certainty through scientific method, dismissed Bancroft's Romanticism. The Spanish sources must be read anew, in the light of scientific ethnology, and the results would certainly reduce the high estimates of Montezuma's world: "Whatever may be said by credulous and enthusiastic authors to decorate this Indian pueblo, its houses, and its breech-cloth people cannot conceal the 'ragged Indian' therein by dressing him in European costume" (quoted in Keen 1971:393). Morgan called for intensive anthropological and archeological work throughout the western hemisphere, beginning in Mexico and the American Southwest, in order to deflate historical and literary hyperbole and place ethnology in the New World on firm ground—by which he meant the "ethnical periods" of subsistence arts, social arrangements, and political and property relations which constituted the basis of *Ancient Society* (1877).

The Morgan-Bancroft dispute marked a significant point in the development of anthropological method. While admitting that they occasionally exaggerated, Bancroft generally trusted the Spanish accounts and, accordingly, deplored the violence committed against peoples who seemed to have been politically, scientifically, and socially advanced. Morgan, on the other hand, saw value in the textual record only when it was confirmed by archeological and ethnographic evidence. While blind to the distorting effect that his own model would have on the fieldwork of his followers, Morgan did bring a certain sobriety to the reading of the Conquest. His general program, which was largely triumphant in the 1880s, was to privilege anthropological experience over historical sources and to associate pueblo societies with the Aztecs by lowering the status of the latter. In doing so he kindled curiosity about connections in the region. Carried forward in its essentials by Bandelier (though with far higher regard for archival sources and with intense sympathy for the Spanish Catholic church), Morgan's program impelled and framed the Southwestern work of Cushing's generation. In the process the Pueblos seemed confirmed as peaceful, "semi-civilized" villagers: neither as savage as their roaming Athapascan neighbors nor as civilized as the natives to the south, in 1880 they occupied the ethnological middle landscape in the American national imagination. When Frank Cushing walked into Zuni pueblo in September 1879, Southwestern Indian peoples had already been carrying for some years the burden of the projected divisions and dissensions of national American politics and mythology.

Myth and Reciprocity:
Cushing at Zuni, 1879–1882

One point on which Bancroft and Morgan agreed was the immediate need for Southwestern ethnography. The Pueblos, Bancroft suggested in 1875, promised high scientific returns; fourteen years later he reiterated that it was "hardly possible to overestimate the importance of these tribes for ethnologic study" (1889:2). As if in response, in September 1879, James Stevenson's collecting expedition for the new Bureau of Ethnology left Cushing at Zuni pueblo. John Wesley Powell, director of the Bureau, had been encouraged by Spencer F. Baird, secretary of the Smithsonian Institution, to include on the expedition an individual whose primary assignment would be to study a single pueblo according to the measures of Morgan: house structure, kinship system, agricultural methods; and Baird offered Cushing. When the rest of Stevenson's party moved on after a few days at the pueblo, Palowaihtiwa, governor of the village of 1,650 people, took Cushing into his living quarters for what he assumed would be a temporary sojourn. Cushing stayed until February 1882 – twenty-nine months.

At the time of Cushing's arrival, Zuni pueblo, like the Rio Grande pueblos to the east and the Hopi villages to the west, was experiencing a rapid increase in contact with non-Indian elements: Mexicans, Mormons, farmers and railway men, miners, missionaries, traders, land speculators, government agents, and scientists. The expedition which brought Cushing was, in fact, only the first of many Smithsonian anthropological foraging efforts in New Mexico and Arizona over the next twenty-five years. These enterprises removed thousands of objects of material culture from the pueblos, especially from Zuni and the Hopi villages – an average of more than five artifacts per person at Zuni between 1879 and 1884 – with profound effects on local economies and social structures (Parezo 1987).

When the Atcheson, Topeka & Santa Fe and Atlantic & Pacific railroads came through New Mexico in 1880, they passed through Gallup directly north of Zuni. Their accelerating impact on the flow of people, goods, and influence in and out of the pueblo was immediate and powerful: the railroad "set about . . . mining the landscape for culture, the culture for artifacts, and the country for tourist traffic" (McLuhan 1985:18). If Palowaihtiwa's father, Pedro Piño, the former governor of Zuni, had seen the military and political disposition of the territory following the Treaty of Guadalupe Hidalgo in 1848, it fell to his son's generation to respond to the more insidious and thoroughgoing invasions of the 1880s (cf. Green 1989).

Traditional ethnographic accounts follow a model of discovery and development in which the fieldworker passes through recognizable stages in "penetrating" the alien culture. Along with Boas, Malinowski, and a few others, Cushing shares responsibility for the design of this strategy. At Zuni, the young man fashioned a compelling and attractive myth of himself as he went along: he appeared as the ethnographer abandoned, struggling, with ever deepening insights, to gain access to Zuni life. Cushing's account of his arrival and early weeks in the pueblo stressed both his decisiveness in choosing to stay, and his hardship and suffering at the hands of both Stevenson and the Zunis—deprived by the first of tobacco, staple and trading goods, and placed at the mercy of the latter, who stripped him of his clothes, dressed him in Zuni costume and forced him to live like an Indian in order to "harden his meat."

Cushing's ethnographic narrative thus clears a critical in-between space, a vantage point forced by betrayal and deprivation. Vital to Cushing's story are isolation and martyrdom, themes which emerge repeatedly in both his private correspondence and public statements. The ethnographer begins socially and psychologically at the bottom, victimized, alone, with no resources but his determination to learn and his physical endurance. He is literally and figuratively denuded. From this point the Cushing myth becomes a story of self-sacrifice, reeducation (into Zuni knowledge) and a dual struggle upward: to acceptance into the secret and powerful orders of the pueblo; and to re-admission into Anglo-American circles of science, society, and politics. Stewart Culin's version tells the story succinctly:

> At the Pueblo of Zuni, . . . he left the expedition and remaining, became a member of the tribe, was appointed one of its high tribal chiefs, and after un-told hardships and privations, returned, broken in health, to tell the world of his epoch-making discoveries. (1904:5)

Such was the form of quest-return narrative which Cushing and his admirers constructed and disseminated (cf. Curtis 1883:25–31).

Cushing's famous *Century Magazine* series, "My Adventures in Zuni" (1882–83), which recounted his first four months in the pueblo, was constructed around stages of abandonment and adoption: new food, new clothes, new family ("father," "older brother," etc.), new knowledge. Adoption by savages has always been deeply problematic in American culture, but it appears acceptable if portrayed as involuntary and temporary (Slotkin 1974). In Cushing's case, the inversion and ambiguity of roles further complicated the meaning of the act for him and for his Indian hosts: he was vulnerable, but he was also a representative and agent of the state power of which the Zunis were themselves wards and to which they were encouraged to look for parental care and protection. In incorporating him as son and brother, certain family groups in the pueblo thereby took to themselves an extension of external power, as well as some risks. From the beginning then, Cushing, too, was problematic: he stood as the brother/son within and the arm of the father without.

Cushing's adoption-by-stages seemed forced upon him, but this interpretation was his own construction. It is always difficult to see behind Cushing, but it does seem clear that the central dialectic at Zuni was reciprocity. For public consumption he emphasized moments of defiance and bravado as the turning points in his acceptance in the pueblo (Cushing 1882:207), but in reality his ethnographic entrée lay in patient attention to the children and, through treatment of their scrapes and sicknesses, to their mothers—a common strategy employed by anthropological visitors before and since, including his Bureau colleagues Washington Matthews and James Mooney (Hinsley 1981:211). Cushing's Zuni name, Tenatsali, or Medicine Flower, indicated as much; *Zuñi Breadstuff*, the most complete product of his Zuni years, testifies to the fruitfulness of his strategy.

Cushing's adoption was in fact personally appropriate, given the strong male and filial bondings that seem to have been essential to his emotional and institutional stability. The youngest of several sons of a strong paternal figure, he reproduced throughout his life filial relations: as a "son" of varying closeness to Powell, Baird, Edward E. Hale, Mary Hemenway, William Pepper, and Phoebe Hearst; as a "brother" to John G. Bourke and Washington Matthews, Sylvester Baxter and Willard Metcalf, and later to Stewart Culin. The most tragic year of his life was 1898, when his father, his brothers, and William Pepper all died (SCP: Cushing to Culin, 2/9, 9/18, 10/10/1898), two years before his own accidental death. As adopted son/brother in Zuni, Cushing thus fell easily into roles with which he was comfortable.

Cushing was not the first Anglo to sojourn at Zuni, nor the first to recuperate from serious illness in the pueblo. In 1865, Albert Franklin Banta, an Arizona adventurer, fell deliriously ill while visiting the pueblo and was nursed to health over a period of two months in the house of the Zuni war chief, Salvador (Pandey 1968:36). At the end of this time he received a Zuni name and considered himself adopted. He returned to Zuni for an indeterminate period in the next few years (1865–73). "The Zunis," he recalled, "desired to make me their War Chief . . . but I declined that honor; nevertheless I went with them against the thieving Navajos on several occasions" (Reeve 1952:213). The Zunis, he concluded, were "the best people in the world; they were honest and truthful, and were the most hospitable people living" (214; cf. Eggan & Pandey 1979:474; Pandey 1972:324).

Early in 1880, Cushing fell seriously ill and was confined to bed for many weeks. He studied Zuni language and etymology daily and began to see the intimate linkages between linguistic practice, history, and social organization. By May he had emerged with a brilliant prospectus of research that envisioned a coordinated approach to language, archeology, history, and ethnohistory. At the same time, though, he had begun to participate, with Palowaihtiwa's encouragement, in the politics of the pueblo, especially the perennial issues of land rights and boundaries. From this point his Zuni experience became complex participation-observation, for it is evident that every advance in his knowledge of the religious and social organization of Zuni life took place with the understanding that in exchange he would serve Zuni purposes—or at least those of the governor and his family (Pandey 1968:71, 74, 103–4).

Judging from Banta's earlier activities and Cushing's own subsequent career as Bow Priest and "First War Chief of the Zunis," those purposes certainly involved protection against Navajo and Anglo encroachment on Zuni land and internal regulation of various kinds of deviance in the pueblo caused by the increase in outside influences. By 1880, several Apache delegations (1868, 1872, 1880) had gone to Washington and even the detested (from the Zuni perspective) Navajos, after pestering the Bureau of Indian Affairs, had been issued an invitation in 1874. Since no Zuni had ever visited Washington, it is likely that an eastern tour had become a prized objective among the Zuni chiefs (Viola 1981:40–41). The 1882 trip was planned, then, as a reciprocal event. It arose as the *quid pro quo* for Cushing's initiation into the Priesthood of the Bow, which had taken place in September, 1881, and as prerequisite to his initiation into the Order of the Kâ-Kâ—which began, in fact, on the beach of Deer Island in Boston Harbor. The visit grew, in short, from complex expectations and obligations that had developed mutually in Zuni over many months. Cushing described the situation most accurately to James C. Pilling, Powell's secretary, when he explained, a few weeks before departing from the pueblo:

> I owe a lasting debt of gratitude to the people of Zuni. They have been forging for me, during the past two years of doubt as to my genuineness, the keys which enable me to open their vast and ancient treasure-house of Ethnologic information, have treated me with strange goodness and distinction; and, in my gratitude, I . . . wish to do all I can toward convincing them that I *am* what I have always claimed to be, their *friend*. (FHCP:FHC/JCP 1/15/1882)

Reciprocity is, however, an ambiguous strategy and position, easily shading over into entangled obligations. It was the entanglement rather than the mutuality of Cushing's Zuni relations that, with his encouragement, came to be a part of public understanding of the trip to the East and subsequently heightened his own mythological status. Following the September initiation as Bow Priest, Cushing found that his new status was complicating his relations in the pueblo, since there were now new expectations of him—one of which may have been marriage. Army lieutenant John G. Bourke, Apache ethnographer and friend of Cushing who spent much of the month of November 1881 at Zuni, reported that Cushing now could not be permitted to leave the pueblo with his secrets, and that he must marry a Zuni girl. According to Bourke, with Cushing's greater knowledge, "the meshes are weaving tighter and tighter about him, and, in the end, his departure from the Pueblo will be a desertion and a flight." Furthermore, he wrote, Cushing understood this fully and moreover had no intention of marriage:

> Time alone can tell; if he deport himself with circumspection, he may for a brief period—six months at the uttermost limit—throw dust in the eyes of the leading

spirits: but they will not long remain deceived and when they discover his du-
plicity, for such it must be, his influence will be destroyed, unless he consent
to the ceremony so long delayed. (Sutherland 1964:961–62)

Bourke may be untrustworthy at such points, for his language is an example of the familiar hyperbolic anticipation of boyish danger that he, Cushing,
and the local military circle engaged in among themselves. Judging from the
subsequent reception of Cushing's Anglo bride, Emily Magill, and her sister
Margaret in the pueblo, Bourke's fears proved unjustifiably alarmist. They
do, though, suggest the tensions that Zuni trust, his new local responsibilities, and his sense of division and possibly hypocrisy had produced in Cushing
by late 1881. The public myth included little hint of this, though. To his
American audiences Cushing explained that he had proposed the trip for
the Zuni chiefs as a means of avoiding marriage into the tribe (Baxter 1882:526).
The story of Cushing's refusal to marry circulated widely and purposefully,
ultimately emerging as a central element in the ethnographer's myth. He spread
it on the eastern trip (e.g., *New York Tribune* 3/6/1882). At the time it served
to confound critics who were anxious to insinuate moral lapse by the ethnographer, and to provide a source of humorous narrative of matrimonial manners and morals, displaced to an exotic locale. The version of William E. Curtis (1883:36–41) reduced Cushing's dilemma to an "attempt to ensnare him
into the matrimonial net," an issue which was staple fare in current potboiler
fiction and theater. Fred Ober, writing in *Wide Awake* (1882:385), repeated
the Cushing/Baxter presentation of the eastern trip as a compromise to avoid
Zuni marriage and remain true to his betrothed, Emily, waiting in Washington. Twentieth-century accounts have further elaborated the story (e.g., Gilbert 1961:12; Sherwood 1979:108).

In the aftermath of the exciting eastern tour Cushing's fame grew, and
the simple story of the marriage dilemma became mythologized as a causal
factor. The complex netting of deeply personal and cross-cultural understand-
ings and misunderstandings that stretched, through Cushing's sickness and
health, over two and a half years at Zuni, was simply too delicate for public
communication.

Theater in the Round:
Zuni Culture-Circles in New England

Cushing brought rich travelling theater eastward in 1882, a year before William F. Cody first took his Wild West show on tour. Charles F. Lummis recalled that Cushing was "epidemic in the culture-circles of New England" that
year:

I remember it very well; and have just been re-reading a large amount of the excitement that came into type. His personal magnetism, his witchcraft of speech, his ardor, his wisdom in the unknowabilities, the undoubted romance of his life of research among "wild Indians of the frontiers," . . . and the impressive dignity and poise of his Indian comrades – all were contagious. The Zunis, in particular, were a sheer revelation to the somewhat waterproof East. . . . Never was tour more skillfully managed. Perhaps never was another quite so curiously mixed between genuine scholarship and the arts of the showman. (1900:11)

If, as Lummis judged, the Zuni tour was "the cleverest thing that has ever been devized and carried out by a scientific student anywhere," it was also a cultural event of serious import.

Much of the "excitement that came into type" during the tour did so through the drawings of a young Boston artist named Willard Metcalf and through the words of Sylvester Baxter, a correspondent for the Boston Herald. Both had been observing Cushing and the Zunis for some time, and their romantic visions help to explain the Cushing "epidemic." In late spring 1881, Baxter and Metcalf undertook a trip through the Southwest in search of colorful and romantic magazine material. Baxter (1850–1927) was a native Bostonian whose family was descended on both sides from the Mayflower migration; Metcalf (1858–1925), who was slightly younger than Cushing, traced his Anglo-Saxon genealogy back nearly 800 years, including paternal ancestors who had landed in Massachusetts Bay in 1636. In 1881, however, the aspiring painter (and future American Impressionist) was struggling to gather sufficient funds for study in Paris. Unlike his contemporary, Frederic Remington, who discovered the American West in the same period and made it a lifelong obsession, Metcalf's affair with the Southwest was merely an early phase, closely tied to Cushing and Zuni; after finally getting to Paris in late 1883, he never returned to the American West (deVeer & Boyle 1987). Baxter's infatuation with Cushing was equally immediate but longer lasting; he became the ethnographer's publicist, amanuensis, and alter ego, announcing his work to the world and serving as the Boston-based corresponding secretary of the Hemenway Expedition from 1886 to 1889.

Cushing came as a revelation to the genteel Boston men. Baxter's oft-quoted first impression, like Metcalf's full-length portrait of Cushing that accompanied it, still has freshness:

a striking figure walking across the parade ground [at Fort Wingate]; a slender young man in a picturesque costume; a high-browed and broad-brimmed felt hat above long blonde hair and prominent features; face, figure, and general aspect looked as if he might have stepped out of the time of King Charles. The costume, too, seemed at first glance to belong to the age of chivalry, though the materials were evidently of the frontier. (1882a:74)

Thus Baxter introduced Cushing to a national magazine public, transforming an initial Southwestern impression into the familiar terms of boyhood
romance. For the Boston men the deep romance with Cushing's Zuni (and
the Zunis' Cushing) was rooted in moments of intense and unforgettable communication and exchange, at Wingate, on the trail, and in the pueblo, in
the months when Cushing's circle of Anglo and Zuni intimates was forming.
John G. Bourke's description of the evening of May 29, 1881, at Fort Wingate,
soon after Metcalf and Baxter's arrival, conveys the special intimacy:

> In the evening, called upon Mr. Hopkins, the post trader, and his charming
> wife; thence to General Bradley's, where I met, besides his family, Mr. Cushing
> with Patricio, the "gobernador" of Zuni, Dr. and Mrs. [Washington] Matthews,
> and Lieut. Chance. Mr. Cushing read us some poetry in the Zuni language,
> an invocation to the spirit of the antelope, showing rhyme, rhythm and mel-
> ody. Patricio said that it was a song they sang to the spirit of the antelope before
> starting out on a hunt and, as we seemed to be so pleased with the words, he
> would sing the song itself, if we so wished. Need I say that we jumped at the
> chance and begged Patricio to gratify us. He sang in a sweet voice, a little bit
> tremulous from nervousness, the invocation or chant beginning: "May-a-wee,
> May-a-wee!" (Spirit of the antelope, Spirit of the antelope!). Just before he began
> his song, Mr. Baxter, the correspondent of the Boston Herald, and Mr. Metcalf,
> an artist of the staff of Harper's Weekly, entered the little circle and took down
> notes of all that occurred. (Sutherland 1964:328–29)

The significant geometrical and psychological figure in Bourke's account
is the "little circle." It recurs again and again in Southwestern encounters.
The circle functions as both locus and moment of magical, spiritual sharing
and transfer of knowledge, set apart from historical conditionality, preciously
preserved by the participants in memory, diary, and published account. In
the more familiar forms of American culture which derive in various ways
from Indian models—the camping circles of geologists or archeologists, the
Boy and Girl Scouts—a blazing campfire is usually the center of the hushed
storytelling. But in the specifically Anglo-Pueblo context it was the secrecy
of the kiva which played the central imaginative role. As seen in Metcalf's
illustration, "Around the Council Fire," which graced the title page of Baxter's
first major popular article on the Southwest, "The Father of the Pueblos"
(1882a), the circle, defined by the fire within and the darkness without and
composed by strong black-white contrasts in the engraving, establishes a series of linked physical and social distinctions: inside/outside, light/darkness,
warmth/cold, inclusion/exclusion, privileged information/general ignorance,
fraternal membership/individual isolation.

Beginning with Cushing's generation, the romantic fascination with the
pueblos, prototypically Zuni, revolved closely around the contrast between
the apparent openness of daily sociability and the secret, regulatory darkness

"Around the Council Fire." Illustration by Willard L. Metcalf for Sylvester Baxter, "The Father of the Pueblos," *Harper's New Monthly Magazine,* 1882.

of the kiva and its associated priestly orders, with their arcane language and exclusive knowledge. In letters to Smithsonian superiors and in some publications, Cushing consciously constructed his ethnographic experience as movement from sunlight to shadow, from exterior to interior—a process of increasingly deep advance/admission into the dark secretive world of Pueblo language and religion. For him, for Matilda Stevenson, for virtually all early Southwestern ethnographers, the ultimate goal became access to the kiva or its equivalent: "Got into the medicine-lodge and saw things I never dreamt of," Washington Matthews typically wrote to Cushing, announcing his discovery of Navajo sand-painting in 1884 (FHCP: 11/4/1884).

The kiva/campfire also offered a central configuration for the circle of knowledge transfer in the Anglo-Pueblo confrontation. As a total phenomenon and in its specific moments and places, the tour was a transfer, from Indian to Anglo, of privileged information, spiritual energy, historical viability, and stewardship. The form in which the act of knowledge transfer usually occurred was the circle. The locus varied widely: churches, theaters, clubs, schools, private homes, a park or a beach. At the moment of knowledge/ energy transfer, those New England spaces took on special status, momentarily transformed to sacred space by the acts: dance, oratory, song, storytelling. If the Zuni was passing from history to theater, the sacred circle was the form of change.

By historical coincidence, the seance–a familiar and powerful form of spiritual communication in contemporary New England circles–seemed to confirm the sense of connection between the circle, spirituality, and knowledge. Willard Metcalf, for example, had grown up in a family deeply influenced by various strands of "spiritism." "Spiritualism suited the artist [Metcalf] for its simple promise of Summerland, where the beauty and serenity of this world was to be repeated in a heightened form" (deVeer & Boyle 1987:18). And for Metcalf, Zuni pueblo was, as it was also for artist William R. Leigh a generation later, "more like a waking dream than reality" (McLuhan 1985:168). Whatever the individual variants of spiritualism, Cushing and Baxter lost no opportunity in attractively suggesting the kinship of spirit and praxis between Zuni and Beacon Street:

> The Zunis have their circles, their mediums, their communications from the spirit world, their materializations–precisely like those of the spiritists of civilized life. Their seances are often so absorbing that they are kept up all night. (BH 6/16/1881)

In an interview with the *Boston Daily Advertiser* during the eastern trip, Cushing went on at greater length:

> In religion the Zuni Indians are Spiritualists, and believe in materialization; they believe that the spirits of their departed friends return to them, and that they hold communication with them; this is the religion of the common people; they are also pantheists, believing that animals, plants, everything, in fact, in nature, has a special god; this is the religion of the select; they believe in one god, "the ruler of the roads of life," as they term him; he is the god of the high priests. The common people pray to the one god. They are very scrupulous in their religious observance, have their special day for one prayer and keep their religious festivals scrupulously. (3/23/1882)

Parlor seance or kiva council, throughout the eastern trip the Anglo-Zuni circle repeatedly reconstituted and re-formed itself in different shapes and contexts: the intimate circle became in effect the social geometry of the Zunis' trip. Two events illustrate the point.

On Thursday evening, March 23, a few days after their arrival in Boston, Cushing and the Zunis accepted an invitation to perform at Wellesley College chapel before an audience of several hundred young women. After Cushing gave the standard account of deprivation and acceptance at the pueblo, the Indians performed dances. There followed an informal reception amidst the tropical greenery of the college "Centre." According to the *Boston Herald* it was a gay time:

> The chiefs listened to the piano playing and singing of some of the young ladies, who had a fine time of it in endeavoring to teach one of the caciques the chorus words of the "Little Brown Jug." The Indians examined with curious wonder

"The Reception." Illustration by Willard L. Metcalf for Sylvester Baxter, "An Aboriginal Pilgrimage," *Century Magazine*, 1882.

the pictures, statuary and everything they saw, and, altogether, they spent a very happy evening, the girls on their part, being most confidingly friendly, and taking a reciprocal interest in everything the chiefs did. (3/24/1882)

The fascination was mutual. While the Zunis constantly exclaimed "E-lu!" [enchantingly beautiful], the women found them "so handsome that they reminded us of Cooper's heroes" (Baxter 1882b:531; *Woman's Home Companion* n.d.). Lucia Grieve, class of 1883, confided to her diary some doubts about Cushing's character—"I don't altogether like the way he has done all this [at Zuni]; it shows sharpness, but does not seem very honorable"—but she enjoyed the Indian show:

They dress well, are an agricultural people, and possess a fine literature and an extremely complicated religion. They danced for us, one of their religious dances, with the bow. They amused the girls immensely, at the Reception, so I heard. (LG: 3/25/1882)

Metcalf's portrayal of the Wellesley reception shows two Zunis surrounded and softened by fronds of greenery and curious, fan-wielding young ladies. Encircled and enchanted, the Indian Other has been tamed and domesticated by the standing, sitting, kneeling females. The anonymous illustrator of Fred Ober's "How a White Man Became the War Chief of the Zunis" (1882) caught

"Decorative." From Fred Ober, "How a White Man Became the War Chief of the Zunis," *Wide Awake*, 1882.

a moment of significant cross-dressing and sublimated sexual exchange be-tween the exotic/erotic in a pose entitled, with deceptive simplicity, "Decora-tive": Nanahe, the Zuni-adopted Hopi, is admired as he stands staunchly with a college woman's fan in the place of his eagle's feather in the headband. "Probably accepting cups of tea from pale-faced squaws was as new to them as handing the tea to dusky braves was to us," recalled the writer for *Woman's Home Companion*. But more than tea was being exchanged in this ceremony: the framing and taming of aboriginal energies, the transfer of autonomous cultural powers was, moment by moment, historically and imaginatively tran-spiring in the Anglo-Zuni circles.

A week later, on the evening of March 29, the Paint and Clay Club of Boston, a private men's artistic and literary group to which Baxter and Met-calf belonged, hosted the visitors. "It was," Baxter reported, "a most picturesque evening, and the scene was one to delight both civilized and barbarous eyes" (1882b:530). The Indians danced, sang, and, through Cushing, supplied vocabulary and related folk-tales until 1:30 in the morning (EEHP: Diary 3/29/1882). "The striking faces and brilliant native costumes of the Indians . . . captivated the artists' eyes, and sketchbooks and pencils were in use all the evening":

> Palo-wah-ti-wah appeared to be the favorite on account of his grim and leonine physiognomy, and at one time in the evening six pencils were busy in noting the lines of his imperturbable countenance. Later, the scene was changed, and the Indians gave exhibition of their singing and dancing. This was returned in kind by the hosts of the evening, so far as the singing was concerned. Several songs of a popular cast were sung by the members with a piano accompaniment, and in the choral part one of the Indians, Na-Na-He, who had previously in N[ew] M[exico] caught the notes through his quick ear, was able to join. No stage effect could exceed in a comic effect and at the same time sympathetic way the vocal and pantomimic demonstration of Na-na-he and Mr. F[rank] D. Millet, who stood face to face beside the piano singing with all the others:
>
> > Hah, ha, hah, you and me,
> > Little brown jug, don't I love thee?
> >
> > (Baxter 1882b:530)

Edward Everett Hale and Julian Olin, who were among those attending and recording the evening, twenty years later still treasured the memory of "that curious night at the Paint and Clay Club" (EEHP: EH/JO 5/4/04). Ober told readers of *Wide Awake* that the Indians "relaxed their dignity and showed themselves the jolly, cheerful fellows they really were." He even suggested that if a motion had been made to make the entire Paint and Clay Club members of the Zuni tribe, it would have carried unanimously (Ober 1882:386).

Accounts of the Paint and Clay Club and other affairs frequently employ theatrical terms—"scene," "effects"—and present events as occurring in circles, or circles within circles, of observers. The drawings of the Paint and Clay evenings by W. L. Taylor, which illustrated Baxter's account in *Century Magazine*, place Cushing and the Indians prominently in a circle of serious, attentive artist/writers. The circle encloses and defines a process in which deep, integrated, cultural knowledge was presumed to be changing form and changing hands: from unwritten, oral tradition to written poetry/narrative, and from Native American priests to secular Anglo artists and writers. Further, it is presented to the public as staged performance. In other words, the Paint and Clay Club evenings were microcosmic moments in an early stage of the aesthetic claiming of the Southwest. It was the transfer of stewardship of Southwestern history and landscape from Native American "caciques" to Anglo aesthetes—from one priestly brotherhood to another—in a time barely prior to mediation by the marketplace. In this transfer of other-worldly knowledge,

"At the Paint and Clay Club." From Fred Ober, "How a White Man Became the War Chief of the Zunis," *Wide Awake*, 1882.

Cushing played diverse roles: showman and shaman, interpreter and familiar, broker and medium. Visually and verbally, he appeared most often seated in the circle of Zuni chiefs, listening and transferring in his own voice the wisdom of the "ancient talks."

Ants in the Whirlwind: History and Pageantry at Old South

Edward Everett Hale, Congregationalist minister of Old South Church, author of *The Man Without a Country*, and by 1882 arguably America's best-known preacher of optimism and uplift, provided the financial backing for Cushing's trip to Boston. At first glance surprising—given Hale's generally low opinion of American "savages" as expressed in various essays and sermons —his support and interest derived ultimately from the minister's sense of American national purpose, a divine plan that seemed to him manifested daily and in countless unexpected ways. For Hale, the Zuni visit was a single act in a long pageant, and he was pleased to play his part in the redemptive transfer of the continent from savage and Catholic hands to the stewardship of civilized Protestantism. Like Baxter and Metcalf, the minister of Old South was a genealogical and spiritual descendant of the Massachusetts migration, and it was as a genial, latter-day Puritan that he accepted Cushing's Indians into his homeland and his home.

As a young man in the 1840s, Hale read for the near-blind William H. Prescott and dreamed of following that great historian's path in presenting the pageantry and manifest purposes of New World history. Hale's own path took other turns, however: to Harvard, newspaper work, the ministry, civic affairs, and the aphoristic literature of uplift (Adams 1977; Holloway 1956). After a decade in the pulpit in Worcester, in 1856 Hale came home to Boston and the South Congregational Church. There he remained, revered as a guardian of American morals and "dean of literary Boston" until well into the twentieth century (Winslow 1902:31–39).

In the late 1870s, as he approached sixty and the end of active preaching, Hale returned to interests of his youth: the history of New Spain and the conquest of Mexico and the Southwest. He chose an opportune time. With the distractions of the Civil War and Southern Reconstruction seemingly behind the reunified nation, the course of commercial empire pointed once again in a southwesterly direction, to Arizona Territory and across the Mexican border (cf. Bishop 1883). "We have in the history of Arizona, a series of questions of the first interest and importance," Hale told an audience in 1878. Silver, the railroad, and firm democratic government, he predicted, would soon release the enormous wealth of the Southwest to national economic purposes. Just as the Puritans had seen future lessons foreshadowed in past deeds, the history of Arizona drew its significance from future prospects. The promised prominence thus justified immediate attention to historical and anthropological investigations: "Gentlemen who have a few weeks of leisure, may well remember that in a fort-night a traveller may now go from Worcester and see the fires of the Aztecs still burning." But, cautioned the minister, only visits by men of intelligence and training were called for; one should not forget "the value, in such affairs, of that personal presence which, indeed, rules the world" (Hale 1878:23–24, 31–33). Southwest knowledge should not be built on hearsay.

Middle child in a large and comfortable family—"warmly sandwiched between six brothers and sisters" (Winslow 1902:34) — Hale instinctively found the unobjectionable middle place, from his Harvard class rank to a genial patriotism. Throughout a long life he consequently enjoyed a blissful self-assurance where his own career or that of his country was concerned. He expressed few second thoughts about either. The destiny of America, he lectured in 1892, had required an empty, clean landscape for the new experiment in human society. Here America would teach new lessons "as to the manufacture of men and women"; to do so "it was necessary rather that there should be an empty land, than a land struggling in the shackles of any half-civilization [i.e., Aztec or Inca]. This empty land was found in North America." In Hale's mental geography the regions northward and eastward of Arizona Territory had presented only moral emptiness:

> When Coronado left the Seven Cities in 1541, he and his troop of brave cavaliers rode east for months, till they struck either the Missouri or the Mississippi ... and they returned to the point from which they started without having seen a single human being except themselves. The desolation of those empty plains and prairies was a terror to them. Here was the opportunity, then, for trying the experiments of the new Christian order. (1900b:159–60)

Not surprisingly, Hale saw most Native Americans in terms of the myths of his childhood: "at their best, dirty, stupid, and mistreated; at their worst, more often, they were cruel and bloodthirsty" (Adams 1977:68). In his later years he found it more convenient simply to depopulate most of the continent from the outset. For Hale the moral meaning of America began only with European settlement: "Man gains no such control of the world, and the world does not prove fit for man, unless he has found out that he is akin to God and can enter into His work. There is no such victory to the savage, who is afraid of God" (Hale 1900a:357).

In such terms Hale's Congregationalism reaffirmed the Puritans' teleology, which even before the Civil War had assumed a secular, nationalistic, and racialist cast. And yet, within the American nation/congregation there were clear signs of declension and disintegration: loss of poetic and aesthetic sensitivity, of pride in work and respect for social position, of physical stamina and purity of stock, of family cohesion. Hale's sermons never reached the intensity of the early Puritan warnings, but they were nonetheless genial jeremiads, Gilded Age exhortations to a more strenuous life and to social reconstruction.

In this crusade Hale found willing lay help among the wealthy parishioners of South Congregational Church, notably Julia Ward Howe and Mary Hemenway. Hemenway's support for the restoration of Old South Church, her enthusiasm for physical education and home economics, and her interest in Cushing's work in Zuni ethnography and archeology were separate ele-

ments in a single concern for social reform and uplift (McChesney n.d.; Mc-
Chesney & Hinsley 1984). Continuity, tradition, cultural integration: these,
so apparently lacking in industrial America, the Zunis might proffer to their
hosts: "What was preserved in Zuni myths, their content, was a system of
belief and religious instruction which formed the basis for the integration of
Zuni society and culture. At least, this was Cushing's argument, and it was
this particular portrayal of Zuni society and culture, as well as the prevalent
and (still) popular belief that in the pueblo societies of the Southwestern
United States lay the remnants of the indigenous ancient American civilization, which captured the heart and mind of Mary Hemenway" (McChesney
n.d.:8)—and of her minister.

The civic concern of Hale, Hemenway, and the Boston reformer/philan-
thropists was merely one instance of a broader antimodernist dynamic in
American culture in the decades surrounding the turn of the century (Lears
1981:60–96). For Hale, who spent his entire life instructing local and national
congregations, it was precisely the obstacles to communicating traditions and
teachings which so threatened social cohesion and probably attracted him
to Cushing's pueblo. The suasive power of rhetoric seemed so important at
one point that Hale seriously suggested teaching Indian language and rhetorical skills in public schools—a proposal that earned him public ridicule (EEHP:
newspaper clipping n.d.).

Hale probably first heard of Cushing's planned trip east from Sylvester Baxter in late 1881; by January he was holding regular "Indian meetings" at the
South Congregational Church to raise money for it (EEHP: 1882 Journal).
"It is edifying for me to see how all the world is excited about them now,
when I found it hard to make people contribute $200 to pay their expenses
hither," he later wrote with some annoyance. During the tour the Indians
danced twice at Old South Church before huge crowds, but the high point
for Hale occurred on Friday, March 24, when they came for lunch at his home.
Hale served them "prairie hens,—which they ought to like—and oysters and
frozen pudding and cake." Cushing and the Indians immediately charmed
Hale: "We have fallen in love with them. Cushing is a modest, simple gentleman; the chiefs remind you of the tenderness of Montezuma." "There is nothing of the N[orth] A[merican] Indian about them,—but the gentleness and
high-breeding of Mexicans," Hale reported (EEHP: EEH/Emily Hale 3/24/
1882). Despite the Zunis' tardy arrival for lunch, the minister found the day
memorable:

Had entertaining afternoon. The Zunis sang, & danced, for our pleasure, &
we gave them shells, beads, etc., for theirs, not to mention ice-cream, etc., of
wh[ich] it was almost their first experience. They are extremely gentle & kindly,
and take to our ways with wonderful quickness. Our rooms were full with in-

vited guests who came after lunch. At 5:30 to Prang's with the Indian party. Evening to entertainment of our Sunday School at Church.*
*I told Zuni story of ants and whirlwind. (EEHP: Journal 24 March 1882)

In the final stanzas of Longfellow's *Hiawatha*, the aging chief admonishes his people not to resist the inevitable dominion of the White Man but to accept graciously and stoically their own supplantation. Hiawatha then paddles off into the sunset to die. It is not difficult to see that Henry Wadsworth Longfellow's romanticization of Schoolcraft's *Algic Researches* established a wishful and comforting scenario of peaceful succession for his own people. The unpleasantness of Mystic Fort now long past, proprietorship of the land would henceforth come about with Indian acquiescence. Hale's asterisked appropriation of the Zunis' ants and whirlwind to the sacred spaces of Old South thus made necessary sense in the New England pageant of succession. Having appropriately lost the land, the Indians, like the Aztecs and Spanish before them, now had one final gesture: to exit gracefully. This Hale was willing, even anxious to assist—with frozen pudding and cake.

Longfellow, after a long and luminous life, died peacefully in his house in Cambridge on Thursday, March 23, while the Zunis were dancing at Wellesley. Shortly thereafter the Reverend Mr. Hale told his Sunday school class about the Zunis' ants and whirlwind. The transfer of knowledge and stewardship was occurring far more subtly and fitfully than either Longfellow or Chief Hiawatha had imagined. Then on Sunday, reassuming the authority of the pulpit, Hale preached to his assemblage about the "Lord of Bethesda" and memorialized the author of "Hiawatha." Cushing and the Zunis were sitting in the Congregationalist pews, listening to the minister (EEHP: Diary 26 March 1882).

Magic People, Sacred Space

John Fiske, Harvard professor and Brahmin historian, was both a close follower and supporter of Cushing's work and an astute critic of his own society. In February 1882, as Cushing was departing from Zuni pueblo, Fiske attempted to explain in *Harper's* the fascination of his generation with the early French and Spanish explorers. Modern knowledge of the globe no longer permitted thought of enchanted ground, he explained:

> Beyond the dark and perilous sea we no longer look for an El Dorado, since maps and gazetteers have taught us to expect nothing better than the beautiful but cruel, the romantic but humdrum, world with which daily experience has already made us sufficiently well acquainted. In this respect the present age,

compared with the sixteenth century, is like mature manhood compared with youth. The bright visions have fled, and naught but the sober realities of life remain. (Fiske 1882:438)

Fiske's lament, with its hint of the loss of enchantment that Max Weber would develop more systematically a few years later into a critique of industrial society, soon became part of the standard case against a neurasthenic overcivilization which had outgrown its youth. In the opening paragraph of *The Ghost Dance Religion* (1896) James Mooney wrote of sinking down, "tired in body and sick at heart, with strength and courage gone," as individuals and as nations, to dream of the lost Arcadia of youth. Mooney was hardly alone in establishing equivalences between dawn, individual/national youth, illusions, and religious enchantment. The deeply felt need for authentic religious experience and the accompanying sacralization of space emerged in telling ways during the Zuni public appearances in Boston.

After a week of grey mist, Tuesday, March 28, 1882, dawned coldly and clearly over Boston harbor. At two in the afternoon a carriage pulled up to Eastern wharf, where a small crowd of spectators had assembled to see Cushing and the five Indians step from the carriage and onto the steamer *J. Putnam Bradlee*. As the steamer left its moorings for the three-mile trip out to Deer Island, Cushing and the Zunis retired to the pilot house to pray "fervently and ceaselessly" (*BH* 3/29/1882). On deck below mingled more than a hundred accompanying notables: Boston's Mayor Green and several city aldermen; officers of Harvard University, Boston University, and Massachusetts Institute of Technology; Professors Eben Horsford, Edward S. Morse, and Frederick W. Putnam; H. L. Cargill, New England agent of the Atcheson, Topeka & Santa Fe Railway; the Reverend Phillips Brooks; journalists from Boston and New York newspapers, *Century Magazine* and some weeklies; and numerous "civic dames and learned ladies." Baxter was on deck; Metcalf was sketching the group in the pilot house.

On arrival at the easternmost point of Deer Island, the Indians and the anthropologist entered a tent, where they put on ornaments and badges of rank. Cushing emerged: "He had on his head a tall bear-skin helmet, with two eagle plumes affixed on the right side – the side of the strong arm. Across his shoulder was the badge of membership of the Order of the Bow. This badge consisted of deer thongs slung over the shoulder and across the chest, and upon it were affixed curious looking flint arrow heads. To it was attached, over the region of the heart, a bunch of the sacred plumes of membership of the same order, made of the strong feathers of the duck, to the base of which was tied a stick with an arrow point upon it, representing lightning" (*BH* 3/29/1882). The others were similarly bedecked.

"At 'The Ocean of Sunrise.'" From Fred Ober, "How a White Man Became the War Chief of the Zunis," *Wide Awake*, 1882.

The ceremonies then began at the seaside, as reported by the *Boston Herald*:

The chiefs, being thus elaborately gotten up, sallied forth and walked down the beach to the edge of the water, where one of them was considerably surprised when an incoming wave suddenly washed over his feet, but without causing him to retreat. The chiefs immediately commenced muttering their prayers and throwing handfuls of prayer-flour onto the water. . . . The chiefs seated themselves on pieces of rock close together, and sang and prayed to the gods of the North, the West, the South, the East, the skies and the lower regions of the world. At the cessation of every prayer the prayer-flour was scattered onto the water. The chiefs also pulled out their feathered prayer-sticks and prayed over them. This lasted about 25 minutes, but in the mean time the tide was rising, and, as it rose, it caused many laughable disasters . . . among the adventurous ones who had taken up positions of peril on the pieces of stone and boulders. Certain enterprising reporters and, also, photographers, who were in attendance with their "instantaneous" apparatus, had innumerable slips off the wet stones into the water, and much confusion ensued.

The tide still rising, Mr. Cushing wished the chiefs to move away, but they told him to remain firm, because the rising of the waters was the manifestation of the satisfaction of the gods, and the ocean was coming to be taken up in reply to their prayers. Finally, the chiefs were persuaded to remove back to the beach, where a wide semicircle of spectators was formed, an open space being kept by a cordon of officers. The next stage of the ceremony was then gone through, consisting of the chiefs sitting on their haunches close together round a sacred painted tray, into which they placed the feathered sticks. Having prayed to the gods of the ocean and to the gods of their ancestors, the chiefs went through the ceremony of the "prayer-smoke." They lit sacred cigarettes, made of cane tubes, moistened with ocean water, and filled with tobacco made and prayed over by the priests of the sun in Zuni.

After some minutes smoke was blown upon the plumes and into them, and then the chiefs rose and threw them into the water. Two of the chiefs, who had taken off their leggings, moccasins and stockings, then waded knee deep into the sea and emptied out from bags quantities of meal, representing the vegetable foods of Zuni, which the spectators imagined to be another kind of prayer flour. This was intended as a sacrifice to the gods of the ocean, as were also the prayer sticks, and in gratitude for the favor shown to them in allowing them to come to that spot. . . .

The auspicious moment had now arrived, and the high priest waved a sacred gourd, which was one of the vessels in which the water was first brought from the gulf of Mexico, to the four quarters of the globe and dipped into the water. Another chief dipped the points of two pieces of hard wood into the water, after which he retained one himself and gave the second to Mr. Cushing. To these pieces of wood were attached long pieces of string, by which they were whirled around, making a "whizzing" noise in so doing. The high priest took the gourd of water in his arms, while another chief carried two vases, presented to the Indians in Boston, also filled with salt water. A solemn procession was then made to the tent, Mr. Cushing and the Zuni whirling their "whizzers" round as they went. On arriving in the tent, the chiefs formed in a row with their faces pointing to the west toward the setting sun, that being the direction in which they were to return to Zuni, bearing with them the sacred water. A few prayers were said, and the rite was then ended, having occupied 43 minutes. (3/29/1882)

In contrast to the *Herald*'s straightforward and rather solemn coverage, the *Boston Daily Advertiser* saw the Deer Island events as a rather lighthearted social outing. In the wheelhouse the Zunis "laughed, chatted, and smoked jovially" as they exchanged remarks about passing steamers and sailboats. As they picked their way from rock to rock in reaching the easternmost point of the island, the crowd followed in a "promiscuous rush," only a few minutes later to retreat pell-mell from the rising tide. Had the ceremony on the beach lasted ten minutes longer, added the paper, "they would have been waist-deep in the cold, sacred sea." By the end of the ceremonies, as it turned out, the surrounding onlookers were "cold and shaking" (BDA 3/29/1882).

Similar contrasts of tone and attitude in public reportage were evident throughout the Zuni trip. The New York Tribune had ridiculed a brief Zuni ceremony in Rock Creek Park on a rainy day in Washington earlier in the month—"three real pagans in their blankets and one counterfeit pagan in the garb of civilization"—and had editorialized that while "worshipping at ant-holes is comparatively harmless," the Indians' excessive smoking was not (NYT 3/6/1882). Two days later, though, the newspaper seriously questioned the purposes of Cushing's work and its effect on his charges: "And yet how can we hope that no harm will come from such an exposition of the effect of civilization upon the minds of these people, brought for the first time into intimate contact with its highest attainments and best results?" (3/8/1882).

Such alternations of sobriety and attempted humor served to create an ironic distance for observers who were (as on Deer Island) literally and figuratively unsure of their footing—that is, of their own aesthetic and psychological positions. At Rock Creek Park, on Deer Island—indeed, all along their itinerary but markedly at places of water—the Zunis engaged in sacralization of place. They were creating sacred spaces, attributing powers to the landscape and its elements—river, beach, and ocean wave. In Euro-American cultures this had been a function long reserved almost entirely to artists. As John Fiske perceived at the time, "all thought of enchanted ground" had long since been crowded out of civilized expectations, but obviously not out of consciousness or desire. Plymouth Rock (originally on the Zuni itinerary) and Old South Church stood as testament to the need for historically sacred ground as charting points to present and future. "Beyond the dark and perilous sea we no longer look for an El Dorado," lamented Fiske, but the Zunis had religiously travelled 2,500 miles for a glimpse and a vaseful of the "Ocean of the Sunrise." The ethnographic field literally had come to the metropolis, and the sacred little circle on the beach found itself surrounded by a larger circle of secular, puzzled well-wishers.

In the evening the locus of performance returned to more familiar ground for the Bostonians: the theater. Here, in the real theatrical space, the Indians became both observers and observed. Accompanied by A. W. Drake of Century Magazine, they attended a performance of The World at the Boston Theater. Promotional advertising for the play highlighted the scenery and effects more than the actors: "The raft tableau is probably the finest ever given in America, if, indeed, it has ever been rivalled anywhere. The entire depth and width of the great stage is seen as the mighty deep, with the rescuing ship approaching by the light of the rising sun. This is emphatically the most effective water scene ever witnessed" (BH 3/26/1882). The packed house greeted the expected Zunis with applause; they acknowledged it by rising from their orchestra seats and shaking their war clubs. It was reported that "they became very excited during the escape from the lunatic asylum" (ibid.), recognized the ocean, and were overcome by the raft scene and the appearance of the sun. When the final curtain fell they impatiently and repeatedly signalled for it to rise again. Afterwards they were taken backstage to examine the set and the curtain mechanism. The theater crowd loved both shows, according to the *Boston Herald* and the *Boston Daily Advertiser* (3/29/1882).

The World performance actually occurred during the Zunis' second evening at the theater. The preceding Friday the Indians had been "astounded at the 'sacred magic' of the minstrels" at Globe Theater (BH 3/25/1882), when Mayor Green had arranged, advertised, and accompanied the Indians' appearance. On that occasion, the program playbill featured (among many acts) "Milt G. Barlow in his celebrated and life-like characteristics of aged colored men," "The colored masquerade, introducing genteel, acrobatic and plantation songs and dances," "Schoolcraft and Coes, in their own and original Ethiopian specialties," and "The Great American Jockey Clog, artistically arranged by those Popular Comedians, Messrs. Primrose and West" (BH 3/29/1882). The theater was crammed with Bostonians anxious to register Pueblo reactions to blackface clowning. They were not disappointed. As soon as they took their seats in the box overhanging the right side of the stage, the Zunis at once became the object of gags and wordplay by the minstrels.

> The corner man, George Wilson, created roars of laughter by the antics and signs he personally addressed to the chiefs, who were only a few feet from him, and who became excitedly responsive. The Zunis were extravagant in their manifestations of pleasure, and at times perfectly shrieked out with delight, giving vent to their feelings by strange cries very much resembling the short barkings of a dog. (BH 3/25/1882)

According to the *Daily Advertiser*:

> They watched the varying performances with wondering eyes, and in their eagerness frequently leaned far out over the railing . . . gave expression to their astonishment and delight in excited gestures and in peculiar, loud, shrill yells, much to the amusement of the actors and audience. (BDA 3/25/1882)

After a short time, however, the Indians became noticeably quiet, a change they later explained as the result of new awareness. At first, Naiiutchi said, "we thought it was the play of clowns, but we saw afterwards that it was the action of a great magic people, and I then told my children and brothers that we must look at it with dignity, and . . . we did not call out any more" (*BDA* 3/25/82). At this point the chiefs made motions that were frequently commented upon throughout their trip—reaching their hands toward the stage and drawing to themselves the influence of the "magic men." "They [the minstrels] know many things, they understand the magic of the voice and body. . . . When we found they were possessed of a knowledge of other things than funny ones, we became grave and only wished to see their actions and draw their breath from them" (*BDA* 3/25/82; cf. Baxter 1882b:532).

The striking aspect of the minstrel evening was the interplay of multiple performance-audience relations. Mayor Green and other notables probably came simply to see and be seen; the Zunis came to see and became a part of the performance. The minstrels/clowns/actors enhanced their program with Zuni-audience repartee. The theater audience enjoyed a rare spectacle: exotic Indians visibly reacting—in accordance with cultural experiences that were incomprehensible to the metropolitan audience—to white men in blackface. Further complicating the triangulated relations (blackface actors, Indian chiefs, white audience), the journalists covering the evening transmitted the entire affair, including audience amusement, to yet another audience, the reading public. The actors on stage, the Zunis, and the theater audience all became actors in a larger public performance.

If the Deer Island rituals revealed Boston's uncertainty in the face of serious ritual and religious fervor, the return to theatrical space may have offered reassurance and a resolution of sorts. The metropolitan theater has for centuries served as a critical locus of safe and socially approved interaction with exotic Others (Foreman 1934). Here the New Englanders could watch themselves watch the Indians and thereby return the focus to their own accomplishments and tolerance. When the Zunis misinterpreted the minstrel stage as sacred space, they and their religious intents returned from active history to theater—a form of live diorama.

The Bow Priest and the Fetishes of Industrial Power

On Friday, March 31, 1882, Cushing's party and the Reverend Mr. Hale left Boston for Worcester, arriving at Union Station at noon. Although two hours late, they were greeted by a crowd of 600, including many children who followed them throughout the afternoon. They toured the high school, where Cushing and the Indians performed their now well-rehearsed songs and dances and Cushing interpreted a brief Zuni speech as follows:

My children: the day has come, when, most unexpectedly to me, I have come to the Eastern country, for the first time, and I look upon you while you look upon me. I am happy to look upon the American people, for they smile on us, which shows the goodness of their hearts. We regard the Americans as great gods,—as we do the sun. They are like our animal gods. However wonderful and precious they are, they show us by their kind looks that they have room for us in their hearts. Today we grasp your hands and hearts. (*WDG* 4/1/1882)

The Zuni speech again brings to the fore Cushing's central role as interpreter, broker, anthropologist, and showman, his unique function in shaping impressions in both directions, and the difficulty that this multiple positioning presents in understanding the Zunis' experience. It was, and still is, impossible to circumvent Cushing. Nowhere was his interpretive role more obvious and determinative than in the day trip to industrial Worcester and its sacred spaces: American factories. Here, through Cushing, the reciprocal balance shifted clearly to the industrialists, and ambivalence gave way to a celebration of industrial capitalism.

Between the severe depressions of 1873–77 and 1893–97, the small mill-towns of America were transformed into the manufacturing metropolises of the Gilded Age (Gutman 1976:3–78; 234–59). By 1886, as a response to government and employer repression, American labor activity had reached unprecedented strength (Akerman & Norman 1983:236). Worcester was typical of the growing manufacturing centers of the Northeast in its "diversified industrial base, a rapid growth rate, and a large immigrant population" (Rosenzweig 1987:215).

Within the old-stock Worcester elite, Stephen Salisbury II and Stephen Salisbury III, father and son, enjoyed a central position. With his funds invested securely in real estate and in Washburn & Moen, the largest wire manufacturer in the United States in 1880 (Akerman & Norman 1983:239), the elder Salisbury was able to serve many years as President of the American Antiquarian Society and trustee/treasurer of the Peabody Museum of Archaeology and Ethnology at Harvard—responsibilities which Stephen III assumed after the father's death in 1884. Stephen the younger inherited his father's antiquarian curiosities, but gave special attention to Yucatan; as a result, the Antiquarian Society supported such explorers as Augustus Le Plongeon, Louis H. Aymé, and Edward H. Thompson. By 1882 the Antiquarian Society on Salisbury Street owned one of the few collections of Mayan artifacts in North America.

Responding to Hale's appeal for funds in January 1882, the elder Salisbury confessed to having little interest in Southwestern ethnography and suggested that money would be better spent on Cushing in New Mexico than in New England. His own current obsession (fired by Thompson and LePlongeon) was the lost island of Atlantis, presumably remote from Zuni pueblo; still, he contributed $50, and a Zuni side-trip to industrial Worcester and the rooms of Antiquarian Hall was agreed to (EEHP: SS/EEH 1/1882). Perhaps the Indians would recognize ancestral similarities in the Mexican antiquities.

After lunch at Worcester's Bay State House, Hale left the party to return to Boston. According to the *Worcester Daily Gazette*, which covered the day assiduously, "their parting with him was very affecting. They embraced and kissed him and made speeches at him full of good wishes" (*WDG* 4/1/1882). The Indians then moved to Antiquarian Hall, where they were greeted by President Salisbury and were photographed, and proceeded to examine photographs, casts, and artifacts from Palenque, Uxmal, Chichen Itza, and other sites.

After Salisbury's brief opening speech, one of the Indians answered— necessarily, of course, through Cushing, sole interpreter and thus the mediate source of all Zuni words and thoughts as experienced by onlookers and readers. The Zunis examined the Society's artifact collection. Through Cushing they claimed to see analogues or versions of their own lifeways: terraced houses, animal figures, pottery whistles and rattles, fiber shoes and cotton garments. What were the Indians really seeing, thinking, and saying? We cannot know. But they must have been impressed, for "in taking leave of Mr. Salisbury each [Zuni] kissed his hand, and one kissed his cane with great reverence" (*WDG* 4/1/1882).

Having kissed the hand of the capitalist/philanthropist, the Indians toured the Worcester factory system. In each place they observed unimagined and mysterious processes, were overwhelmed by the experiences, exclaimed their admiration and delight, and were rewarded with product samples to take back to the pueblo—souvenir fetishes of magical industrial power. At Washburn & Moen's wire factory they were told of "the magnitude of the business" and were shown "one ledger in which all the business of the establishment is consolidated, to which the Chief answered: 'our ears are being taken from us by your figures.' They have never before seen anything of the power of the industrial machinery, and were amazed at everything shown them." They wondered at a hydraulic elevator and saved bits of snipped iron. Everything, according to the newspaper, was wonderful to them: "In passing about the premises amid piles upon piles of wire in the process of manufacture, one said: 'There is enough blue metal throughout here to make the giant cob-web which stretched all over the world,' alluding to one of their own fairy legends [K'yan'asdebi, or Water-strider]" (*WDG* 4/1/1882).

The power of industrial machinery to desensitize and dehumanize found ironic expression in Cushing's interpretation of the Zuni visitors' reactions. "What is the use of seeing more; what we have seen has taken out our eyes," they reportedly exclaimed: "But when they saw the giant rolling mill which takes inch bars of iron and draws them to a small wire at the rate of half a mile a minute, they were wild with wonder, calling to each other and jumping about in ecstasy of astonishment" (*WDG* 4/1/1882).

Zuni reactions, as reported, could be publicly received only as childish and ignorant. The tour was not one of education but of diminution, and the Indian Others returned to Moen & Washburn's business office, business cards stuck foolishly in their headbands, to concede the might of American technological and organizational power:

> In bidding farewell the head chief said:—"My *Father*: Thanks. This day through your will we have seen your many works, wonderful, and our hearts have been turned with gladness toward you, and we thank you, and wish the light of the gods to always meet you in return."
>
> Another said:—"My *Father*: this day through your will we have seen a tribe of workers, and a world of works, and we thank you that you have made our hearts glad and put into our minds that which we will take away today to our country, and tell our children, and astonish them with wonder for many days."
>
> ... Mr. Washburn responded to the "talks" of the Indians, telling them that what they had seen had, through industry, enterprise, and sound judgment, grown up in a single half century from an establishment which made four hundred pounds of wire a day to one making 300,000 pounds, and employing 3,000 men, representing with their families a community of 15,000 people. (*WDG* 4/1/1882)

At Witherby, Rugg and Richardson's wood-working shop the Zunis were amazed at the rapidity of the planes and saws. At Whitcomb and Co. envelope factory they admired the cutting, folding, gumming, and counting machines and received bunches of envelopes. At J. H. and G. M. Walker's boot factory the pegging and crimping machines left them groping for words: "It is thus that the Americans jest with the gods" and "Alas, my heart," the reporter overheard (through Cushing). At Crompton Loom Works they took turns holding the beam of a loom, following the shuttle: "they ran from one loom to another like children," scarcely willing to believe that the samples they held had come from such contraptions. At the end of the day, departing from industrial Worcester, "they left the city carefully treasuring the specimens of manufactured goods gathered during the afternoon and profoundly impressed with the wonderful power of organized industry as they had witnessed it for the first time." They had seen, the *Gazette* boasted, "Worcester in its shirt sleeves" (4/1/1882).

The sacred rituals of the American factory system had indeed overwhelmed the Indians, as its products already had taken over and secularized so much of their sacred space. Washburn & Moen was in 1882 the largest manufacturer of barbed wire, the company's main product and the American invention that since 1874 had drastically changed the physiographic and economic face of the continent (Jackson 1972:23). There was, indeed, enough blue metal to stretch giant, rectilinear cobwebs all over the world of Native America—and still have some left over for fetish-souvenirs.

The Worcester visit became a serious business trip. Although President Salisbury remained unconvinced of Cushing's reliability (SSP: S. Baird/SSIII, 4/4/1882), the anthropologist drew crowds and favorable notice. Most important, through the eyes of preindustrial innocence a flattering, even worshipful attitude toward technology and capital enterprise received confirmation. It is worth pausing over the *Gazette*'s italicized *"My Father"* Zuni salutations, so familiarly prayerful and textually doxological. The cultural meanings of the Zunis' trip owed much to Cushing's archaic and biblical phrasing and the journalistic practices of the day. The bow priest became the priest of the machine power. The Zunis, it seemed, recognized power in all its mysterious configurations.

Return to Zuni

The Zuni leaders returned to a pueblo already riven by factionalism and dissension, in the first stages of disintegration caused by external pressures and interests that had come upon it only a few years before. By the mid-nineties, the Bow Priesthood was in steep decline and a permanent division between sacred and secular authorities had set in. The Piño family probably drew temporary status from the travels of father and son. But Pedro, already failing, was showing signs of senility; he returned advocating Anglo ways and causing some consternation. Palowaihtiwa (Patricio Piño), his son, proud of new knowledge and linguistic abilities, spoke for his people at a Santa Fe Independence Day celebration the following summer. His vision of history and current relations now bespoke an astute pragmatism:

> I am told that this is a feast of my father in Washington, and that he wished it. Hence I have come with my children and speak here this day, for I know that my people are poor among men, and if they smile not on Washington and his children, then they will pass away, or like dogs, lie hungry at the doors of strangers. (*New Mexican Review* 7/18/1883)

The governor returned to the East for several months in 1886, but neither his worldly knowledge nor his political pragmatism could halt the acceleration of change in Zuni pueblo. As the mythicization of an Apollonian Southwest began to take hold in cosmopolitan circles of the East, Zuni society was falling apart through drunkenness, disease, dissension, and death.

Cushing wrote of his own return to Zuni: "I rode up to my doorway, rushed in, and was plunged in the embraces of my family almost instantly. . . . about fifty or sixty Indians were gathered outside riotously awaiting my exit" (HCP:

FHC/Baxter [Draft] 10/3/1882). Acting in his enhanced capacity as war chief of the Zunis, within a week the anthropologist became involved in the political controversies that would lead to his recall to Washington fifteen months later. At the same time he wisely cultivated the Boston connections that had been so promisingly established, aided by Baxter's newspaper and magazine reports of life at Zuni (Baxter 1882a–g, 1883). He curried Hale's favor, for instance, in filial fashion:

> The life and language, the religion of the Zunis are intensely poetic. With no amount of poetry to which my words or pen may aspire, can I hope to give to the world as I feel it, in listening to the rituals, folklore, or even councils of this innocent people, their imagery and their poetry and their quaintness. (EEHP: FHC/EEH 4/16/1882)
> Two weeks since I was married to a very brave little girl who has faithfully remembered me through all my long years of exile among the Zunis, and who wishes to share my future labors and life among them. She has read many of your works and loves them as I do; she loves their author, for the good he has done the world, and for his friendship toward me. (EEHP: FHC/EEH 7/24/1882)

Even as he turned to Boston for future support, Cushing's Zuni reality, too, was undergoing change. Returning with Emily, her sister, and a cook, the anthropologist erected a new house and new limitations to his participant-observation. Cushing's Anglo enclave grew within the pueblo. No longer a lone fieldworker, Cushing was already partly myth, and the myth was being quickly elaborated. Thus both the anthropologist and the Indians attained mythical status from the 1882 trip, and both myths denied or hid realities—but with far different consequences. The ambiguous, often duplicitous role of the anthropologist as broker and mediator fell to the background as the struggling ethnographer came forward. The structural and historical asymmetry of Anglo-Zuni confrontation was masked by the growth of a mythology of sunny Southwestern pueblo life.

The cost of this process to Zuni culture was enormous. The Zunis became the special property of artists and poets, and their pueblo has served as the playground for mimetic anthropologists from Cushing to Dennis Tedlock. For Aldous Huxley it became the rest-cure reservation from a brave new world of regimentation. Not surprisingly, Baxter was one of the first to formulate this view of a conflict-free, communal order; he did so both in his ruminations on the landscape and in his more direct observations of pueblo life:

> But whence came one lovely trait that pervades all their myths and folk-lore, as related by Mr. Cushing, like an interwoven golden thread, gleaming through every fabric—the idea of the ultimate good existing in everything, and that even evil-working causes are but transitory, and become the means to the accomplishment of final good? It seems strange to find a feature like this in the faith of

a barbaric race, and it appears to be a proof of an innate gentleness of spirit. (Baxter 1883:124)

"As related by Mr. Cushing"—the phrase hints and hides the difficulties with cultural in-betweenness. Cushing too was enmeshed, translating into a world of established images, economic interests, and widespread wishful thinking. His words and those of his followers remind us that the intellectual and aesthetic struggle to find breathing space within the suffocating philosophies of nineteenth-century evolutionism and Gilded Age economic relations took many forms. One was a romantic public anthropology that came to center on the Southwest. The dominant—domineering—utilitarian attitude toward the continent as resource to be invested in and used up seemed to call forth some need for imaginative balance. It would be an Other place and an Other people set aside, an Other serving as reassurance of good intentions and better selves—not simply a place of recuperation from the industrial world. The loss of sacred landscape and transcendent purpose required a counterpoise.

Ultimately ambiguity gave way to reassertion of historical necessity. Words were hard to find, because doubts were outcast, but Bostonians of 1882 evidently felt the loss. Enmeshed in seemingly ineluctable historical movement, Anglo observers could only distance their unease by, in effect and in fact, staging the Zunis. With Cushing as dramaturge, history became theater and anthropology became myth.

Acknowledgments

This essay owes a great deal, in inspiration, language, and structure, to Barbara Babcock. George Stocking clarified my ideas and made critical suggestions. Jesse Green permitted me to consult his forthcoming work on Cushing at Zuni, and Elizabeth deVeer was most generous with her materials on Willard Metcalf. Warren Wheeler of Hamilton, New York, and Peter Bloomer of Flagstaff, Arizona, provided fine photography. The Colgate University Research Council and Northern Arizona University gave financial support. Special thanks to Sanda Luthy.

References Cited

Adams, J. R. 1977. *Edward Everett Hale*. Boston.
Akerman, S., & H. Norman. 1983. Political mobilization of the workers: The case of the Worcester Swedes. In *American labor and immigration history, 1877–1920s: Recent European research*, ed. D. Hoerder, 235–58. Urbana, Ill.
Bancroft, H. 1875. *The native races of the Pacific states*. 5 vols. New York.
———. 1889. *The history of Arizona and New Mexico, 1530–1888*. San Francisco.
Baxter, S. 1882a. The father of the Pueblos. *Harper's New Monthly Mag*. June: 72–91.

————. 1882b. An aboriginal pilgrimage. *Century Mag.* 24:526–36.

————. 1882c. F. H. Cushing at Zuni. *Am. Arch. & Build. News.* 11:319 (February 4): 56–57.

————. 1882d. Mr. Cushing and the Zunis at Washington. *Am. Arch. & Build. News.* 11:325 (March 18): 121–22.

————. 1882e. [no title]. *Am. Arch. & Build. News.* 11:327 (1 April): 146–47.

————. 1882f. Some results of Mr. Cushing's visit. *Am. Arch. & Build. News.* 11:331 (29 April): 195–96.

————. 1882g. The tenacity of Indian customs. *Am. Arch. & Build. News.* 12:356 (21 October): 195–97.

————. 1883. Zuni revisited. *Am. Arch. & Build. News.* 13:377 (17 March): 124–26.

BDA. *Boston Daily Advertiser.*

Berkhofer, R. 1978. *The white man's Indian: Images of the American Indian from Columbus to the present.* New York.

BH. *Boston Herald.*

Bishop, W. H. 1883. *Old Mexico and her lost provinces: A journey in Mexico, Southern California, and Arizona, by way of Cuba.* New York.

Culin, S. 1904. The Indians of the Southwest: A course of lectures delivered in the museum of the Brooklyn Institute of Arts and Sciences. Unpublished typescript. Brooklyn Museum Archives.

Curtis, W. E. 1883. *Children of the sun.* Chicago.

Cushing, F. H. 1882. *My adventures in Zuni.* Santa Fe. Reprinted, Palo Alto (1970).

————. 1920. *Zuñi breadstuff.* New York.

de Veer, E., & R. J. Boyle. 1987. *Sunlight and shadow: The life and art of Willard Leroy Metcalf.* New York.

Dwyer, K. 1982. *Moroccan dialogues: Anthropology in question.* Baltimore and London.

EEHP. See under Manuscript Sources.

Eggan, F., & T. N. Pandey. 1979. Zuni history, 1850–1970. *Handbook of North American Indians,* ed. W. C. Sturtevant. Vol. 9: *Southwest,* 474–81.

FHCP. See under Manuscript Sources.

Fiske, J. 1882. The romance of the Spanish and French explorers. *Harper's New Monthly Mag.* February: 438–48.

Foreman, C. 1934. *Indians abroad.* New York.

Gilbert, H. 1961. 1882: Zuni pilgrimage to the Atlantic Ocean. *Desert Mag.* 24 (5):12–15.

Green, J. Forthcoming. *Cushing at Zuni: Correspondence and diaries of Frank Hamilton Cushing, 1879–1884.* Albuquerque.

Gutman, H. G. 1976. *Work, culture, and society in industrializing America: Essays in working class and social history.* New York.

Gutman, H. G., & D. H. Bell, eds. 1987. *The New England working class and the new labor history.* Urbana, Ill.

Hale, E. E. 1878. Report of the Council. *Proc. Am. Antiq. Soc.*

————. 1900a. The colonization of the desert. In *The works of Edward Everett Hale.* Vol. 8:355–71. Boston.

————. 1900b. The results of Columbus's discovery. In *The Works of Edward Everett Hale.* Vol. 8:131–62. Boston.

Hale, E. E., Jr., ed. 1917. *The life and letters of Edward Everett Hale.* 2 vols. Boston.

Holloway, J. 1956. *Edward Everett Hale: A biography*. Austin.

Hunt, H. [Jackson]. 1882. A midsummer fête in the pueblo of San Juan. *Atlantic Monthly*. January: 101–8.

Jackson, J. B. 1972. *American space: The centennial years, 1865–1876*. New York.

Janowitz, T. 1987. *A cannibal in Manhattan*. New York.

Keen, B. 1971. *The Aztec image in Western thought*. New Brunswick, N.J.

Keyssar, A. 1987. Unemployment and the labor movement in Massachusetts, 1870–1916. In Gutman & Bell 1987:233–50.

Lears, T. 1981. *No place of grace: Antimodernism and the transformation of American culture, 1880–1920*. New York.

LG. See under Manuscript Sources.

Lips, J. E. 1937. *The savage hits back: The white man through native eyes*. London.

Lummis, C. F. 1900. The white Indian. *Land of Sunshine*. June: 8–17.

McChesney, L. n.d. The vision of Mary Hemenway. Unpublished paper.

McChesney, L., & C. M. Hinsley. 1984. F. H. Cushing and the Hemenway Southwestern Expedition. Paper presented at the 1984 Meeting of the American Ethnological Society, Asilomar, Ca.

McLuhan, T. C. 1985. *Dreamtracks: The railroad and the American Indian, 1890–1930*. New York.

Mooney, J. 1896. *The ghost-dance religion and the Sioux outbreak of 1890*, ed. A. F. C. Wallace. Chicago (1964).

Morgan, L. H. 1877. *Ancient society; or researches in the lines of human progress from savagery through barbarism to civilization*, ed. E. B. Leacock. Cleveland and New York (1963).

NMR. *New Mexican Review*.

NYT. *New York Tribune*.

Ober, F. 1882. How a white man became the war chief of the Zunis. *Wide Awake*.

Pandey, T. N. 1968. Factionalism in a southwestern pueblo. Doc. diss., Univ. Chicago.

———. 1972. Anthropologists at Zuni. *Proc. Am. Philos. Soc.* 116 (4): 321–37.

Parezo, N. J. 1987. The formation of ethnographic collections: The Smithsonian Institution in the American Southwest. *Adv. Archaeol. Method & Theory.* 10:1–47.

Reeve, F. D. 1952. Albert Franklin Banta: Arizona pioneer. *New Mexico Hist. Rev.* 27:200–252.

Rosenzweig, R. 1987. Middle-class parks and working-class play: The struggle over recreational space in Worcester, Massachusetts, 1870–1910. In Gutman & Bell 1987: 214–30.

———. 1983. *Eight hours for what we will: Workers and leisure in an industrial city*. New York.

Said, E. M. 1981. *Covering Islam: How the media and the experts determine how we see the rest of the world*. New York.

SCP. See under Manuscript Sources.

Sherwood, J. 1979. Life with Cushing: Farewell to desks. *Smithsonian* 10 (5): 96–113.

Simpson, J. H. 1852. *Journal of a military reconnaissance from Santa Fe to the Navajo country*. Philadelphia.

Sitgreaves, L. 1853. *Report on an expedition down the Zuni and Colorado rivers*. 32nd Cong., 2nd Sess., Senate Exec. Doc. 59. Washington, D.C.

Slotkin, R. 1974. *Regeneration through violence: The mythology of the American frontier.* Middletown, Conn.

SSP. See under Manuscript Sources.

Sutherland, E. 1964. The diaries of John Gregory Bourke: Their anthropological and folklore content. Doct. diss., Univ. Pennsylvania.

Viola, H. J. 1981. *Diplomats in buckskin: A history of Indian delegations in Washington City.* Washington, D.C.

WDG. Worcester Daily Gazette.

WHHP. See under Manuscript Sources.

Whipple, A. W. 1853–54. Report of explorations near the 35th parallel. In *Pacific Railroad Rep.* vols. 3–4. Washington, D.C.

Winslow, H. M. 1902. *Literary Boston of today.* Boston.

Ziff, L. 1973. *Puritanism in America: New culture in a new world.* New York.

Manuscript Sources

EEHP   Edward Everett Hale Papers, New York State Historical Library, Albany.

FHCP   F. H. Cushing Papers, Southwest Museum, Los Angeles.

SCP   Steward Culin Papers, Brooklyn Museum, New York.

LG   Diary of Lucia Grieve, Wellesley College Archives, Wellesley, Mass.

SSP   Stephen Salisbury Family Papers, American Antiquarian Society, Worcester, Mass.

WHHP   William Henry Holmes Papers, Library of the National Museum of American Art, Smithsonian Institution, Washington, D.C.

THE ETHNOGRAPHIC
SENSIBILITY OF THE 1920S
AND THE DUALISM OF THE
ANTHROPOLOGICAL TRADITION

GEORGE W. STOCKING, JR.

Like individual memory, the recollected or reconstructed past of a human discipline reflects mythistorical processes of archetypification, which characteristically coalesce around nodes of person and of moment. Archetypically, the endeavors of pattern-making figures, at critical moments of discipline formation (or reformation), mold the models and write the rules of subsequent inquiry, embodying the discipline's fundamental methodological values in their own heroic efforts. In the case of psychoanalysis, the archetypifying forces are powerfully condensed around particular episodes in the career of a single individual (cf. Sulloway 1979; Pletsch 1982). But the process may be more diffuse and pluralistic: alternate (or competing) archetypes—not always tied to the personage of a single historical figure—may be associated with particular phases (or tendencies) within the discipline, or within the undisciplined chaos that preceded it.

In the most potent version of the mythistory of anthropology (cf. McNeill, 1986), three looming archetypes contest the stage of the disciplinary past: the amateur ethnographer, the armchair anthropologist, and the academically trained fieldworker. Each of these archetypes can be linked to a particular moment, developmental and/or chronological, in the history of the discipline. Thus the defining moment of the ethnographic amateur is a vaguely temporal

George W. Stocking, Jr., is Professor of Anthropology and Director of the Morris Fishbein Center for the History of Science and Medicine at the University of Chicago. He is currently at work on a sequel to his book, *Victorian Anthropology* (1987), entitled *After Tylor: The Reformation of Anthropology in Post-Victorian Britain, 1888 to 1938*.

preprofessional phase, beginning with the accounts of early explorers, travellers, and missionaries, but persisting on into the twentieth century out beyond the margins of the academic realm in which professional values were domesticated. In contrast, the defining moment of the armchair anthropologist is the "late-nineteenth century," when E. B. Tylor and J. G. Frazer, at their desks in Oxbridge studies, synthesized the reports of ethnographic amateurs (to some of whom they offered an encouraging epistolary supervision) in comparative evolutionary studies of the customs and beliefs of the "Amongthas"– "Among the Watchandis of Australia . . . ," "Among the Esquimaux . . . ," "Among the Aryan nations of Northern Europe . . ." (Tylor 1871:II, 200–201). The defining moment of the archetypal academic fieldworker is harder to fix in time, because that role has been attributed to, or claimed by, more than one anthropological prometheus: Bronislaw Malinowski, William Rivers, Franz Boas, Frank Hamilton Cushing, Nikolai Miklouho-Maclay, even Lewis Henry Morgan, could be called forth as candidates. But a case can nevertheless be made that the emergent "moment" of the archetypal fieldworker is the decade or so following World War I.

This is not to say that the method of modern fieldwork, as promulgated by Malinowski in 1923 in the opening chapter of *Argonauts*, had in fact been "invented" by him in the Trobriand Islands seven years before. Indeed, as the above list of putative paters suggests, the emergence of modern fieldwork was a multifaceted process to which many individuals before and after Malinowski contributed (cf. *HOA* 1). But Malinowski's deliberate archetypification of the role of "the Ethnographer" offered, both to prospective anthropologists and to various publics at the boundaries of the developing discipline, a powerfully condensed (yet expansive) image of the anthropologist as the procurer of exotic esoteric knowledge of potentially great value – an image potent even in the United States, where the students of Franz Boas were inclined to insist that they were already practicing what Malinowski preached (Stocking 1983). The academicization of the discipline, which had gained its first real momentum in the decade after 1900, and survived a period of wartime and postwar retrenchment, was in the later 1920s reinforced by substantial support from major philanthropic groups (Stocking 1985; cf. 1976a). By that time, one could speak of a second generation of academic anthropologists – students of the students of those who brought anthropology into the academy. Although the doctoral dissertation based on fieldwork was not yet the norm, and academically trained fieldworkers were still few in number, those who went out from the university to the field in the 1920s were confident that they were doing ethnography in a different, more efficient, more reliable, more "scientific" way than the travellers, missionaries, and government officials whom they were pushing to the margins of the discipline. Expressed in the metaphor of the ethnographic field as a "laboratory," in which a distinctive method was employed to test previously assumed comparative (or merely culturally traditional) generalizations about human behavior, this disciplinary self-image was projected with considerable success outward to the surrounding social sciences, and even beyond to the general intellectual and literate public.

As the defining moment of the fieldworker archetype, the 1920s may be regarded also as the beginning of the "classical" period of modern anthropology (cf. Stocking 1989). With the critique of social evolutionism already established, and the succeeding phase of historical diffusionism rapidly passing, a powerful movement had begun within the Anglo-American tradition toward a largely synchronic anthropology. Allowing for the temporal vagueness inherent in the idea of the "ethnographic present," the focus of ethnographic and theoretical concern was henceforth increasingly to be on the study of culture and social structure as manifest in current rather than remembered or reconstructed custom and belief (Burton 1988; cf. HOA 2). It was during this defining moment that modern anthropology's fundamental "methodological values"—the taken-for-granted, pretheoretical notions of what it is to do anthropology (and to be an anthropologist)—began to be established: the value placed on fieldwork as the basic constituting experience both of anthropologists and of anthropological knowledge; the value placed on a holistic approach to the entities that are the subject of this form of knowledge; the value placed on a relativistic valuation of all such entities; and the value placed on their uniquely privileged role in the constitution of anthropological theory (Stocking 1982a:411–12, 1983:174).[1] Method itself was still evolving—Margaret Mead's Samoan research was seen by Boas as marking "the beginning of a new era of methodological investigation of native tribes" (MP: FB/MM 11/7/25); to more conservative historical diffusionists, Redfield's community study of Tepoztlán was a "sociological" departure from traditional ethnographic approaches (Kroeber 1931). But although "laundry lists" of cultural elements continued to be required tools in the ethnographic kits of Kroeber's students at the University of California on into the late 1930s, the more "sociological" (and psychological) approaches were clearly beginning to carry the day (cf. HOA 1; HOA 2; HOA 4).

Given the sense of urgency that has characterized ethnographic endeavor since the early nineteenth century, and the consequent commitment to the importance of "salvaging" the (presumed) pristine human variety facing obliteration by the march of European civilization (Gruber 1970), it is scarcely sur-

---

1. These methodological values of the "classical" period are a modification of David Mandelbaum's listing of basic postulates derived from the concept of culture: holism, fieldwork, a comparative approach, and micro- to macro-theorizing (Mandelbaum 1982:36). In addition to the four primary methodological values noted here, I have elsewhere suggested a secondary triad, products of an earlier evolutionary phase of the discipline, which still retain a considerable potency (Stocking 1982a; see below, p. 266).

prising that the ethnography of academic anthropologists tended to follow a "one ethnographer/one tribe" pattern. The number of aspiring anthropological professionals was far fewer than the number of unstudied tribes, and the methodological values of the new ethnography encouraged a "my people" syndrome—the effects of which were reinforced by a strong sense of institutional territoriality among emerging academic centers. In areas of ethnographic concentration, several academic anthropologists might study closely related peoples, or different aspects of the same culture—sometimes for training purposes (cf. Stocking 1982b). But if the salvage imperative (and the ultimate vision of a comparative science of man) encouraged some academic ethnographers to work among more than one people, it did not encourage competition among academic ethnographers. In contrast, it did allow them to study peoples who had been studied previously by "amateurs," whose work might be mined for facts but was likely to be superficial and/or systematically flawed by ethnocentric assumptions. In this context, the problem of the reliability of ethnographic data—which might perhaps have been suggested by the laboratory metaphor and by the frequent self-identification of the new academic professionals as "scientists"—was largely forestalled by the archetypal distinction between the ethnographic amateur and the academic professional. University-trained fieldworkers might talk of a "personal equation," but they did not allow such concerns to keep them from "getting on with the work" of documenting the ethnographic variety of humankind before it was effaced.

A generation further on, when the distinction between amateurs and professionals was an accomplished historical fact, the problem of ethnographic reliability was not so easily sidestepped. As professional anthropologists increased in numbers, they became more differentiated theoretically, methodologically, and institutionally. Less inhibited by the forceful founding figures of earlier professional generations, they began occasionally to tread in each other's ethnographic territories, and sometimes to map them in rather different ways. Even so, when ethnographic reliability first presented itself as a serious issue to modern anthropologists, it did so indirectly, as a consequence of interpretive differences between students of groups in the same culture area (Bennett 1946) or as a by-product of the attempt to study culture change using a previous study as base point (Lewis 1951). And despite the growth of the discipline over the succeeding four decades, the "my people" ethic remains very strong. Although ethnographic method has upon occasion been the subject of systematic consideration (e.g., Lewis 1953; Naroll 1962; Pelto 1970; Werner 1987), ethnographic data are still characteristically produced by individual investigators, using relatively unsystematic and subjective methods, whose reliability is only rarely at issue.

There are, however, a small number of classic "restudies" in which the problem of ethnographic reliability has presented itself in a compelling fashion—

instances in which ethnographic work of particular significance in the development of the discipline has been called into question by another ethnographer studying the same people. Every anthropologist is aware of the differing interpretations of Pueblo culture in the American Southwest and the criticisms by Oscar Lewis of Robert Redfield's study of Tepoztlán in central Mexico. Given the recent furor surrounding Derek Freeman's critique of Margaret Mead's study of Samoa, it seems likely that in the future this will be regarded as a third such case.

There are of course compelling methodological and epistemological grounds for defending the idiographic character of ethnographic inquiry in contrast to that which is generally presumed to be characteristic of the natural sciences (e.g., Ulin 1984). But regardless of its methodological significance, the fact that different observers of what in a general sense may be regarded as the same phenomenon should have represented it in what seem to be radically differing ways does present an interesting interpretive problem, especially when major figures in the history of a discipline are involved (cf. Heider 1988). In the present instance, the interpretive significance is perhaps enhanced by the fact that all three classic cases originate in a single cultural historical moment: the 1920s—which, as has been suggested here, is also the defining moment of the academic fieldworker as a disciplinary archetype. From this point of view, an attempt to consider the three cases together, in historical context—even if it should leave many issues unexplored or unresolved—may still cast some light on the historical development and perhaps even the nature of anthropological inquiry.[2]

Culture and Civilization in the 1920s

If the emergence of the fieldworker archetype in the 1920s was one marker of the beginning of the "classical period" of anthropology, another was the recognition of "culture" as its focal concept and subject matter.[3] Prematurely

2. A fourth case could easily be added: that of Malinowski himself, whose interpretation of the Trobriand oedipal complex has recently come under attack along lines that could be encompassed within the present argument (Spiro 1982)—and whose archetypical status as "the Ethnographer" has now for twenty years suffered from the self-exposure of his ethnographic diaries. But since I have discussed Malinowski's diaries elsewhere (Stocking 1983, 1986), and since his inclusion here would require a consideration of the postwar milieu in Britain as well as in the United States, I have not treated him in the present essay.

3. This statement requires qualification for one of the two dominant anthropological traditions of the "classical" period. Within British social anthropology, where Boas had little or no influence, the culture concept had an aborted development. Although current in the immediate postevolutionary moment in the work of Rivers and then of Malinowski, "culture" was by the 1930s replaced by Radcliffe-Brown's concept of "social structure" (cf. Stocking 1984, 1986).

proclaimed in an evolutionary form by E. B. Tylor in 1871, intellectually grounded in the work of Franz Boas and the first generation of his students, "culture" burst into flower in the 1920s (cf. Stocking 1968). As its analytic bibliographic chronologists have shown (Kroeber & Kluckhohn 1952), this was the moment when citations burgeoned: save for five precursory figures, whose usage they suggest may only have had a "formal or verbal resemblance" to the anthropological concept, without actually having "'meant' the same" (149–50), the opening entry in most of their categories dates from this period. It was at this time that, building on Boas' critique of evolutionary culture, anthropologists (e.g., Boas' student Clark Wissler [1923]) and sociologists (e.g., the Boas-influenced William Ogburn [1922]), joined forces in fashioning and making fashionable what was later described by one influential popularizer as "the foundation stone of the social sciences" (Chase 1948:59).

However, one need only consult an historical dictionary to realize that, like some other central concepts in the human disciplines, "culture" was from the beginning entangled with the categories, the discourse, and the experience of the "outside" world—and that it only gradually achieved a certain (inherently limited?) independent conceptual status. In the 1920s it was also still closely (and problematically) tied to its conceptual sibling "civilization"—which in Tylor's definition had been its synonym, and which Kroeber in 1917 had used as pseudonym to avoid the unpatriotic resonance of the German "Kultur" (Kroeber & Kluckhohn 1952:28–29). And in the 1920s, beyond (and at) the margins of disciplinary discourse, these linked concepts were the subject of widespread discussion and debate among American intellectuals.

To put the matter in a nutshell, world (and national) historical experience seemed no longer to sustain either the easy absolutism implied in the popular Arnoldian notion of culture ("the pursuit of perfection . . . the best that has been thought and known" [1869:69–70]), or the easy evolutionary synonymity of Tylor's "ethnographic" definition ("Culture, or civilization, . . ." [1871:I, 1]). For many intellectuals, the values to be cultivated by the individual in the pursuit of perfection could no longer be taken for granted; and the "permanent distinction and occasional contrast" between such cultivation and the idea of civilization—on which Coleridge had long before insisted (Williams 1958:67)—had become painfully evident.

There have been various attempts to encapsulate the values associated with the idea of civilization in the later Victorian era. One influential interpretation grouped them in a triptych, with "progress" and "culture" (in the Arnoldian sense) flanking the central panel of "practical idealism": "the reality, certainty, and eternity of moral values" (May 1959:30, 9). A more recently proposed trio included the "ethic of self-control and autonomous achievement, [the] cult of science and technical rationality, [and the] worship of material progress" (Lears 1981:4). But linked to (or implicated in) these triads were also other value commitments: the ethnic values of white Anglo-Saxon racial superiority, the political values of liberal representative government, the economic values of free capitalist enterprise, the religious values of Protestant Christianity, and—perhaps most centrally, in terms of the transmission of cultural character, the familial, gender, and sexual values of patriarchal respectability (cf. Hale 1971; Stocking 1987:187–237).

By 1920, many intellectuals had begun to question both these values and the idea of civilization in which they were embodied. The timing, extent, and thoroughness of this intellectual rebellion has been a matter of historiographical debate. The "revolution in morals" has been associated with flappers, jazz, speakeasies, and the "lost generation" as a characteristic phenomenon of the 1920s itself (Leuchtenberg 1958). In contrast, the "end of American innocence" has been associated with the "scoffers" and "questioners" of the turn-of-the-century decades, and with the "innocent rebellion" of younger American intellectuals between 1912 and 1917 (May 1959). More recently, the development of an antimodernist "revolt against overcivilization" (which in fact promoted "new modes of accommodation to routinized work and bureaucratic 'rationality'") has been traced throughout the four decades prior to 1920 (Lears 1981:iv, 137). Against all this has been argued the persistence of the older values and the constructive role of a "nervous generation" of American intellectuals in reshaping them during the 1920s itself (Nash 1970). But even a staunchly self-proclaimed revisionist has acknowledged that a "moral earthquake" shook Western civilization in the years after World War I (ibid.: 110). Whatever questioning of Victorian values had taken place prior to the war's outbreak, it was the horrible spectacle of the civilized nations of the West engaged in the mutual slaughter of their youth that forced many intellectuals to wonder if there were not some alternative to the values of what Ezra Pound called "a botched civilization" (1915).

If Pound's adjective implied an alienated despair, the indefinite article could also imply a regenerative relativity, which in fact had been reflected previously in the prewar sense of cultural self-discovery epitomized in Van Wyck Brooks' *America's Coming-of-Age* (1915). Thus when "civilization" became "the center of interest" in the postwar decade (Beard 1942:10ff.), the issue was not simply the content of a painfully problematic universal category, but the possibility of now, finally, realizing a civilization that would truly embody the maturing American experience—rather than the worn-out values of the "Puritan" tradition, or the hypocrisy of small-town Babbittry, or the acquisitive commodity culture of big cities and their suburbs. In the fall of 1920, Brooks and Harold Stearns, responding to the "common enemy of reaction" in the "hysterical post-armistice days," got together a group of "like-minded men and women" who would attempt to "speak the truth about American civilization as we saw it, in order to do our share in making a real civilization possible"

(Stearns 1922:iii–iv). Dividing the domains of American culture among themselves, they covered topics ranging from "the city" and "the small town" to "the alien" and "racial minorities," from "art" to "advertising," from "philosophy" to "the family," and from "science" to "sex"—with the notable omission of "religion," about which no one was willing to write, because they felt that "real religious feeling in America had disappeared, . . . and that the country was in the grip of what Anatole France has aptly called Protestant clericalism . . ." (vi). From these contributions, Stearns distilled three major themes: hypocrisy, the suppression of heterogeneity, and "emotional and aesthetic starvation" (vii).

Noting the "sharp dichotomy between preaching and practice" in "almost every branch of American life," Stearns suggested that rather than submitting the "abstractions and dogmas which are sacred to us" to "a fresh examination," Americans worshipped them "the more vociferously to show our sense of sin." Arguing that "whatever else American civilization is, it is not Anglo-Saxon," he insisted that "we shall never achieve any genuine nationalistic self-consciousness as long as we allow certain financial and social minorities to persuade us that we are still an English colony." Asserting that "we have no heritages or traditions to which to cling except those that have already withered in our hands and turned to dust," and that "the whole industrial and economic situation [was] so maladjusted to the primary and simple needs of men and women" that it was futile to attempt a "rationalistic attack" on our "infantilisms of compensation," Stearns proposed that

> There must be an entirely new deal of the cards in one sense; we must change our hearts. For only so, unless through the humbling of calamity or scourge, can true art and true religion and true personality, with their native warmth and caprice and gaiety, grow up in America to exorcise these painted devils we have created to frighten us away from the acknowledgment of our spiritual poverty. (vii)

The overlapping of anthropological discourse and the discourse of cultural criticism in the early 1920s is evidenced by the inclusion of two important Boasians among the thirty participants in the Stearns symposium: Robert Lowie, who offered Boas' "transvaluation of theoretical values in the study of cultural development" as the exemplar of modern anthropology's contributions to contemporary science (Stearns 1922:154); and Elsie Clews Parsons, who attacked Puritan "attitudes of repression or deception" toward sex as an expression of "arrested development," in which women, classified "by men on an economic basis," were "depersonalized" as "creature[s] of sin" or "object[s] of chivalry" (310, 314–15, 317). And there were other Boasians who, in other venues, were also important contributors to the discourse of cultural criticism in the early 1920s, in tones resonant of the Stearns volume.

The most notable of these was Edward Sapir, whose seminal essay "Culture, Genuine and Spurious"—as its publication history suggests—was at once a part of that critical cultural discourse and a major document in the development of the anthropological culture concept (cf. Handler 1983:222–26; Kroeber & Kluckhohn 1952, where Sapir is the third most cited author). Published in part in two of the better known "little magazines" of the period (Sapir 1919, 1922), the essay appeared in full in 1924 in the *American Journal of Sociology*, where it was perhaps the most important contribution to the sociological discussion of the anthropological culture concept in the middle and late 1920s. Although drafted a year before the Stearns symposium was conceived, it could in fact be viewed as a conceptual commentary on the relationship of the symposium's central concern ("civilization") to another concern which appeared occasionally and unsystematically throughout, and which Sapir (like Coleridge) insisted was quite a different matter ("culture").

Sapir began by distinguishing three different meanings of the term "culture": the "ethnologist's," which included "any socially inherited element in the life of man, material and spiritual" (in which terms "all human groups are cultured, though in vastly different manners and grades of complexity"); the "conventional ideal of individual refinement"; and a third which was to be his own concern. Sharing aspects of the first and second usages, it aimed "to embrace in a single term those general attitudes, views of life, and specific manifestations of civilization that give a particular people its distinctive place in the world" (1924:308–11). "Civilization," in turn, was the progressive "sophistication" of society and individual life resulting from the cumulative sifting of social experience, the complication of organization, and the steadily growing knowledge and practical economic mastery of nature. It stood in sharp contrast to "genuine culture," which was an "inherently harmonious" and "healthy spiritual organism," free "of the dry rot of social habit," in which "nothing is spiritually meaningless" for the human individual: "civilization, as a whole, moves on; culture comes and goes" (314–17). It was clearly gone from modern American life, in which the "vast majority" were either "dray horses" or "listless consumers":

> The great cultural fallacy of industrialism, as developed up to the present time, is that in harnessing machines to our uses it has not known how to avoid the harnessing of the majority of mankind to its machines. The telephone girl who lends her capacities, during the greater part of the living day, to the manipulation of a technical routine that has an eventually high efficiency value but that answers to no spiritual needs of her own is an appalling sacrifice to civilization. As a solution of the problem of culture she is a failure—the more dismal the greater her natural endowment. As with the telephone girl, so, it is to be feared, with the great majority of us, slave-stokers to fires that burn for demons we would destroy, were it not that they appear in the guise of our benefactors. The

American Indian who solves the economic problem with salmon-spear and rabbit-snare operates on a relatively low level of civilization, but he represents an incomparably higher solution than our telephone girl of the questions that culture has to ask of economics. There is here no question of the immediate utility, of the effective directness, of economic effort, nor of any sentimentalizing regrets as to the passing of the "natural man." The Indian's salmon-spearing is a culturally higher type of activity than that of the telephone girl or mill hand simply because there is normally no sense of spiritual frustration during its prosecution, no feeling of subservience to tyrannous yet largely inchoate demands, because it works in naturally with all the rest of the Indian's activities instead of standing out as a desert patch of merely economic effort in the whole of life. A genuine culture cannot be defined as a sum of abstractly desirable ends, as a mechanism. It must be looked upon as a sturdy plant growth, each remotest leaf and twig of which is organically fed by the sap at the core. (Sapir 1924:316)

Despite Sapir's denial of "sentimentalizing regrets" for "natural man," a strong residual aroma of romantic primitivism hangs heavily over this rhetorically tangled bank of critique and concept. If "a genuine culture was perfectly conceivable in any type or stage of civilization," it was "easier, generally speaking," for it to "subsist on a lower level of civilization" (Sapir 1924:318). There was a "geography of culture," which reached "its greatest heights in comparatively small, autonomous groups"—not in the "flat cultural morass" of New York, Chicago, and San Francisco, but in Periclean Athens, Augustan Rome, the city-states of the Italian Renaissance, Elizabethan London—and the typical American Indian tribe, where the "well rounded life of the average participant" could not escape the notice of "the sensitive ethnologist" (328–31, 318). Sapir's thought on the idea of culture and its relation to personality departed in important respects from that of many of his fellow anthropologists in the 1920s and 1930s—including several who were most influenced by him (Handler 1986; Darnell 1986). But in these passages, he was clearly speaking for other "sensitive ethnologists" who were critical of the civilization of their day. From this point of view, "Culture, Genuine and Spurious" was a foundation document for the ethnographic sensibility of the 1920s, and it is perhaps more than coincidental that the authors of its three most problematic ethnographic cases were all strongly influenced by Sapir—who was an intimate poetic confidant of Ruth Benedict and Margaret Mead, and a teacher of Robert Redfield.

The Geography of Genuine Culture

For intellectuals searching for genuine culture in the postwar period, there were several localities in the cultural geography of the United States that were clearly marked off from the surrounding "flat cultural morass." In New York

"Easter Eve, Washington Square, 1926." Etching and aquatint by John Sloan. (Courtesy of the Delaware Art Museum, Wilmington.)

City, there was Greenwich Village, where just before the war the cheap rents of a disintegrating traditional neighborhood (Ware 1935:93) had opened a cultural space for rebel-seekers who were by temperament (or by gender) excluded from "business, big-time journalism, university life, and other corporate pursuits" (Lynn 1983:89, 83). Finding "the traditional Anglo-Protestant

values inapplicable and the money drive offensive," they set out on an eva-
nescent urban frontier "to make for themselves individually civilized lives according to their own conceptions" (Ware 1935:235). Much of their rebel energy
was spent in "free love, unconventional dress, erratic work, . . . all-night parties, . . . plenty of drink, living from moment to moment"—"rationalizing their
conduct with the aid of Freud and of art" (ibid.: 95, 262). And their "counter-
culture" was soon to a considerable extent coopted by middle class culture, with
the *New Yorker* adapting the style of the *New Masses*, and the Theatre Guild
evolving from the Washington Square players (Lynn 1983:91). But if "the village"
offered more of individualistic escape than of "genuine" cultural alternative,
it was also for a time a bubbling oasis of cultural modernism, in which intellectuals alienated from the spurious culture of contemporary business civilization could savor heterodox ideas, discover new aesthetic modes, and experiment
with alternative life styles (cf. Lasch 1965)—directly, as residents or occasional
habitues, or vicariously, through the various media of cultural criticism.

It has been argued that one "longing" that served to bring together all factions of the cultural rebellion was an "aesthetic" fascination with "the culture
of poverty"—a manifestation of a more general "preoccupation with primitive
vitality" among many intellectuals in this period (Lynn 1983:87–89). For those
intellectuals, like Mabel Dodge, whose primitivist urges required a more "genuine" culture than urban bohemia could provide (Lasch 1965:119), there was
another oasis far out across the great cultural desert of middle America: the
pueblo Southwest. Against a backdrop of arid ochre scarps and arching crystal
skies, the crisp adobe lines of Spanish churches and Indian pueblos—artifacts
of cultural traditions more deeply rooted than colonial New England—provided
the setting for a resonantly exotic cultural life in the present.

Starting in the late 1890s, when the advertising department of the Santa
Fe Railway began to "mine the landscape for culture" and to present the Santa
Fe Indian as "a prototype of preindustrial society" (McLuhan 1985:18), a small
group of painters, playwrights, poets, and writers had settled in Santa Fe and
Taos. Twenty years later Harriet Monroe, the editor of the "little magazine"
which was the major outlet for the new American poetry, complained that
"we Americans, who would travel by the many thousand, if we had the chance,
to see a Homeric rite in Attica, or a serpent ceremony in old Egypt, are only
beginning to realize that the snake-dance at Walpi, or the corn-dance at Cochiti,
are also revelations of primitive art, expressions of that original human impulse toward the creation of beauty" (ibid.: 41).

By 1924 the Santa Fe Railway was transporting 50,000 tourists a year to
the rim of the Grand Canyon, and two years later it had begun the "Indian
Detours" in which Packard touring cars drove the richer and more venture-
some to witness "spectacles which can be equaled in very few Oriental lands"
(McLuhan 1985:43). Others found a deeper message of spiritual regeneration.

When Mabel Dodge heard the singing and drumming at Taos pueblo, she felt herself suddenly "brought up against the tribe, where a different instinct ruled, and where virtue lay in wholeness instead of in dismemberment" (ibid.: 156); within several years she had cast off her artist third husband to marry the Pueblo Indian Tony Luhan. For D. H. Lawrence, whom she lured to "the edge of Taos desert" in 1923, it was a matter of "true nodality":

> Some places seem temporary on the face of the earth: San Francisco for example. Some places seem final. . . . Taos pueblo still retains its old nodality. Not like a great city. But, in its way, like one of the monasteries of Europe. . . . When you get there, you feel something final. . . . the pueblo as it has been since heaven knows when, and the slow dark weaving of the Indian life going on still . . . and oneself, sitting there on a pony, far-off stranger with gulfs of time between me and this. And yet, the old nodality of the pueblo still holding, like a dark ganglion spinning invisible threads of consciousness. (ibid.: 162)

In the 1920s, the mapping of the "geography of culture" of cultural criticism overlapped that of cultural anthropology to an extent that we may not appreciate today, when the boundaries between academic anthropology and the outside world are more sharply imagined. The routinization of anthropological charisma had not yet reduced the careers of its devotees to years in the university punctuated by ever more infrequent episodes of fieldwork. A number of the New York anthropologists were frequenters of the culture of Greenwich Village, participants in the New School of Social Research, contributors to little magazines. When these same anthropologists went into the field, it was not into a generalized laboratory but into particular exotic places, some of them heavy with the musky scent of "primitivistic longing."

The single most-visited venue was the pueblo Southwest. With the post-evolutionary changing of the institutional and theoretical guard in American anthropology, this favored preserve of anthropologists associated with the Bureau of American Ethnology became more accessible to the Boasians. The pueblo at Zuni, which from 1879 on was studied by Frank Cushing, Matilda Stevenson, Jesse Fewkes, and F. W. Hodge, began to attract Boasians in 1915, when Elsie Clews Parson arrived, to be followed during the next nine years by A. L. Kroeber, Leslie Spier, Boas himself, and then Ruth Bunzel and Ruth Benedict (Pandey 1972). It may be that Boas' on-going shift from historical diffusionism toward the psychological study of the individual and culture made more attractive an area where the culture seemed still vibrantly "alive and well" (Stocking 1976a:15–17). But if there was a disciplinary dynamic that drew Boasians to the area, it seems also clear that some of them—sharing to a considerable extent the backgrounds, motives, sensibilities, experiences, and impressions of nonanthropologist intellectuals—also felt the pull of Lawrence's "invisible threads of consciousness."

The Delectable Mountains
of the Apollonian Southwest

For Ruth (Fulton) Benedict, these threads ran back to a dark ganglion of childhood fantasy. As she later recreated it for Margaret Mead, the story of her life began when her father, a young surgeon interested in cancer research, died twenty-one months after her birth in 1887 (Benedict 1935:97).[4] Her mother, a Vassar graduate who later supported herself as teacher and librarian, took tiny Ruth and her infant sister in to view her father in his coffin, "and in an hysteria of weeping implored me to remember" (98).[5] Benedict later recalled it as her "primal scene": "Certainly from earliest childhood I recognized two worlds, . . . the world of my father, which was the world of death and which was beautiful, and [my mother's] world of confusion and explosive weeping which I repudiated" (99). Benedict marked that repudiation by "ungovernable tantrums" and "bilious attacks" (which followed the same six-week rhythm as her later menstrual periods)—"protests against alienation from my Delectable Mountains" (108). In her other, calmer world, she had an "imaginary playmate" who enjoyed "a warm, friendly family life without recriminations and brawls" in "the unparalleled beauty of the country over the hill"—until, at age five, she was taken by her mother to the ridge of her maternal

4. The fact that this manuscript was prepared for Mead in 1935, "at a time when life histories were becoming a matter of anthropological interest" (Mead 1959a:97)—and after *Patterns of Culture* (Benedict 1934) was already in print—might be used to argue for limiting its status as independent source material about that volume's genesis, since Benedict may have been consciously or unconsciously patterning her own life in relation to one of the patterns of her book. But if so, it can still be argued that the interpretation here given to these two sources has a basis in her own self-understanding. Although I have also drawn information from Modell's biography (1983), and have consulted Caffrey's dissertation (1986), the interpretation here derives from my own long-standing concern with Benedict's career (Stocking 1974a, 1976b).

5. Collecting information on the "perceptions of their parents" of eighty-eight Greenwich Villagers, Kenneth Lynn found that two-thirds of them "were raised in households which they considered to be female-dominated" due to the "personal force of the mothers" and "the absence or startling weakness of the fathers." Lynn used these data to attack the idea that they were rebelling against "patriarchal authority," and suggested that their family backgrounds had in fact encouraged them to be nonconformist, and to place a high value on personal freedom and self-realization: "Strong mothers taught their gifted daughters to believe that women in America could not be fulfilled unless they ignored restrictive definitions of their social role . . . [and] inflated their [gifted sons'] egos to the point where [they] were unprepared to accept the discipline of any organization not put together for their own benefit . . ." (Lynn 1983:78–79). While this may represent an important sophistication of our understanding of the rebelling or questioning intellectuals, the image of all those "strong mothers" seeking vicarious release from "restrictive definitions of their social role" suggests that the issue of "patriarchal authority" may have been lurking somewhere in the background. Be that as it may, it is worth noting that Benedict, Redfield, and Mead all came from families with strong mothers (and grandmothers), although in the case of Benedict, her emotional relationship to her mother was markedly antagonistic.

family's upstate New York farm, and she saw that beyond it lay a territory that was "all familiar and anything-but-romantic" (100). From then on, her other world was "made up mostly out of my Bible," and peopled "by people of a strange dignity and grace," who moved like Blakean figures, "skimming the ground in one unbroken line" (107, 109). Her isolation heightened by partial deafness after an infant bout with measles, Benedict allowed no one to pass beyond her "physical and emotional aloofness." The one partial exception was Mabel Ganson (later Mabel Dodge), who went to the same girls' school in Buffalo; although Benedict was six years younger and their acquaintance was slight, she remembered "knowing that [Mabel Dodge] lived for something I recognized, something different from those things for which most people around me lived" (109). And while she introduced this recollection with the comment "amusingly enough," the present context suggests a greater symbolic significance.

Their routes to the Southwest were, however, to be quite different. In 1905, Benedict matriculated at Vassar, where as a freshman she abandoned formal religious belief for Walter Pater's humanistic vision of culture, and as a senior lamented the loss of "the sense of reverence and awe" in the realistic "Modern Age" (Mead 1959a:116, 135). After a year in Europe, another doing charity work in Buffalo, and three more teaching in girls' schools in California, she tried to come to terms with the "very terrible thing [it was] to be a woman" (120) and to "master an attitude toward life which will somehow bind together these episodes of experience into something that may conceivably be called a life" (129). Putting aside, for the moment, the youthful idea that "we were artificers of our own lives," she decided that "a woman has one supreme power—to love" (130); in 1913 she married Stanley Rossiter Benedict, a brilliant biochemist, and tried to live the life of a housewife in a suburb of New York. There she dabbled with literary projects, including "chemical detective stories" she hoped to publish under the pseudonym "Stanhope," and a manuscript on "New Women of Three Centuries." But when fate denied her the "man-child" who might "call a truce to the promptings of self-fulfilment," Benedict was unwilling to "twist" herself into "a doubtfully useful footstool" (135); "Stanhope" died, to be reborn later as "Anne Singleton" (the name under which she published poetry in the 1920s).

After armistice brought an end to "this tornado of world-horror," when it had "seemed useless to attempt anything but a steady day-by-day living" (Mead 1959a:142), Benedict searched once more for expedients to "get through the days." Although she rejected the advice of a friend to "move to the village and have a good time, and several love affairs" (ibid.: 7), she did in 1919 begin to attend lectures at the New School, where she was quickly attracted to Elsie Clews Parsons' course on "Sex in Ethnology," which offered a comparative study of the "distinctive distribution of functions between the sexes" (Modell

1983:111; cf. Hare 1985; Rutkoff & Scott 1986). She also took a number of courses from the brilliant Boasian maverick, Alexander Goldenweiser, who during this period was at work on "the first book by an American anthropologist which was to present cultures briefly as wholes" (Mead 1959a:8). To one whose psyche was grounded in an opposition between radically different emotional worlds, and whose life and marital experience had undercut the value-absolutes sustaining the central institution of her culture, the implicit relativism of the anthropological approach offered a principle of order; and in 1921, Benedict was taken uptown to Columbia by Parsons, to be introduced to Boas and to begin study for a doctorate in anthropology.

Quickly sensing the vigorously imaginative mind veiled by her "painfully shy" demeanor, Boas waived credit requirements to hurry Benedict through the Ph.D. Her dissertation, a library study of American Indian religion, was an analysis of the "observed behavior" of a single "well-recognized cultural trait," the guardian spirit concept, which she argued was "the unifying religious fact of North America" (Benedict 1923:6, 40). Rejecting all generalized origin theories, Benedict found that the guardian spirit was associated with other cultural elements in a series of "essentially fortuitous" and "fluid recombinations" defying any single causal explanation (56, 82). The dissertation showed various precursory traces of the later Benedictine viewpoint. Thus, although she concluded with an attack on "the superstition that [a culture] is an organism functionally interrelated" (85), Benedict insisted that in any given culture area, the vision-complex was "formalized" into "definite tribal patterns" under the influence of dominant values and activities (41–43)—to such an extent that in the American Southwest, where every other element of the complex was present, the notion of the individual guardian spirit experience had almost totally disappeared "under the influence of group ceremonial as the proper way of approaching the gods" (35–40). For the most part, however, the dissertation remained within the conventional mold of Boasian historicism, in which the approach "toward a more just [i.e., nonevolutionary] psychological understanding of the data" depended first on an adequate reconstruction of which one "of all these indefinitely numerous plausible potentialities . . . did actually and historically secure social recognition among a given people" (7).

Hampered by deafness and diffidence, Benedict did not find fieldwork congenial, and the small amount that she did (no more than eight months altogether) fell into a rather conventional early Boasian mold. In 1922, she combined a visit with her sister's family in Pasadena with a memory ethnography of the "broken culture" of the Serrano of Southern California, working primarily with one seventy-year-old woman (Mead 1959a:213). The following February, after some hesitation, she yielded to Boas' urging and accepted a fellowship for folklore research from Elsie Clews Parsons, who funded ethnographic work through her personal anthropological philanthropy, the South-west Society (Mead 1959a:65; Hare 1985:148); but it was not until August of the next year that Benedict actually went to Zuni, at the same time that Ruth Bunzel (the second of Boas' departmental secretaries to turn anthropologist) was beginning her study of Pueblo potters (cf. Mead 1959b:33–35). A year later, Benedict returned to the Southwest for another six weeks of folklore research, divided between Zuni (where her stay again overlapped Bunzel's), and then Peña Blanca and Cochiti. Although she was subsequently to lead parties of students among the Mescalero Apache and the Blackfoot, the last fieldwork Benedict did on her own was among the Pima of Arizona in 1927 (Modell 1983:169–79).

Margaret Mead later suggested that Benedict had never seen a "living flesh-and-blood member of a coherent culture" (Mead 1959a:206), and Benedict herself commented on "the disintegration of culture" at the Rio Grande Pueblos. But she did so in the course of contrasting them with Zuni, which she was grateful to have gotten to "before it's gone likewise" (RFB/Mead 9/16/25, in Mead 1959a:304). When Benedict arrived at Zuni, it was, as Bunzel later noted, "in one of its periodic states of upheaval": the "progressives," who were tradi-tionally friendly to ethnographers, "had been ousted after unsuccessful at-tempts by [B.A.E.] anthropologists to photograph the mid-winter ceremonies," and were now discredited, so that Benedict and Bunzel were forced to find informants "among the conservative and traditionally hostile group that was now in power" (as quoted in Pandey 1972:332). Assisted by interpreters, Benedict worked with paid informants, for eight or nine hours a day, taking down the myths and folktales they dictated to her. Although one "amorous male," ready to play the role of Tony Luhan, hoped she would be "another Mabel Dodge" (RFB/MM 9/8/25, in Mead 1959a:301), most of Benedict's in-formants were old men, and it has been suggested (and indirectly acknowl-edged by Benedict herself) that the vision of Zuni culture which emerged through the double haze of memory and myth may have been somewhat ideal-ized (Pandey 1972:334; cf. Mead 1959a:231). Benedict herself clearly sensed the mythopoeic power of the place, remarking after leaving Zuni that she felt as if she had "stepped off the earth onto a timeless platform outside today"; after a walk with Bunzel under the "sacred mesa" along "stunning trails where the great wall towers above you always in new magnificence," she exclaimed: "when I'm God I'm going to build my city there" (RFB/MM 8/29, 8/24/25, in Mead 1959a:295, 293).

While Zuni provided the site for a lapsed Puritan's "city on a hill," the development of a conceptual framework for its construction took some time. Although Boas' intellectual shift away from historical reconstruction toward problems of cultural integration and the relation of individual behavior and cultural pattern had already begun, anthropologists were still, as Mead later

Zuni Pueblo, 1916. Wall of graveyard in front of church ruin; Corn Mountain in the distance. From Elsie Clews Parsons, *Pueblo Indian Religion* (1939). (Courtesy of the University of Chicago Press.)

noted, searching for a "body of psychological theory" adequate to the analysis of cultural materials (Mead 1959a:16). One of the most important searchers was Sapir, who, for Boas' more conservative taste, had "read too many books on psychiatry" (FB/RFB 7/16/25, in Mead 1959a:288), and to whom Benedict apparently sent a copy of a preliminary version of her dissertation (ES/RFB 6/25/22, in Mead 1959a:49). Over the next several years, during which the mental illness of his first wife occasionally took him from Ottawa to New York in connection with her treatment, Sapir and Benedict developed a close relationship, carried on largely by correspondence, in which they discussed the "poetries of passion and despair" they were each writing "to express the agony of marriages unravelling": "Lovers have nothing left, the incomparable worth of flesh become a shifting ash that covers love's utmost grief with characterless earth" (in Mead 1959a:161; cf. Handler 1986:138, 143). Sapir offered detailed appreciative criticisms of Benedict's poems (in the Puritan tradition, "but with a notable access of modernity"), and cautioned her against using a pen name: "you know how I feel about even toying with the idea of dissociation of personality" (ES/RFB 2/12/24, 3/23/26, in Mead 1959a:166, 182). He also seems to have encouraged her to move toward psychology, suggesting that "the logical sequel" to her dissertation would be a study of "the historical development of the guardian spirit in a particular area, the idea being to show how the particular elements crystallized into the characteristic pattern"—a task which he felt required "room somewhere from psychology," unless "you balk at psychology under all circumstances" (ES/RFB 6/25/22, in Mead 1959a:49).

The psychology Sapir first commended to Benedict was Jung's theory of *Psychological Types*, which had just been translated into English (1923), and which was the subject of "continuing excitement" in conversations at the anthropological section of the British Association for the Advancement of Science meeting in Toronto in 1924 (ES/RFB 9/10/23; MM/RFB 8/30, 9/8/24, in Mead 1959a: 54, 285–86; cf. 207, 552). Benedict did not fully share the enthusiasm Sapir and several others had for Jung, speaking disparagingly of Paul Radin's "lecturing" her about "the great god Jung" (RFB/MM 3/5/26, in Mead 1959a:305; cf. 206, 546). And there were other important influences on her work—including the Gestalt psychologist Kurt Koffka, whose *Growth of the Mind* (1925) Sapir commended as "the real book for background for a philosophy of culture, at least your/my philosophy" (ES/RFB 4/15/25, in Mead 1959a:177). However, it seems likely that Jung's book, which was heavily heavily influenced by Nietzsche (whose *Zarathustra* Benedict had read twenty years before), was the immediate source of the Apollonian/Dionysian opposition which in 1928 was to structure her discussion of "Psychological Types in the Cultures of the Southwest" (cf. Benedict 1939:467), where she mentioned Jung's book as a starting point for the interest in culture and personality).[6]

Having earlier noted the hypertrophy of the vision quest among the Plains Indians, and its attenuation in the Pueblo Southwest, and having been strongly impressed by the contrast between the Zuni and the neighboring Pima, for whom "intoxication is the visible mirroring of religion, . . . and the pattern of its mingling of clouded vision and of insight" (Benedict 1928:250; cf. Mead 1959a:206), Benedict now elaborated a contrast that echoed the two worlds of her childhood. On the one hand, there were the Dionysian Pima, pushing ritual to excess in order to achieve "the illuminations of frenzy"; on the other, the Apollonian Zuni, distrusting of excess, minimizing to "the last possible

6. According to Mead, Benedict's characteristic conceptualization of culture as "personality writ large" was worked out during the winter of 1927–1928, in long conversations the two of them had about "how a given temperamental approach to living could come so to dominate a culture that all who were born in it would become the willing or unwilling heirs to that view of the world" (Mead 1959a:206–12; 246–47)—and was first applied by Mead in *The Social Organization of Manu'a*. Although the issue is not germane to the present argument, it is worth noting that the phrase ("personality writ large") was first used by Benedict in "Configurations of Culture Growth in North America" (1932), which Mead suggests (and textual evidence confirms) was written after "most of *Patterns of Culture* [1934] had been completed" (Mead 1959a:208); although Benedict included "certain paragraphs" from "Configurations" in *Patterns*, they did not in fact include the phrase that was to be her theoretical *leitmotif*.

vanishing point any challenging or dangerous experiences," allowing "the individual no disruptive role in their social order" (Benedict 1928:249–50). Separated by no "natural barriers from surrounding peoples," Pueblo culture could not be understood by tracing "influences from other areas," but only in terms of "a fundamental psychological set which has undoubtedly been established for centuries," and which "has created an intricate pattern to express its own preferences"; without such an assumption, "the cultural dynamics of this region are unintelligible" (261).[7]

Without implying that it had no basis in her own observations, or no confirmation in those of others, it seems evident that the picture Benedict painted of Zuni reflected the personal psychological set established at the moment the story of her life began, and the patterning and dynamics of her subsequent personal and cultural experience. The resonance is richest in *Patterns of Culture*, a work written for a popular audience, in which Benedict was, as it were, speaking to the culture in which, after much pain, her personality had found a suitable niche—"Papa Franz" having got her appointment at Columbia regularized after she and her husband finally separated in 1930. Not the least of these resonances is that of sexuality, which in Benedict's own life had moved from a passionless marriage through the distanced passion of a poetic intimacy to a settled lesbian relationship with a younger woman (Modell 1983:188). Thus one of the prominent features of the matrilineal Pueblo pattern was the ease of sexuality, in which menstruation made "no difference in a woman's life" (Benedict 1934:120), in which houses built by men "belong to the women" (106), in which marital jealousy was "soft-pedalled" (107), in which divorce was simply a matter of placing the husband's possessions "on the doorsill" (74), in which there was no sense of sexual sin and no "guilt complexes" (126), and in which homosexuality was an "honourable estate" (263). Just as sex was "an incident in the happy life" (126), so also was death "no denial of life" (128); never the occasion for "an ambitious display or a terror situation," it was got past "as quickly and with as little violence as possible" (109). Homicide was virtually nonexistent, suicide too violent even to contemplate (117); save for witchcraft and revealing the secrets of the kachinas, there were "no other crimes" (100). Economic affairs and wealth were "comparatively unimportant" (76, 78); controversies, whether economic or domestic, were "carried out with an unparalleled lack of vehemence"; "every day in Zuni there are fresh instances of their mildness" (106). Although Zuni was

7. Superficially, this position echoed Sapir's call for the application of psychology to make understandable the historical process by which "particular elements crystallized into the characteristic pattern"; but at a deeper level, Benedict's hypostatization of an underlying psychological set for each culture contrasted sharply with Sapir's developing thought on the relation of culture and personality, which was increasingly critical of any tendency to reify culture, or to view it as "personality writ large" (Handler 1986; Darnell 1986).

"a theocracy to the last implication" (67), everyone cooperated, and "no show of authority" was ever called for, either in domestic or religious situations. Save for the ritual whipping of initiation—which was "never in any way an ordeal" (103)—children were not disciplined, even by the mother's brother, and there was no "possibility of the child's suffering from an Oedipus complex" (101). There was no striving for ecstatic individual experience, "whether by the use of drugs, of alcohol, of fasting, of torture, or of the dance" (95), and no culturally elaborated "themes of terror and danger" (119); the Pueblo way of life was the Apollonian middle way "of measure and of sobriety" (79, 129). Small wonder, then, that the Pueblos did not "picture the universe, as we do, as a conflict of good and evil" (127).

Zuni society was "far from Utopian"; it manifested also "the defects of its virtues" (Benedict 1934:246)—most notably, from our own cultural perspective, "the insistence on sinking the individual in the group" (103): there was no place for "force of will or personal initiative or the disposition to take up arms against a sea of troubles" (246). But for one for whom the achievement of individual identity had been so painfully problematic, and at a cultural moment when "rugged individualism" had come up against the painful reality of massive economic disaster, even this defect had its attractions, especially in view of the broader purpose for which Benedict had written the book. Primitive cultures were "a laboratory of social forms" in which the "problems are set in simpler terms than in the great Western civilizations" (17). Studying them should teach us not only "a greatly increased tolerance toward their divergencies" (37), but could also train us "to pass judgment upon the dominant traits of our own civilization" (249). And when placed against the "cut-throat competition" of the paranoid puritans of Dobu (141) and the "conspicuous waste" of the megalomaniac Kwakiutl (188), there could be little doubt as to which of the three provided the positive reference point for that task of cultural self-criticism.

In reviewing the book, Alfred Kroeber emphasized that it was written for the "intelligent non-anthropologist," arguing that here Benedict had used "pattern" in a "wider sense" than in the article she had published for a professional audience (Kroeber 1935). But as "propaganda for the anthropological attitude," *Patterns of Culture* was a powerful statement of the anthropological conception of cultural plurality, integration, determinism, and relativity, and it did a great deal toward accomplishing Benedict's goal of making Americans "culture-conscious" (1934:249). Selling well over a million copies during the next thirty years, it was widely used as a college text, and served for many later anthropologists as an introduction to the discipline, even after its portrayal of Zuni culture had come under sharp criticism (cf. Smith 1964:262).

Tepoztlán, as photographed by Robert Redfield from the house which he and his family occupied in 1926. (Courtesy of the Department of Special Collections, University of Chicago Library.)

The Long-Imagined Avatar of Tepoztlán

During the 1920s, the geography of United States cultural anthropology, which with a few exceptions had until then been coextensive with that of the nation itself, began to expand its horizons—although it was not until after World War II that it became substantially international. As ethnography moved tentatively into new areas, it encompassed other nodes of primitivistic longing, the nearest of which were the transfigured remnants of Aztec Mexico. Objects of ambivalent regard over the centuries, they were then entering a phase of rediscovery, in the eyes of both Mexican *indigenistas* seeking a more viable basis for national identity, and United States intellectuals yearning for a more "genuine culture" (Keen 1971:463–92; cf. Warman 1982:90; Hewitt 1984). One of the centers of *indigenista* interest was the village of Tepoztlán, on the southern side of the mountain rampart rimming the valley of Mexico, where the four thousand inhabitants ("Indians of almost pure blood") still spoke Nahuatl as well as Spanish, and the "folk culture [was] a fusion of Indian and Spanish elements" (Redfield 1930:30, 13; Godoy 1978:61)—and where Robert Redfield undertook his first anthropological fieldwork late in 1926.

Like the cultural history of Tepoztlán, Redfield's personal history was a fusion of two traditions. In a biographical statement elicited in 1950 by Anne

Roe for a comparative psychological study of prominent natural and social scientists, he described himself as "conscious from the first of belonging to two pasts": the "frontier tradition" of his father's "old American" family, and the "European tradition" of his mother, the "hyperrefined" daughter of the Danish consul in Chicago—where Redfield was born in 1897 (Roe 1950; cf. 1953a, 1953b; Stocking 1980). This dual cultural heritage was symbolized in the calendric cycle of his childhood: the six warmer months close to nature in the "clan community" that had developed on land his paternal great-grandfather had settled northwest of Chicago in 1833; the rest of the year in city apartments among Danish-speaking maternal kinfolk who kept alive a strong European tradition (reinforced by occasional trips abroad). Kept "secure from the world" by an "intensively protective father" (a successful corporate lawyer), the "inward facing" family life was marked by "intense intimacy combined with a certain aloofness from the ordinary world." A shy and timid boy, Redfield had little contact with children other than his younger sister, and was tutored at home throughout his somewhat infirm childhood. In 1910, he entered the University of Chicago Laboratory School, where his earlier natural historical interests took a marked literary turn, and he became part of a "somewhat precocious group of literati," before enrolling in the University of Chicago in 1915.

The only conflicts Redfield later recalled with his father were about his "over-protection," and in 1917 he went "went down one day" without prior consultation to enlist in an ambulance unit being organized to support the French army—for which his father then arranged the purchase of an ambulance. In France, Redfield took a "salutary beating" from his "hoodlum" buddies, and heard about (though he did not join) their trips to Paris; he also saw "some hard service"—memorialized in poetry later published by Harriet Monroe: "Are all men dead but me, or is this Death by my side?" (Redfield 1919:243). When the unit was disbanded, Redfield returned to the United States "very confused and disorganized," and convinced that "war was unspeakably bad"—although he did make speeches for the Liberty Loan drive after a heart murmur kept him out of the army. Accepting his father's suggestion that he go to Harvard, Redfield briefly studied (and disliked) biology, and then joined his family in Washington, where he served as a Senate office boy and worked in the code room at Military Intelligence. When the family returned to Chicago after the war, Redfield again followed paternal advice and studied law. Upon taking his degree the year after his father's death, he went to work in what had been his father's firm, where he did ill-paid drudge work in the city records for cases involving the sewer system ("I knew more about manhole covers than anyone in the city of Chicago") (Roe 1950).

By this time, Redfield had married the daughter of the Chicago urban sociologist Robert Park, and (at his own father's expense) had enjoyed a honeymoon in the Pueblo Southwest. In 1923, when Redfield was in a "state of great restlessness" over his work, and had begun to be excited by his father-in-law's ideas about a "science of society," his wife suggested that they accept an open invitation to visit Mexico previously extended to the Park family by Elena Landazuri, a feminist *indigenista* who had studied under Park. While there, they met other *indigenistas*, including the artist Diego Rivera, the folklorist Frances Toor, who had recently done research in Tepoztlán, and Manuel Gamio, a Boas-trained anthropologist then carrying on archeological and ethnographic research at Teotihuacán. Observing Gamio at work in the field, Redfield decided to become an anthropologist—happily, at the very time when his father-in-law wrote to announce that the Chicago Department of Sociology and Anthropology was taking steps to develop a training program in the latter field (Godoy 1978:50–51).

Redfield began his studies in the fall of 1924, the second year of Fay-Cooper Cole's effort to revitalize Chicago anthropology, which under Frederick Starr had been moribund for twenty years. Cole was an early Boas Ph.D. of rather traditional archeological and ethnological orientation; but he was also a talented academic entrepreneur, sensitive to changing trends within anthropology and to emerging funding patterns in the social sciences. Within a year he had succeeded in bringing Edward Sapir to Chicago. While most of Redfield's anthropological work was with Cole, he took several courses with Sapir, as well as courses in sociology with Ellsworth Faris, William Ogburn, Edward Burgess, and his father-in-law. His early anthropological orientation clearly reflected Park's personal intellectual heritage, which was an amalgam of the pragmatism of John Dewey and William James, the sociological concepts of Georg Simmel, Ferdinand Tönnies, and William Graham Sumner, and the epistemological thought of Wilhelm Windelband. Accepting the Germanic distinction between idiographic and nomothetic sciences, and acknowledging the Boasian critique of evolutionism, Redfield associated himself with the emerging anthropological interest in "processual generalizations," which he felt was exemplified in the work of William Rivers, Clark Wissler, and Sapir (Stocking n.d., 1979).

Perhaps his most significant experience, however, was in Burgess's practicum in sociological research, which in a department noted for its empirical work in the "laboratory of the city" was required of every student. During his first year of graduate study, Redfield made more than forty visits to the Chicago Mexican community, recording his experiences in a lengthy typed diary. After Redfield completed two years of course work and a year of teaching at the University of Chicago, his experience in Burgess's practicum became the basis for a research proposal that Cole forwarded to the recently formed Social Science Research Council, in the hope that field research might be made a standard part of graduate training in anthropology. Redfield's previous "survey of Mexicans in Chicago" suggested the need for a study of the "conditions under which the Mexican has been raised" in "semi-primitive village communities" in order to understand "the problems arising out of the growing Mexican immigration into the United States." To this end, he proposed an inquiry that touched the four bases of his own (and his father-in-law's) social scientific interests: a "nomothetic study" of the problem known "to sociologists as assimilation and to the anthropologists as culture-borrowing"; a more subjective understanding of native culture by entering "the lives of people and learn[ing] the problems which occupy their minds"; a functional study of the various social institutions and their interrelations; and a study of "comparative mentality" (Godoy 1978:54–60; cf. Stocking n.d.).

Aided by a $2500 Social Science Research Council fellowship, and accompanied by his wife, their two small children, and his mother-in-law, Redfield left Chicago in November 1926 for Tepoztlán, which Gamio had suggested as a field site. After travelling the sixty miles from Mexico City by rail, they were met at nearby San Juan by Jesús Condé, a member of the expatriate "Colonia Tepozteco" formed in Mexico City during the latter days of the Mexican Revolution. Condé had subsequently returned to his native village to push a program of civic reform and Indian cultural regeneration, and was to be Redfield's primary informant. After a four-hour mountain trek to Tepoztlán, the Redfield family settled quickly into simple (but by local standards "elegant") domesticity in a one-room brick-floored house. Savoring the vista of the valley spread out before their doorway, and the visibly embedded history of the "stillest, quietest place" he had ever seen, Redfield and his wife filled their days with ethnographic work among barefoot people who moved "in crooked lanes, where never runs a wheel, like figures in a dream." It was so much what Redfield had "for so long imagined" that it felt like "a repetition of an experience in some earlier avatar" (RP: RR/R. Park, 12/2/26).

But as Redfield also noted, Tepoztlán had been a focal point of revolutionary violence, and it was still "very Zapatista in sentiment." Beneath the surface of its "relatively homogeneous and well-integrated" society, the village was divided between religious and "bolshevik" factions, and the "Cristero" rebels in the surrounding region made the Redfields' position insecure almost from the first. On February 18, forty armed men rode into the village shouting "Viva Cristo el Rey," and before the "battle of Tepoztlán" was over, two locals had been wounded and one rebel left dead in the gutter (RP: RR/Clara Park 2/20/27; Godoy 1978:67–68). The Redfields retreated to sanctuary in the Federal District, from which Redfield carried on a commuter ethnography —despite fits of "profound depression," the serious illness of his wife, and continuing rebel activity that made his informants "reluctant to give information." By the end of June he was physically and emotionally exhausted, and

Robert Redfield in Tepoztlán, 1926. (Courtesy of the Department of Special Collections, University of Chicago Library.)

over Cole's objections that it would not "look good" to his funders, he took his family back to Chicago (Godoy 1978:70–72).

Redfield looked back upon the rebellion as a "minor disturbance of a life as delightful as it is remote, and as scientifically provocative as it is delightful" (Redfield 1928:247). He had collected a fair amount of rather traditional ethnographic information on such topics as festal cycles and the social organization of the barrios, as well as a large number of "corridos" (contemporary folk ballads), which he saw as playing the same integrative role his father-in-law (a former journalist) attributed to the newspaper in urban society. But in general Redfield's ethnographic corpus was somewhat thin and spotty, and the frankly sketchy synthesis he defended as a dissertation in the summer of 1928 (and published with slight revision two years later) showed at various points not only the influence of the personality and values that predisposed him to romanticize Tepoztecan life and to repress its less "enjoyable" aspects, but also the influence of prior conceptual and theoretical assumptions.

Redfield regarded Clark Wissler's *Man and Culture* (1923) as "the best piece of anthropological writing" he had read (RP: RR/Wissler 2/9/25), and *Tepoztlán* is clearly influenced by Wissler's concepts, which were quite congenial to the "ecological" approach Park had adopted for the study of the city. In interpreting the diffusion of culture traits in Tepoztlán, Redfield redefined the notion of the "culture area" in terms of a modification of the concentric ecological zones Park had laid upon the map of Chicago, with the central plaza serving as the "periphery of change" from which to trace "the diffusion of city traits." Like Park, Redfield conceptualized cultural units and processes in terms of different styles of mental life and personality types, transforming the Tepoztecan descriptive adjectives "tonto" and "correcto" into polar personality and class categories. Redfield's conception of the "folk community" as a type "intermediate between the primitive tribe and the modern city" (1930:217) was strongly influenced by Park (and the German traditions on which Park drew), and by the modified social evolutionism that structured Park's thinking. Thus "the disorganization and perhaps the reorganization" of Tepoztecan culture "under the slowly growing influence of the city" was merely an example "of the general type of change whereby primitive man becomes civilized man, the rustic becomes the urbanite" (Redfield 1930:14; cf. Stocking n.d.; Breslau 1988). But Redfield showed a greater tendency than Park to romanticize the *gemeinschaftlich* organicism of the folk community, and the relation to Sapir's dichotomy of cultures was subsequently suggested by one of Redfield's students: "To the degree that a culture is folk it is also genuine; and, to the degree that a culture departs from its folk attributes, to that degree is it moving toward a condition of spuriousness" (Tumin 1945:199).

By the time *Tepoztlán* appeared, Redfield had embarked on a long-term study of four communities in Yucatan, distributed "along the scale of modernization," which exemplified the process by which small, isolated, closely integrated folk communities underwent a regular process of disorganization, secularization, and individualization as they came in more frequent cultural contact with heterogeneous urban society (Stocking 1980). Both the "folk-urban continuum" and the ethnography of Tepoztlán were to come under sharp criticism from a later generation of meso-American anthropologists. Even at the time, Ruth Benedict (who must have had in mind Malinowski and Mead rather than her own rather traditional memory ethnography) criticized Redfield for relying on informants rather than on his own "actual participation in the life of the community" (Benedict 1930). But the leading Boasian historicist greeted Redfield's book as a "landmark" study, which might provide a "model" for future inquiry (Kroeber 1931:238). And although Redfield, unlike Benedict and Mead, did not direct his study to popular audiences, or himself use Tepoztlán for purposes of cultural critique, several of his readers did. For Stuart Chase, the influential cultural critic and popularizer of social scientific ideas—who drew extensively on Redfield's work—*Tepoztlán* became an archetype to be posed against *Middletown* (Lynd & Lynd 1929) as contrastive Other in his ongoing critique of "mechanical civilization."

> Middletown is essentially practical, Tepoztlán essentially mystical in mental processes. Yet in coming to terms with one's environment, Tepoztlán has exhibited, I think, the superior common sense. . . . These people possess several qualities the average American would give his eyeteeth to get; and they possess other things completely beyond his purview—human values he has not even glimpsed, so relentlessly has his age blinded and limited him. (Chase 1931:17, 208)

Lithe Brown Bodies Silhouetted against the Sunset

From the time that Captain Cook returned from Tahiti, the focal ganglion in the world geography of European primitivistic longing was the islands of the "South Seas," where handsome brown-skinned natives led untroubled lives, finding ready sustenance in the fruit of palm trees under which they made a free and easy love (Fairchild 1961; Smith 1960). But although the islands of the Pacific were also the locus of anti-primitivist missionary enterprise throughout the nineteenth century (Boutelier et al. 1978; Garrett 1982), and were touched by the United States Exploring Expedition in the 1840s (Stanton 1975), they did not become an object of serious American anthropological interest until immediately after World War I (Te Rangi Hiroa 1945; cf. Stocking 1976a). In a postwar context of cultural criticism, moral questioning, and sexual experimentation, it is scarcely surprising that this anthropological interest became entangled, in the work of Margaret Mead, in "invisible threads" of primitivist consciousness.[8]

Four years younger than Redfield, Mead was also the firstborn child in a family securely set off from the rest of the world; she later recalled taking "pride in living in a household that was itself unique," but also longing "to share in every culturally normal experience" (Mead 1972:20). And while both her parents came from "old American" backgrounds, the rather dramatic contrast between the strong women and the weak men within her family environment must have reinforced a sense of the possibilities of culturally conditioned difference. But if her father's life had been "cut down" to "the pattern of academic and social virtues in which [her] mother believed" (40), his marginal involvement in the entrepreneurial world as professor in the University of Pennsylvania business school and editor of *Railway Age* nevertheless assured the family a comfortable middle-class existence, and he found outlet for a somewhat anxious masculinity in occasional infidelities. Overprotective of his "fragile" and disaster-prone son, he left most of the supervision of his daughters to his wife. While Mead resented his occasional "arbitrary intrusions into our lives" and his "conservative, money-bound judgments" (39), she quickly learned how to get what she wanted from him—and as "the original punk" was easily able to dominate her younger brother. Her mother, a graduate student at the University of Chicago when she married at the age of twenty-nine, moved the family to Hammonton, New Jersey, in 1902 so that she could continue her never-completed dissertation research among Italian families. A feminist radical who combined "fury at injustice" with "deep personal gentleness" (25), she retained a strong Old New England sense of the distance between "people with some background" and the "common herd" (28)—but also "danced for joy" at the outbreak of the Russian revolution (97). That Mead in her own life "realized every one of her [mother's] unrealized ambitions" (29) was in large part due to the "decisive influence" (45) of her paternal grandmother, a one-time school teacher, who was responsible for Mead's education until she entered high school, who taught her "to treat all people as the children of God" (54), and who set the ten-year-old Mead to work taking notes on the behavior of her younger siblings (just as Mead's mother had previously taken notes on Mead's). Within the "overriding academic ethos [that] shaped all our lives," in which "the enjoyment of the intellect as mediated

8. Although they did not achieve the same degree of anthropological notoriety, Ralph Linton's observations on Marquesan sexuality were also based on fieldwork done in this period, and provide an interesting gender contrast to those of Mead in Samoa. Whereas Mead emphasized the freedom of female premarital sexuality, Linton emphasized the treatment of women as sexual objects, and the man's "playing up to her erotic wishes" (Linton 1939:173)—a characterization that was to be called into question by a later ethnographer, on methodological grounds not dissimilar to those raised in the case of Mead (Suggs 1971).

by words in books was central," Mead was "the child who could make the most of this," and was never "asked to constrain or distort some other gift" (90).

Child of pragmatic rationality and confident privilege, Mead's only remembered experience with "a possibly punitive authority" came at the age of two when her mother made her show a stolen violet to a park policeman, who "only smiled" (Mead 1972:120). Her archetypal experience of the formation of irrational prejudice came when Midwestern sorority members at DePauw University in Indiana rejected her for her exotic Eastern mannerisms and the ritualistic Episcopalianism she had embraced in mild adolescent rebellion against her agnostic parents—if not also for her feeling that "from this position of security" she could "dictate egalitarian behavior" (94). Although Mead responded characteristically "by setting out to see what I could do within this system" (98), she experienced her year at DePauw as a small-town "exile" from "the center of life" in New York City (100), and in the autumn of 1920, she transferred to Barnard College.

There she quickly found a subculture she could fit into: an unusually talented literary "intelligentsia" set off from their "mediocre" and "reactionary" classmates, who lived in an off-campus apartment and went down to "the Village" ("a most delightful place"), who refused to attend a dinner with Columbia's president "Nicky Butler" because evening dress was required, who (after some hesitation) "bobbed" their hair, who listened to Scott Nearing and "organized a meeting for two Italians framed up for murder because they are radicals," and who called themselves first the "communist morons" and then the "Ash Can Cats" (MP: MM/E. F. Mead, 1920–23). Although they were "still remarkably innocent about practical matters relating to sex," they read Margaret Sanger, talked about Freud, and knew that "repression was a bad thing" (Mead, 1972:103). They also "learned about homosexuality"—as "Euphemia," Mead received passionate letters from a classmate who signed herself "Peter" (MP: Box C1). Mead later spoke of her friends as "part of a generation of young women who felt extraordinarily free"—refusing to "bargain with men," delaying marriage until they felt like it, and carrying on affairs with older men who were somewhat perplexed by their freedom (Mead 1972:108; cf. Fass 1971:260–90). She herself, however, had been engaged since shortly after her sixteenth birthday to Luther Cressman, whose own moral odyssey took him from army training camp into training for the Episcopal priesthood, and thence into graduate training in sociology (Cressman 1988). Until (both still virgins) they were married after her graduation, the major nonverbal outlet for her libidinal energy was apparently a persistent neuritis of the right arm (Mead 1972:104; cf. Howard 1984:47–48; Cressman 1988:92). From the beginning, the emotional commitments in what she later called her "student marriage" seem to have been a bit asymmetrical. However, Mead did not have her own affair with an older man until her poetry had begun to reveal her marital discontent: "You could dampen my joy with your reason, My ecstasy cool with a glance" (MP: Poems; cf. Mead 1972:123). When she did, it was with " the most brilliant person" and the "most satisfactory mind I ever met" (Mead 1972:50); but when Edward Sapir "implored" her, after the death of his wife, to "be mama" to "his three motherless children" (quoted in Howard 1984:52), Mead had by that time already committed her own life to anthropology.

At Barnard, Mead's ambitions had shifted from writing to politics to science, through which she hoped both to understand human behavior and "be effective in the world of human events" (Mead 1962:121). Although she majored in a rather scientistic quantitative psychology, at the beginning of her senior year she took two classes that were to lead her towards anthropology: Ogburn's course on the psychological aspects of culture, which—despite his strong statisticalist bent—was the first in which "Freudian psychology was treated with respect" (111); and Boas' introductory course in anthropology, in which Mead so impressed him by her "helpful participation in class discussion" that Boas excused her from the final exam (112). Despite Boas' anti-evolutionism, what moved her most about anthropology was the "sense of the millennia it had taken man to take the first groping steps toward civilization" (112)—and the prospect of studying one of the "primitive cultures" that were fast being killed off by "contact with modern civilization" (MP: MM/M. R. Mead 3/11/23; cf. Mead 1959b). "Dr. Boas"—not yet "Papa Franz"—remained a somewhat distant and unapproachable figure, and it was Ruth Benedict who "humanized Boas' formal lectures" (Mead 1962:113) and recruited Mead for anthropology—and who, in the aftermath of a classmate's shocking suicide, Mead began to know "not only as a teacher but also as a friend," and later for a time as lover (115; cf. Bateson 1984:140).

Although Mead's master's thesis was formally in psychology, the problem was set by Boas, as part of his on-going critique of hereditarian racial assumption. Carried on in the same community her mother had studied two decades before, Mead's research on "Group Intelligence Tests and Linguistic Disability Among Italian Children" showed that test scores varied in proportion to the amount of English spoken in their homes (Mead 1927:642). Her doctoral research, eventually published as *An Inquiry into the Question of Cultural Stability in Polynesia* (1928a), reflected another part of Boas' developing agenda: the attempt, in response to the hyperdiffusionism of certain British and German ethnologists, to test the relative stability of different elements of culture. Like Benedict's dissertation, it was a library study of the association of cultural elements over a broad geographical area, and led toward a more integrative study—inasmuch as the form and meaning of elements was "particularly subject to reinterpretation in terms of the prevailing pattern of each group" (84).

At the end of her first year of graduate study, Mead was initiated into the then rather intimate world of professional anthropology at the Toronto meetings of the British Association. There she heard Sapir and Goldenweiser arguing about Jung's psychological types, met Erna Gunther (whose "avant-garde 'contract marriage'" with Leslie Spier in 1921 had occasioned shocked comment in the New York press), and discovered that everyone "had a field of his own, . . . a 'people' to whom he referred in his discussions" (Mead 1972: 124). Already immersed in the ethnographic literature of Polynesia, and no doubt aware that few professional claims had been staked in the area, Mead decided to do fieldwork there on the question of cultural change. Although Mead hoped that the psychogalvanometer (the forerunner of the lie detector) would enable her actually to measure "the individual's emotional responses" to change, (125), Boas regarded such quantification as "premature" (Mead 1962:122). By this time his research agenda was shifting from diffusionary questions to "the set of problems that linked the development of individuals to what was distinctive in the culture in which they were reared" (Mead 1972: 126), and he proposed instead that Mead undertake a study of "the relative strength of biological puberty and cultural pattern" (Mead 1962:122).

In the era of "flaming youth," the phenomenon of adolescence was a center of cultural concern, and the discussion was strongly influenced by the recapitulationist evolutionary arguments of G. Stanley Hall (1907) – who had in fact been *persona non grata* to Boas since Boas' acrimonious departure from Clark University back in 1892. Boas may have felt that adolescence was a particularly appropriate problem for Mead, who at twenty-three knew what it was to be a "flapper," and who still had a slight, adolescent figure and a childish gait. A bargain was struck, and Mead accepted Boas' problem, which they presented to the National Research Council as "A Study in Heredity and Environment Based on the Investigation of the Phenomena of Adolescence among Primitive and Civilized Peoples" (MP: Fellowship application, 1925). In return, Boas – overriding Sapir's objection that she was "too high strung and emotional" – agreed that Mead might go to an area he himself regarded as "too dangerous," provided she chose an island "to which a ship came regularly" (Mead 1972:128–29). Mead picked American Samoa, which since 1900 had been under the governance of the U.S. Navy, and where her father-in-law had contacts (cf. Cressman 1988:114). When April 30, 1925, brought the news that she had been awarded a Research Council fellowship, Mead and the Ash Can Cats were able to join its celebration to another they had already planned: a midnight visit to Greenwich Village, where they hung a Maybasket of flowers on the front door of a surprised and delighted Edna St. Vincent Millay – though they lost the nerve to recite her verse in chorus (Howard 1984:56–57).

Three months later, Mead set off by rail across the country, accompanied

part way by Benedict, who was returning to Zuni. Passing through Los Angeles (a city "run by real estate men for other real estate men"), Mead embarked from San Francisco for Honolulu (where "wandering mists" hid "all
the signs of industrial civilization"). From there she sailed to Pago Pago, where
she stayed in the hotel that had been the setting for Somerset Maugham's
Rain, and went to dances aboard a U.S. Navy cruiser (Mead 1977:21, 23; cf.
MP: "Field Bulletins"). During the next few weeks in Pago Pago and in nearby
villages on the island of Tutuila, she practiced the language and saw "the principal social ceremonies," remarking the contrast between what was visible on
the surface to the "transient white man" and the underlying "fabric of their
culture," and concluding that it was "much easier to derive aesthetic pleasure
from contemplating the ideas underlying their culture than from looking at
the human embodiments of those ideas" (MP: "Field Bulletins," 10/3/25). She
decided to transfer in November to Ta'u, the easternmost island of the Manu'a
district, which several years before had been the center of a rebellion against
U.S. rule—"an insane procedure fostered by an unstable officer and a schem-
ing carpetbagger" (MP: "Field Bulletins," 10/31/25). "More primitive and
unspoiled than any other part of Samoa," Ta'u nevertheless had a resident
Navy medical officer, with whose family Mead could live, so that she could
be "in and out of the native homes" all day and "still have a bed to sleep
on and wholesome food" (Mead 1977:28).

Although Boas felt that Mead's study was a methodological innovation,
marking the "first serious attempt to enter into the mental life of a group in
a primitive society" (MP: FB/MM 11/7/25), he had given her only one half-
hour of methodological instruction before she sailed for Samoa, emphasizing
that she should stick to her problem and not waste time "studying the culture
as a whole" (Mead 1972:138). Mead did in fact collect general ethnographic
material, but she concentrated on performing psychological tests and collecting systematic data on a group of fifty girls, twenty-five of them postpubertal
(Mead 1928b:260; cf. MP: MM/FB 2/15/26). The most problematic data were
of course those on sexual behavior, which were collected by various means.
Mead's notes on the Samoan language include a lengthy and highly explicit
list of sex terms recorded sixty years before by the missionary George Pratt;
her general notes include a long and vividly detailed interview with one adult
male informant covering all aspects of Samoan sex life, including techniques
of masturbation and foreplay, sexual positions, frequency of married and
premarital intercourse, and female behavior at the height of orgasm; one of
her bulletin letters home includes an account of an evening with adolescents
that ended with one of the girls, amid much banter about her numerous lovers, picking out a boy to accompany her home; the records Mead kept of her
fifty girls include a column headed "Sex," in which she made such notes as
"admits a lover," "the other girls say she sleeps with . . . ," "promenades a great

Margaret Mead and unidentified Samoan friend, Manu'a, 1926. (Courtesy of the Institute of Intercultural Studies, Inc.)

deal." Mead's bulletin accounts suggest that although she had some trouble with the language, she worked without an interpreter (being in fact coopted for that role by the chaplain), and that she was able to establish good rapport with young Samoans, who visited her from five in the morning until midnight. Indeed, a key component of her "method" seems to have been the kind of late-night gossip she must have enjoyed with the Ash Can Cats.[9]

After five months in Ta'u – during which a severe hurricane had disrupted her work for two weeks – Mead felt that she had really experienced Samoan life from the inside. She had avoided entanglement in the "toils" of the rank system in her own village, where the children called her "Makelita" and treated her as "one of themselves." But elsewhere on the island, where she was treated as *taupou* (or ceremonial virgin), she had "rank to burn," and "could order the whole village about." At the end, she felt that she had not only watched Samoans, but had "been them":

> I have been dressed to dance by the whole village as they tied the ti leaves around my wrist and ankles and smeared the cocoanut oil over my arms and shoulders. . . . I haven't watched a group of boys flirt with the visiting lady, I've flirted myself as the visiting lady . . . and I've listened to my talking chiefs quarrel and scheme over the return presents and shared the humiliation of high chiefs too poor to properly validate their privileges.

When it came time to leave, Mead was ready to go home: "nine months of isolated labor in an uncongenial climate are quite enough for me." But as she told her grandmother, who had taught her "to appreciate the infinite detail of existence," she felt a deep sense of loss that soon there would be "no more palms, no more lithe brown bodies passing and repassing, silhouetted against the sunset": "if Samoa were nearer to you all, and there were no dull white people and mosquitos, it would be a pleasant paradise" (MP: MM/M. R. Mead 4/15/26).

---

9. Derek Freeman has suggested that the Samoan participants in these late evening sessions "plied Mead with . . . counterfeit tales" in order to "amuse themselves, and had no inkling that their tales would ever find their way into a book"; they were simply manifesting the behavior called *tau fa'asse'e*, "the action of deliberately duping someone, a pastime that greatly appeals to the Samoans as a respite from the severities of their authoritarian society" (Freeman 1983a:290). More recently, he has offered evidence of interviews with several elderly Samoan women who recalled those evenings of sixty years ago in very much the same terms: "I think some girl told her a wrong story. The Samoan people you know wants to laugh to a foreigner or someone, so they told a wrong story to influence her to listen to the story but it's not a true story." "Yes, she asked us what we did after dark. We girls would pinch each other and tell her that we were out with the boys. We were only joking, but she took it seriously. As you know, Samoan girls are terrific liars and love making fun of people, but Margaret thought it was all true." (Freeman, personal communication, 11/22/88, quoting passages from the post-production script of the film *Margaret Mead and Samoa*, by Frank Heimans.) There is little doubt that the matter of Samoan sexuality is one where Mead seems to have been particularly susceptible to scotomization (blind spots) and/or projection (cf. Devereux 1967) and she might also have been the victim of misinformation. On the other hand, the elicited octogenarian recollections of adolescent informants as to the events of sixty years before may also be subject to distortions of various sorts.

Two months into her stay on Ta'u, in a moment of methodological angst, Mead had written to Boas wondering how she might present her material so that "no reader should have to trust my word for anything," but would be offered "an array of facts from which another would be able to draw independent conclusions." The "Ogburns of science" would not be satisfied with anything other than a "semi-statistical" presentation, but this would be "misleading" because the sample was too small, and "isolated facts" had meaning only in the context of "my final conclusion as to submission and rebellion in the family circle." Alternatively, she could use case histories—but to fill them "with all the minutiae which make them significant to me when they are passing before my eyes is next to impossible," and it was not clear in any case that they would "prove a point" (MP: MM/FB 1/5/26). In response, Boas suggested that a "statistical treatment of such an intricate behaviour" would "not have very much meaning." He recommended instead giving a "summarized description" of "the conditions under which the behaviour develops" and then setting off "the individual against the background"—which he compared to "the method that is used by medical men in their analysis of individual cases on which is built up the general picture of the pathological cases that they want to describe." While "complete elimination of the subjective attitude of the investigator is quite impossible in a matter of this kind," Boas felt Mead would undoubtedly "try to overcome this so far as that is possible" (MP: FB/MM 2/15/26).

Mead returned from Samoa westward via Europe, and on the trip fell passionately in love with an aggressively masculine young New Zealand psychologist, Reo Fortune, who was on his way to England to study anthropology with Malinowski. For the moment, she "re-chose Luther," but the sense of "common vocation working with people within the framework of the church" was gone, and Mead, who had planned to have six children, was told by a gynecologist that a tipped uterus would prevent her ever giving birth. She continued to live with Cressman through an "odd winter," finishing an account of her Samoan research during time free from her new job at the American Museum of Natural History. But after another "tempestuous" month with Fortune in Germany the following summer, she decided to marry him, and wrote to Cressman insisting on a divorce (Mead 1972:157–67; Cressman 1988:189–91).

Back in New York that fall, Mead worked on revisions of the rather prosaically titled manuscript on "The Adolescent Girl in Samoa" which she had previously sent to the publisher William Morrow. In that version, cross-cultural comparisons were relegated to a brief set of "conclusions" in which Mead suggested that "only by criticizing our own civilization in terms of the behavior of other human beings in civilizations having different patterns of behavior can we arrive at any knowledge of how great a part of our attitudes and behavior is due, not to the accident of humanity or even of sex, still less of race, but rather to the accident of being born in America, or in Samoa, in the America of 1927 instead of the America of 1729" (MP). Morrow was interested in the manuscript, but he wanted something that might have the impact of the recent best-selling anthropological popularization *Why We Behave Like Human Beings* (1926)—whose author, George Dorsey, had introduced Mead to Morrow (Howard 1984:87–88). Somewhat ambivalently, Mead "finally decided" to go along with a number of proposed revisions and provided Morrow with new material in which she pushed speculation "to the limit of permissibility" (MP; MM/WM 1/25/27, 2/11/28).

The result was *Coming of Age in Samoa: A Psychological Study of Primitive Youth for Western Civilisation* (Mead 1928b).[10] The worrisome methodological issues Mead had discussed with Boas were now relegated to an appendix on problems of sampling and the "personal equation," where, accepting Boas' clinical analogy, she acknowledged that the "student of the more intangible and psychological aspects of human behavior is forced to illuminate rather than demonstrate a thesis" (260). In rather striking contrast, her new introduction confidently asserted the validity of the "anthropological method" as the only option for those "who wish to conduct a human experiment but who lack the power either to construct the experimental conditions or to find controlled examples of those conditions." By choosing "quite simple, primitive peoples," whose "fundamental structure" a "trained student" could "master" in a "few months," and in which "one girl's life was so much like another's," it became possible to answer the question "which sent me to Samoa" (7, 8, 11).

Mead's ability to do this depended in part on relegating another potentially troublesome issue to the back of her book, where "Samoan Civilisation as it is Today" (originally her final chapter) also appeared as an appendix. In it, she minimized the impact of missionaries and emphasized the naval administration's "admirable policy of benevolent non-interference in native affairs," concluding that while "the new influences" had "drawn the teeth of the old culture" (cannibalism, blood revenge, the "cruel defloration ceremony," etc.) they had not introduced "economic instability, poverty, the wage system, the separation of the worker from his land and from his tools, modern warfare, industrial disease, the abolition of leisure, the irksomeness of a bureau-

10. During the same period when Mead was working on revisions of *Coming of Age in Samoa,* she wrote a more conventional ethnography, *The Social Organization of Manu'a,* which was published in 1930 as a museum bulletin. While it seems evident that certain of the more questionable aspects of her interpretation of Samoa reflect the attempt to popularize her findings in response to Morrow's urging, it is doubtful that all the issues that have been raised regarding her Samoan ethnography can be resolved by compartmentalizing the "popularized" and the "professional." Although the substance and the style of the second work were clearly directed to a specifically professional audience, Mead did not at the time insist on the difference. She cited her earlier study (1930:126), and insofar as the two studies overlap, their interpretations seem consistent with one another.

cratic government," or the "subtler penalties of civilisation" such as neuroses, philosophical perplexities, and individual tragedies (Mead 1928b:270, 276–77). Granting that precontact Samoan culture had been "less flexible" and "less kindly with the individual aberrant," and cautioning the reader against mistaking the conditions she described for "aboriginal" or "typical primitive ones," Mead suggested that "present day Samoan civilisation" was simply the result of the "fortuitous" and "fortunate" impact of "a complex intrusive culture upon a simpler and most hospitable indigenous one" (272–73). But in the body of the book itself, such ambiguities of cultural historicity were subordinated to purposes of cultural archetypification.

The tone was set right at the beginning in a brief account Mead had inserted of "A Day in Samoa," which opened at dawn with "lovers slip[ing] home from trysts" and closed long past midnight with "the mellow thunder of the reef and the whisper of lovers" (1928b:14–19). This archetypifying sense of cultural contemporaneity was sustained throughout the next ten chapters by the consistent use of the "ethnographic present," except when Mead referred in the past tense to the behavior of particular individuals she had studied. Similarly, most of her infrequent comments on "former days" or processes of cultural change had the effect of accounting for anomalies in the pattern she was constructing—for example, the reference to rape as an "abnormal" result of contact with "white civilisation" (93), or the explanation of the "curious" attitude toward virginity as the result of the "moral premium on chastity" introduced by Christianity (98).

When at the end Mead undertook more explicit comparison of the "civilisation of America and the civilisation of Samoa," this archetypifying atemporality had (paradoxically, for a disciple of Boas) an evolutionary as well as a culturally particular aspect: what made the life of the Samoan adolescent girl different was partly the "shallowness" of Samoan (as opposed to other) "primitive civilisations," and partly the limitation of individual choice that was characteristic of "all isolated primitive civilisation" (1928b:198, 200). The presentation of cultural relativism in an evolutionary package ("A Study of Primitive Youth for Western Civilisation") made it possible to appeal simultaneously to motives of romantic primitivism and ethnocentric progressivism. On the one hand, Mead insisted that "our own ways are not humanly inevitable or God-ordained" (233) and that we "pay heavily for our heterogeneous, rapidly changing civilisation" (247). But in return, we gained "the possibility of choice, the recognition of "many possible ways of life, where other civilisations have recognized only one." By accepting the "downfall of a single standard" and educating our children for choice, "we shall have realised the high point of individual choice and universal toleration which a heterogeneous culture and a heterogeneous culture alone can attain" (248).

Mead felt that she had written a book about the cultural determination

Dust jacket illustration for an early edition of *Coming of Age in Samoa*. (Courtesy of William Morrow & Co., Inc., and the Institute of Intercultural Studies, Inc.)

of individual choice, and that message was surely there. But a more specifically sexual message was suggested by the dust jacket illustration of a bare-breasted maiden rushing an apparently nude young man to a tryst beneath a moonlit palm. And the text itself, resonating both to contemporary cultural and her own personal experience, did a great deal to sustain this reading: "romantic love as it occurs in our civilisation, inextricably bound up with ideas of monogamy, exclusiveness, jealousy and undeviating fidelity" was absent among Samoans, who "scoff at fidelity to a long absent wife or mistress, [and] believe explicitly that one love will quickly cure another" (Mead 1928b:104–5). When Robert Lowie suggested that the "free love" of modern Samoa might be the abnormal result of cultural contact and should not be offered as evidence for Mead's "pedagogical theses" (Lowie 1929:533), Mead insisted that she had never intended to imply that "Samoans are free from conflict principally because they are 'sexually uninhibited'" (MP: MM/RHL 11/5/29). Similarly, she was amazed that the students of a professor at a Tennessee teachers' college should have thought that her book was "mainly about sex education and sex freedom," when "out of 297 pages there are exactly sixty eight which deal with sex" (MP: MM/W. Brownell 3/10/30). But as the dust jacket comments, the almost uniformly favorable reviews in the popular press, and the many news accounts of Mead's adventure suggest, there were many others who got the same impression—including Edward Sapir, whose neo-conservative essay on the "discipline of sex" was written with Margaret Mead in mind (Sapir 1930: 413; cf. 1928:523; Handler 1986:143–47).

Despite Mead's initial "amazement" that it had been used as a college text (MP: MM/W. Brownell 3/10/30), *Coming of Age in Samoa* served that purpose from the moment of its publication. And although there was from the beginning an undercurrent of professional criticism of its ethnographic adequacy, it has been, like *Patterns of Culture*, one of the most influential anthropological works of the twentieth century. This, despite (or perhaps because of) the fact that it, too, was strikingly marked by personal and cultural concerns at once particular to an historical moment and resonant of a more general cultural tradition (cf. Jones 1988).[11]

The Critique of Apollonian Ethnography

Although their career patterns followed rather different trajectories, Benedict, Redfield, and Mead all became major figures in American anthropology. But

11. Three decades later, Mead herself acknowledged the embeddedness of her book in the cultural context of the mid-1920s, which she recalled as both "young and hopeful," but filled with "the rebellion and self-criticism, the hatreds and the cynical despair which were nourished by the growing crisis of the post-World War I world." For many, her book was "an escape in spirit that paralleled an escape in body to a South Sea island where love and ease were the order of the day." Furthermore, this was a reading her own "inexperience" had encouraged: because she herself had "yet to come to terms with other primitive people, fear-ridden and hungry and harsh to their children, the Samoans inevitably stood for 'the primitive'"—despite the fact that she "was not advocating a return to the primitive but rather greater knowledge which would give modern man more control over the civilizing process itself" (1961:xi–xii).

over the decades, each of their early ethnographic interpretations was to become the subject of systematic (and controversial) criticism. Widely spaced
in time, these critiques were not themselves the products of a single cultural
historical moment. Nevertheless, there are certain common threads that run
through them, and by considering them here together, we may perhaps cast
light not only on the "Apollonian" ethnography of the 1920s,[12] but on certain
more enduring aspects of the modern anthropological tradition, regarded both
as a professional discipline and as a cultural ideology.

The fieldwork on which the first of these critiques was based was actually
begun before Benedict herself had gone to the Southwest, when in 1920 Franz
Boas' young secretary, Esther Schiff, coaxed him to allow her to join him on
a field trip to the Laguna pueblo, where the previous summer he had begun
a study of the Keresan language. Born in 1897 to one of the German Jewish
financial families from whom Boas occasionally sought research support, Schiff
had taken his introductory course during her senior year at Barnard. Although
she continued as his secretary after her month in the Southwest, she also
attended anthropology classes, and the following summer was invited to accompany him again. This time she began fieldwork at Cochiti, where she was
struck by the occasionally violent factionalism between the "progressives" and
"conservatives." In 1922, she again accompanied Boas to Cochiti, where she
was adopted into the clan of her hostess, and continued the research that
eventuated in a monograph on social and ceremonial organization (Goldfrank 1927). In the fall of 1922, Schiff gave up her secretarial position (to Ruth
Bunzel) in order to pursue an academic career. However, that career was interrupted by her marriage in December to Walter Goldfrank, a widower with
three sons—although she did manage a trip to Isleta pueblo in 1924 (Goldfrank 1978, 1983).

When her husband died suddenly in 1935, Esther Goldfrank felt free to
return to anthropology in the Columbia department, which was then sharply
divided between the students of Ruth Benedict and those of Ralph Linton,
the hiring of whom had forestalled Benedict's inheritance of Boas' mantle.
Goldfrank became a participant in the extramural seminars on culture and
personality in which Linton had joined the psychoanalyst Abram Kardiner,
and in which a more differentiated and processual approach to culture and
personality than Benedict's was being developed (cf. Manson 1986). However,
Goldfrank took her theory courses from Benedict and joined Benedict's field-

12. Although I have used the term "ethnography" here to characterize the work of both the
Apollonians and their critics, several of the works at issue are not in a conventional sense
ethnographic monographs—and one of the authors has specifically disavowed the idea that his
work constituted "an alternative ethnography" (Freeman 1983a:xii); from this perspective, "ethnographic interpretations" is perhaps the more appropriate term, since the problem of interpretation is undeniably at issue in every single case.

work party among the Plains Indians in the summer of 1939. Although Gold-frank found *Patterns of Culture* conceptually interesting, she argued vehemently with Benedict about her view of Zuni society, which Benedict tended to generalize to the pueblos Goldfrank herself had studied. By this time Bene-dict's interpretation had, somewhat tentatively, been called into question in print by the Berkeley-trained Chinese anthropologist, Li An-che (1937). But Goldfrank herself did not develop a systematic critique until after 1940, when she met and married the brilliant German Marxist sinologist Karl August Wittfogel, who had just left the Communist Party in the aftermath of the Hitler-Stalin pact. Long convinced that "the fundamental question" of social development was "the effect of water control on societal structure," Wittfogel had scarcely met Goldfrank before he asked her "what about irrigation among the pueblos?" (Goldfrank 1978:156, 146). In 1943 they produced a collaborative article in which pueblos were discussed as "miniature irrigation societies"– but which did not yet directly confront Benedict.

Following this joint effort, Goldfrank wrote a series of articles on differ-ent American Indian tribes, each challenging prevailing interpretations from a Marxist-influenced perspective. The first drew on historical accounts to argue (to Benedict's considerable displeasure) that among the prereservation Teton Dakota "wealth was important for status recognition; that warfare was no 'game'; and that in-group violence was well documented" (Goldfrank 1978: 161; cf. 1943). The second argued that "Navajo leadership, like Navajo com-munity cooperation, had developed out of the requirements of agriculture in a semi-arid environment," and was "no mechanical replica of Pueblo or-ganization" (1978:165, cf. 1945a). The third, an analysis of Hopi and Zuni child-rearing patterns, "called into question the image of Pueblo society and per-sonality that Benedict had been so insistently presenting since 1928" (1978: 171). Drawing on historical documents, autobiographical accounts, and psy-chological tests, Goldfrank argued that the achievement "of the cooperation necessary for a functioning irrigated agriculture" was "the end of a long pro-cess of conditioning, often persuasive, but frequently harsh, that commences in infancy and continues throughout adulthood." The anxiety-ridden adult Pueblo personality was "moulded not so much by parental permissiveness dur-ing infancy as by the severe disciplines imposed after infancy by external agents – by impersonators of the supernaturals and by the priesthoods" (1945b: 527, 519, 523, 536).

Benedict herself never responded in print, or to Goldfrank privately, "ex-cept to say that the Pueblos 'bored' her" (Goldfrank 1978:171). But Goldfrank's critique, along with the previous one by Li An-che, did stimulate the first systematic consideration of the influence of personal values on ethnography, in an article by John Bennett, who had studied with Redfield while taking his doctorate at Chicago in the late 1930s. Reviewing "The Interpretation of

Pueblo Culture" in 1946, Bennett drew a sharp contrast between what he called the "organic" and the "repressed" views. On the one hand, there had been several studies of Pueblo Indians (primarily Hopi and Zuni) which saw their culture as "integrated to an unusual degree, all sectors being bound together by a consistent, harmonious set of values," with "an ideal personality type which features the virtues of gentleness, non-aggression, cooperation, modesty, [and] tranquility"—"virtually a fulfillment of the ideal-typical folk-preliterate homogeneous, 'sacred' society and culture" (Bennett 1946:362–63). On the other, the Pueblos had been viewed as "marked by considerable *covert* tension, suspicion, anxiety, hostility, fear and ambition," with children "coerced subtly and (from our viewpoint) brutally into behaving according to Pueblo norms," and with "authority in the hands of the group and chiefs, the latter holding the power of life and death," so that the adult individual must "repress his spontaneity, originality, enthusiasm, out-goingness, individualism, . . . and become neurotic" (363, 367). Although Bennett charged the organic approach with "the sin of omission of certain important sets of data," with "a tendency to distort or misrepresent some facets of the Pueblo configuration [and] to make the interpretation in the long run an entirely personal, subjective affair," he did not conclude that it was "wrong." Rather, he argued that it was not possible to say that "one side or the other is less-influenced by values," and left it to the sociologist of knowledge to "make a reflexive analysis of the meaning of the respective interpretations in the culture of which they are a part" (373, 374). Nevertheless, the effect of the article was to make it thenceforth rather difficult for Pueblo culture to be interpreted in systematically harmonious Apollonian terms.

Although Bennett called attention to Redfield's concept of the "folk society" as part of the context of theory in which the organic view should be understood (1946:364), he made no reference to Redfield's study of Tepoztlán. However, within several years that, too, was subjected to systematic criticism by a young anthropologist who had also received his training in the faction-ridden pre–World War II Columbia department. Born in 1914, Oscar Lewis (né Lefkowitz) was the son of a Polish immigrant rabbi who for reasons of health moved to a small town in upper New York state, where he managed a somewhat marginal subsistence by converting a farm into a summer hotel. Introduced to Marxism by a Communist Party organizer who summered nearby, young Lewis went on to a take a bachelor's degree in 1936 at the City College of New York, where he studied with the Marxist historian Philip Foner before going on to do graduate work at Columbia Teachers College. But he soon became disillusioned with the limited historical perspective he found there, and at the suggestion of his brother-in-law, the psychologist Abraham Maslow, had a long talk with Ruth Benedict, which led him into anthropology. However, Lewis, like Goldfrank, was also influenced by Kardiner and

Linton, and while he greatly admired Benedict as a person, and for her critique of racism (1940), he too, became somewhat critical of her approach. Although his doctoral dissertation was to be a library treatise on "The Effects of White Contact upon Blackfoot Culture," he, too, had accompanied Benedict on the field school of 1939. Out of that experience came a study of the Piegan "manly-hearted women," in which Lewis expressed scepticism of "theories of culture which play down the role of economics and which stress homogeneity at the expense of the range of behavior and values" (Butterworth 1972:748; cf. Rigdon 1988:9–26).

During the early years of World War II, Lewis worked with the Strategic Index for Latin America of the Human Relations Area Files at Yale University and briefly as propaganda analyst for the U.S. Department of Justice. In 1943, he and his psychologist wife moved to Mexico City in connection with a large-scale comparative study of Indian culture and personality, and there also assumed administrative duties in the Inter-American Indian Institute headed by Manuel Gamio. Seeking a nearby site to study, and hoping to take advantage of Redfield's monograph as the ethnographic base for his own research, Lewis chose Tepotzlán, which by then had been linked by highway to the Federal District. With the help of his wife and more than a dozen native Mexican researchers, Lewis carried out a systematic investigation during seven months in 1944, with return trips during the summers of 1947 and 1948. The team collected extensive data on representative families from different income groups in each barrio, using schedules of questions that extended to a hundred pages. From the beginning, the project was oriented toward problems of rural development; and to overcome the resistance of villagers who were suspicious that he was an agent of the government, Lewis organized meetings at which he encouraged them to talk "about their needs and problems" in order that he might "draw up proposals for the improvement of conditions in Tepoztlán." This orientation "set the tone for the entire investigation," which soon suggested that while Redfield's material was "adequate" regarding religious and ceremonial matters, "the picture of Tepotzlán as written by Redfield and Stuart Chase has been highly romanticized" ("Progress Report," 2/44, as quoted in Rigdon 1988:32–35).

From the time he chose the Tepoztlán site, Lewis was in correspondence with Redfield, who wrote letters supporting his applications for funding, and (though he considered Lewis "probably not a man of first rank") also endorsing Lewis's candidacy for the job he got at the University of Illinois in 1948 (RP: RR/Carl Taylor 11/11/46, RR/J. W. Albig 4/26/48). By that time, however, serious "differences in interpretation and in field data" had arisen. Responding to the suggestion (made by Redfield's wife) that "if culture is seen as that which gives some order and significance to life," then Lewis's account of a particular Tepoztecan family had "very little of culture in it," Lewis argued that "much of the unity and bonds of family life in Tepoztlán flow from what might be called negative factors rather than positive ones":

> What I mean is that in a village where most people are withdrawn and suspicious and view the world as a hostile place to live in, the family unit by comparison with the non-family represents a relatively close in-group and in this sense is a haven. But it would be missing many of the crucial aspects of Tepoztecan family life and the quality of human relationships in Tepoztlán not to see the great amount of internal tensions and conflict that exists, as well as the frustrations and maladjustments. Nor do I believe that this is to be explained entirely in terms of the break-down of an earlier folk culture. The idea that folk cultures produce less frustrations than non-folk cultures or that the quality of human relationships is necessarily superior in folk-cultures seems to me to be sheer Rousseauean romanticism and has not been documented to my knowledge. (Quoted in Rigdon 1988:205)

Lewis in fact doubted that Tepoztlán was really a "folk culture": "It seems to me that Tepoztlán is not now and in all probability has not in the last four hundred years been a folk culture in the sense that you have defined the term in your writings." Rejecting the implication "that he was guilty of middle-class bias" because "my picture of family life turns out to be so similar to family life as it has been reported in our own culture," Lewis insisted that it was "possible to have valid standards which cut across all cultures without thereby being ethnocentric, by which the quality of human relationships can be measured and appraised," noting "Fromm's recent book 'Man for Himself' [as] a step in this direction" (RP: RR/OL 6/8/48; OL/RR 6/11/48, quoted in Rigdon 1988:205–6).

When it appeared in 1951, Lewis's book bore a dedication to Redfield, who in return offered a somewhat double-edged jacket comment: "In putting before other students my errors and his own [sic] in a context of intelligent discussion, he has once more shown the power of social science to revise its conclusions and move toward the truth." In the volume itself, Lewis drew a sharp contrast between Redfield's view of Tepoztlán as "a relatively homogeneous, isolated, smoothly functioning and well-integrated society" and his own findings, which emphasized "the underlying individualism of Tepoztecan institutions and character, the lack of cooperation, . . . the schisms within the village, and the pervading quality of fear, envy, and distrust in inter-personal relations" (428–29). Granting the influence of "the personal factor," and allowing something also for cultural change and differences in the "general scope" of the two studies, Lewis was inclined to emphasize instead "differences in theoretical orientation," and especially "the concept of the folk-culture and folk-urban continuum" which was "Redfield's organizing principle in the research" (431–32), and which since 1930 had been further elaborated in his studies of The Folk Culture of Yucatan (1941).

Unlike Benedict, Redfield spent a good deal of effort, both in correspondence and in print, in responding to Lewis's critique, which in the early 1950s precipitated a considerable discussion of folk culture, peasant societies, and the folk-urban continuum (Miner 1952; Foster 1953; Mintz 1953; Wolf 1955; Wagley & Harris 1955; cf. Redfield 1953, 1955, 1956). Although Redfield insisted that it was not prior hypothesis, but "some experience with Tepoztlán" which led him to develop the concept of a "folk society," his general approach was to insist on the abstractive nature of his "ideal type," which was "a mental construction of imagined societies that are only approximated in particular 'real' societies" (RP: RR/OL 6/22/48; RR n.d., response to OL's "six objections"). And while he did not "recall any intention to suggest that everything about savages or about Tepoztecans has my approval nor that with civilization came the fall of man" (RP: RR/OL correspondence, n.d.), in the end Redfield was inclined to explain the empirical differences in terms which were clearly value-laden: the "hidden question" of his own research had been "What do these people enjoy?", whereas that of Lewis's had been "What do these people suffer from?" (Redfield 1955:136). On that basis, the two men were able to minimize their differences (RP: OL/RR 4/25/54; RR/OL 4/27/54) – though Lewis later insisted that *his* hidden question was "more productive of insight about the human condition, about the dynamics of conflict and the forces of change" (1960:179).

When a conference was held in 1952 to evaluate the general state of "anthropology today," Lewis was asked to present a paper on fieldwork method, in which he argued at some length for the importance of systematic restudy as an essential feature of anthropological method (Lewis 1953). During the next few years there was to be a flurry of studies that were undertaken (or reconceptualized) as restudies. One of these was in fact a study of the same Samoan village in which Mead had worked – although, here, as in Lewis's own case, the work was apparently not originally intended as a restudy. Lowell Holmes, a graduate student of Melville Herskovits at Northwestern, had intended to do research in Rarotonga, but two weeks before his planned departure the University of Hawaii, which was funding his work, suggested that he go to American Samoa instead. Suddenly left "without a definite research problem," Holmes decided, in consultation with Herskovits (who had been Mead's contemporary under Boas at Columbia), to carry on an acculturation study of the Manu'a group, working in Mead's village, and using her material "as a base line." To facilitate this, he asked Mead for some of her field data (MP: LH/MM 9/2/54). While she refused to divulge the real identities of the girls she had studied, she indicated that Holmes could determine them from her village census, which she would send if he would first send her a copy of one that she suggested he should make to provide an independent point of comparison (MP: MM/LH 6/22/54). Holmes seems not to have taken up this offer (Mead 1969:xix), relying instead on Mead's published work as his base point. After five months in Ta'u, where he worked largely in English, and four in Pago Pago, Holmes came back ready to write a dissertation rather critical of Mead's work, but as he later recalled, "was forced by my faculty advisor [Herskovits] to soften my criticism" (LH/DF 8/1/67, as quoted in Freeman 1983b:134). Although Holmes disputed Mead on a number of factual issues—later suggesting that she had discovered "what she hoped to find"—he nevertheless concluded that "the reliability of Mead's account is remarkably high" (1957a:232). Holmes's posture was roughly that of the general anthropological community for the next several decades: whatever reservations may have been held in Oceanist circles about the quality of Mead's Samoan ethnography (cf. Mead 1969), these did not affect its public status, which was sustained by her own position as the single most visible American anthropologist (cf. McDowell 1980; Rappaport 1986).

By 1967, however, Holmes was warning Mead of the "present activities" of another Samoanist, Derek Freeman, who was seeking to "discredit you, me, Boas and all of American anthropology" (MP: LH/MM 10/23/67). Mead had in fact been aware of Freeman's work at least since 1964, when after a somewhat heated debate, in a seminar at the Australian National University, over the significance of Samoan defloration ceremonies, Freeman told her he intended to do further research on "the realities of adolescent and sexual behaviour in Samoa" (MP: DF/MM 11/11/64; MM/DF 12/2/64). Born in 1916 in Wellington, New Zealand—where during adolescence he developed a passion for exploration and mountain climbing—Freeman had attended Victoria University College and the Wellington Training School for Teachers. In 1938 he became a member of the graduate seminar of Ernest Beaglehole, who held a Ph.D. degree in sociology from the London School of Economics and who had come under the influence of Boasian anthropology as a postdoctoral student of Sapir's at Yale in the early 1930s. Like Beaglehole, Freeman was at that time very much a cultural determinist, concluding from a study of the socialization of school children that "the aims and desires which determine behavior" were all derived from the social environment (Freeman 1983b:109). Under Beaglehole's influence Freeman began to think seriously of doing anthropological work in Polynesia, and in 1939, he obtained a position in the Education Department of Western Samoa, where he hoped also to carry on ethnographic research that would extend the work of Margaret Mead (Appell & Madan 1988:5). After two years during which he became fluent in Samoan, Freeman began intensive research in the settlement of Sa'anapu, where he was adopted into the family of a senior talking chief and given the title and status of the heir apparent (a young man who had Freeman's English middle name, John, and who, fortuitously, had died just before his arrival on the scene). Gradually becoming aware of serious discrepancies between his own observations and Mead's, Freeman was at first inclined to explain them as due to the fact that he worked in Western and she in Eastern Samoa. But by the time he left in November 1943 to serve in the New Zealand navy, he had concluded that he would "one day face the responsibility of writing a refutation of Mead's findings" (1983a:xiv).

After the war (and a brief return to Samoa in the summer of 1946), Freeman went to the London School of Economics to study anthropology under the leading British Polynesianist, Raymond Firth. There he continued studies of manuscript sources on Samoa in the archives of the London Missionary Society, and in 1948 produced a diploma thesis on "The Social Structure of a Samoan Village Community." However, when Firth dismissed as "structure ad nauseam" a paper of Freeman's that was highly praised by Meyer Fortes, Freeman shifted his intellectual allegiance (Appell & Madan 1988:6). When he left Britain in 1948 to carry out research among the Iban in Sarawak— whom he had previously encountered during his war service—he was strongly under the influence of Fortes' more orthodox Radcliffe-Brownian structuralism, which continued to condition the analyses of Iban society that occupied him during the next decade.

After receiving his doctorate under Fortes at Cambridge in 1953, Freeman returned to New Zealand as visiting lecturer at the University of Otago, from which he was invited to the Australian National University in 1955. During the next few years, Freeman became dissatisfied with the way in which British social anthropology set up methodological barriers against most of the other behavioral sciences (cf. MacClancy 1986), which he found particularly inhibiting in the interpretation of the symbolism of the Iban headhunting cult. His dissatisfaction climaxed during the visit of Max Gluckman to A.N.U. in the summer of 1960, and that fall Freeman wrote Fortes suggesting that social anthropologists should acquire "systematic training in psychoanalysis" (Appell & Madan 1988:12). The following February, he was asked by the vice-chancellor of A.N.U. to alter his plans for study leave in order to go to Kuching, Sarawak, to investigate a problem that had arisen between the curator of the Sarawak Museum, Tom Harrisson, and a research scholar from the A.N.U. When he arrived, Freeman found himself "in the center of a complicated social situation in which he was able to study at first hand a whole series of deep psychological processes." Although the details of the situation have not been specified, the result was a "cognitive abreaction" so "momentous" that he "suddenly saw human behavior in a new light" (ibid.; cf. Freeman 1986).

Departing from Sarawak in March 1961, Freeman broke off his fieldwork plans in order to embark on systematic reading in ethology, evolutionary biology, primatology, the neurosciences, psychology, and genetics. Writing to Fortes in October 1962, Freeman suggested that his approach to anthropology was now "very much that of the natural historian," insisting that "anthropology, if it is to become the science of man, must be biologically based" (quoted in Appell & Madan 1988:13). In the aftermath of this conversion to a "naturalistic approach to human behavior," Freeman underwent certain other dramatic intellectual changes. Arguing that "dereistic thinking and irrational behavior are not one whit the less dereistic because they happen to be shared and accepted," he abandoned the doctrine of cultural relativism (Freeman 1962:272; cf. 1965), embraced the scientific epistemology of Karl Popper, studied ethology under the guidance of Konrad Lorenz, and undertook a year's training and personal analysis at the London Institute of Psychoanalysis – although his later attempt to apply Popperian principles in a series of psychoanalytic papers led to his ostracization by the Australian Society of Psychoanalysts in 1965 (Appell & Madan 1988:15–16).

It was in the context of these changes – and the rereading of Mead's *Coming of Age* when he was returning to Australia from Europe in July 1964 – that Freeman decided he must reexamine and test the evidence Mead had offered for her conclusion that adolescent behavior could not be explained in terms of biological variables. Returning to Western Samoa in December 1965, he carried on further fieldwork in Sa'anapu, and in 1967 made a visit to the site of Mead's fieldwork in Manu'a. By the time he went back to Australia in January 1968, Freeman had concluded that Mead's work was "pivotal to the development and acceptance in the United States of the doctrine of cultural determinism" (Appell & Madan 1988:17). Turning to investigations of the historical background of Boasian anthropology, he soon became convinced that "these men were not really interested in dispassionate scientific enquiry, but rather in the dissemination and support of certain doctrines, of an idealistic, metaphysical and quasi-political kind, in which they passionately believed" – and he suggested to Mead that he might have to write a book devoted to the reexamination of "some of these doctrines" (MP: DF/MM 3/20/69).

By 1971, Freeman was able to submit to an American publisher a summary of the proposed work, but the negative responses of anonymous reviewers led him to delay its completion while he carried on further research (Appell & Madan 1988:19). In 1978, Freeman offered to send Mead a preliminary draft of an "*acutely* critical" paper on Samoan sexual values and behavior (MP: DF/MM 8/23/78). But her illness and death intervened, and to Freeman "made it obvious that the publication of [his] refutation would have to be deferred" – presumably in order to let a decent interval elapse (as quoted in Appell & Madan 1988:21). It was only late in 1981, after Freeman had gained access to the archives of the High Court of American Samoa, that the manuscript was finally sent off to the Harvard University Press.

Even before its publication in 1983, Freeman's book had become a cause célèbre. Despite (or perhaps because of) her immense public stature, Mead had always been somewhat ambivalently regarded by professional anthropologists, and her work had been controversial at least since the early 1950s debate around the "swaddling hypothesis" interpretation of Great Russian personality (Mead 1954). Had Freeman's critique been limited to what he described as a "formal Popperian refutation" of her Samoan ethnography, the professional response might have been much more restrained—although many anthropologists would surely have been put off by his strident scientism. But his book was quite explicitly a frontal attack—in a rather abrasively polemical style—on what he insisted was the evidential linchpin of the paradigm of "absolute cultural determinism" which had dominated American anthropology for fifty years.[13] While for the most part rejecting Freeman's characterization of their discipline's history, American anthropologists were clearly concerned that a critique of cultural determinism might support a resurgence of hereditarian thought and racialist politics. Although Freeman insisted that his goal was to clear the way for a new "interactionist" paradigm that would give appropriate weight to the influence of both biological and cultural factors and had himself been somewhat critical of sociobiology (Freeman 1980), his book was seen by many as giving aid and comfort to the ideological enemy. In this context, American anthropologists rallied to the defense of their discipline and of the figure who was publicly most prominently identified with it.[14]

13. Since my own work has been drawn on to buttress this characterization (Freeman 1983, passim), I offer here a brief comment on this issue. There is no doubt that cultural determinism (in some sense) was an essential feature of the anthropological idea of culture, which since the 1920s has had a pervasive influence in the social sciences and in American culture generally (cf. Stocking 1968). There is no doubt also that Mead's study was conceived as an inquiry into the power of cultural determinism, and that it played an important role in the dissemination of that notion. On the other hand, the addition of the modifier "absolute" raises serious historiographical problems, which can scarcely be dealt with by citing a single instance in which Mead used that word in a phrase in which neither the noun "culture" nor the adjective "cultural" appeared (Freeman 1983b:169). It is no doubt the case that some anthropologists (notably Kroeber), in particular polemical contexts, made statements to which Freeman's phrase might seem an appropriate gloss. But its use, either directly or by implication, to characterize the Boasian school, or any individual Boasian, is to say the least extremely problematic.

14. Although portions of the present argument clearly bear on issues in the Samoan controversy, it is not intended as a systematic treatment of those issues or of that discussion. For reasons indicated in part in the text below, many of the more important issues are beyond my competence to judge, and will probably remain so; some others closer to my competence can only be touched on in the present argument. However, the whole episode is surely one of the more illuminating ones in the history of anthropology, and, at a later point, when the dust has settled somewhat, and more of the sources are available, I hope perhaps to attempt a more systematic treatment. Major items in the debate so far include the "special section" of the December 1983 number of *American Anthropologist*, "Speaking in the Name of the Real: Freeman and Mead on Samoa"; the two numbers of the 1984 volume of *Canberra Anthropology*, "Fact and Context in Ethnography: The Samoa Controversy"; Rappaport 1986; Holmes 1987. At every point along the way, Freeman has offered his own commentaries and rebuttals, as well as additional evidence

For present purposes, however, the broader issues of the controversy are less germane than some of the specifics of Freeman's critique, which resonates strongly of the earlier critiques of Benedict and Redfield. Charging that Mead had failed to appreciate the "bitter rivalries" generated by the rank system (1983a:135), Freeman insisted that far from eliminating "interest in competition," Samoans showed an intense competitiveness not only in ritualized contests, but "in virtually all other areas of their society" (147). Rather than being one of the "most peaceful peoples in the world," Samoans were prone to aggressive behavior (163). Instead of wearing their religion lightly, they were "a highly religious people" (179). Contrary to Mead's suggestion that the Samoan child was succored by "women of all ages . . . none of whom have disciplined it," Samoans shared the biologically based "primary bond between mother and child" that was characteristic of all humans, and were subject to "quite stringent discipline" (203, 205). Far from lacking "deeply channeled emotions," they were people of "strong passions" (212, 215). Instead of condoning casual adolescent lovemaking, their sexual mores emphasized the "cult of virginity" (234); male sexuality, far from being unaggressive, was manifest in one of the world's highest incidences of rape (244). Rather than enjoying a carefree time of gradual adjustment to adult roles, Samoan adolescents had a delinquency rate ten times higher than that of England and Wales (258). In short, the Samoans were not a Polynesian version of Benedict's Apollonian Zuni; like all mankind, they were a complex mixture of Apollonian and Dionysian motives (302).

When Ethnographers Disagree . . .

Although he wrote before the critiques of Redfield's Tepoztlán and Mead's Samoa, John Bennett's 1946 account of the contrastive "interpretations of the basic dynamics of Pueblo society and culture" may nevertheless serve as a convenient reference point for more general remarks on the Apollonian ethnographies of the 1920s. "Lacking any close familiarity with Pueblo research," Bennett eschewed an assessment of the "organic" and "repressive" interpretations "from the standpoint of excellence of field work and general scientific operations." Assuming that "the workers on both sides" were "careful students of culture" and "respectable" members of the "academic fraternity" of "professional anthropologists," he did not attempt to say that one side represented "good" and the other "bad" ethnography (Bennett 1946:370).

---

supporting his critique, both in print (e.g., Freeman 1987) and in extensive correspondence with participants and other interested parties, including myself; having recently claimed "closure" of the controversy (personal communication 7/7/88), he is himself currently at work on a study of the debate.

Four decades ago, when the relatively small community of professional anthropologists faced the future full of confidence that "the science of man" could meet the challenges of expanding ethnographic opportunity in the postwar world, one could perhaps take for granted that they shared a methodological consensus. But intervening history—by now precipitated in several genres of anthropological writing about the problems of fieldwork and of ethnographic representation (cf. Gravel & Ridinger 1988)—has made such consensus much more problematic. By the time of Lewis's critique of Redfield, methodology was implicitly very much at issue; and in the case of Freeman's critique of Mead, so also was the nature of the "professional fraternity" itself (Rappaport 1986).

For the positivistically inclined—and for those postpositivists who still cherish the conviction that there may be criteria for judging the relative adequacy of conflicting factual or interpretive statements about human action in a social world—the possibility must be acknowledged that "when ethnographers disagree . . . someone is wrong" (Heider 1988:75). But with the ante of ethnographic competence now trebled, and issues of method and epistemology more explicitly problematic, an historian without ethnographic experience has even more reason than Bennett had in 1946 to refrain from evaluative judgments of ethnographic adequacy. This is even more the case in view of other issues that Bennett did not discuss: whether the ethnographic "objects" subject to differing interpretations may have "actually" differed, insofar as the observers had focussed on different subcultural groups or regional variants, or as the result of cultural change over time (cf. Heider 1988); or whether the response of the people under study to the ethnographers studying them may have led them to present themselves differently to different observers.[15]

Despite these caveats, certain contrasts between the Apollonians and the critics do suggest themselves, even to an ethnographic outsider or, for that matter, to a nonethnographer. If one compares the six anthropologists involved in terms of such obvious factors as time in the field, linguistic competence, or number of informants, one may easily note differences among them, which *prima facie* incline one to regard the Apollonian ethnographies as perhaps

---

15. On this issue, Gartrell (1979) is extremely suggestive, along lines that are surely relevant to the present discussion. Contrasting her own ethnographic experience with that of another woman ethnographer who studied the same African people during the same period, Gartrell explained the factual and interpretive differences between them in terms of differences in their expectations of fieldwork, their local sponsorship, their choice of interpreters, their perceived gender roles, etc.—all of which elicited quite differing "exclusionary maneuvers" from the people they were trying to study. Significantly, the interpretive consequences were especially marked in regard to cultural personality and ethos—the areas most at issue in the critique of Apollonian ethnography.

more open to question (cf. Narroll 1962). The more so, since fieldwork was
never the forte of either Benedict or Redfield; and while Mead was to become
a highly productive, innovative, and methodologically self-conscious fieldworker, Samoa was her maiden effort, which she herself came later to regard
as the product of a methodologically less sophisticated era (Mead 1961:xv).

But if this might lead us to believe that the anti-Apollonians were on the
whole more reliable ethnographers, it does not resolve all the factual or interpretive differences at issue. The truth or falsity of any given ethnographic
"fact" (or even the definition of such an entity) is not so simple a matter as
the more positivistically inclined critics would seem to feel; and this is even
more true of ethnographic interpretations, which may relate to ethnographic
facts in ways that are by no means straightforward. Simply as an instance,
we may briefly consider the problem of the incidence of forcible rape in Samoa,
which has been a much debated issue in the Mead/Freeman controversy. According to Mead, rape was "completely foreign to the Samoan mind" (1928c:487),
but had occurred "occasionally" since "the first contact with white civilization" (1928b:93). In contrast, Freeman was at some pains to argue that forcible
rape had been frequent in Samoa at the time Mead was there, and gave as
the reason for his delay of publication the fact that it was only in 1981 that
he was able to get into the archives of the High Court of American Samoa,
where he found documentary evidence on the issue (Freeman 1983a:xvi). In
a later commentary, he noted that these records had revealed that "during
the years 1920–29 twelve Samoan males (five of them in American Samoa
and seven of them in Western Samoa) were tried and convicted of forcible
rape or (in two cases) of attempted rape" (1983b:119). Granting that Freeman's
work has succeeded in calling into question not only some of the specifics but
also the general tenor of Mead's account of Samoan sexuality (cf. Romanucci-
Ross 1983), the evidence on rape in the 1920s remains somewhat problematic,
especially to anyone epistemologically disinclined to accept Freeman's dogmatic assertion that "even a single verified case" would refute Mead (1983b:119).
Even disregarding the problem of the influence of "white civilization," or of
the quality of the court records, or of the location of the two attempted rapes—
not to mention that of the cross-cultural definition of such a category—we
might ask whether five rapes in American Samoa during a ten-year period
is merely "occasional" or a "high incidence," and wonder whether this is a
matter that can be settled by comparing Samoan figures from a later date with
those elsewhere in the world. If interpretation must intervene to give meaning to "facts" even in one (not so) simple quantitative case, how much more
so in judging the "wrongness" or "rightness" of facts/interpretations in three
different ethnographic situations. Clearly, that is not a task to be undertaken
in the present essay.

On the other hand, one cannot ignore the (interpretive) fact that the contrasts Bennett found between the "organic" and "repressive" interpretations of Zuni—harmonious integration vs. covert tension, tranquility vs. hostility, cooperation vs. individualism, voluntarism vs. authority, permissive vs. coercive childrearing—are echoed in the later Redfield/Lewis and Mead/Freeman debates. Clearly, the contrast is of more than local ethnographic significance, and in attempting to contextualize it, we must look beyond the specific cases. Although there are distinct limitations to the interpretation that can be offered here, we may take a few steps toward their more adequate historical contextualization by looking at the Apollonians and their critics with a view to contrasts of personal biography and of cultural moment.[16]

Considered first in terms of biographical commonalities among the six anthropologists, the present materials allow only limited generalization. Thus neither class nor gender nor nationality will distinguish all of the Apollonians from all of the critics. One the other hand, the fact that the Apollonians, unlike the critics, were all presidents of the American Anthropological Association, may suggest a more general contrast in terms of professional and personal marginality: whereas the Apollonians were (save Redfield on the maternal side) "Old Americans," the critics (two Jews and a New Zealander) may perhaps be thought of as cultural (as well as professional) outsiders. One might speculate that the former, insofar as they became alienated from the dominant culture, would be inclined to value cultural alterity—while simultaneously taking for granted the possibility of reform within their own culture. In contrast, the latter were more concerned with the problem of mobility within a dominant culture, and therefore emphasized commonalities of human capacity—even as they tended to view society in more conflictual terms. And the fact that the critics—younger in each case by half a generation—were people whose work in a particular ethnographic area was in some sense forestalled by a personally significant other of major professional reputation may have

16. Among these limitations, the most striking is the obvious asymmetry in the contextualization of the Apollonian ethnographers and their later critics. The treatments of the former—all of them now dead—have not only been much lengthier, but have also drawn more extensively, if unsystematically, on less public sorts of source materials (including Benedict's reconstruction of her primal scene, Redfield's Rorschach, and the "outtakes" from Mead's published autobiographical writings). If, as Bennett suggested, it is up to the sociologist of knowledge (or, in this case, the historian of anthropology) "to seek out biases and stresses obviously not completely apparent to the researchers" (1946:374), a fully adequate approach to that task would require the same sort of treatment (and the same sorts of source materials) for the critics as for the authors of Apollonian ethnographic interpretations. Failing that, there is a risk of implying that Goldfrank, Lewis, and Freeman were unencumbered by unconscious bias—a proposition they might find flattering, but which the historian of anthropology must regard as questionable. I take it for granted that members of the "repressive" school are not immune to scotomization and projection (cf. Devereux 1967)—though the question of the relative strength of such tendencies in different observers remains an open (and a difficult) one.

helped to motivate or to sustain their critiques. In Freeman's case, this motive may have been enhanced by an identification with Mead's New Zealander second husband, who was also a critic of Mead's ethnography (Fortune 1939).[17]

The fact that the Apollonians were all published poets might suggest a metamethodological predisposition toward what Bennett spoke of as "logico-aesthetic integration" (1946:371). And there is perhaps other evidence to support this, including the Rorschachs of Benedict (Goldfrank 1978:126) and Redfield (Roe 1950), and the often-noted propensity of Mead for the quick apprehension of cultural totality—evidenced in a remark to Boas three weeks after arriving in Manus on her second fieldwork expedition: "The outlines of the culture are emerging more and more each day" (BP: MM/FB 1/6/29). The obverse of this atemporal integrative inclination might be a tendency to minimize the importance of disruptive historical event—be it factional struggle, revolutionary foray, or tropical hurricane. In contrast, the critics seem to have been impelled to call up against integrating cultural totalizations controverting evidence of an historical or a quantitative character. Granted that this may have been motivated by the demands of argument, and that the critics were not without totalizing agendas of their own. Granted also the avowed nomothetic goals of the early Redfield, and the strong strain of scientism present in the early Mead and recurrent throughout her career. Nevertheless, the fact that Mead relegated historical change and quantification to an appendix (and that they did not reappear in the second more "professional" monograph) suggests that a basic methodological commitment had been made. No doubt it was, as Boas' comments on the statistical and clinical methods suggest, a defensible one. But as Mead's own later comment on "the historical caprice which had selected a handful of young girls to stand forever like the lovers on Keats' Grecian urn" reminds us (1961:iii), her interpretation depended very much on the subjective apprehension of a cultural pattern frozen in a timeless moment. While it would not do to reduce the matter to a simple contrast of humanist and scientist, it does seem that some underlying meta-methodological opposition was, or came to be, at issue between the Apollonians and their critics.

The two groups may also be contrasted in terms of certain theoretical and attitudinal presuppositions. As a starting point, we may note that all of the anthropologists involved were, in the early phases of their careers, identifiable as Boasian cultural determinists. For the Apollonian ethnographers, that view-

---

17. Since Mead's Samoan research has been contextualized here in relation to her early biography and American cultural currents in the 1920s, interpretive symmetry might suggest a similar contextualization of Freeman's critique. Although extended consideration of this issue would obviously depend on much fuller biographical and cultural historical information, a suggestive starting point can be found in the discussion of gender roles, sexual mores, adolescent aggression, attitudes to authority, etc. in New Zealand in Ausubel (1960).

point was certainly a part of the context of research—in Benedict's case, less perhaps in the original fieldwork than as the critical factor in subsequent ethnographic interpretation; in Redfield's, simply as a general orienting assumption; in Mead's, in the very formulation of the fieldwork problem. But it is worth noting among them also the major orienting influence of a more diffuse body of evolutionary assumption that seems in retrospect quite un-Boasian (though in fact expressions of it can also be found in Boas' work). Especially in the cases of Redfield and Mead, it was the opposition of the "civilized" and the "primitive" (the "folk" being intermediate between the two), as much as any specific cultural determinism, which conditioned the interpretation of ethnographic data.

The attitudes of Apollonian ethnographers toward the contrast implicit in that opposition were more complex than the terms "primitivist" or "cultural relativist" might suggest—primitivism, like relativism, being a very relative matter. Even in what has come to be regarded as its *locus classicus* (Benedict 1934), cultural relativism was a problematic concept; a double-edged sword, it could be wielded both in the cause of cultural tolerance and in the cause of cultural criticism. When used to justify the established ways of "primitive" others to the denizens of a "civilization" threatening to eradicate them, it presented those practices in a generally favorable light. But when used to question the established ways of "this crazy civilization," the "limits of outrage" that might be "plumbed" in "scandalous" cultures became negative reference points rather than positive models (Benedict, in Mead 1959a:330–31). Benedict made a point of disavowing "any romantic return to the primitive"—"attractive as it sometimes may be" (Benedict 1934:19–20). For her, as for Mead, cultural integration could be negative as well as positive, and two of her three cultural cases were presented in starkly negative terms. Thus the "paranoid," "treacherous," "Puritan" Dobu lived out "without repression man's worst nightmares of the ill-will of the universe" (172), and the "megalomaniac paranoid" Kwakiutl "recognized only one gamut of emotion, that which swings between victory and shame" (222, 215). The common denominator of comparative characterization was less the Apollonian Zuni than an implicitly critical vision of American civilization. What Benedict yearned for was not so much homogeneity as a more tolerant individuation.

In the case of Redfield, there are signs of similar ambivalence. In the study of Tepoztlán, the idealization of the folk was largely implicit in the general descriptive material, the contrastive aura of place—surfacing in such comments as the opposition between "the folk, a country people among whom culture is built up, and the urban proletariat, among whom it tends to break down" (Redfield 1930:6). At the same time, it also seems clear that Redfield identified with the process of "sophistication" by which the folk were transformed; and over time, he was to become troubled by the concept of cultural relativism.

There is a similar tension in the case of Mead. One can find in *Coming of Age* strikingly pluralistic passages, resonant more of Herder than Rousseau, including a foreshadowing of Benedict's "great arc" of culture: "each primitive people has selected one set of human gifts, one set of human values, and fashioned for themselves an art, a social organisation, a religion, which is their contribution to the history of the human spirit" (Mead 1928b:13). But many of the contrasts that Mead drew were quite conventionally evolutionary: Samoan culture was "simpler," lacking in "individualization" and "specialized feeling." What it offered was not so much a general cultural alternative as a point of critical comparison: "granting the desirability of [the] development of [a] sensitive, discriminating response to personality, as a better basis for dignified human lives than an automatic, undifferentiated response to sex attraction, we may still, in the light of Samoan solutions, count our methods exceedingly expensive" (211). In the end, Mead's purpose was to realize "the high point of culture that a heterogeneous culture and a heterogeneous culture alone can attain" (248).

Clearly, the matter is more complex than the contrast Bennett drew between the "value orientation" of the "organic" school toward the "solidified, homogeneous group life" of preliterate culture and that of the "repressive" school in favor of the "greater individuation" and heterogeneity of "urban life" (1946: 366). And yet a certain romantic primitivist spirit was clearly manifest in the Apollonian ethnographies – in the very process of denial ("attractive as it may sometimes be"); in the specific descriptive material; in what Bennett called "the general linguistic atmosphere," and in the strikingly ambivalent attitude toward "the heterogeneity of modern life" (364–65). Confirmed by the response of contemporary readers, it was also evident by contrast in the response of their later critics, none of whom could be called romantic primitivists, and all of whom became critical of the doctrine of cultural relativism.

Despite their evolutionary residues and their varying receptivity to psychoanalysis, the Apollonians were disinclined to view human behavior in terms of three notable "isms" of modern social theory: Darwinism, Marxism, and Freudianism – the more so, perhaps, since their own characteristic "ism," that of cultural determinism, had been advanced as an antidote to prevailing determinisms of biology, economics, and psychology (cf. Lowie 1917). In contrast, each of the three critics seems to have been strongly influenced by one or more of these eponymic "isms" at critical points in their intellectual development.

From this point of view, it is tempting to continue the argument in terms of cultural moment, with Marxism especially in mind. Just as the Apollonian ethnographies may be contextualized as expressions of a certain tendency within Boasian anthropology in the 1920s, when the nature of culture and its relation to civilization were particularly problematic for American intellectuals, so the critiques of those ethnographies might be seen as expressions of the 1930s. Boasian influence was by this time well established in American anthropology, and the discipline was entering a more differentiated phase; externally, the Great Depression overrode issues of American cultural identity, facilitating a view of culture that was more differentiated, more conflictual, more subject to economic and environmental determinants. In support of such an interpretation one might note the fact that Lewis and Goldfrank were both resident in the Columbia department in the factional period after Boas' retirement in 1936, and that, in differing ways, both were strongly affected by the Marxist radicalism so influential among intellectuals in the 1930s (Goldfrank 1978; Rigdon 1988; Kuznick 1988).

However, the fact that in Freeman's case, the relevant eponymic "isms" are those of Freud and Darwin, and that his move away from cultural relativism and determinism came two decades later, suggests that the critique of Apollonian ethnography must be contextualized in terms of other cultural moments than the 1930s. Although it is beyond the scope of this essay to do more than mention them, two later cultural moments seem especially worthy of brief comment: the early 1950s, when Lewis published his critique of Redfield and Holmes undertook his restudy of Ta'u; and the early 1980s, when Freeman published his critique of Mead.

In contrast to the response of Apollonian ethnographers in the earlier post–World War I decade, that of anthropologists to the experience of World War II was a movement away from cultural relativism. This time, the transvaluing impact of war was not to call into question the verities of European Western civilization but rather to reassert the values of universal humanity and the controlling promise of scientific knowledge against the horror of the Holocaust and the universal terror of the atomic bomb. The turn/return was evident even in the three Apollonians. In the short period before her death in 1948, Benedict seems to have experienced a resurgence of the "faith of a scientist," and she became involved in a large-scale comparativist project on "Contemporary Cultures" (Mead 1959a:431, 434). Redfield wrote a book on *The Village that Chose Progress* (1950), and also organized a large-scale comparativist project, which he viewed as part of a "great conversation" of civilizations which might contribute to the permanent establishment of a peaceful world community (Stocking 1980). Mead did a restudy of the New Guinea community she had studied on her second field trip, which the war in the Pacific had catapulted from the "stone-age" into the "modern world" (1956:xi); the neo-evolutionary impulse of the 1950s was even more evident in her general work on *Continuities in Cultural Evolution* (1964). Looking backward at the postwar period, Eric Wolf noted "the repression of the romantic motive in anthropology" and the resurgence of universalistic and scientizing tendencies in the postwar period (1964:15). In this context, the problem of ethnographic reliability was handled by calls for more rigorous methods and the systematization of "restudies"; although the period was one of optimistic interdisciplinary cross-fertilization, the professional identity of cultural anthropology was never really at issue.

In contrast, Freeman's critique of Mead's ethnographic adequacy came after a decade of "crisis in anthropology" and the end of its "classical" period (cf. Stocking 1982a, 1989), and in the context of a resurgence of biological determinism in the human sciences (Caplan 1978). Furthermore, his critique explicitly called into question the cultural determinism which (although never "absolute") had been central to the discipline's definition during the preceding half century. From the beginning, it seemed clear that the professional identity of cultural anthropology was at issue, and the resistance to Freeman was widespread among American anthropologists, despite the ambivalence many of them felt toward Margaret Mead. From the perspective set forth at the beginning of the present essay, what was at issue was not only the basic conceptual orientation of cultural anthropology, but also its methodological values (and the mythistory that sustained them).

From another perspective, however, it might be argued that Freeman was simply reasserting other methodological values that are also very much a part of the anthropological tradition: the value placed on a comparative study of human variation; the value placed on the potential integration in a single embracive discipline of a number of approaches to the study of human variability (traditionally, the "four fields" of biological, linguistic, archeological, and cultural anthropology); the value placed on the "scientific" character and status of such an integrated comparative enterprise; and the value placed on general statements about the nature and causes of human diversity as the goal of such a scientific inquiry (cf. Stocking 1982a:411–12). Just as the four methodological values previously mentioned (above, p. 210) were products of the "ethnographicization" of anthropology in the early twentieth century, these four are products of the previous evolutionary period, and may be regarded as its enduring residue (cf. Stocking 1989). Although pushed into the background during the "classical" period, they have never been erased completely from the disciplinary identity, and were in fact expressed at various points in the work of the Apollonian ethnographers. Paradoxically—in view of the vehemence of Freeman's attack—they were quite strongly evident in much of the work of Margaret Mead. And it might be argued that they have in fact been reasserted by defenders of the American discipline, who have insisted, contra Freeman, that it has always assumed an "interaction" of culture and biology.

All of which might lead one to argue that, just as there are limits to the easy contextualization of the Apollonians and their critics in terms of personal biography, so are there limits to easy contexualization in terms of cultural moment.[18] Just as the case of Freeman suggests that the "repressive" critiques were not all expressions of a single cultural milieu, so also the case of Goldfrank reminds us that not all 1920s Boasians can be characterized as "organicists," even to the extent that term is appropriate for the Apollonians. What has been called here "*the* ethnographic sensibility of the 1920s" might more accurately be spoken of as "*an* ethnographic sensibility"—strikingly manifest in certain individuals in a particular cultural historical moment, but not necessarily peculiar to it or invariably in them.

Shifting, thus, the axis of contextualization away from the historically specific, we may ask whether the organic orientation might be an expression of a more enduring anthropological viewpoint. Bennett seems to have been inclined to identify the "organic" orientation with the anthropological outlook itself, arguing that it must be "seen in a context of theory basic to much of anthropology," which was "an expectable outgrowth of the anthropological preoccupation with preliterate communities" (Bennett 1946:364). Wolf's later comment on the subsequent "repression of the romantic motive in anthropology" (1964:15) suggests another alternative—the more so, another generation on, when a reaction against scienticizing tendencies that began in the later 1960s has become quite widespread, and the issue of relativism has been reinscribed on the agenda of anthropological discussion (Geertz 1984; Hatch 1983). Eschewing "cycles" or "pendulum swings," or any notion of recurrence that cannot be grounded in specific historical context, we may nevertheless wonder if there is not some enduring relationship between anthropology and outlooks similar to those Bennett called "organic" and "repressive."

Here we may take a clue from the opposition Franz Boas described a century ago between the methods of the physicist and of the cosmographer/historian, between a fragmenting analytic method and one based on an empathetic integrative understanding. On the one hand, the physicist studied phenomena that had an "objective unity," resolving them into their elements, which were investigated separately and comparatively, in the hope of estab-

18. On the matter of cultural moment, it may be worth commenting briefly on the failure of this essay to emphasize the racialist and hereditarian milieu of the 1920s as a factor in the formation of Apollonian ethnography (cf. Weiner 1983). While it is undoubtedly true that the emergence of Boasian cultural determinism cannot be adequately understood historically without reference to immigration restriction, the eugenics movement, and Nazism, as well as various other currents of racialist and hereditarian thought and social action in the late nineteenth and early twentieth centuries (cf. Stocking 1968, 1978), the contextual factors emphasized in the present essay seem to me more directly relevant to an interpretation of the Apollonian ethnographies. (It is perhaps worth noting, in this connection, that the biological determinism Mead confronted in her Samoan ethnography was a generically human rather than a racially specific one—cf. Mead 1928b.)

lishing or verifying general laws. On the other, the cosmographer/historian insisted on the validity of a holistic study of complex phenomena that had "a merely subjective unity"–whose elements "seem to be connected only in the mind of the observer." Motivated by "the personal feeling of man towards the world" around, such study required the observer "lovingly" to "penetrate" into the secrets of the phenomenon, until its "truth" could be affectively apprehended–without concern for "the laws which it corroborates or which may be deduced from it." Boas did not propose a resolution of the epistemological and methodological issues separating the physicist and the cosmographer/historian; rather, he granted the equal validity of the two approaches, each of which originated in a fundamental tendency of the human mind (Boas 1887:642–45; cf. above, pp. 4, 30–32).

Although Boas wrote "The Study of Geography" at a point when his own transition from physics to ethnology was still in process (Stocking 1968:133–60; cf. 1974c:9–10), his remarks may tell us something about the discipline toward which he was moving, as it has developed in the century since he wrote. More obviously than in the case of many other "ologies," cultural anthropology focusses on complex phenomena whose elements seem to be connected only in the mind of the observer. Insofar as their study is necessarily motivated by the personal feeling of the observer, and conditioned by the experience of the observer in the process of observation, these highly subjective objects of study must be perceived and conceived in terms that reflect this subjectivity. It may well be that not all aspects of these phenomena are equally so conditioned (cf. Gartrell 1979); but so long as anthropologists continue to be interested in broadly contrastive characterizations of otherness, subjectivity will be both the object and the instrument of their endeavor. If methodological sophistication may to some extent bring that subjectivity under control, it seems unlikely that method can ever eliminate entirely the anxiety aroused by the subjective encounter with otherness; and, as Boas' opposition implies, it may in fact be that our understanding is in some profound sense dependent on that anxiety (cf. Devereux 1967).

If this is the case, then it seems unlikely that the tension between the "organic" and the "repressive" orientations–any more than that Boas postulated between the methods of analysis and understanding–will ever disappear from anthropology. Just as the latter opposition is long traditional in the epistemology of the human sciences, so the former is long traditional in the history of Western attitudes toward the processes of culture and civilization. And just as anthropology has traditionally been a field of epistemological contention, so has it been a field of attitudinal ambivalence. In the future, as in the past, advocates of one or the other epistemological or attitudinal position will attempt to claim the field; and in that contending process, the bounds of generally accepted knowledge of human unity and diversity will no doubt enlarge.

But in the area beyond those bounds, where the reach into otherness continues to exceed the anthropologist's grasp, we can expect the tension to be manifest, within and between individual anthropologists and within and between phases in the history of the discipline. From this point of view, what has been called here the ethnographic sensibility of the 1920s may be viewed in culturally perduring as well as historically specific terms: on the one hand, as the manifestation of a particular moment, on the other as an expression of one of several dualisms inherent in the Western anthropological tradition.

Acknowledgments

The research and writing of this paper were supported by The Getty Center for the History of Art and the Humanities (Santa Monica, California) and the Marian and Adolph Lichtstern Foundation for Anthropology (of the Department of Anthropology, University of Chicago). A brief paper containing a portion of the argument was given to the American Anthropological Association meetings in Chicago in 1983. A longer draft was discussed in 1986 by the Chicago Group in the History of the Human Sciences (sponsored by the Morris Fishbein Center for the History of Science and Medicine); other versions were presented at the Getty Center, March 1989, and the symposium on "Disciplinarity: Formations, Rhetorics, Histories" of GRIP (Group for Research into the Institutionalization and Professionalization of Literary Studies), University of Minnesota, Minneapolis, April 1989. I am indebted for suggestions and criticisms to Bernard Cohn, Raymond Fogelson, George Marcus, Martin Orans, and Robert Richards. Others who helped in various ways include George Appell, Mary Catherine Bateson, Derek Freeman, Neil Harris, Curtis Hinsley, David Koester, Shari Segel, Virginia Yans-McLaughlin, and Bill Young. I would also like to express my appreciation to the officers and staffs of the manuscript archives in which I worked.

References Cited

Appell, G. N. & T. N. Madan. 1988. Derek Freeman: Notes toward an intellectual biography. In *Choice and morality in anthropological perspective: Essays in honor of Derek Freeman*, ed. Appell & Madan, 3–26. Buffalo, N.Y.

Arnold, M. 1869. *Culture and anarchy.* Cambridge (1957).

Ausubel, D. P. 1960. *The fern and the tiki: An American view of New Zealand national character, social attitudes, and race relations.* North Quincy, Mass. (1977).

Bateson, M. C. 1984. *With a daughter's eye: A memoir of Margaret Mead and Gregory Bateson.* New York.

Beard, C. A., & M. R. Beard. 1942. *The American spirit: A study of the idea of civilization in the United States.* New York (1962).

Benedict, R. F. 1923. *The concept of the guardian spirit in North America.* New York (1964).

———. 1928. Psychological types in the cultures of the southwest. In Mead 1959a: 248–61.

———. 1930. Review of Redfield 1930. N.Y. Herald Trib. 11/2.

———. 1932. Configurations of culture in North America. Am. Anth. 34:1–27.

———. 1934. Patterns of culture. Boston.

———. 1935. The story of my life. In Mead 1959a:97–117.

———. 1939. Edward Sapir. Am. Anth. 41:465–77.

———. 1940. Race: Science and politics. New York.

Bennett, J. W. 1946. The interpretation of Pueblo culture: A question of values. Southwest. J. Anth. 2:361–74.

Boas, F. 1887. The study of geography. In Race, language, and culture, 639–47. New York (1940).

Boutilier, J. A., et al. 1978. Mission, church and sect in Oceania. Ann Arbor, Mich.

Breslau, D. 1988. Robert Park et l'écologie humaine. Actes Rech. sci. soc. 74:55–63.

Brooks, V. W. 1915. America's coming-of-age. New York.

Burton, J. W. 1988. Shadows at twilight: A note on history and the ethnographic present. Proc. Am. Philos. Soc. 132:420–33.

Butterworth, D. 1972. Oscar Lewis, 1914–1970. Am. Anth. 74:747–57.

Caffrey, M. M. 1986. Stranger in this land: The life of Ruth Benedict. Doct. diss., Univ. Texas, Austin.

Caplan, A. L., ed. 1978. The sociobiology debate: Readings on ethical and scientific issues. New York.

Chase, S. 1931. Mexico: A study of two Americas. New York.

———. 1948. The proper study of mankind. New York.

Cressman, L. 1988. A golden journey: Memoirs of an archaeologist. Salt Lake City, Utah.

Darnell, R. 1986. Personality and culture: The fate of the Sapirian alternative. HOA 4:156–83.

Devereux, G. 1967. From anxiety to method in the behavioral sciences. The Hague.

Dorsey, G. A. 1926. Why we behave like human beings. New York.

Fairchild, H. 1961. The noble savage: A study in romantic naturalism. New York.

Fass, P. 1971. The damned and the beautiful: American youth in the 1920s. New York.

Fortune, R. 1939. Arapesh warfare. Am. Anth. 41:22–41.

Foster, G. 1953. What is folk culture? Am. Anth. 55:159–73.

Freeman, D. 1962. Review of Trance in Bali, by Jane Belo. J. Polynesian Soc. 71:270–73.

———. 1965. Anthropology, psychiatry and the doctrine of cultural relativism. Man 65:65–67.

———. 1972. Social Organization of Manu'a (1930 and 1969), by Margaret Mead: Some errata. J. Polynesian Soc. 81:70–78.

———. 1980. Sociobiology: The 'antidiscipline' of anthropology. In Sociobiology examined, ed. A. Montagu. New York.

———. 1983a Margaret Mead and Samoa: The making and unmaking of an anthropological myth. Cambridge, Mass.

———. 1983b. Inductivism and the test of truth: A rejoinder to Lowell D. Holmes and others. Canberra Anth. 6:101–92.

———. 1986. Some notes on the development of my anthropological interests. Unpublished typescript. [This essay contains some further information on the incident in Sarawak in March 1961, but since it only became available to me at a point when this volume was already in page proofs, and since any use of it would have involved further letters back and forth to New Zealand, I have not been able to draw on it here. GWS.]

————. 1987. Comment on Holmes's *Quest for the real Samoa. Am. Anth.* 89:903–35.

————. Forthcoming. Fa'a pu a'a Fa'a mū and Margaret Mead.

Garret, J. 1982. *To live among the stars: Christian origins in Oceania.* Geneva.

Gartrell, B. 1979. Is ethnography possible? A critique of *African Odyssey. J. Anth. Res.* 4:426–46.

Geertz, C. 1984. Anti-anti-relativism. *Am. Anth.* 86:263–78.

Godoy, R. 1978. The background and context of Redfield's *Tepoztlán. J. Steward Anth. Soc.* 10(1): 47–79.

Goldfrank, E. S. 1927. The social and ceremonial organization of Cochiti. *Am. Anth. Assn. Mem.* 33. Menasha, Wis.

————. 1943. Historic change and social character: A study of the Teton Dakota. *Am. Anth.* 45:67–83.

————. 1945a. Irrigation agriculture and Navaho community leadership: Case material on environment and culture. *Am. Anth.* 47:262–77.

————. 1945b. Socialization, personality and the structure of Pueblo society (with particular reference to Hopi and Zuni). *Am. Anth.* 47:516–39.

————. 1978. *Notes on an undirected life: As one anthropologist tells it.* New York.

————. 1983. Another view: Margaret and me. *Ethnohistory* 30:1–14.

Gravel, P. B., & R. B. Ridinger. 1988. *Anthropological fieldwork: An annotated bibliography.* New York.

Gruber, J. W. 1970. Ethnographic salvage and the shaping of anthropology. *Am. Anth.* 72:1289–99.

Hale, N. 1971. *Freud and the Americans.* New York.

Hall, G. S. 1907. *Adolescence: Its psychology and its relations.* 2 vols. New York.

Handler, R. 1983. The dainty and the hungry man: Literature and anthropology in the work of Edward Sapir. *HOA* 1:208–31.

————. 1986. Vigorous male and aspiring female: Poetry, personality, and culture in Edward Sapir and Ruth Benedict. *HOA* 4:127–55.

Hare, P. H. 1985. *A woman's quest for science: Portrait of anthropologist Elsie Clews Parsons.* New York.

Hatch, E. 1983. *Culture and morality: The relativity of values in anthropology.* New York.

Heider, K. G. 1988. The Rashomon effect: When ethnographers disagree. *Am. Anth.* 90:73–81.

Hewitt de Alcantara, C. 1984. *Anthropological perspectives on rural Mexico.* London.

Holmes, L. 1957a. The restudy of Manu'an culture: A problem in methodology. Doct. diss., Northwestern Univ.

————. 1957b. Ta'u. Stability and change in a Samoan village. *J. Polynesian Soc.* 66: 301–38, 398–435.

————. 1987. *Quest for the real Samoa: The Mead/Freeman controversy and beyond.* South Hadley, Mass.

Howard, J. 1984. *Margaret Mead: A life.* New York.

Jones, E. M. 1988. Samoa lost: Margaret Mead, cultural relativism, and the guilty imagination. *Fidelity* 7(3): 26–37.

Jung, C. G. 1923. *Psychological types: Or, the psychology of individuation.* Trans. H. Baynes. New York.

Keen, B. 1971. *The Aztec image in western thought.* New Brunswick, N.J.

Koffka, K. 1925. *The growth of the mind: An introduction to child psychology.* Trans. R. M. Ogden. New York.

Kroeber, A. L. 1931. Review of Redfield 1930. *Am. Anth.* 33:286–88.

———. 1935. Review of Benedict 1934. *Am. Anth.* 37:689–90.

———. 1952. *The nature of culture.* Chicago.

Kroeber, A. L., & C. Kluckhohn. 1952. *Culture: A critical review of concepts and definitions.* Cambridge.

Kuznick, P. J. 1988. *Beyond the laboratory: Scientists as political activists in 1930s America.* Chicago.

Lasch, C. 1965. *The new radicalism in America (1889–1963): the intellectual as a social type.* New York.

Lears, J. 1981. *No place of grace: Antimodernism and the transformation of American culture, 1880–1920.* New York.

Leuchtenberg, W. E. 1958. *The perils of prosperity, 1914–1932.* Chicago.

Lewis, O. 1951. *Life in a Mexican village: Tepoztlán restudied.* Urbana, Ill. (1963).

———. 1953. Controls and experiments in anthropological fieldwork. In *Anthropology today,* ed. A. L. Kroeber, 452–75. Chicago.

———. 1960. Some of my best friends are peasants. *Human Organ.* 19:179–80.

Li An-Che. 1937. Zuni: Some observations and queries. *Am. Anth.* 39:62–76.

Linton, R. 1939. Marquesan culture. In *The individual and his society: The psychodynamics of primitive social organization,* ed., A. Kardiner, 137–95. New York.

Lowie, R. H. 1917. *Culture and ethnology.* New York.

———. 1929. Review of Mead 1928b. *Am. Anth.* 31:532–34.

Lynd, R. S., & H. M. Lynd. 1929. *Middletown: A study in American culture.* New York.

Lynn, K. S. 1983. *The air-line to Seattle: Studies in literary and historical writing about America.* Chicago.

MacClancy, J. 1986. Unconventional character and disciplinary convention: John Layard, Jungian and anthropologist. *HOA* 4:50–71.

McDowell, N. 1980. The Oceanic ethnography of Margaret Mead. *Am. Anth.* 82: 278–302.

McLuhan, T. C. 1985. *Dream tracks: The railroad and the American Indian, 1890–1930.* New York.

McNeill, W. H. 1986. *Mythistory and other essays.* Chicago.

Mandelbaum, D. 1982. Some shared ideas. In *Crisis in anthropology: View from Spring Hill, 1980,* ed. E. A. Hoebel et al., 35–50. New York.

Manson, W. C. 1986. Abram Kardiner and the neo-Freudian alternative in culture and personality. *HOA* 4:72–94.

May, H. 1959. *The end of American innocence: A study of the first years of our time, 1912–1917.* New York.

Mead, M. 1927. Group intelligence tests and linguistic disability among Italian children. *School & Soc.* 25:465–68.

————. 1928a. *An inquiry into the question of cultural stability in Polynesia.* New York.

————. 1928b. *Coming of age in Samoa: A psychological study of primitive youth for Western civilisation.* New York.

————. 1928c. The role of the individual in Samoan culture. *J. Roy. Anth. Inst.* 58: 481–95.

————. 1930. *The social organization of Manu'a.* Honolulu (1969).

————. 1954. The swaddling hypothesis: Its reception. *Am. Anth.* 56:395–409.

————. 1956. *New lives for old: Cultural transformation—Manus, 1928–1953.* New York.

————. 1959a. *An anthropologist at work: Writings of Ruth Benedict.* Boston.

————. 1959b. Apprenticeship under Boas. In *The anthropology of Franz Boas,* ed. W. Goldschmidt, 29–45. San Francisco.

————. 1961. Preface to reprint of Mead 1928b, pp. xi–xvi.

————. 1962. Retrospects and prospects. In *Anthropology and human behavior,* ed. T. Gladwin & W. Sturtevant, 115–49. Washington, D.C.

————. 1964. *Continuities in cultural evolution.* New York.

————. 1969. Introduction to the 1969 edition, xi–xix; Conclusion 1969: Reflections on later theoretical work on the Samoans, 219–230, in reprint edition of Mead 1930.

————. 1971. Preliminary autobiographical drafts, in MP (see under Manuscript Sources).

————. 1972. *Blackberry winter: My earlier years.* New York.

————. 1977. *Letters from the field, 1925–1975.* New York.

Miner, H. 1952. The folk-urban continuum. *Am. Soc. Rev.* 17:529–36.

Mintz, S. 1953. The folk-urban continuum and the rural proletarian community. *Am. J. Soc.* 59:136–43.

Modell, J. 1983. *Ruth Benedict: Patterns of a life.* Philadelphia.

MP. See under Manuscript Sources.

Naroll, R. 1962. *Data quality control—a new research technique: Prolegomena to a cross-cultural study of culture stress.* Glencoe, Ill.

Nash, R. 1970. *The nervous generation: American thought, 1917–1930.* Chicago.

Ogburn, W. F. 1922. *Social change, with respect to culture and original nature.* New York.

Pandey, T. N. 1972. Anthropologists at Zuni. *Proc. Am. Phil. Soc.* 116:321–37.

Paddock, J. 1961. Oscar Lewis's Mexico. *Anth. Quart.* 34:129–50.

Pelto, P. J. 1970. *Anthropological research: The structure of inquiry.* New York.

Pound, E. 1915. E.P. Ode pour l'election de son sepulchre. In *Personae: The collected poems of Ezra Pound,* 187–91. New York (1926).

Pletsch, C. 1982. Freud's case studies and the locus of psychoanalytic knowledge. *Dynamis* (Granada) 2:263–97.

Rappaport, R. A. 1986. Desecrating the holy woman: Derek Freeman's attack on Margaret Mead. *Am. Scholar* 55:313–47.

Redfield, R. 1919. War sketches. *Poetry* 12:242–43.

————. 1928. Among the middle Americans: A Chicago family's adventures as adopted citizens of a Mexican village. *Univ. Chicago Mag.* 20:242–47.

————. 1930. *Tepoztlán, a Mexican village: A study of folk life.* Chicago.

————. 1941. *The folk culture of Yucatan.* Chicago.

————. 1950. *Chan Kom: The village that chose progress.* Chicago.

————. 1953. *The primitive world view and its transformations.* Ithaca, N.Y.

―――. 1955. *The little community.* Chicago.

―――. 1956. *Peasant society and culture.* Chicago.

Rigdon, S. M. 1988. *The culture facade: Art, science and politics in the work of Oscar Lewis.* Urbana, Ill.

Roe, A. 1950. Interviews with R. Redfield. (See under ARP in Manuscript Sources.)

―――. 1953a. A psychological study of eminent psychologists and anthropologists, and a comparison with biological and physical scientists. *Psychol. Monogr.* 67:1–55.

―――. 1953b. *The making of a scientist.* New York.

Romanucci-Ross, L. 1976. Anthropological field research: Margaret Mead, muse of the clinical field experience. *Am. Anth.* 82:304–17.

―――. 1983. Apollo alone and adrift in Samoa: Early Mead reconsidered. *Rev. Anth.* 10:86–92.

RP. See under Manuscript Sources.

Rutkoff, P. M., & W. B. Scott. 1986. *New School: A history of the New School for Social Research.* New York.

Sapir, E. 1919. Civilization and culture. *Dial* 67:233–236.

―――. 1922. Culture, genuine and spurious. *Dalhousie Rev.* 2:358–68.

―――. 1924. Culture, genuine and spurious. *Am. J. Soc.* 29:401–29 (as reprinted in Sapir 1949:308–31).

―――. 1928. Observations on the sex problem in America. *Am. J. Psychiatr.* 8:519–34.

―――. 1930. The discipline of sex. *Am. Mercury* 19:13–20.

―――. 1949. *Selected writings of Edward Sapir in language, culture and personality,* ed. D. G. Mandelbaum, Berkeley.

Smith, A. G. 1964. The Dionysian innovation. *Am. Anth.* 66:251–65.

Smith, B. 1960. *European vision and the South Pacific: A study in the history of art and ideas.* London.

Spiro, M. 1982. *Oedipus in the Trobriands.* Chicago.

Stanton, W. 1975. *The great United States exploring expedition of 1838–1842.* Berkeley.

Stearns, H. ed. 1922. *Civilization in the United States: An inquiry by thirty Americans.* New York.

Stocking, G. W., Jr. 1968. *Race, culture and evolution: Essays in the history of anthropology.* New York.

―――. 1974a. Benedict, Ruth Fulton. *Dictionary of American Biography, Supplement IV, 1946–1950.* 70–73. New York.

―――. 1974b. Growing up to New Guinea. *Isis* 65:95–97.

―――. 1974c. The basic assumptions of Boasian anthropology. Introduction. In *The shaping of American anthropology, 1883–1911: A Franz Boas reader,* 1–20. New York.

―――. 1976a. Ideas and institutions in American anthropology: Thoughts toward a history of the interwar years. In *Selected Papers from the American Anthropologist, 1921–1945,* ed. G. W. Stocking, Jr., 1–53. Washington, D.C.

―――. 1976b. Patterns, systems, and personalities. *Times Literary Supplement,* Mar. 12.

―――. 1978. Anthropology as Kulturkampf: Science and politics in the career of Franz Boas. In *Anthropology and the Public,* ed. Walter Goldschmidt, 33–55. Washington, D.C.

―――. 1979. *Anthropology at Chicago: Tradition, discipline, department.* Chicago.

―――. 1980. Redfield, Robert. *Dictionary of American Biography, Supplement VI, 1956–1960,* 532–34. New York.

————. 1982a. Anthropology in crisis? A view from between the generations. In *Crisis in anthropology: View from Spring Hill*, ed. E. A. Hoebel et al., 407–19. New York.

————. 1982b. The Santa Fe style in American anthropology: Regional interest, academic initiative, and philanthropic policy in the first two decades of the Laboratory of Anthropology, Inc. *J. Hist. Behav. Sci.* 18:3–19.

————. 1983. The ethnographer's magic: Fieldwork in British anthropology from Tylor to Malinowski. *HOA* 1:70–120.

————. 1984. Radcliffe-Brown and British social anthropology. *HOA* 2:131–91.

————. 1985. Philanthropoids and vanishing cultures: Rockefeller funding and the end of the museum era in Anglo-American anthropology. *HOA* 3:112–145.

————. 1986. Anthropology and the science of the irrational: Malinowski's encounter with Freudian psychoanalysis. *HOA* 4:13–49.

————. 1987. *Victorian Anthropology*. New York.

————. 1989. Paradigmatic traditions in the history of anthropology. In *Companion to the history of modern science*, ed. G. N. Cantor et al. London.

————. n.d. On the influence of Robert Park on Robert Redfield. Unpublished manuscript.

Suggs, R. C. 1971. Sex and personality in the Marquesas: A discussion of the Linton-Kardiner report. In *Human sexual behavior*, ed. R. S. Marshall & R. S. Suggs, 163–86. New York.

Sulloway, F. 1979. *Freud, biologist of the mind: Beyond the psychoanalytic legend*. New York.

Te Rangi Hiroa (Peter Buck). 1945. *An introduction to Polynesian anthropology*. Bishop Museum Bull. 187. Honolulu.

Tumin, M. 1945. Culture, genuine and spurious: A reevaluation. *Am. Soc. Rev.* 10: 199–207.

Tylor, E. B. 1871. *Primitive culture: Researches into the development of mythology, philosophy, religion, language, art and custom*. 2 vols. London.

Ulin, R. C. 1984. *Understanding cultures: Perspectives in anthropology and social theory*. Austin, Tex.

Wagley, C., & M. Harris. 1955. A typology of Latin American subcultures. *Am. Anth.* 57:428–51.

Ware, C. 1935. *Greenwich Village, 1920–1930: A comment on American civilization in the post-war years*. Boston.

Warman, A. 1982. Indigenist thought. In *Indigenous anthropology in non-western countries*, ed. H. Fahim, 75–96. Durham, N.C.

Weiner, A. 1983. Ethnographic determinism: Samoa and the Margaret Mead controversy. *Am. Anth.* 85:909–18.

Werner, O., et al. 1987. *Systematic fieldwork*. 2 vols. Newbury Park, Cal.

Williams, R. 1958. *Culture and society, 1780–1950*. New York (1960).

Wissler, C. 1923, *Man and culture*. New York.

Wittfogel, K. A., & E. S. Goldfrank. 1943. Some aspects of Pueblo mythology and society. *J. Am. Folk.* 56:17–30.

Wolf, E. 1955. Types of Latin American peasantry: A preliminary discussion. *Am. Anth.* 57:452–71.

————. 1964. *Anthropology*. Englewood Cliffs, N.J.

Manuscript Sources

In writing this essay, I have drawn on research in several bodies of manuscript materials, to whose archivists I would like to express my appreciation for their assistance at various points along the way—and which are here cited by the following abbreviations:

ARP   Anne Roe Papers, which contain the records of her interviews with Robert Redfield, American Philosophical Society Library, Philadelphia.

BP   Franz Boas Papers, American Philosophical Society Library, Philadelphia.

MP   Margaret Mead Papers, Library of Congress, Washington, D.C.

RP   Robert Redfield Papers, Department of Special Collections, Regenstein Library, University of Chicago.

Index